Inquiry
into
Math, Science, and Technology
for Teaching
Young Children

Inquiry into Math, Science, and Technology for Teaching Young Children

Arleen Pratt Prairie

**With contributions by
Warren Buckleitner**

THOMSON
*
DELMAR LEARNING   Australia Canada Mexico Singapore Spain United Kingdom United States

KH

Inquiry into Math, Science and Technology for Teaching Young Children
Arleen Pratt Prairie

Vice President,
Career Education SBU:
Dawn Gerrain

Director of Production:
Wendy A. Troeger

Director of Marketing:
Wendy E. Mapstone

Production Editor:
J.P. Henkel

Cover Design:
Andrew Wright

Director of Editorial:
Sherry Gomoll

Acquisitions Editor:
Erin O'Connor

Any additional questions about permissions can be submitted by email to thomsonrights@thomson.com

Library of Congress Cataloging-in-Publication Data

Prairie, Arleen.
   Inquiry into math, science, and technology for teaching young children / Arleen Pratt Prairie, with contributions by Warren Buckleitner.
      p. cm.
   Includes bibliographical references and index.
   ISBN-13: 978-1-4018-3359-6
   ISBN-10: 1-4018-3359-4
      1. Mathematics—Study and teaching (Preschool)—United States. 2. Science—Study and teaching (Preschool)—United States. 3. Technology—Study and teaching (Preschool)—United States. 4. Curriculum planning—United States. 5. Education—Curricula—United States. I. Buckleitner, Warren. II. Title.

QA135.6.P69 2005
372.35'049—dc22   2004017299

NOTICE TO THE READER

1/28/08

This book is dedicated to
my grandchildren, Michael and Alana,
who continue to show me the joys of childhood.

Table of Contents

Chapter 11   Technology in the Classroom   161

Chapter 12   Approaches to Curriculum   185

Part II   Inquiry Curriculum

Chapter 15 Exploring Math in Shape, Space, and Time   239

Foreword

In 1997 Congress passed the National Goals Initiative, the first of which states that all young children will start school ready to learn. This goal recognizes a half-century of research showing that young children's development and learning influences later school achievement. This research is well summarized in *Eager to Learn*, a publication from the National Research Council.* The report suggests the following principles to guide the education of young children: (1) Social engagement and learning are essential aspects of school readiness. Teachers need to understand that much of what children learn they learn through their relationships with the people they love and admire. Establishing a loving relationship with a young child energizes their wish to be like and to please another. By showing interest in objects and ideas, loved teachers help direct children's attention toward important concepts and appropriate social behavior. (2) Children need environments rich in explicit opportunities to observe and manipulate objects and to have adults and older children to explain and model how objects are used. This means making sure that environments have interesting and usable objects and adults who encourage children's attempts to understand and use them. (3) Teachers need to recognize children's interests. Often, we are so anxious to give information, we don't notice that we have lost our audience. It is best to keep our information for young children brief and wait for more questions. (4) Teachers need to build on what children already know. Young children are predisposed to learn some things—like loving, and language, and motor skills. But they still need opportunities to extend what they learn easily. For example, while typically developing children acquire language with little effort, school requires them to have words for complex ideas and relationships among objects. They need experience with these. (5) Performance and understanding need to go hand in hand. If new opportunities to learn are too narrow or too meager, children may not be able to use their past experience to make sense of new ones. For example, when children are encouraged to memorize without understanding, they may memorize the invariant order of number tags (they can say 1 to 5 in order) but they may not

---

*Bowman, B., Donovan, M. S., and Burns, M. S. (Eds.). (2000). *Eager to Learn: Educating Our Preschoolers*, Washington, DC: National Academies Press.

understand how to count five objects. It is critical to not only expose children to opportunities to learn but to make sure that the opportunities are frequent enough and coherent enough not only to ensure correct performance but also to support underlying understanding. (6) Children are capable of learning quite complex ideas when they have had sufficient prior experience. While there are age constraints on children's ability to learn, these are not as inflexible as we once thought. For example, children have been shown to develop more mature judgments regarding space and numbers when given a chance to build on their naturally acquired knowledge. Thus, the opportunity to learn can extend children's competence in areas we have yet to fully appreciate. (7) It is important to maintain children's natural zest for learning while providing them with a coherent curriculum designed to support school success.

This volume attends to these principles. The author has combined theory and practice, development and learning in a highly readable and well-organized book. The in-depth curriculum is coherent and based on sound research principles. Through exploration and inquiry, it will engage children in activities that are both interesting and motivating. The novice teacher will find a wonderful aid for planning and implementing a program that meets learning standards. The experienced teacher will find a broad array of ideas on which to build in order to adapt to the needs of diverse students. Novice and experienced teachers alike will find the book helpful as they meet the challenge of building a solid foundation for children in the world of math, science, and technology. I expect to keep this book in my library for years to come, and I am sure you will, too.

Barbara T. Bowman
Erikson Institute

Preface

BACKGROUND

Some books may live a long time in the mind before becoming a book. The beginnings of this text originated when faculty at Harold Washington College developed a new course, Math and Science for the Young Child. As my colleague, Rhoda Olenick, and I continued to develop and teach the course, I began to write articles on how children approach learning in math and science in order to enable students in developing appropriate math and science learning. Rhoda Olenick, Gemma Selman, and I worked with students to develop appropriate activities for graphing, making a weekly calendar, and experiencing physical science. As I worked along with the students in laboratory experiences in math, science, and technology for the young child and in their student teaching experiences as they implemented science and math learning, the process became increasingly apparent in how to engender success for students learning to teach science and math. So this became the basis for the book.

Recent developments in National and State Standards have a far-reaching impact on the teaching practices and expectations in preschool and kindergarten classrooms. Focus on math and science is driven by both the ever-expanding knowledge in cognitive development in the young years and the realization that education is not keeping up with the demand for the science and mathematics needed by young adults entering various fields of work. The Reggio Emilia schools of Italy, the project approach, the constructivist approach, and the emergent curriculum each bring a vision of deep exploration and learning brought about through interesting study by and with children. My respect for these current developments has impacted the writing of this book.

PURPOSE

This text will prepare current and future teachers of young children in preschool and kindergarten to create curriculum that follows children's interests and involvement. Teachers and children together will be intrigued by the wonders of math, science, and technology. Teachers can participate in the discoveries children make and facilitate the direction of their learning. Because the adult is tuned in and turned on, the child will become deeply engaged in this learning process at his own level of understanding.

Students preparing to teach at the associate level and for licensure (Baccalaureate level) will need to know the child, the effective learning processes, and the subject matter they teach. The book attempts to guide students as they construct their ideas in teaching by presenting theory of learning, recent curriculum developments, and an array of curricula for their practice. Interlaced throughout the book are the concepts of what and how children learn and practical approaches to subject matter.

Professional teachers can enhance their teaching skills through the thorough study of current approaches in early childhood education and exposure to the experiences of curriculum planning. The theory and curriculum found in this text will assist teachers in reassessing the constructs of their practice.

SECTIONS AND FEATURES

This text has two main sections: Part I, Theory and Inquiry, and Part II, Inquiry Curriculum. In Chapter 1 the reader is introduced to the constructivist approach to learning and to the inquiry process and is given an opportunity to examine her own response to math, science, and technology. Chapter 2 looks at cognitive development and integrates the steps of inquiry with young children's thinking. Chapters 3 and 4 look at ways of learning with others in the context of community and culture and applying assessment to build on children's interests and skills.

In Part I, Chapters 5 through 9 build the inquiry process into logical and appropriate steps with young children. In Chapters 5, Exploring; 6, Identifying Materials and Processes; 7, Classifying, Comparing, and Contrasting; 8, Hypothesizing and Generalizing; and 9, Communicating Results, each portrays a step of the inquiry process. Chapter 10, The Number Sense of Math, delves further into math by depicting the number sense in young children. Chapter 11, Technology in the Classroom, explains the appropriate technology to enhance curriculum. Chapter 12, Approaches to Curriculum, and Chapter 13, Environments, introduce the rich curriculum choices and environments for learning in preschool and kindergarten classrooms.

In Part II, Chapters 14 through 19 are studies of curriculum in the areas of math and science. Chapters 14 and 15 focus on the various math experiences. Chapters 16 through 19 portray in-depth experiences in the following areas of science: Physical Science, Earth Science, Life Science: Plants, and Life Science: Animals. Chapter 20, Inquiry as Approach to Life, brings the reader back to reflect on the relevance of teaching in science and math.

As you browse through this text you will find several features in each chapter that will help in organizing your learning:

- Objectives provide the focus for each chapter and serve as guides to what the reader will learn.

- Ideas to Ponder can organize your query for each chapter. These can organize your focus when approaching the chapter either through self-reflection or as guides for discussion.
- New terms are highlighted and defined as they occur in the text or in a nearby side bar. These also appear in the Glossary in alphabetical order.
- National Standards are interspersed in chapters as they refer to specific components in learning.
- To Further Your Thinking provides thoughtful experiences to foster development of your constructs in teaching and learning.
- Additional Resources list several references to current works that can take you further in exploring concepts and curriculum. Web sites cited provide current resources on the Internet. Videos are suggested where appropriate. In the chapters on curriculum, relevant children's books are included.

The National Standards referenced throughout the book are as follows:

1. National Science Education Standards: Professional Development Standards, Teaching Standards and Content Standards, Grades K–4
2. Principles and Standards for School Mathematics: Chapter 4. Standards for Pre-K–Grade 2, from the National Council for Teachers of Mathematics
3. Preparing Early Childhood Professionals: NAEYC's Standards for Initial Licensure from National Association for the Education of Young Children.

In Appendix A you will find the full reference to each of these Standards cited in the text. Find Web sites to access your State Standards.

The Inquiry Topics that appear in Chapters 14 to 19 are a springboard to developing study topics in depth. In following the premise of selecting topics of study that pique children's interest and involvement, these Inquiry Topics provide a general focus on beginning a possible inquiry. Teachers can use these as guidelines for developing the study that evolves from the group of children and flows naturally with them.

In Chapter 11, Technology in the Classroom, Warren Buckleitner and I explain appropriate technology use for young children and explore various ways of enhancing curriculum through technology. Throughout Part II you will encounter practical application of technology in curriculum. In Appendix B you will see suggested products for classrooms. Because of the fast-paced technology industry, the innovative uses of technology will continue to advance rapidly and may outpace the information contained in this book.

 Additional resources and activities can be found in the Online Companion for this text at http://www.delmarlearning.com.

APPROACHES TO USING THE TEXT

The layout of the book is evident from the contents: Part I presents first theories of learning and processes to facilitate learning and then the steps of inquiry. The next four chapters examine the number sense, technology, kinds of curriculum, and environments to lay the groundwork for presenting curriculum. Part II articulates the practical aspects of presenting curriculum in the areas of math and science.

The use of the book can be organized in different ways to accomplish the approaches of a particular course. One approach or a combination of options can be selected.

To group the text materials by subject, the following arrangement is suggested:

1. For mathematics, materials can be sequenced: Two sections in Chapter 2, Early Mathematical Thinking and One-to-One Correspondence, along with Chapters 7, 10, 14, and 15 on the learning of math concepts and curriculum experiences in math.
2. The study of science can be built from sections of Chapter 2, on the development of cognition; and Chapters 5 through 9, on the steps of inquiry; and finally, Chapters 16 through 19, the experiences in science inquiry.
3. For technology, Chapter 11, Technology in the Classroom, along with Appendix B can be included at the last. Students will easily recognize how technology is integrated to enhance the Inquiry Topics within Chapters 14 through 19.

Another approach can be used if students begin this class with depth of understanding of stages of cognitive development, theory of learning, and assessment, as well as approaches to curriculum and environments. In this case Chapters 2, 3, 4, 12, and 13 can be referred to for instructive review and used in making curriculum decisions.

A different approach can be followed by combining both theory and practical application in each class session. The chapters in Part I can be correlated with the practical curriculum chapters of Part II. In this way the class sessions can integrate the theory with laboratory experiences. For a course where there is less time to spend on math, science, and technology, this is a worthwhile option.

For professional preparation and in-service training led by staff and consultants, this book can serve as a resource for a particular concentration of study in math, science, or technology. In pinpointing a selection of theory in Part I and a selected area of math, science, or technology in Part II, trainers can effectively present theory and practice together. Training can easily be constructed from the hands-on learning experiences and detailed processes of planning curriculum found in the *Instructor's Guide.*

Professional teachers who are searching for current theory and curriculum focus will find interesting and readable research and practice in inquiry. Part II will be particularly useful in developing in-depth math and science curriculum.

ACKNOWLEDGMENTS

It is an impossible task to include all who inspired and guided me in the writing of this book. I recognize the many students in child development at Harold Washington College who were invariably teaching me about their learning over many years. I am particularly thankful to teachers at North Avenue Day Nursery in Chicago (NADN) who studied the process of preparing science and math curriculum in their classrooms. The result of their inspiring curriculum planning is that the teachers and children from NADN appear in many of the photos throughout the book. These dedicated teachers are Yvonne Alvarado, Miltrona-June Brown, Hattie Cooper, LaTherese Clay, Thamara Estrada, Larissia Hughes-Milton, Brenda Johnson, Janice Johnson, Irene Orozco, Jacqueline Quiles, Bertha Rutley, Cynthia Stevens, and Norbella Valadez. I am extremely grateful to Pat Jackson and B. J. White, who worked step-by-step with me on the in-service training with these fine teachers at NADN.

Special thanks go to Warren Buckleitner, Editor of Children's Software Review, who contributed the current concepts and resources on technology in Chapter 11 and Appendix B. His appreciable expertise on technology and knowledge about the ways young children approach computers makes the technology information credible.

I am particularly thankful to Diane Colwyn, the editor who devoted her energies and expertise to make this book ready to be published, and to Ivy Ip, who answered my many queries to enlighten me on the publishing process and who faithfully served as my important connection with Delmar Learning during the course of preparing the text. Both have been extremely supportive.

Three of my colleagues took the beginning form of this book into their classrooms to pilot the project. I thank Adrienne Edlin, Meredith Chambers, and Karen Roth for their informative feedback on what works in the college classroom. I appreciate all of these reviewers who gave sound advice on making this book relevant in the field: Mary Banbury, Bellevue Community College, Bellevue, WA; Kim A. Bozenhardt, Ed.D., DWUMC Child Development Center, Mobile, AL; Meredith Chambers, Truman College, Chicago, IL; Adrienne K. Edlen, City Colleges of Chicago, Chicago, IL; Teresa Frazier, Thomas Nelson Community College, Hampton, VA; Mary Henthorne, Western Wisconsin Technical College, La Crosse, WI; Helene J. Silverman, Ph.D., Lehman College, Bronx, NY; Karen Roth, National-Louis University, Evanston, IL; and Frances H. Squires, Ph.D., Indiana University Southeast New Albany, IN.

I am grateful to photographer extraordinaire Patrick Clark and am thankful for the able assistance of Betty Clark, Kim and Kendal Kroes, and Linda Siewart.

Many friends, guides, and contributors have given their support and knowledge in innumerable ways: Elizabeth Alvarez, Barbara Bowman, Yvonne Carlisle, Irmgard Gruber, Cynthia Hoisington, Patty Horsch, Vanessa Rich, Rhoda Olenick, Myra Cox, Gemma Selman, Delores Rix, Wendy Coulson, Meredith Chambers, Karen Haigh, Jane Cecil, and Janice Woods. I am deeply indebted to Skip VerDuin for his ongoing support during the writing of this book.

Letter to the Student

Dear student,

Welcome to this journey of experiencing the subjects of math, science, and technology for teaching children ages three through six. This book is about understanding the learning process and applying this to your teaching. The place to begin is with you as author of your beliefs and style of teaching.

As you approach the subjects of math, science, and technology for the young child, you may be aware of the personal feelings you have, both positive and negative, about these subjects. The openness to examine these topics will strengthen your ability to provide an atmosphere for inquisitiveness and exploration that is so important for children's learning. In this book the goal is for you to explore learning math and science and to bring your sense of inquiry into both your understanding of the topic and the knowledge of young children in the learning process.

In the area of technology you may be so familiar with the computer and photography that you are comfortable with uses of these in the classroom. If so, you will welcome these tools and your challenge will be to expand your knowledge in their uses. Whether or not you are comfortable with new technology, your openness to learn will model inquiry into technology use.

As you further explore your approach to teaching through this text, you will have many opportunities to question, examine ideas and materials, research children's understandings, and compare ideas with others. With this process you will be examining the math and science materials and be looking at approaches that you can use to provide the involved experiences needed in children's learning. For math you will work with the various concepts young children will learn. For science you will develop the sense of inquiry for yourself and use that to analyze what children do in developing their sense of inquiry. For technology you will see how children best learn from the technology available and implement this to enhance their learning. You will facilitate learning through sharing thought processes, asking probing questions, and investigating science and math along with the children. This will enable children to think about making relationships, seeing cause and effect, making inferences, and describing their discoveries. As we bring these ideas together, you will have the opportunity to apply your process of helping children learn within a variety of curriculum approaches.

Along the way, you will develop your education construct in math and science and technology for the young child. It will become integral to your teaching. Hopefully you will gain a deeper appreciation for your involvement in teaching as well as a genuine respect for the children you teach.

Your author,
Arleen Pratt Prairie

Part One

Theory and Inquiry

Chapter 1

The Process of Inquiry into Math, Science, and Technology

OBJECTIVES Through the process of discovery in this chapter, you will be able to:

1. Discern inquiry in the child and yourself.

2. Recognize sources of national standards in science, math, and early education.

3. Compare your process of self-reflection to the constructivist approach to learning.

4. Describe social constructionist learning and three elements of social context.

5. List the Inquiry Processes Used by Children and compare these with constructivist thinking.

6. Discern what determines a process in inquiry as math or science.

7. Discuss how technology can be integrated into the math and science process of inquiry.

8. Discover some of your attitudes of math, science, and technology and processes for changing these attitudes.

9. Discover sources of social influences on attitudes of learning in math, science, and technology.

10. Discuss current inequities that may exist, especially related to gender, culture, and family background.

IDEAS TO PONDER

- What is the process of my thinking?

- How does the young child think?

- How do my attitudes about math, science, and technology affect the way I teach?

- How can I make education equitable for all children I reach?

"I don't think I have to teach math and science in preschool, do I? I hated math in high school, and in science all we ever did was read and answer the questions in the back of the book."
(Melissa, college student, personal communication, September 21, 2001)

"I just love getting into looking at all kinds of stuff. My daughter just brought home a tree branch that had all kinds of leaves on it, green and yellow and dead ones."
(Sandra, college student, personal communication, September 21, 2001)

WHAT IS INQUIRY?

Inquiry is a close investigation in a quest to find out.

Inquiry is the process of finding out. The child explores, compares, investigates, and repeats his actions in an attempt to discover. The infant puts the ball in the cup and turns it over, repeating the process over and over again. The toddler looks at what her grandmother takes out of the refrigerator to make dinner. As she climbs up on the stool she asks, "Nana, What's dis?" while poking at each vegetable. The preschooler gently pours rivulets of wet sand on top of the emerging sand tower. The kindergartner tries out the matchbox cars to see which will travel the full length of the floor. He measures the length traveled by the last car with his arms, then declares this as "the winner." These are processes of inquiry by the child. Your understanding and support of these will unfold in the book.

YOU AS INQUIRER

First and foremost this is a book about you as an adult who searches for answers in the world, in children, and in the process of learning itself. It is about you as you understand your own processes of inquiry especially in the broad subjects of math and science.

As a teacher of young children you will be the one who sets the stage for children's experiences in math, science, and technology. As inquirer you will become an important role model. As children go about pursuing what they strive to learn you will provide the language that will bridge their understanding to labeling and communicating. In short, you will be one who determines what is important to learn and ways for children to learn.

NATIONAL STANDARDS

Your role in preparation for teaching young children can be compared to the teacher preparation described in the National Science Education Standards.

Professional development for teachers should be analogous to professional development for other professions. Becoming an effective science teacher is a continuous process that stretches from preservice experience in undergraduate years to the end of a professional career. Science has a rapidly changing knowledge base and expanding relevance to societal issues, and teachers will need ongoing opportunities to build their understanding and ability. Teachers also must have opportunities to develop understanding of how students with diverse interests, abilities, and experience make sense of scientific ideas and what a teacher does to support and guide all students.

Reprinted with permission from the *National science education standards.* (1996). The National Academy of Sciences, courtesy of the National Academies Press, Washington, DC (p. 56).

This textbook reflects this statement of the National Standards for Science for K–12. As you move from the first chapters of understanding the child to the content of science, math, and technology, you will have the opportunity to develop inquiry in the subject areas as well as look at the way young children learn. With an understanding of inquiry yourself and the ability to study all the vast content presented in this text, you will be able to approach the teaching of young children with the same sense of inquiry.

National standards are incorporated into the text so that the relevance of what you accomplish through this book is tied to the broad standards developed by experts in the fields of mathematics (National Council of Teachers of Mathematics [NCTM] Principles and Standards for School Mathematics), science (National Science Education Standards [NSES]), and early childhood education (National Association for the Education of Young Children [NAEYC], Standards for Initial Licensure in Professional Preparation in Recognition and Accreditation). The National Council for Accreditation of Teacher Education (NCATE) works in conjunction with NAEYC in the review process for accreditation of higher education institutions with early childhood education. This same framework of professional preparation standards is also presented to institutions with advanced and associate degree programs.

PURPOSE OF THIS TEXT

For this study of *Inquiry into Math, Science, and Technology for Teaching Young Children,* you will uncover a wealth of information about how young children learn, what they may learn, and the processes of teaching them. You will be observing children to see what and how they comprehend and trying out various teaching ideas. You will be exposed to a variety of curricula. You will be guided to reflect on what you are learning and the decisions you will make in composing your teaching style. There will be some curriculum methods from which to choose for your current situation or future way of teaching. You will have a large selection of **inquiry topics** you can try out. In this **reflective thinking** you will be developing your way of teaching.

Inquiry topics are curricula based on the inquiry process.

REFLECTION ON PAST LEARNING

It is helpful to gain some understanding of your past learning experience. This will highlight what you bring to your thinking about the learning of young children. For this exercise,

Reflective thinking is the process of using past information and knowledge combined with new information to compose new understanding.

> Think of a positive learning experience you have had in the past. This can be in any place at any age.

What were the circumstances? What did you learn? What expectations were there (if any)? Was another person involved with you in this learning situation? If so, how did that impact your learning?

What was your process to understand in a new way?

What did you do with that understanding? If there was another person involved, was there a shared recognition of that learning?

How does this experience affect the way you learn today?

A PARALLEL PROCESS IN THINKING

As you consider reflective thinking in the preceding exercise, you may be aware of mentally rearranging ideas in your mind to organize a way to express them. Perhaps you "see" putting ideas in a certain order. There is a parallel process for the child. However, because of differing ability in cognitive development, the child may actually move objects around in space before constructing the idea in her mind. The parallel here is that adult thinking uses images; the child uses objects. In both cases the individual is putting together ideas or processes. Because her thinking is different, the child may not use perceptions like yours or arrive at the same answer you would in her process.

CONSTRUCTIVIST APPROACH TO LEARNING

Constructivist learning is putting together (hence constructing) one's own ideas through action and thought processes.

The preceding parallel points out the constructivist approach to learning. **Constructivist learning** is a scientifically researched theory of learning that is both a physically and mentally active process. In this process the young child constructs knowledge (understanding concepts) through his own activity, as opposed to simply being told (Bowman, 1999). Each learner (both adult and child) constructs knowledge through observing, questioning, documenting, and reflecting. In constructivist learning theory, knowledge is not acquired through transmission from others (Chaillé & Britain, 2003). The child acts on objects to construct her own ideas in learning.

There are many steps to constructivist learning, as seen in Table 1–1. Young children may use only some of these processes. Yet at times adults may find patterns in the information to analyze, and after analyzing, may move to synthesize (Branscombe, Castle, Dorsey, Surbeck, & Taylor, 2000).

ANECDOTE

Tara is stacking cylinder blocks on the floor next to Caitlin. She uses the thin cylinders, placing them vertically end to end. Quietly she watches them fall each time she places the third one on top. After the third try Tara stops in gathering the fallen blocks to watch Caitlin. Caitlin says to her, "Do this," as she starts at the bottom with a fat cylinder. "These ones stack better." Tara watches solemnly, then follows Caitlin's idea by stacking only the fat ones. With this new understanding Tara builds her tower high, and she stands up to place the last one on top.

The child does not use constructivist processes in isolation. For the young child, input comes from manipulating objects, from trial and error, from input of others (both peers and adults), from listening, and from observing.

This approach to learning is titled **social constructionist** because of the involvement with peers through observing and listening. For Tara this learning was accomplished through sharing ideas.

Tara moved quickly into accomplishing her goal of stacking the cylinder blocks through observing, listening, and following another's thought processes. Her advances here moved much more quickly than if she had worked to develop this idea on her own.

THE SOCIAL CONTEXT

The **social context** can encompass more than the immediate experience to include Tara's individual social history. Tara has two older brothers whom she learns from by watching their play on many occasions. She has learned to view another's process as ways to learn for herself.

Another part of the social context is the overall social history of how things are learned in the child's community and in the larger society. Included in this are

Social constructionist learning is involvement with others in the construction of ideas.

Social context includes sharing in the immediate experience, the individual social history, as well as the cultural social history.

TABLE 1–1 A Constructivist Approach to Learning

Question	Search to build understanding and figure out causes, origins, and rules.
Observe	Look closely at phenomena to gain an understanding.
Analyze	Find patterns in information, find evidence, and draw conclusions.
Synthesize	Combine data found at present with other data to compare and put into a whole to make predictions or create hypotheses.
Reflect	Think about the past and future as well as the present to consider a different way of organizing thoughts.
Research	Take formal or informal steps to look closely at phenomena to search for answers.
Communicate results	Share the results of a learning process through means of written correspondence or pictorial or graphic representations.

Branscombe, Castle, Dorsey, Surbeck, & Taylor, 2000, pp. 3, 9, 21, 25–37.

such things as the use of language and the importance of accomplishment. Both Tara and Caitlin share this social understanding. If Caitlin had challenged Tara on building taller or had simply moved over and built Tara's tower for her without saying a word, Caitlin would be operating from a different social context.

What children learn and the ways children learn are affected by these three aspects of social context: the experience of sharing in the immediate experience, the individual social history, and the cultural social history. People in Western society often assume that all children learn the same way. Research has shown that children learn in different ways (Berk & Winsler, 1995; Bodrova & Leong, 1996; New, 1999; Rogoff, 2003).

THE INQUIRY PROCESSES

The inquiry processes as developed by Stephanie Feeney (Feeney, Christensen, & Moravcik, 2001) take their form from the formal scientific process. This adaptation of the scientific process fits the young child's process of scientific inquiry. Here you are introduced to Inquiry Processes Used by Children (Table 1–2), and you will be using an adapted form in future chapters. These steps of the inquiry process form the basis of inquiry in understanding and applying science and math curriculum.

COMPARE INQUIRY PROCESSES AND CONSTRUCTIVIST THINKING

These Inquiry Processes Used by Children are similar to the terms used to describe the Constructivist Approach to Learning (Table 1–1). In comparing these for example, questioning and observing are descriptors of the inquiry process of exploring. And analyzing, synthesizing, reflecting, and researching are processes used in hypothesizing and generalizing. Whether using the inquiry processes or the processes in constructivist thinking, both describe the kinds of thinking the young child uses in actions and thought.

TABLE 1–2   Inquiry Processes Used by Children

Exploring	Using the senses to observe, investigate, and manipulate.
Identifying	Naming and describing what is experienced.
Classifying	Grouping objects or experiences by their common characteristics.
Comparing and contrasting	Observing similarities and differences between objects or experiences.
Hypothesizing	Using data from experiences to make guesses (hypotheses) about what might happen.
Generalizing	Applying previous experience to new events.

Who am I in the lives of children? (6th ed.) by Feeney, Christensen, & Moravcik, © 2001. Reprinted by permission of Pearson Education, Inc., Upper Saddle River, NJ, p. 316.

Both the Inquiry Processes Used by Children and Constructivist Approach to Learning are not stages; so they are processes both the child and adult may experience. As children mature they are able to accomplish more of the processes listed in Tables 1–1 and 1–2, but these are not dependent entirely on age-related abilities.

PLACING AN INQUIRY STEP INTO MATH AND SCIENCE CATEGORIES

The question arises as to what makes up the subjects of math and science. The Inquiry Processes Used by Children are generated from the study of science; yet because they encompass math as well as science, it is not simple to determine whether an inquiry process fits the math or science categories. In many instances of the thinking processes of children, math and science are joined. Math and science endure as distinct topics but also are combined into the full process of inquiry.

ANECDOTE

In a preschool classroom busy four-year olds are actively placing the collection of rocks from their walk onto a large tray placed on the floor. The children jostle each other to place their items.

"I got that one. It's the biggest."

"That's heavy."

"That's the littlest."

"The big rocks go here."

"And the medium ones go here."

"Look, there are only two baby ones."

What is being processed here? Is it science or math? What do you see the children doing? While this is part of the inquiry process, the ways the children approached this was through use of math. They classified, compared, contrasted, and counted. Where do these fit in the inquiry process?

Later in the day in this classroom, the children, with the assistance of the teachers, are using a flashlight, steel file, sandpaper, pan of water, tripod magnifier, small hammer, and safety goggles to work with the rocks they had found. They shone a strong beam from a flashlight on several rocks and put others in the water. A couple of children sanded the rocks and another used a steel file. With one teacher working with them two children took the largest rock to the woodworking table and, while wearing goggles, cracked open the rock. This new surface—the inside of the rock—was placed under the magnifier. Now, is this science or math? What influenced your decision? Can you fit the processes here into the inquiry processes used by children? (See Table 1–2.)

INTEGRATING TECHNOLOGY INTO MATH AND SCIENCE INQUIRY

Now let's consider the use of the computer and other technology in the preschool classroom. One current practice places the computer in the preschool classroom as a separate entity, isolated from other learning. It becomes the instrument for a child or a small group to explore different software games or exercises for learning and fun. How limiting a view for this versatile instrument. Instead, think of the computer as a tool to enhance children's learning in various areas:

Working with math concepts from sorting or counting to software math programs

Expanding knowledge in any aspect of science

Emerging literacy for individuals or the group

Communicating with people near and far

Emerging literacy: The beginnings of communication and understanding language, especially through reading and writing in the early childhood years.

Software programs, the Internet, e-mail, and the word processor can be put to use to foster learning in these areas and more.

In addition, both new and existing technology can also enhance the learning process in the preschool and kindergarten classroom. Possibilities include the following:

A transparency projector to view another way of seeing things

A digital camera to bring instant photographic images to view, record, enhance, and share

A video and an audiocassette recording to hear and view ideas and projects for reviewing and sharing with others

Regardless of how you feel about utilizing technology, the items on this list open up new paradigms for technological advances using the process of inquiry. From glancing at the list, whether or not you know some of these tools you may be challenged to learn more about them.

ATTITUDES TOWARD MATH, SCIENCE, AND TECHNOLOGY

As you saw in the preceding introduction of technology in the classroom, you naturally bring with you attitudes toward technology. In addition, you also bring your viewpoints on the subjects of math and science.

These affect your approach to teaching and the time and effort you will give to these subjects. Children will learn the attitudes you bring to the classroom.

By examining attitudes in each of the areas of math, science, and technology, you can begin to recognize and correct outmoded responses. First look at the approach to math, science, and computer use while you were in primary school, secondary school, and college. Was math understandable or incomprehensible, from the times tables to algebraic formulas? Did you learn through knowing why

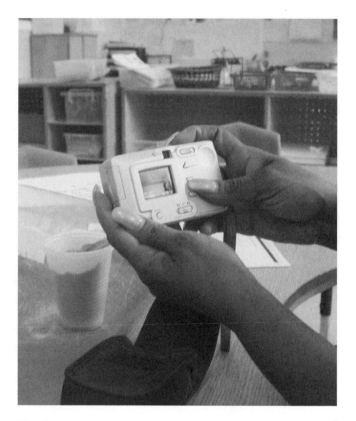

The digital camera enhances curriculum.

each math fact was true or did you accept these facts as rules and then do just what you were supposed to do?

Did you experience science as a set of facts to learn? Were these subjects seen as dry and separate from the world as you knew it? Were you actively involved in using the scientific method by exploring, observing, investigating, and drawing conclusions? Were these studies integrated with the world you knew?

Did you experience technology as an innovative and a fun way to learn? With each new software program, were you motivated to uncover its benefits? If you grew up with computers readily available, you may approach the computer with

---

STANDARDS

Build on the teacher's current science understanding, ability, and attitudes.

Reprinted with permission from *National science education standards*. (1996). The National Academy of Sciences, courtesy of the National Academies Press, Washington, DC (p. 59).

curiosity and an eagerness to explore what it has to offer. If you were introduced to the computer during adulthood, you may hesitate to explore new techniques for fear of making a mistake.

SOCIAL INFLUENCES ON ATTITUDES IN MATH, SCIENCE, AND TECHNOLOGY

How did your teachers, family members, and friends treat the topics discussed in the preceding section? What did you learn from the people around you about how you should handle these areas? Were you encouraged to be curious, to ask questions, and to talk about some very different ideas? In math, if you arrived at the correct answer in a different way, did you receive approval? In science, were you told it is not safe to handle objects that you found, or that you were not to ask questions, or that your thoughts were trivia—or just completely wrong? In technology, were you able to explore the computer freely? Many of the attitudes held as adults were learned very early in life. Well-meaning people may pass along values and beliefs that inadvertently affect attitudes about learning in these areas. A child may be told he will be punished in no uncertain terms if he crosses the street alone. A child may find that the only way to respond to his innate curiosity is to explore on his own. Or he deems it best not to respond to the childlike queries he has, as this is the only way to be accepted. Being teased or silenced may cut off a youngster's attempts to explain her emerging thought processes. The people in your life while you were young may have had valid reasons for what they taught you. Or it may simply be that what was passed along to them as children were, without thinking, given to you.

What are your attitudes about aspects of plant life and living beings? Examine your response to the common earthworm. Earthworms are beneficial to the garden because their digestion process leaves the soil richer. "If you define the tickle and scrunch in your hand as a 'bad' feeling, look back and see where you acquired the psychological burden" (Holt, 1989, p. 106). Unfortunately, some of our abhorrence for certain textures, such as soft and mushy things, foul smells, and unsightly ooze, are just learned from others. What comes to mind is the grade school boy who chases the girl with the worm. The dark color and soft texture of the worm really is not abhorrent in and of itself.

What causes these negative responses to things in nature? Some of this has to do with our food chain. The repulsion of finding the worm in the apple may stem from the belief that the apple was meant for you. This negative response may stem from survival issues. Insects that eat our food and spoilage of food both interfere with our ability to consume food. Basic concepts, yes. In addition, some may cause risk of illness or disease. Animals and insects that can carry disease are rightfully disliked (Holt, 1989).

THE FEAR OF NOT KNOWING

Because of previous experiences, or lack of them, you may approach teaching with the belief that you have insufficient background in math, science, or technology—or all three—to be knowledgeable for the discussion and investigation at the

Ashley shows enjoyment of a big earthworm.

preschool and kindergarten level. This is a valid concern. Yet there are actions that can be taken to alter this. Teachers do not have to be the experts. While it is important to obtain knowledge in areas of study that you will teach, it is more important to have a **disposition** of questioning and exploring. This opens up the motivation to find resources and the will to access information for current questions. When we do this, children learn some important life lessons: It is okay not to know (and adults certainly do not know everything); one can access a variety of resources to find out; and one gains new competence in the process of the search.

Disposition is a prevailing inclination or a habit of mind.

ACCESSING INFORMATION

How do you access information? Look around at available resources. Use people as resources: colleagues, family members, friends, and other contacts. Call on extension services, librarians, computer technicians, museum, and zoo personnel for knowledgeable people to provide answers. Some of these experts are there to provide answers just for the asking. And those "experts" you personally know may feel privileged that you asked.

Books are resources. Hopefully you will work in a school where you will find resource books, such as children's encyclopedias, bird and insect books, and information books on flora and fauna, industries, and occupations in your area. For your personal use, obtain some of these information books including those on your locale. Use the library for additional resources. The Internet takes you

This teacher exhibits the disposition to question and explore.

beyond the print material into vast resources of knowledge. Use informational Web sites to research basic information and answer detailed questions you have. Web sites in the Additional Resources at the end of each chapter will get you started using this convenient resource.

To expand your personal expertise, explore an area of math, science, or technology for your own inquiry. Play around with materials so you can gain firsthand knowledge about materials. This can involve examining dandelion seeds under a magnifying glass or trying out a paint program on the computer. Take a young friend to the zoo, a local park, or nearby farm. By taking a child on an excursion, in addition to learning yourself, you can learn through the eyes of a child.

GENDER INEQUITIES

There are gender issues that go far beyond the scene of the boy chasing the girl with a worm. Even though today attempts are made not to be gender specific, this tends to be perpetuated in some ways. The process of recognizing your own attitudes can provide insight into **gender inequities.** Do you tend to think of a group of children as girls and boys or as a group of individuals holding distinct characteristics? Do you ask boys to carry something big and heavy and ask girls to clean up after cooking? If a teacher decides to separate play groups according to gender lines to provide equity, conversely, the differences between the sexes are promoted. If a group of boys or girls tends to invade the block area daily, a frank discussion about making this open to all may show that some girls and some, but not all, boys would prefer to build in that area.

Gender inequities are attitudes that show a difference in expectations of boys' and girls' experiences.

Beyond play and activities in the classroom, stereotypes are promoted through attitudes, modeling, and cultural expectations. Unfortunately, this will not be erased in even the current generation. In presenting choices in life, you can honor that choices may be influenced by society but recognize that not all people need to actualize their choices the same way. As a woman, one can say, "I would like someone else to fix the sink, although it is something I can do." And as a man, one can say to a group of children, "I particularly liked raising my own children, so I decided to be a teacher." A teacher may say to the children, "It is okay for Stephano's family to take him and his older sister hunting. Other families can make other choices." When equitable gender choices are made in the classroom and seen in the larger society as choices that a girl and a boy, a woman and a man would make freely, this can be treated matter-of-factly. Research says that children can know "the difference between what people can do and what they usually do" (New, 1999, pp. 147–148).

While gender choices are made more freely today, inequity remains in science and math occupations, health care, technology, and education. **Equitable** handling of math, science, and technology with young children may help either gender to expand its interests in these topics. This would open up more possibilities for both sexes to choose these areas in future occupations (New, 1999).

Equitable is dealing fairly and equally with everyone.

In the classroom "teacher attitude and knowledge may also account for much of the inequitable treatment of preschool mathematics, science, and technology" (New, 1999, pp. 144–145). The majority of teachers in early childhood education are women who may lack interest and experiences in math, science, and technology. In addition, early childhood education has stressed child development and psychology rather than those topical areas. "Indeed, many early childhood educators readily admit their reticence to explicitly incorporate science and technology into their curriculum, because of their own incomplete understandings of these academic domains" (New, 1999, pp. 144–145).

INEQUITIES IN A PLURALISTIC SOCIETY

In the effort to plan curriculum around the expressed interests and abilities of the children we teach, another inequity may arise. The interests and abilities of children may be influenced by gender, culture, and family background.

Early childhood education has stressed a "different strokes for different folks" philosophy . . . which supports educational practices that respond to children's individual differences and family lifestyles. It is difficult to find fault with a pedagogy that is grounded in knowledge about and response for children and their families. If implemented uncritically, however, this sensitivity to differences can further exacerbate inequities in children's learning. At the least it can interfere with another principle central to an education for a democratic, pluralistic society: that all children are entitled to gain access to the skills and knowledge regarded as social capital in the dominant culture. (New, 1999, p. 142)

While responding to diversity is essential, it is necessary to provide equity in science, math, and technology across culture, economic, and geographic areas in all programs for young children. Early education needs to provide the beginning for all children to advance in areas of science and mathematics as well as to inspire interest and motivation for study in these areas.

SUMMARY

Dispositions for learning are more important than the acquired learning. Whether it is concerned with you as a teacher or with young children in the classroom, the process is much more important than learning a set of facts. If you ask the child a question with the expectation of a certain answer, such as, "Triangle" or "The triangle has three corners," the emphasis is in the wrong place. Asking the child to compare the triangle with the square or to make a square from triangles changes the emphasis to constructivist thinking processes. Even the wrong answer can provide fodder for constructivist thinking. A teacher who asks, "How did you find that three triangles make the square?" may be rightfully challenged to see the child's thinking. The next chapter will exemplify the development of thinking in young children. From this you will have a clearer view of how children think differently from adults.

TO FURTHER YOUR THINKING

1. In your reflection on past learning presented in this chapter, continue by considering a current learning situation and how this can be (or is) a positive learning experience. How would this be structured? What would your role be in the learning situation? If this involved another person, what role would the

other person play? Write a vision of positive future learning experiences for yourself and state what learning is for you.

2. Think of a recent time you have been reflective. What were the thought processes you used? How do you think this is the same or different from a child's thinking?

3. From the Constructivist Approach to Learning (Table 1–1), reread the description of the terms and add an example of each from the viewpoint of either a child or an adult. For example, following the term *synthesize*, you could write, "Children asked for the magnifying glass when they wanted to look more closely at the ladybug. They remembered and applied the experience of using the magnifier to examine the worm."

4. Think of a specific activity you did with a friend or family member such as planning a purchase or planning weekend activities.
   a. How did involvement with another influence the way you planned?
   b. How did your previous experiences with others affect your planning process?
   c. How does social learning from the community and larger society affect how you make these decisions?

   Your responses to these questions indicate the social context of this kind of activity for you.

5. Using the Inquiry Processes Used by Children (Table 1–2), first list synonyms for each term, then provide some examples of each. When you are familiar with the terms, discuss these with classmates.

6. From the comments the children made while placing the rocks in the tray (page 9), decide what each child is doing according to the inquiry processes used by children. For the quote by each child, label the specific inquiry process. In the same way, continue this exercise by commenting on what children did later in the day with the rocks (page 9).

7. Consider your personal responses to math studies in your primary, secondary, and college studies. What did you like, and not like, about them? Do the same for your studies in science.

8. What is your attitude toward computers and other current technology tools? What influences these attitudes?

9. What are your attitudes toward living plants and animals? Are there things you love and things you abhor? What may cause these current attitudes?

10. What are your earliest memories about learning? How did others respond to this learning? Do you relate in some ways to the meaning of that learning today?

11. What gender inequities did you experience as you were growing up? What beliefs about the roles of males and females stayed with you to the present?

12. Select a classroom from your memory or one you know today. How were/are gender issues treated? Make a table of equitable and inequitable treatment of boys and girls. How does this treatment influence the thinking of both genders?

13. Canvas classmates and friends about the number of males and females they know in various gender-biased careers. Consider the health professions, engineering, education, and technology. Has this changed in the last ten years? Twenty years?

REFERENCES

Berk, L. E., and Winsler, A. (1995). *Scaffolding children's learning: Vygotsky and early childhood education.* Washington, DC: National Association for the Education of Young Children.

Bodrova, E., and Leong, D. J. (1996). *Tools of the mind: The Vygotskian approach to early childhood education.* Englewood Cliffs, NJ: Prentice Hall.

Bowman, B. T. (1999). Policy implications for math, science, and technology in early childhood education. In American Association for the Advancement of Science, *Dialogue on early childhood science, mathematics, and technology education* (pp. 40–49). Washington, DC: Author.

Branscombe, N. A., Castle, K., Dorsey, A. G., Surbeck, E., and Taylor, J. B. (2000). *Early childhood education: Constructivist perspective.* Boston: Houghton Mifflin.

Chaillé, C., and Britain, L. (2003). *The young child as scientist: A constructivist approach to early childhood science education* (3rd ed.). Boston: Allyn and Bacon.

Feeney, S., Christensen, D., and Moravcik, E. (2001). *Who am I in the lives of children?* (6th ed.). Upper Saddle River, NJ: Prentice Hall.

Holt, B. J. (1989). *Science with young children.* Washington, DC: National Association for the Education of Young Children.

National Academy of Science. (1996). *National science education standards* [book version, on line]. Washington, DC: National Academies Press. **www.nap.edu**

New, R. (1999). Playing fair and square: Issues of equity in preschool mathematics, science, and technology. In American Association for the Advancement of Science, *Dialogue on early childhood science, mathematics, and technology education* (pp. 138–156). Washington, DC: Author.

Rogoff, B. (2003). *The cultural nature of human development.* New York: Oxford.

ADDITIONAL RESOURCES

American Association for the Advancement of Science. (1999). *Dialogue on early childhood science, mathematics, and technology education.* Washington, DC: Author. This current look at the state of science, math, and technology is the outcome of a forum in which these authors presented. www.project2061.org

Delpit, L. (1995). *Other people's children: Cultural conflict in the classroom.* New York: The New Press. This author presents a vision of cultural dissonance in education from more than one cultural perspective.

Forsman, G. E., and Kuschner, D. S. (1983). *The child's construction of knowledge: Piaget for teaching children.* Washington, DC: National Association for the Education of Young Children. This thorough text delves into the questions that form the basis for constructivist thinking.

Holt, B. J. (1989). *Science with young children.* Washington, DC: National Association for the Education of Young Children. This classic text approaches attitudes in science and ecology that are very relevant.

Moriarty, R. (2002, September). Entries from a staff developer's journal: Helping teachers develop as facilitators of three- to five-year-olds' science inquiry. *Young Children,* 57(5), 20–24. From a series of workshops for teachers, concepts of inquiry are explored.

Wadsworth, B. J. (1996) *Piaget's theory of cognitive and affective development* (5th ed.). New York: Longman. In addition to the Piagetian theory, this book lays the groundwork for constructivist theory.

Web Sites

www.naeyc.org and www.ncate.org NAEYC Standards for Early Childhood Professional Preparation. Baccalaureate or Initial Licensure.

www.naeyc.org NAEYC Standards for Early Childhood Professional Preparation. Advanced and Associate Degree Standards.

www.nap.org National Science Education Standards [book version].

www.nctm.org National Council of Teachers of Mathematics, Principles and Standards for School Mathematics.

Chapter 2

The Thinking of the Young Child

OBJECTIVES Through the process of discovery in this chapter, you will be able to:

1. Identify changes in brain development in the early years including synapses, pruning, myelination, and growth of the corpus callosum.

2. Discuss characteristics of the child's thinking from infancy through early school age.

3. Discuss gains of representational thinking and limitations of intuitive thinking in the preschool child.

4. Describe examples of one-to-one correspondence.

5. Identify three kinds of knowledge in the thinking of young children.

6. Identify physical knowledge criteria that can enable children to understand cause and effect.

7. Discuss implementing learning for the young child according to the three kinds of knowledge.

8. Recognize and provide examples of children using steps of the inquiry processes.

9. Compare inquiry for preschoolers and kindergarteners to science standards.

IDEAS TO PONDER

- How well do we understand young children's thinking?

- How does brain development affect the way children think?

- How does children's thinking affect how they understand their physical world?

- How does children's thinking affect how they understand math?

- How will young children use, or not use, the inquiry processes?

"When I walked into the kitchen last night there was my daughter, Carta. She had just laid all the chairs down on the floor. 'What are you doing, Carta?' 'They're sleeping,' she answered," Scott related.
"That's real cute!" Roseanne added.
Scott replied, "I couldn't figure out what in the world she was doing."
(R. Roraback, personal communication, July 15, 2003)

BRAIN DEVELOPMENT

Since Carta's actions and thoughts are so different from the adult's, one doesn't really understand this child's thinking at two-and-one-half years. What makes this thinking so different? Why is this development so at odds with the child's gradual growth in height from infancy to adult stature?

The brain is the one organ of the human body that has early rapid growth, developing faster than any other part of the body in the first few years. In comparison to adult size, the brain at age two has reached 75 percent of its adult weight and by age five it has grown to 90 percent of adult weight. By age seven the brain is full grown (Berger, 2001; Eliot, 1999).

Even though the brain of the human infant has grown tremendously in size by age two, that rapid growth does not correlate with the child being able to master thinking like an adult. "We have an alien in our midst," suggests Elkind (1993) (as quoted in Gopnik, Meltzoff, & Kuhl, 1999), so it would do well to get acquainted with the way that alien approaches thought. Young children's thinking must be understood in the context of the child, not the adult (Elkind, 1999).

Yet even more dramatic than the rapid physical growth of the brain, the magnitude of changes taking place inside the brain is even greater. At birth the baby has most of the **neurons** that he will have throughout his life. But at birth, the connections between neurons have just begun. The branching of the neuron and the connections made possible through this branching are growing exponentially in the first two years.

The point of connection between one cell and another is the **synapse,** and these are multiplying rapidly. "During infancy and early childhood the **cerebral cortex** actually overproduces synapses, about twice as many as it will eventually need" (Eliot, 1999, p. 29). This overproduction makes a very inefficient system of communication in the brain. As the child grows older, the unused connections will be pruned away. "Children lose on the order of 20 billion synapses *per* day between early childhood and adolescence. While seeming harsh, it is generally a good thing. The elimination of stray synapses and the strengthening of survivors is what makes our mental processes more streamlined and coherent as we mature" (Eliot, 1999, p. 32). The expression "use it or lose it" follows this pruning and strengthening.

Another amazing process of brain development is the insulation of the axons or long parts of the neuron. This insulation is a fatty substance called myelin. The covering with myelin will prevent the loss of some of the message that is being

Each neuron is a cell of the nervous system where messages are transferred from one to another or to a particular part of the body.

Synapse is the connection between two neurons where the transfer of information takes place.

Cerebral cortex is the area of the brain where conscious behavior and thinking occur.

Myelination is insulation (myelin) of the long parts of the neuron that makes the transfer of information in the brain efficient and fast.

transferred from one neuron to another. This **myelination** also means that the transfer of the message is efficient and fast (Eliot, 1999). Myelination takes place rapidly during the preschool years.

Another advance relates to the young child's thinking. This is the growth in the **corpus callosum,** a band of neuron fibers that connect the right and left hemispheres of the brain. Because of the connections and myelination, the left and right hemispheres are able to communicate with each other. This means that the child can process incoming messages in several parts of the brain at once. The child is able to retrieve information from several senses: thoughts, emotions, actions, and memory. At about five years of age, the child begins to show more coordinated thinking because of these connections along with myelination (Berger, 2001).

Corpus callosum is the connection between the right and left hemispheres of the brain. It is made up of a large band of neuron fibers.

The executive part of the brain, the prefrontal lobe of the cerebral cortex, is where the most advanced cognitive processing takes place. This important area develops later as pruning, synapses, and myelination are still developing in this area from early childhood into the teens. As a result, it takes a long time for the human brain to use advanced thought processes.

STANDARDS

Candidates use their understanding of young children's characteristics and needs, and of multiple interacting influences on children's development and learning, to create environments that are healthy, respectful, supportive, and challenging for all children.

Standard 1. Reprinted with permission from National Association for the Education of Young Children. NAEYC standards for early childhood professional preparation: Initial licensure programs (2003). In *Preparing early childhood professionals: NAEYC's standards for programs,* M. Hyson (Ed.). Washington, DC: Author, (p. 29).

COGNITIVE THINKING: INFANCY THROUGH EARLY SCHOOL AGE

Sensorimotor is the first stage of cognitive development in which the child learns through senses and action on the environment.

Scientists correlate the changes in the brain with changes in thought capabilities. The brain development described previously is one way to picture changes in cognitive thinking. Observing behavior is another way to track the advancement in the way children think.

Infants and Toddlers

During infancy the exploration of the world is through his senses and actions. The first two years are called the **sensorimotor** stage by Jean Piaget, a Swiss psychologist, who developed a stage theory of cognitive development (Berger, 2001).

ANECDOTE

Baby Michael mouths a large rubber softball. He obtains sensory information by tasting the large ball, feeling its shape against the mouth, feeling the softness of the ball against the tongue, seeing the pattern and lines, and smelling the surface of it. When he accidentally drops the ball he hears the soft thud. He also watches the ball move and stop.

Beginning Cause and Effect From about six months to two years, the infant acts on objects. He knows that his own actions produce a result.

ANECDOTE

When Michael bats at the ball with his hands, he causes it to roll away from him. Because he likes this, he will bat the ball away over and over again.

The infant learns a basic cause and effect. The action he does has a certain effect on the ball. We can see that, if it pleases him, he will act to reproduce this same result. These actions will be repeated and elaborated to accomplish gradually more complex feats. As the toddler gains more cognitive skills, he can carry out more complicated behaviors.

Object Permanence Through the first two years an understanding of the **permanence of objects** develop. As young as 4½ months infants will stare longer at the trajectory of a screen passing through a box than if it is stopped by the box. The baby seems to know (observers can tell by the way she looks longer at the impossible event) that the moving screen could not go past the box (Baillargeion & DeVos, 1992, as cited in Berger, 2001).

Object permanence is the knowing that an object continues to exist when out of sight.

ANECDOTE

From birth Michael can see and hear the music mobile over his head every time he is placed in his crib. At five months he smiles the moment his mother winds up the mobile. It appears to be a comfort to him because of its familiarity.

The infant at six to nine months begins to go after an object he wants as it moves away from him. This is the continuing development of the young child, gradually knowing the object exists even when he can no longer see it.

ANECDOTE

At six months Julio would whimper when his empty bottle was removed from his mouth. His father would say, "All gone," and place the bottle on the floor where Julio could not see it. In a moment Julio would give a toothless full smile to his father.

At seven months Julio cried when his empty bottle was taken away from him. Even though his father hid the bottle and played with him, Julio continued to whimper for a minute or two.

It was at nine months that Julio began to cry after his mother went out the front door on her way to work. Now the child recognizes that his mother still exists when she is gone.

Knowing objects exist continually provides a base. From there the understanding of characteristics of objects grows. So the rubber softball that is pushed away, then retrieved and sucked on emits the same sensory information. The child builds on this information through the day-to-day experience of handling the ball as well as his other toys.

Beginning Communication   The toddler's language helps her to recall basic concepts in memory, to communicate about objects, to say what she wants as well as understand the adult. A few words help with recalling objects not in her sight.

ANECDOTE

Toddling to the kitchen after his father, baby Julio murmurs, "Ba-ba," as he grabs hold of his father's pant leg. His father stops and smiles at him, "So you want your bottle."

While the toddler hears meaningful language in his family, his concept of meaning gradually grows. An understanding of meaning is often gained through meaningful actions more than with words alone.

```
                        ANECDOTE
```

At 18 months, Andrew is interested in the Swedish clogs on my feet. Andrew is not yet talking. I slip my foot out of one shoe and invite him, "Try it on your foot." Andrew quickly complies. Then he pushes the shoe to my foot. I respond to his gesture, then move it toward him again. "Do you want to try it again?" The game of trying on the shoe continues.

The toddler's understanding of the language comes from the context, including the gestures, movements, and vocal intonation, not from the words alone.

Dawn of Representational Thinking According to Piaget, the child makes a big change in thinking abilities from about 18 months to 2 years. At this time the child begins to use mental symbols in her mind as **representations** of actions and objects. One of the first things observed is language. The word *kitty* stands for the animal the child sees skirting about the house. She can use the word to communicate to others her thoughts of kitty. She can also pretend to be a kitty as she crawls under the dining room table. She can take another object, such as a small block, and pretend the block is a kitty. When she turns the pages of her animal book, she correctly labels the pictures of the kitty. She now has the ability to represent objects in her mind and tell this to others.

Representation is the ability to use a mental symbol to stand for an object or an action.

She can also use thoughts to accomplish simple problem solving of a situation at hand.

```
                        ANECDOTE
```

Corey, an active, eager two-year-old, arrives in the kitchen, alone for the moment. He looks up to where the cereal is stored on a closed shelf above the counter. He clumsily drags a chair over to the counter. Corey easily climbs the chair and struggles to climb up on the counter. Then he slowly moves from a squat into a standing position on the counter. He opens the cupboard, finds his favorite Cocoa Puffs, and carefully slides it out from the boxes of cereal. As Corey turns around holding the cereal box over his tummy, his father discovers and rescues him.

At two, most toddlers can think an action through before doing it. The toddler is able to solve a basic problem by planning actions he already knows how to do. This helps with rudimentary problem solving, such as getting one's favorite cereal. Yet this thinking is closely related to the events of the moment—the here and now. He cannot plan what he will do in the future, but he can decide what to do now (Ginsberg & Opper, 1979).

Preschoolers' Use of Preoperational Thought

Preoperational thought is a cognitive stage during the years from two to six, in which thought processes are prelogical and intuitive.

Three- and four-year-olds advance to use thought to plan and to problem solve. Yet reasoning at ages three and four is prelogical. One form of **preoperational thought** is called **magical causality** (Wolfinger, 1994). The child attributes magic as the cause of events.

ANECDOTE

Devonte grabs the smooth black box with the words "The Lion King" on it. He skillfully slips it into the hole in the machine (VCR) under the television. Devonte deftly pushes the buttons to begin the movie. Devonte accepts this technology without question, assuming it is magic. If the movie does not appear as usual, he has no way of fixing it without his mother's help. She will rewind the video for him (Prairie, 1994a).

Magical causality is attributing actions to magic when those actions cannot be understood logically.

In the child's way of thinking, there is no reason for him not to believe in Santa Clause and many reasons for it.

ANECDOTE

Two weeks before Christmas, in the classroom, four-year-old Karen announces authoritatively that there is no Santa Claus. "He's just a man dressed up in a red suit." Even though she repeats these nuggets of knowledge, they have absolutely no effect on the twelve classmates who are eagerly anticipating Santa's visit (Prairie, 1994a).

Egocentrism is seeing events and experiences only from one's viewpoint.

At age four, the contradicting evidence concerning Santa has absolutely no effect on the beliefs. Causality is magic. At four, the effect is accepted without question and logic is not even a passing thought.

Children see objects and events from their point of view, without consideration of others' beliefs. Karen cannot grasp how the others will be disappointed if they believe her. Knowing what she does from her family, who does not celebrate Christmas, she only wants to tell what she understands. The others cannot take in what Karen says because they can only see their point of view. In their families, they know this special visit is approaching. Thus, **egocentrism** affects children's thinking (Prairie, 1994a).

Realism is the belief that what is imagined is real.

Young children approach beliefs of **realism** with a different picture than ours. What goes on in their heads is real. For them dreams really take place. If they imagine the monster in their room, it is really there (Piaget & Inhelder, 1969).

ANECDOTE

When she was six, my granddaughter, Alana, talked a lot about what she feared in monsters. She fought these fears with self-talk of beating them up. "When that monster comes, I will kick him with my feet." One summer night after dark we turned off all lights in the house and looked at the shapes of the furniture in the living room as they appeared in the dark. Then the lights were turned on and she recognized what those shapes were. Again and again, Alana could see the representation of obscure shapes as something familiar. Through this she displaced a lot of her fear of the dark. At four and five those shapes had still represented the fearful monster shapes in her thoughts. At six, Alana was ready to relate the real to what she perceived in the dark.

During the early years what moves is alive, and what does not move is not alive. This is called **animism** (Piaget & Inhelder, 1969).

> *Animism is the belief that what moves is alive and objects take on human characteristics.*

ANECDOTE

Carlisle and Diamond were picking up the two big rocks they had brought in from the walk and were holding them above their heads. Adrienne suggested they put them in a large clear plastic peanut butter jar, which she placed in front of them. "Let's try putting water in the jar and see what your large rocks look like then." They rushed to the sink, and Diamond held the jar while Carlisle turned on the faucet. Slowly and steadily Diamond brought the full jar back to the table, slid it onto the table, and leaned over to peer in it. The water moved back and forth as Diamond brought the jar closer to her. As Carlisle now had a chance to look closely, he stared, then shouted, "Look, they're alive. They're movin'!" Carlisle moved back quickly. Entranced, Diamond looked, too. After a moment she looked at him and said, "No, just the water's movin'. That's all."

Children give human motives to objects.

- The ball stops because it is tired.
- The thunder makes noise because the clouds are angry.

Another type of thinking is **artificialism.** Objects and events are either caused by humans or made for human benefit.

> *Artificialism is the belief that objects and events are caused by humans or are made for human benefit.*

- Why does the boat float on water? Because the people made it to float.
- It is sunny today because we want to play outside.

- Why does the television go on? So we can watch it.
- Why does the sun shine? To keep us warm and so the plants will grow.

If we provided a scientific explanation, young children would not follow it (Elkind, 1999).

Cause and effect is the belief that if two events happen together, one has caused the other.

Understanding **cause and effect** presents some difficulty in preschoolers' logic. At this stage they believe that if two things happen together, one thing causes the other. Other possibilities in a hypothesis are not considered. If Daddy comes home when the sun goes down, then Daddy caused the sun to set. (Doesn't Daddy have the power to do anything?) From our adult logic this kind of thinking brings up a problem because the sun will set at different times in the calendar year, so Daddy will not always "have that power." It is important to see that the child will not consider these as problems, just as he will not consider that there may be a Santa in several places during the Christmas season; or that it is impossible to get to all children before midnight on Christmas Eve; or that it would be impossible for Santa to get to the child (even considering egocentrism) by going down a chimney to get to an apartment in a high-rise building. Usually the family provides another explanation that is quite plausible for the child. It is the child's prelogical reasoning that makes these beliefs possible, not the clever adult (Prairie, 1994a).

Transductive Reasoning All these characteristics of thinking can be summed up in the understanding of transductive thinking (Elkind, 1999, pp. 64–65). Young children tend to think of objects and events as equal to each other. These are not hierarchical or caused by logical deductions.

Transductive reasoning is thinking of relationships from object to object or event to event without a hierarchy of relationships.

ANECDOTE

Jessica, a four-year-old girl, was thinking out loud to her mother on the way home from preschool. Jessica (who was white) said, "When I grow up I want to be a teacher like Mrs. Matthews. Will that mean that my skin will be brown like hers?"

Centration is focusing on one aspect of a situation and not considering any others.

The thought processes in magical causality, realism, animism, artificialism and cause and effect all occur because of **transductive reasoning.** With this view of how children perceive relationships, adults can understand that prelogical thought presents a different view of how events happen in everyday life. Adults relate best to this difference in thinking by accepting children's ideas and explanations. By being involved in ongoing experiences and discussions about what they see and understand, children gradually perceive other viewpoints. And, according to Piaget, there are other limitations in their thinking.

Centration Another characteristic described by Piaget that contributes to limitations in the child's thinking is **centration.** The child focuses on one aspect of a

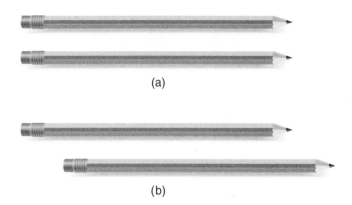

(a)

(b)

Figure 2–1 Centration is seen (a) when the child identifies that two pencils are of equal length and, (b) when one pencil is moved to the right, the child centers on one end of the pencil only.

situation and not any others. You can do a simple task of showing two identical pencils to a young child, first holding them horizontally, exactly one above the other. Then move one a little to the right and ask if they are the same now. Invariably the preschooler will answer that one is longer. It depends which end he centers on for his answer. He is centering on one end of the pencils only and answering what appears to him to be longer (Fig. 2–1).

In the example shown in Figure 2–2, the child uses centration by looking at the length of the line (b) instead of the number of objects in it.

Static States While looking at a classic experiment that is done with young children, Piaget provides another glimpse of ways young children think. For this, ask a young child to watch you place seven pennies in row. Match a second row next to them using one-to-one correspondence. Is this row the same amount or does one have more than the other? The child will answer that they have the same. Then while the child is watching, take the second row of pennies and spread them out. Ask again if this row is the same as the first or does one have more than the other. The preschool child will say that the second row has more. Using adult logic, you would say it is the same; you only moved the objects around. The young child must see it differently, and in fact she does. She sees the situation as **static,** that is, as if still pictures were taken of the event before and after. She knows that you only moved them, but she is paying attention to the last picture only. In that glimpse the row that is spread out looks like more. To make her decision she does not connect the two separate images before the pennies were moved and after (Bjorklund, 1995; Piaget & Inhelder, 1969) (Fig. 2–2).

Irreversibility In the pennies experiment just presented, if the child would think about and use the information that occurred first in this experiment, she would answer differently. She would see that the seven pennies were still there. With that answer you would understand her logic. According to Piaget, this is

Static states is the process of believing the appearance of what is seen at the moment, not using information of the process to understand the result.

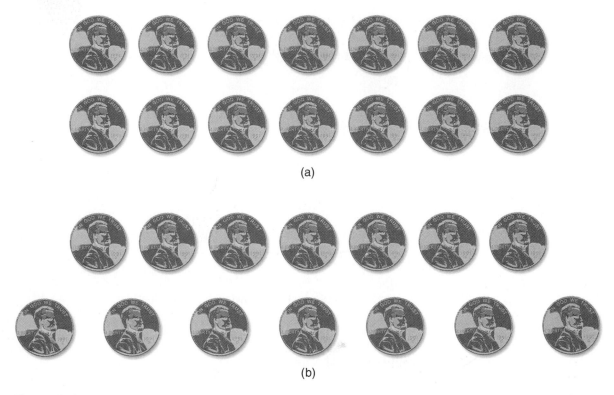

(a)

(b)

Figure 2–2 The preschool child sees static states, so in the second example (b), the child says that the second row is longer because it looks longer.

Irreversibility is the lack of ability to see that reversing a process will bring it back to its former state.

one of the abilities children lack. They can remember earlier scenes but cannot use them in these decisions. With **irreversibility** they cannot reverse steps in the experiment to accomplish logical thinking (Piaget & Inhelder, 1969).

The child from two to five has made giant gains in her thinking. She can do simple problem solving, communicate ideas, pretend, and think about the events in the world she knows. **Intuitive thinking** of the preschool child results from the limitations of seeing in static states, transductive thinking, centration, and irreversibility. She uses this information that she gains from appearances over logic (Table 2–1).

Intuitive thinking is using appearances over logic.

Concrete Operations of the School-Age Child

As the child moves toward kindergarten, she will begin to see other ways of seeing things though she will not always be certain of her perception. And she will become more logical in her responses. During the years from ages five to seven, the child will gradually take on a different vision in thinking. During her kindergarten

TABLE 2–1	Cognitive Development in the Early Years	
Age Range	**Stage**	**Ability in Thinking**
Birth to two years	Sensorimotor	Learning through actions and senses
		Beginning cause and effect
		Object permanence
		Beginning communication
		Representational thinking
Two to six years	Preoperational	Intuitive and prelogical thought
		Magical causality
		Realism
		Animism
		Artificialism
		Cause and effect
		Transductive reasoning
		Centration
		Static states
		Irreversibility
Seven to eleven years	Concrete operations	Logical thinking
		Conservation

year, this logic will gradually develop and become the basis for **concrete operations** in the primary grades

The young child moves into logical thinking tentatively, as she seems to glimpse the logical view, but may become confused when trying to explain the logic. When the row of seven pennies (Fig. 2–2) is spread apart, the child will say that the number of pennies is the same. But when asked why they are the same, she cannot give a reason and may even change her mind to say that the longest row has more. She begins to see the logic but remains unsure.

Officially, the beginning of concrete operations is at age seven, the age of reason. As the child becomes more logical, he no longer sees things in static states. He **decenters** in the way he looks at situations and objects and his thought processes become **reversible.**

This logical ability in concrete operations is based primarily on the understanding of constancy, or **conservation.** By seven, the child now knows, without a doubt, that if nothing is added or taken away from a substance, such as the seven pennies, then the amount stays the same no matter what appearances tell her. Because amounts remain constant in the stage of concrete operations, adding and subtracting are now understood.

Concrete operations occur as the third stage of cognitive development when the child has the ability to apply logical processes to concrete problems.

Decentering is taking in more than one aspect of a situation.

Reversibility is the ability to reverse operations and use information presented earlier.

Conservation is the understanding that amounts remain the same if nothing is added or taken away.

The child has the ability now, during concrete operations, to consider more than one aspect of a situation at a time. Inconsistencies that did not phase him at earlier times now become a problem to be solved. It is sometime after seven that the child figures out the real story of Santa. The problems in the story of Santa that did not bother him at an earlier age now logically counter his earlier belief system.

With this new stage of concrete operations, the child is able to complete mental operations, or thought processes, in her head on situations that are tangible or real. At eight years of age, a child would approach looking at a simple float and sink situation concretely. She finds that a small paper clip and a two-inch square wood block do not behave in predictable ways when dropped into water. If she has the opportunity to experiment with these and other objects made of metal and wood, she could gradually see that wood objects float and metal objects sink. She is dealing with tangible things that she can perform actions on. However, this experimentation does not prepare her for a new, more complex, consideration (e.g. that large steel tankers float). This would take her into new considerations needed in formal operations, the thinking of an eleven- or twelve-year-old who can consider the hypothetical.

EARLY MATHEMATICAL THINKING

Adult thinkers have the concept of the consistency of amount, that is, they know that the number or amounts of things stay the same unless altered.

ANECDOTE

If you remember putting $20.00 in your billfold, you expect it to be there until it is spent. When you find only $16.00, you will search for the missing four dollars until they are found. Of course, there might be some faulty memory working here, like forgetting the stop at McDonald's or lending $4.00 to a friend. But when going over the day's events, you can relax after you recapture where the money was spent.

As adults we accept this as a given, but the young child does not know consistency in amounts, or conservation, until she is seven. Because the preschool child does not consider consistency in amounts, the total sum is irrelevant (Prairie, 1994b).

The young child has a long way to go in development to reach adult mathematical concepts. Yet even young babies show us that they understand some basic concepts. In the same way that researchers discern if a baby understands the consistency of objects as described earlier, it is also seen that young babies have a rudimentary concept of number and of characteristics of objects.

Infants have demonstrated a firm concept of the difference between one and two objects. A five-month-old registers surprise that there is only one little doll in front of her when a moment ago she saw two being placed there (Wynn, 1992, as cited in Bjorklund, 1995).

By the end of the first year, babies can distinguish between photographs of birds as distinct from horses (Roberts, 1988, as cited in Berger, 2001). Mandler and McDonough also report that babies see dogs as distinct from cats (as cited in Berger, 2001). The research seems to show that the child has the beginnings of organization for categories and of counting within the first year. This rudimentary ability to recognize differences will be defined more as the child grows into the preschool years.

ONE-TO-ONE CORRESPONDENCE

In the first year, the child is actively placing one object to go with another one.

ANECDOTE

Jerlean stops in her crawling and pulls on the toe of her sock until she triumphantly jerks it off her foot. She puts it over her toe in a half-hearted attempt to put it on her foot again.

The next morning when her mother dresses her, she makes an attempt to put a sock on one foot. She laughs, pushing her foot toward her mother to finish the job.

At this young age, Jerlean is making a relationship with an object that belongs with another object.

ANECDOTE

Jerlean plays a game with her mother by pointing to her mother's nose, then to her own. Her mother laughs with her and then adds eyes, ears, and chin to the game.

One-to-one correspondence is putting two objects into relationship; one item goes with one item.

A sock belongs to a foot, a nose matches a nose. Jerlean matches one item to one item. She is making the relationship of **one-to-one correspondence** (Piaget, 1965). Preschoolers play out this same basic concept, giving a plate to every doll, a cup to every plate.

Thus the foundation for mathematics is laid. The very act of counting includes one-to-one correspondence. By putting a finger on each card as Hue Lee says the number, this enables him to count correctly (Kamii, 1982).

ANECDOTE

Ms. L. has set out a row of six cards and asks four-year-old Hue Lee to count them. Hue Lee gently places his finger on each card as he correctly counts them.

THREE KINDS OF KNOWLEDGE

Young children are involved in many different types of activity and explore many different types of thinking in their day-to-day experiences. Within these three kinds of thinking are categorized. The first, **physical knowledge,** is involved with the cognitive processes experienced as children act on objects. Given a group of shells in a basket, the child does actions on various shells and observes the results. He feels the shape and smoothness. He clinks them together and tries dropping one on the table. What he learns is knowledge basically outside him. It is in the physical properties (shape, texture, sounds that they make) of the objects that he finds through exploring. By exploring the objects and performing some actions on them, the child has learned about physical knowledge of the shells.

Mathematics is included in **logicomathematical** knowledge, the second kind of knowledge. This is created when the child makes relationships between and among objects. The one-to-one correspondence described previously and classifying, comparing, and numbering are all about the objects as they are in relationship to each other. The child handling the shells compares the sizes of several shells, matches the clam shells that are just alike, and classifies some of them into groups according to shapes. In addition to manipulating the objects to see relationships, the child considers these relationships in his mind.

Social knowledge is knowledge shared by people. It is information decided on by groups. That the item the child is holding is called *concha* in Spanish and *shell* in English is information gathered from people around the child. The number name in math is social knowledge as is the name of the act, whether it is called counting the shells or adding them. The decision that we should return sea creatures back to the sea is also social knowledge. The distinction of social knowledge is that it comes from people, not from the objects themselves (Chaillé & Britain, 2003; Kamii & DeVries, 1993; Williams & Kamii, 1986).

Applying the Three Kinds of Knowledge

Preschoolers' thinking is tied to the real, logical, here and now. This is important to see in understanding the child's grasp of physical knowledge as well as other processes in learning. As first proposed by Kamii and DeVries, the young child can understand cause and effect when these four criteria are present:

1. The child must be able to produce the movement by his or her own actions. The connection of the action and reaction is because of what the child does, not the intervening force (like a magnet) causing the reaction.
2. The child must be able to vary his or her actions on objects. The ability to change the effects on the outcome makes experimentation possible.
3. The reaction of the object must be observable. In some examples of physical science materials, only the end result is observable; the cause is not, as in gravity, magnetism, and electricity.
4. The reaction of the object must be immediate. This means there is an immediate reaction of the object because the action and reaction are close in time and space. (Chaillé & Britain, 2003, pp. 68, 69; Kamii & DeVries, 1993, pp. 8, 9)

With these guidelines, teachers can prepare physical science activities (see Chapter 16) so the child can directly act on materials and obtain information that occurs because of what the child does. You can see that this refers to the ways that preschool children think about cause and effect.

For logicomathematical knowledge, the child puts things in relationships and uses her understanding to make those relationships. It is with her thinking that she puts items into one-to-one correspondence. It is through many experiences that she makes sense of making sets or counting. This understanding comes through her actions and thinking combined, not through direct teaching. If adults teach the child how to count, he learns it as facts outside of himself, not integrated into his way of thinking. The mainstream social concept in the United States is that adults *teach* children numbers. Because of this belief, it is particularly hard for adults to grasp that learning logicomathematical knowledge develops through children handling materials. You will see in later chapters that the teacher supports the logicomathematical process of counting by teaching skills of counting, then providing ample opportunity for the child to practice—and accepting his mistakes (Kamii, 1982; Kamii & DeVries, 1993).

During the early years social knowledge comes from adults, peers, and siblings. Teachers are actively teaching social knowledge through talking about what children are doing, naming the items they are using and promoting the children's discussion which will provide practice in using newly acquired social knowledge. This does not mean teaching words didactly, but it does mean providing a rich language environment that expands vocabulary while talking about what children are doing (Kamii & DeVries, 1993).

ANECDOTE

Angela, age four, is arranging three large cylinder blocks in the block area. By herself she lifts each block, then lets it roll. She stands each one on its end and they stay put. The characteristics she feels and experiences (feel of wood, roundness, rolling ability, or standing ability) are physical knowledge.

Angela lines up the three blocks on end making a line. She then groups the three blocks close together. This relationship (the set of three) is logicomathematical. She can also form this group in her mind, seeing the threeness of the group.

Angela looks up as Ms. A. approaches her. "You put the three cylinder blocks together."

"They stand together," replies Angela pointing to the blocks.

"Yes, three blocks together." Ms. A. nods.

With her experiences handling the blocks, Angela advances in two types of knowledge. In addition, Angela hears the labeling words in her teacher's conversation. By naming the number (three), the type (cylinder) and the class (blocks), the teacher can also help Angela gain social knowledge (Williams & Kamii, 1986).

REVISITING THE INQUIRY PROCESS

Returning to the inquiry processes used by children that you encountered in Chapter 1, you can apply your knowledge of how children learn. What do you know about young children's thinking that assists you in knowing how children will use these steps? Preschoolers

- Are prelogical in their thinking
- Are bound to here and now
- Learn through concrete, or real, experiences to grasp concepts about things that concern them
- Understand cause and effect when it is easily observable
- Are nonlineal, which means the steps they take will not be in order
- Are fluid as they move from one step to another
- Are intuitive in that they will use their perceptions instead of logic

As you move forward in this text, you will continue to be observant of the individual child. Use this to understand his thinking, his way of processing his experiences, and to help him understand the next step in learning. In this way you will be able to structure the learning experiences, the dialog around his learning, and take the next steps in inquiry with him.

SOME REAL VIEWS INTO THE INQUIRY PROCESS

From looking at many aspects of how young children learn, you now can combine what you have read with real views of children learning. Table 2–2 shows examples of what preschoolers do in these steps.

TABLE 2–2   Examples of Inquiry Process

■ Exploring	A child pats the sand after pouring water on it.
	A child runs the car down the ramp over and over again.
■ Identifying	"I made an airplane. It goes up and zooms."
	"The two triangles made a square."
■ Classifying	"You found the small rocks."
	"Why did you put these in this box?"
	"I have the green plates."
■ Comparing and contrasting	"Is your block tower taller than you?"
	"Do you both have the same amount?"
	"How is this one different?"
■ Hypothesizing	"You used all the cylinder blocks to make it this high. What can you do to make it higher?"
	"What will happen if we swing the pendulum from your side?"
	"You gave two crackers to everyone and we have some left. I wonder what we can do to use the ones that are left?"
■ Generalizing	"Now when you want to make a tower even higher you can use smaller blocks."
	"Look I made pink!" "Now you know that you can make pink by mixing red and white paint."
	"If we pass around the crackers again I think each one can get one more."

(Terms of Inquiry Processes used by Children from *Who am I in the lives of children*?, 6th ed., by Feeney, Christensen, & Moravcik, © 2001. Reprinted by permission of Pearson Education, Inc., Upper Saddle River, NJ, p. 316.)

After spending time observing young children at play, you will be able to see the steps of inquiry being accomplished by the children themselves. You can add your own observations to this list. Through this you can develop the skill of looking for these steps throughout your involvement with children.

The science standards go on to say that children in K–4 have difficulty with the process of experimentation. With preschoolers and kindergartners, expectations are that a full process of experimentation would not take place, but that aspects of experimentation occur and, later on, older children will focus on the concrete results of their experiments (National Academy of Sciences, 1996).

STANDARDS

Full inquiry involves asking a simple question, completing an investigation, answering the question and presenting the results to others. . . . However, children in K–4 have difficulty with experimentation as a process of testing ideas and the logic of using evidence to formulate explanations.

Content Standard A1. Reprinted with permission from *National science education standards.* (1996). The National Academy of Sciences, courtesy of the National Academies Press, Washington, DC (p. 122).

SUMMARY

By looking closely at the ways the young child thinks, you see how different these ways are from our modes of thinking. You can also appreciate these thought processes and be better able to respond appropriately. Now, with this understanding, you can accept the different ways young children will use the inquiry process. In view of constructivist learning, the focus is on the child learning through his experiences. In the next chapter, you will see how the child learns in the context of others and within the context of a culture. From this view of the individual learning, we can see how this same child is learning with others.

TO FURTHER YOUR THINKING

1. After reviewing the significant changes in the development of neurons, explain these changes to a classmate or a friend. Describe the following processes: branching in neurons, overproduction of synapse, pruning, myelination, growth in corpus callosum. How does this growth enable the changes in the young child's thinking abilities?
2. Discuss with a classmate or friend the following cognitive abilities of infants, toddlers, and preschoolers:
   a. Early cause and effect
   b. Object permanence

     c. Representational thinking

     d. Magical causality

     e. Egocentrism

     f. Realism

     g. Animism

     h. Artificialism

     i. Cause and effect

     j. Transductive reasoning

     k. Centration

     l. Static states

     m. Irreversibility

3. Discuss the difference in thinking for the child five to seven years of age compared with the preschool and primary age child.

4. Discuss advances in concrete operational thinking as compared to preschool thinking.

5. If presented with the situation of having less money at the end of the day, why would the young child think differently than you would about the lesser amount?

6. Describe examples of a young child accomplishing one-to-one correspondence.

7. Using the example of Angela handling the three cylinder blocks, describe the three kinds of knowledge she encounters. Apply the three kinds of knowledge to a child pretending to set a table with plates, spoons, and cups.

8. In revisiting the inquiry processes (page 36), compare each bullet point with the description of preschoolers' thinking discussed earlier in the chapter. How would the understanding of young children change the structure of learning experiences for them?

REFERENCES

Berger, K. S. (2001). *The developing person through the lifespan* (5th ed.). New York: Worth.

Bjorklund, D. F. (1995). *Children's thinking: Developmental function and individual differences* (2nd ed.). Pacific Grove, CA: Brooks/Cole.

Chaillé, C., and Britain, L. (2003). *The young child as scientist: A constructivist approach to early childhood science education* (3rd ed.). Boston: Allyn & Bacon.

Eliot, L. (1999). *What's going on in there? How the brain and mind develop in the first five years of life.* New York: Bantam.

Elkind, D. (1999). Educating young children in math, science, and technology. In American Association for the Advancement of Science, *Dialogue on early childhood science, mathematics, and technology education* (pp. 62–70). Washington, DC: Author.

Feeney, S., Christensen, D., and Moravcik, E. (2001). *Who am I in the lives of children?* (6th ed.). Upper Saddle River, NJ: Pearson Education.

Ginsberg, H. P., and Opper, S. (1979). *Piaget's theory of intellectual development* (2nd ed.). Englewood Cliffs, NJ: Prentice Hall.

Gopnick, A., Meltzoff, A. N., and Kuhl, P. K. (1999). *The scientist in the crib: What early learning tells us about the mind.* New York: HarperCollins.

Kamii, C. (1982). *Number in preschool and kindergarten.* Washington, DC: National Association for the Education of Young Children.

Kamii, C., and DeVries, R. (1993). *Physical knowledge in preschool education: Implications of Piaget's theory.* New York: Teachers College Press.

National Academy of Science. (1996). *National science education standards* [book version, on line]. Washington, DC: National Academies Press. www.nap.edu

National Association for the Education of Young Children. (2003). NAEYC standards for early childhood professional preparation: Initial licensure programs. In M. Hyson (Ed.), *Preparing early childhood professionals: NAEYC's standards for programs* (pp. 17–63). Washington DC: Author.

Piaget, J. (1965). How children form mathematical concepts. In R. C. Anderson and D. P. Ausubel (Eds.). *Readings in the psychology of cognition* (pp. 406–414). New York: Holt, Rinehart & Winston.

Piaget, J., and Inhelder, B. (1969). *The psychology of the child.* New York: Basic Books.

Prairie, A. P. (1994a). *Do children understand science?* Unpublished.

Prairie, A. P. (1994b). *The very basics of mathematics for young children.* Unpublished.

Williams, C. K., and Kamii, C. (1986, November). How do children learn by handling objects? *Young Children, 41*(1), 23–26.

Wolfinger, D. (1994). *Science and mathematics in early childhood education.* New York: HarperCollins.

ADDITIONAL RESOURCES

Allen, K. E., and Marotz, L. R. (1994). *Developmental profiles: Pre-birth through eight.* Clifton Park, NY: Delmar Learning. This list of developmental characteristics of children through eight years of age adds to the elements of cognitive development in this chapter.

Berger, K. S. (2001). *The developing person through the life span* (5th ed.). New York: Worth. In the section on preschool you will find illustrations of Piagetian tasks for young children and descriptions of complex brain development.

Bransford, J., Brown, A. L., and Cocking, J. (Eds.). (2000). *How people learn: Brain, mind, experience, and school: Expanded edition*. National Research Council. Washington, DC: National Academies Press. A thorough presentation of current understanding of cognitive development.

Charlesworth, R. (2004). *Understanding child development* (6th ed.). Clifton Park, NY: Delmar Learning. Solid foundation of development from ages birth to eight in this text.

Eliot, L. (1999). *What's going on in there? How the brain and mind develop in the first five years of life*. New York: Bantam. A readable book that clearly explains the complex brain development from prenatal to school age.

Gopnick, A., Meltzoff, A. N., and Kuhl, P. K. (1999). *The scientist in the crib: What early learning tells us about the mind*. New York: HarperCollins. An easy-reading book for parents that clearly discusses thinking in young children.

Piaget, J. (1973). *To understand is to invent: The future of education*. New York: Grossman. There are numerous texts by Piaget, but this text and the following one are good sources for causality and for understanding thinking.

Piaget, J. (with R. Garcia) (1974). *Understanding causality*. New York: Norton. While the books by Piaget translated from French are rather difficult, this classic is easily understood.

Shonkoff, J. P., and Phillips, D. A. (Eds.). (2000). *From neurons to neighborhoods: The science of early childhood development*. Washington, DC: National Academies Press. A thorough presentation of brain development and how this relates to education and the social community for optimum development.

Wadsworth, B. J. (1978). *Piaget for the classroom teacher*. New York: Longman. This readable text explains Piagetian theory and outlines the tasks the reader can explore with children.

Williams, C. K., and Kamii, C. (1986, November). How do children learn by handling objects? *Young Children, 42*(1), 23–26. This article reviews the three kinds of knowledge and applies this thinking to the classroom.

Web Sites

http://ecrp.uiuc.edu Hosted at University of Illinois, this current on-line journal provides opportunity to respond to articles.

www.exploratorium.edu Exploratorium Institute for Inquiry has posted a description of inquiry.

Chapter 3
Socially Shared Learning

OBJECTIVES Through the process of discovery in this chapter, you will be able to:

1. Discuss how young children learn in the social context.

2. Describe components of zone of proximal development and scaffolding.

3. Describe the role of play in young children's cognitive development.

4. Discuss how expectations are transferred in the culture.

5. Discuss the way that learning to think is embedded in the social context.

6. Describe how approaches to learning involve the social context.

IDEAS TO PONDER

- How can adults assist children in the thinking process?

- How does learning occur in play?

- How are adult expectations transferred to the child?

- How does culture affect learning?

- How can we discover the ways of learning in a culture?

- How can the child's education include her way of learning?

"I do not know when I began telling stories to my own young children. As a child I recall listening to my grandmother tell stories. These were stories based on living, on traditions, and especially about our religion. For my children I created an imaginary character named Lulu who taught lessons to my children in ridiculous situations. Lulu has taught my children that leaving the faucet running is not a good idea. She has taught the names of various clouds. My children

do not realize that Lulu has taught them so much. Hardly a day goes by that they do not ask, 'Mommy, can you tell us a Lulu story?'"
(E. Alvarez, parent and teacher, personal communication, April 22, 2003)

THE SOCIAL CONSTRUCTS OF LEARNING

Building on Chapter 2's discussion of the child learning as an individual, this chapter examines the child learning in a context and connected to family, culture, and the wider social world. Like the Lulu stories from the preceding quote, the stories children hear in their families become part of the rich cultural context. "People are products of their social and cultural worlds and that to understand children, we must understand the social, cultural and societal contexts in which they develop" (Berk & Winsler, 1995, p. 1).

In the **sociocultural theory,** Lev Vygotsky proposes that learning occurs within the social and cultural contexts and is shared by the members of that group. "Vygotsky argued that children learn to use the tools for thinking provided by culture through their interactions with more skilled partners" (Rogoff, 2003, p. 50). In these complex interactions, children learn the processes of thinking used (and promoted) by that culture (Berk & Winsler, 1995; Cole, John-Steiner, Scribner, & Souberman, 1978).

Sociocultural theory is the concept that learning occurs in a social context.

ZONE OF PROXIMAL DEVELOPMENT

Through observing the child the adult can see what the child can accomplish on his own. There is a next level that can be reached with assisted performance

Scaffolding supports the child in learning new abilities.

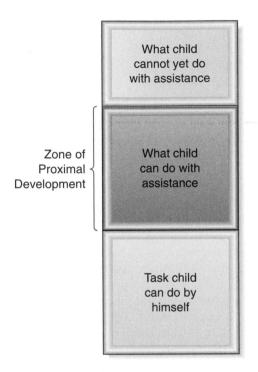

Figure 3–1 Zone of proximal development.

The zone of proximal development is the area of learning at the point where the learner can accomplish the task with the help of another.

through the help of a peer, older child, or attentive adult. In this level the child can learn with the help of another above what the child can do on his own; this is the **zone of proximal development** (ZPD). This is constantly changing as the child builds skills (Bodrova & Leong, 1996) (Fig. 3–1).

SCAFFOLDING

Scaffolding is the structure the teacher provides so the child can master the task with help.

In using ZPD, the teacher can choose to use **scaffolding.** When the teacher is aware that the child falters in one or more steps, he can help the child just enough so the child can accomplish the task with help. Later, the child will accomplish this task on his own.

ANECDOTE

The following is an example of scaffolding:

Devonti dumps out his He-Man figures from the bag he has brought from home. He kneels down close to the table and counts them rapidly and randomly.

"1-2-3-4-5-9-10!" he announces as Jon, his teacher, moves to sit down with him. "You've counted all your He-Man figures. How about standing each one up as you count them. That way you can see them."

Devonti nods and places one at the edge of the table. Jon says, "That's one."

"Ya, one."

"Now the next one. Still want to count them?"

Devonti nods and carefully lines the second one at the edge of the table and adds, "Two!"

"You are making a line of them. That makes them easy to count."

Devonti continues slowly. At the fourth figure, he looks up at Jon and Jon supplies the number four. As Devonti continues he matches a number name to each figure but not in correct order. His total count goes as this: "1-2-3-4-6-8-9-10."

"You counted them all lined up." At this, Devonti beamed.

During this incident we can see that Devonti's ability is changing. With more practice using the skill of matching the number name to each figure, he will gradually self-correct counting errors (see Chapter 10). This task of scaffolding accomplishes more than assisted completion of the task. The child now has skills to accomplish on his own and will feel confident to forge ahead.

In scaffolding, all or some of the steps shown in Table 3–1 may occur.

TABLE 3–1   Steps in Scaffolding

1. Observe to ascertain what the child is doing. From observing you can follow the child's intent.
2. Ask the child what he intends to do. Asking respects the child and provides verbal input on his intent.
3. Comment on the child's actions. Through your comments he knows you are paying attention to what he is currently doing.
4. Scaffold verbally or through action to provide a way to solve the problem. This input opens up possibilities for the child to try out new ways. Ask permission before making a move to change his work.
5. Once the child enters the process of accomplishing the task, move back from the child's work. This will help him "own" his work.
6. Comment specifically on the child's accomplishment. He will value his new skill from your statement.

In managing scaffolding, Wood, Bruner, and Ross (1976) explain that the structure varies depending on the particular aspect the child needs in order to accomplish the task. There are several approaches to consider:

> Reduce or simplify the number of steps required to solve the problem so the child can manage them, maintain the child's interest in pursuing the goal, point out the critical features that show the difference between the child's performance and the ideal performance, control frustration, and demonstrate the idealized version of what the child is doing. (Wood, Bruner, & Ross, 1976, p. 60)

Peers sometimes provide the best scaffolding. It seems that they more readily understand the steps that the child needs because it was not long ago that the child needed that herself. Yet scaffolding is not outside the realm of the adult teacher. The teacher can focus on exactly what the child is doing, what the child needs in order to learn, and give just that help, no more. This takes an ability to step outside oneself for the moment to understand the thinking of another.

STANDARDS

Candidates know, understand, and use a wide array of effective approaches, strategies, and tools to positively influence children's development and learning.

Standard 4b. Reprinted with permission from National Association for the Education of Young Children. NAEYC standards for early childhood professional preparation: Initial licensure programs. (2003). In *Preparing early childhood professionals: NAEYC's standards for programs,* M. Hyson (Ed.). Washington, DC: Author, (p. 29).

ANECDOTE

PERCEPTIVE VERSUS INTRUSIVE ADULT-TO-ADULT TEACHING

In contrast to learning about the camera, the learning of PowerPoint™ was a positive experience that furthered autonomous learning.

> When I first looked at my new camera I was so pleased, yet overwhelmed at all the knowledge needed to operate it even at the basic level. So I handed it to my brother and asked him how to load film, and he began teaching me from step one all aspects of using the camera. I became bored and resented this help because he did not perceive what I requested of him.

> When I was first learning to use PowerPoint, a colleague asked me to begin by opening up the program. At the point I was stuck he was ready to show me what to do next. From that one session I felt I knew how to operate it. So when I took it to the classroom, I knew the needed steps to present the PowerPoint lesson.
>
> (Author)

PLAY

Play is essential in the learning of the young child. Both Piagetians and followers of Vygotsky uphold play as essential in young children's lives. In *Mind in Society: The Development of Higher Psychological Processes* by L. S. Vygotsky, the editors propose that the child in pretend play develops his own zone of proximal development to advance his abilities.

> In play a child always behaves beyond his average age, above his daily behavior; in play it is as though he were a head taller than himself. As in the focus of a magnifying glass, play contains all developmental tendencies in a condensed form and is itself a major form of development. (Cole, John-Steiner, Scribner, & Souberman, 1978, p. 102)

LEVELS OF COGNITIVE PLAY

Play is important for children from infancy to school age. While play is naturally a part of the preschool, there needs to be more emphasis on play in kindergarten. The four levels of cognitive play are seen in children from infancy to school age (Table 3–2).

TABLE 3–2   Levels of Cognitive Play

- **Functional Play**   Repeat movement of the body or objects for the sake of movement or to experience the sensory aspect of the motion. Examples: Shaking a tambourine or splashing water.
- **Constructive Play**   Physical manipulation of objects to build or construct an object that represents the child's ideas. Examples: Building a road with blocks, making tortillas from play dough (Forman, 1998).
- **Pretend Play**   Playing roles or using objects to take on imaginary roles seen in everyday life or learned through the media. Examples: Playing roles of teacher and students or he-man characters.
- **Games with Rules**   Board games or outdoor games that have a set of rules, including turn-taking and a prescribed way to complete the actions of the game. Examples: Jump rope, checkers. (Piaget, 1962; Smilansky & Shefatya, 1990)

Through play the young child learns in many areas: physical skills, social interactions, emotional expression, and cognitive understanding. While all these areas are important considerations whenever play is observed, this text emphasizes the cognitive area of play. All levels of play advance cognitive learning, including advancing skills in math and science.

In functional play children handle objects and materials and explore their properties and find out what they can do with these materials. Exploring (see Chapter 5) is a main outcome of functional play.

Constructive play offers the most opportunities for working to understand how objects relate to each other, how to combine them to form desired outcomes. These, in turn, may evolve into pretend play (Forman, 1998). In constructive play mathematical learning may involve one-to-one correspondence, classification, comparing, counting, adding and subtracting, and geometry. Physical science opportunities are part of the play as children manipulate and move objects to accomplish goals.

Mathematical learning occurs in constructive play with blocks.

In pretend play, specifically **sociodramatic play** in which children play together in role-taking situations, new areas of cognitive growth emerge. In Piagetian terms, sociodramatic play enables young children to develop and practice decentration and reversibility. For example, in the following anecdote Tasha is both the child in real life and the teacher in play. Tasha can move back and forth from being child (real) and teacher (pretend) as the play moves along.

Sociodramatic play is pretend play with one or more peers where children take on social roles they know.

ANECDOTE

In Tasha's pretend play, she (as teacher) tells children to sit, then opens the book to read the story. When another child wants to be the teacher, she (as Tasha) tells the child that she is the teacher now. When that child walks away from the small group of listeners, Tasha (as Tasha) can determine if the child is leaving the play because she has truly lost interest or (as teacher) whether the child is *playing* at not following the teacher's directions.

Sociodramatic play offers opportunities to take on roles.

In checkers children learn about following rules, taking turns, and another's point of view.

In moving in and out of pretend and in consideration of others in the pretend or real mode, the young child can use skills of decentration and reversibility. These are skills that will not appear in reality modes until the child is six to eight years old (Rubin, Fein, & Vandenberg, 1983). Pretending promotes flexible thinking and enables the child to deal with contradictory information (Fromberg & Bergen, 1998).

In games with rules, children learn skills such as reciprocity (in acknowledging the need to follow rules). Strategy develops logical thinking and reversibility in planning ahead. Various math concepts are also employed (see "Board Games" in Chapter 14).

WAYS OF TRANSACTING EXPECTATIONS IN SOCIAL CONTEXT

The child learns about what is expected of her in all sorts of ways. Through observation she sees adults, siblings, and peers act in a particular way to accomplish a particular outcome. The child sees how others respond to her behavior, some of which bring approval and others which bring disapproval. In day-to-day experiences she learns what is best to learn. Much of the expected behavior is learned through nonspoken interaction. A story from my parenting experiences shows this clearly.

ANECDOTE

THE EXPECTED BEHAVIOR

When my two children were quite young, we lived near a grocery store that was on the other side of a very busy city street. As usual I would take my two children to the store, fill up two bags of groceries, then take the two bags and the children to cross the street. My action would simply be to hold out one arm to each of them, watch for the break in traffic, and then cross the street with them. The two would respond without a word from me and we would cross safely. (Never mind the message at crossing where there was not a stoplight.) Once across they would gaily run ahead on the sidewalk for the block to home. Even though I was a rather easygoing parent in discipline, the children readily obeyed these expectations implicitly.

(Author)

This anecdote conveys how situational behavior drives behavior and learning. Circumstances dictated certain actions; hence the children easily complied without hearing a word. How much more is passed from adult to child on what is important for learning.

LEARNING EMBEDDED IN THE SOCIAL CONTEXT

While much has yet to be understood about learning in the cultural context, research shows that the subjects that are important to learn and the way they are to be learned are embedded in the culture. Within the theory of Piaget, it is assumed that the child has the freedom in the sociocultural context to explore many avenues of his curiosity. When the child has a lot of freedom from adult supervision, this can be true to some extent. Yet the availability of materials and space to learn may deter the possibilities. Goodnow (1987) points out that there may be many implicit understandings of what is important to learn and what is acceptable to learn. These can be influenced by constraints that a particular group may place on gender or social class.

In sociocultural theory, the teacher (i.e., parent, any adult, sibling, older child, or peer) also presents to the child what is important to learn and how it is learned. In studies by Rogoff, Guatemalan children learned from family members through observation more than through information presented verbally or through scaffolding. In contrast, children in Salt Lake City, Utah, were given more verbal enticement, instructions, and opportunity to try the activity (Rogoff, Mistry, Göncü, & Mosier, 1993).

Goodnow (1987) discusses what determines what is learned in a particular society. Perhaps this is governed by both what the people with power deem is appropriate and valuable to learn and by the position the learner holds in society.

THE USE OF QUESTIONS IN TWO CULTURES

Although the questions about how different children learn are just beginning to be asked, the findings from the following research completed by Heath (1983, 1989) show how use of language in two cultures impacted the children's behavior in school.

ANECDOTE

As their children attended school in Trackton, a southeastern U.S. city, parents were disturbed about their children's dislike of school. Researchers followed the white teachers at home and school as well as the African American children at home and school to search for answers. One of the differences they found was in the way African American and white adults used questions. In observing the white teachers at home, they found that 50 percent of their utterances were interrogatives, and these questions were "teaching questions" or the known-answer type, such as "What kind of truck is that?" These teaching questions, used in both the school and home of the white teachers, were questions for which the adult already knew the answer.

The African American children in Trackton were not used to these kinds of questions. In fact, their parents did not ask young children questions until they were seen as competent sources of information. Black parents asked "real" questions, ones to which they themselves did not know the answer. Trackton children developed complex verbal skills at home, but at school they were confused by the teaching questions in the classroom and often withdrew into silence. The outcome of this study was that teachers added informative questioning and through this process the children became active participants in the classroom. (Berk & Winsler, 1995; Delpit, 1995; Heath, 1983, 1989)

SUPPORTING CHILDREN'S LEARNING STYLES

Leaders in education have pinpointed several approaches to meet culturally diverse learning styles of some African American children and incorporate culture into the teaching practices of the school. Ladson-Billings (2001) proposes culturally relevant pedagogy by blending home and community experiences into teaching. For example, Lisa Delpit (1995) explains that math is learned successfully when the math problem is put in the context of a real-life problem.

```
ANECDOTE
```

Following this idea in presenting math within the context of real life, Juanita Copley approaches five-year-old children with, "I have a problem . . . ". She then shares the problem and these eager young learners work diligently to find the answer. One child told her, "Ms. Copley, you sure have a lot of problems!" (Clements, Sarama, & Copley, 2003).

Wade Boykin (2002) continues in this vein by evaluating the meaning of children's everyday cultural practices and drawing on these to study culturally relevant topics and ideas. This style of teaching affects the learning by validating the participation patterns of black children in their families through collaborative learning, fostering mutual support and emphasizing communal over individualistic learning (Boykin, 2002; Delpit, 1995; Ladson-Billings, 2001).

Afro-cultural influences in the school should include movement, tied to the mosaic of expressiveness in dance, percussiveness, and rhythm. Also there will be communalism and a sensitivity to the fundamental interdependence of people with identity and esteem in group membership (Boykin, 2002). In contrast, the mainstream cultural themes are autonomy, individualism, individual recognition, solitude, and competition (Ellison, Boykin, Towns, & Stokes, 2000). These aforementioned Afro-cultural themes should not replace the mainstream themes (Ellison, Boykin, Towns, & Stokes, 2000). "Rather what is suggested is that the cultural contexts in schools need to be diversified so that a fuller range of expectations is available. Moreover, if teachers made explicit mainstream expectations, then over time the children can become more flexible in the application of their talents, skills, and effort" (Boykin, 2002, p. 55). Variations of many of these principles have been implemented in schools.

TEACHING WITH STORIES

Really listening to children can open up discourse and disclose understanding from the students' point of view. In discussion of her teaching, Gallas (1995) perceived Latino students' learning not to utilize the type of discourse normally used in science. She had been used to presenting science concepts to students and expecting students to respond in discussion. She discovered that the first rule in teaching through discourse was to find out what she did not know about her students. "My sense of responsibility for helping my students place science into the immediate context of their lives grew as I realized that the only way to do that was to uncover their 'stories about science'" (Gallas, 1995, p. 11). She learned their stories from listening to her students' informal conversations among each other.

In a similar vein, Elizabeth Alvarez (personal communication, June 20, 2003) learned to listen to her students' stories brought out in class by the lessons. Her

ANECDOTE

A STORY OF LEARNING THROUGH TEACHING, BY ELIZABETH ALVAREZ

I never fathomed that a monolingual, Spanish-speaking, eighth-grade class from a marginalized community would change my ideals and practices in teaching science. As a bilingual Mexican-American teacher accustomed to American schooling, I began teaching science to this group of Mexican students who were new to the country and barely understood English. In one of the 45-minute lessons during a lesson about the phases of the moon, a student raised his hand and began sharing this story.

Arturo: Maestra, ¿conoce la historia del conejo que vive en la Luna?
Teacher, do you know the story about the rabbit that lives on the moon?

Martín: Ah, sí. Es el cuento de un conejo que sube hasta la Luna y pone su sombra enfrente de la Luna y por eso tenemos los cambios de la Luna.
Oh, yeah. It is the story about a rabbit that climbs to the moon and places his shadow in front of the moon and that is why the moon changes.

Sra. Alvarez: No, no conozco la historia, pero no vamos hablar de eso.
I don't know that story and we are not going to talk about it.

Arturo: Pero, maestra, de veras, este conejo cambia la aparencia de la Luna. Por eso tenemos el cuarto creciente, la Luna llena, el cuarto menguante y la Luna nueva.
But, Teacher, it's true; this rabbit changes the appearance of the moon. That is why we have the first quarter, full moon, the last quarter, and the new moon.

Sra. Alvarez: Está bien, pero no hay un conejo que vive en la Luna. Yo nunca he oído de eso. He oído del hombre que vive en la Luna y el primer hombre que subió a la Luna en 1969, pero nunca de un conejo. Dejemos de hablar de este cuento y vamos a continuar con la lección.
That is fine, but there is no rabbit that lives on the moon. I never heard of that. I heard about a man on the moon, and the first man to go to the moon in 1969, but never a rabbit. Let's forget talking about that story and continue with our lesson.

I was intrigued, yet reluctant to hear this story. Yet through "Rabbit on the Moon," he remembered the four phases of the moon before the lesson of the moon had even started.

My upbringing was very similar to that of Richard Rodriguez, who describes "public society" pertaining to the outside world, where inside his house was purely private. "Just opening or closing the screen door behind me was an important experience" (Rodriguez, 1982, p. 17). In the same way I had learned to repress and silence the culture La de Mexicana and to separate the two cultures that lived within me. I had felt that in order to succeed, I needed to oppose my intimate culture and become immersed with my American or "public society" culture. My schooling had taught me to provide the factual meaning behind the phases; that telling stories concluded that students knew nothing of the subject. Yet these stories were part of their traditions, their culture, and style of learning (Smolen & Ortiz-Castro, 2000).

The student's story about the rabbit on the moon became the revelation to my new teaching approach in science. Because I am Mexicana, I had the potential to make the shift between my two cultures: my "public society" schooling culture and my private life culture, which I denied and hid away for many years. This experience caused me to realize it is imperative first to understand students' culture before the students understand the teacher's culture (Cazden, 1988).

Since then I began seeing stories embedded in all subjects, where it held the key in aiding Latinos' pursuit in succeeding in science, a bridge to grasping the English language and science language and eventually fitting in United States schooling. (E. Alvarez, personal communication, June 20, 2003)

story relates her eventual understanding of how stories were important for her Latino students.

These stories tell how teachers came to realize how a particular group of children learned. The stories the students shared were based on Mexican folk tales, myths, tales told by their grandparents and parents, as well as life experiences at home and while visiting Mexico. "My caring for my students by listening to their stories encouraged the students to become enthusiastic about science which led them to achieve and succeed in science" (Alvarez, personal communication, June 20, 2003). Through personal search and reflection on what children were saying, teachers changed their approach to meet the ways children learned.

LEARNING THE SOCIAL CONTEXT OF THE CHILD

In a classroom there will often be children of diverse cultures. In the first few years of life children have already experienced the way of knowing and the "what of knowing" from family and community. When teachers search for understanding these ways, children and adults will learn from each other.

Here are some steps teachers can take to embrace ways children learn:

1. Ask parents what is important for their children to learn and how they expect them to learn.
2. Ask parents to share stories of their children.
3. Listen to the interactions of parents and their children, and among the children's peers and siblings. Pay attention to the language style and form.

4. Learn as much about the particular culture as you can through families, acquaintances, the Internet, articles, and books.
5. Observe and listen to children. Welcome children's stories. It is children themselves that will tell you how they learn.

EMBRACING HOME AND SCHOOL CULTURES

Teaching is necessarily a two-way process. From you, the child will learn something of what is important to learn, what is expected of her, and how to accomplish the task. At the same time, the teacher will learn what the child knows, what she wants to know, and her way of learning. Once in relation with the child, the teacher becomes part of her social context. By embracing the ways the child has already learned in her early years, the adult can effectively bring these ways into the teaching process and then gradually introduce the cultural expectations of the school. The cultural learning of expectations occurs for both teacher and learner.

According to Wade Boykin (2002, p. 55), "If African American themes frame contexts in schools, then their presence may facilitate higher achievement for the black children." Mainstream themes like individualism and competition would also be included in order "that the cultural contexts in school . . . be diversified so that a fuller range of expectations is available" (p. 55).

LEARNING IN THE SCHOOL CULTURE

Learning through real-world experiences is not a new idea. In her study of cultural impact on development, Barbara Rogoff (2003) proposes change in the conception of teaching and learning in schools. Schools can build the concept of communities of learners where teachers and children engage in integrated projects often selected by the children and teachers. In this learning through real-world experiences the application of learning grows from the context of children communicating with teachers and peers and together accomplishing goals. This approach "involves complex group relationships among students who learn to take responsibility for contributing to their own learning and to the group's projects" (Rogoff, 2003, p. 361). This concept takes form in the integrative approach to curriculum and development of math and science inquiry as seen in this text.

SUMMARY

Learning is a highly individual matter and teaching is a highly individualized interactive process. With the teacher focusing on the child and assisting her in what she cannot yet grasp, she can master the next step. There are many questions regarding cultural ways of learning that teachers can ask about their students. These questions can lead to an understanding of how the child learns as well as what he needs to learn through both cultural and mainstream society expectations. As you move on to the next chapter, you will be examining observation and assessment as powerful processes in teaching. You will encounter the interactive process of effective questioning and listening as a means to guide learning.

TO FURTHER YOUR THINKING

1. From the Steps in Scaffolding (Table 3–1), determine the steps Jon used to scaffold Devonti's counting (see box on pages 44–45). For each step you find, write Jon's statement or action. Was this scaffolding effective for Devonti? Would you add to or subtract from the steps Jon used?

2. Reflect on your past experiences of scaffolding.
   a. When have you realized that another has been helpful by scaffolding to assist you in learning something new? How did that feel? What did you gain from this interaction?
   b. When have you realized you have helped another (child or adult) through scaffolding? How did the other person respond? How did you feel once the other completed the task?

3. What do you think of when you think of play? Recall some of your play experiences as a child. What play do you remember of children you know? How do you think play helps a child in developing thinking skills? What importance does play have in the life of the young child?

4. For each of the Levels of Cognitive Play (Table 3–2), observe young children at play and write specific examples of the kinds of cognitive play observed. Label them according the four levels of cognitive play and compare these with your classmates' findings.

5. Write your own story of how you understood learning as a child. What do you remember about how you were expected to learn? How was that communicated to you? What were you expected to learn? Did you meet the expectations of those around you? Compare your remembrances with others in the class.

6. Consider the place of stories in your family. How did story pass along the culture and family history? How can story be used for learning in a classroom for young children?

REFERENCES

Berk, L. E., and Winsler, A. (1995). *Scaffolding children's learning: Vygotsky and early childhood education.* Washington, DC: National Association for the Education of Young Children.

Bodrova, E., and Leong, D. J. (1996). *Tools of the mind: The Vygotskian approach to early childhood education.* Englewood Cliffs, NJ: Prentice Hall.

Boykin, A. W. (2002). Integrity-based approaches to the literacy development of African American children: The quest for talent development. In B. Bowman (Ed.). *Love to read: Essays in developing and enhancing early literacy skills of African American children* (pp. 47–61).Washington, DC: National Black Child Development Institute.

Cazden, C. (1988). *Classroom discourse, the language of teaching and learning.* New York: Heinemann.

Clements, D., Sarama, J., and Copley, J. (2003). *Teaching the young thinker: Integrating learning, development, and high-quality practices in mathematics.* Paper presented at NAEYC Conference, Chicago, November 5–8, 2003.

Cole, M., John-Steiner, V., Scribner, S., and Souberman, E. (Eds.) (1978). *Mind in society: The development of higher psychological processes. L. S. Vygotsky.* Cambridge, MD: Harvard.

Delpit, L. (1995). *Other people's children: Cultural conflict in the classroom.* New York: New Press.

Ellison, C. M., Boykin, A. W., Towns, D., and Stokes, A. (2000). *Classroom cultural ecology: The dynamics of classroom life in schools serving low-income African American children (Technical Report No. 44).* Baltimore, MD and Washington, DC: Johns Hopkins University & Howard University, Center for Research on the Education of Students Placed at Risk, Report No. 44.

Forman, G. (1998). Constructive play. In D. P. Fromberg and D. M. Bergen (Eds.), *Play from birth to twelve: Contexts, perspectives, and meanings* (pp. 392–400). New York: Garland.

Fromberg, D. P., and Bergen, D. M. (Eds.). (1998). *Play from birth to twelve: Contexts, perspectives, and meanings.* New York: Garland.

Gallas, K. (1995). *Talking their way into science: Hearing children's questions and theories, responding with curricula.* New York: Teachers College Press.

Goodnow, J. J. (1987). *The socialization of cognition: What's involved?* Paper presented at Culture and Human Development Conference, Chicago, November 5–17, 1987.

Heath, S. B. (1983). *Ways with words: Language, life, and work in communities and classrooms.* Cambridge, England: Cambridge University Press.

Heath, S. B. (1989). Oral and literate traditions among Black Americans living in poverty. *American Psychologist 44,* 367–373.

Ladson-Billings, G. (2001). The power of pedagogy: Does teaching matter? In W. H. Watkins, J. H. Lewis, and V. Chou (Eds.), *Race and education: The roles of history and society in educating African American students* (pp. 72–88). Boston: Allyn & Bacon.

National Association for the Education of Young Children. (2003). NAEYC standards for early childhood professional preparation: Initial licensure programs. In M. Hyson (Ed.), *Preparing early childhood professionals: NAEYC's standards for programs* (pp. 17–63). Washington, DC: Author.

Piaget, J. (1962). *Play, dreams, and imitation in childhood.* New York: Norton.

Rodriguez, R. (1982). *Hunger of memory.* New York: Bantam Books.

Rogoff, B. (2003). *The cultural nature of human development.* New York: Oxford.

Rogoff, B., Mistry, J., Göncü, A., and Mosier, C. (1993). Guided participation in cultural activity by toddlers and caregivers. *Monographs for the society for research in child development, 58*(7), 69–165.

Rubin, K. H., Fein, G. G., and Vandenberg, B. (1983). Play. In W. M. Hertherington (Ed.), *Handbook of Child Psychology: Vol. 4, Socialization, personality, and social development* (pp. 693–744). New York: Wiley.

Smilansky, S., and Shefatya, L. (1990). *Facilitating play: A medium for promoting cognitive, socio-emotional, and academic development in young children.* Geithersburg, MD: Psychosocial and Educational Publications.

Smolen, L., and Ortiz-Castro, V. (2000). Dissolving borders and broadening perspectives through Latino traditional literature. *The Reading Teacher, 53*(7), 566–578.

Wood, D., Bruner, J. C., and Ross G. (1976). The role of tutoring in problem solving. *Journal of Child Psychology and Psychiatry, 17,* 89–100.

ADDITIONAL RESOURCES

Butterfield, P. M., Martin, C. A., and Prairie, A. P. (2004). *Emotional connections: Teaching how relationships guide early learning.* Washington, DC: Zero to Three. This book has an interesting section on scaffolding for very young children. www.zerotothree.org

Delpit, L., and Dowdy, J. K. (Eds.). (2002). *The skin that we speak: Thoughts on language and culture in the classroom.* New York: The New Press. This book gives many accounts of influences of the language of African American children in education today.

Johnston, T., and dePaola, T. (1994). *The tale of rabbit and coyote.* New York: The Putnam & Grosset Group. This is the Mexican legend that portrays the rabbit causing the four phases of the moon.

Ladson-Billings, G. (1997). *The Dreamkeepers: Successful teachers of African American children.* San Francisco, CA: Jossey-Bass. These are stories of teachers that highlight effective teaching in diverse cultures.

Web Sites

http://ask.elibrary.com eLibrary is a subscription-based research tool that allows you to search an archive including documents on sociocultural theory and educational subjects (one-week free trial).

www.nbcdi.org The National Black Child Development Institute (NBCDI) is a national organization that serves as a resource to childcare professionals and educators.

Chapter 4

Learning to Look, Listen, and Respond

OBJECTIVES Through the process of discovery in this chapter, you will be able to:

1. Use reflective thinking to understand children's ideas and actions.

2. Describe the usefulness of authentic assessment in teaching.

3. Describe documentation, portfolios, and photography as tools for assessment.

4. Identify the zone of proximal development as an assessment tool.

5. Explain how assessment can be accomplished through group discussion.

6. Discuss using assessment to drive what you teach.

7. Give examples of curriculum possibilities based on assessment.

8. Describe how preoperational thought can be processed through dialogue.

9. Describe the co-construction of knowledge through dialogue.

IDEAS TO PONDER

- How do I observe to understand children's thinking?

- How can assessment be used to decide curriculum?

- How can I learn about children's ideas from leading group discussions?

- What is the teacher's role in promoting dialogue?

- How can ZPD be used for individual planning?

Three children start adding more cubes to the boat to make it sink in a physical science project. Then they change the activity to playing captain and crew using the cubes and boats.
(Author)

Amanda shows off her new running shoes. "These make me run faster than anybody. See?" And she takes off running.
(Author)

As Lee Chung waters the plants, he tells them, "Umm, you were thirsty. Feel better? That's good." He puts down the mister and gently pats the leaves.
(Author)

In the water table, two three-year-old children slowly fill up a large jar by pouring small cups of water into the jar over and over again.
(Author)

Rhonda, age six, concentrates on making combinations that equal a quarter. For one row she matches a quarter with twenty-five pennies. For the next row she quickly places ten dimes and the next, five nickels. When her teacher asks about her decisions, she looks up and quietly says, "The dimes are smaller than nickels. So I need more."
(Author)

REFLECTIVE THINKING IN OBSERVATION

In the act of teaching, the adult will watch and listen with his whole self to catch the process of inquiry in the making. The first step is to tune into the actions, the thought processes, and the ideas of children. Teaching involves actively looking and listening for these occurrences. It is almost as if you see with a third eye.

Once attuned to this thinking occurring in a specific moment, you can listen and then briefly record the way a child explores an object or what transpires in a conversation. By carrying a small notepad or having sticky notes available, you can quickly jot down the words spoken in an incident and, using this quote, develop the incident into a full anecdote later.

In reflective thinking teachers use their knowledge of young children's thinking to perceive the way children are processing their experiences. In the snippets of actions and thoughts, at the beginning of this chapter, words and actions were caught and recorded. Why would a child turn cubes placed in a plastic boat into captain and crew? Does it make the action more understandable to have the objects perform as people? Children use pretending as a means to understand their world.

Authentic assessment is capturing the individual or group process, concerns, and current thinking in order to implement applicable curriculum.

In the brief comments that began this chapter, you can see the transductive reasoning (Elkind, 1999) in the animistic, egocentric, and intuitive thought. It is evident in these instances that the child is working on making sense of her world. By letting go of the usual adult expectations, you can better understand how a child is thinking.

AUTHENTIC ASSESSMENT

As the assessment standards emphasize, **authentic assessment** can be effective in understanding the child at the present moment in order to prepare her for the next steps in learning. According to NAEYC (Bredekamp & Rosegrant,

1992, p. 10), "Assessment is the process of observing, recording, and otherwise documenting the work children do and how they do it, as a basis for a variety of educational decisions that affect the child, including planning for groups and individual children." Determining that assessment can be constructively used to "guide planning for children in groups and individual planning makes it authentic, real in its day-to-day usefulness and resemble the activities of the preschool and primary classroom" (Mindes, Ireton, & Mardell-Czudnowski, 1996, p. 21).

Documentation

What process is used to determine what children are questioning, what they are thinking, and what they are curious about? "**Documentation** is an approach to assessment that attempts to build directly upon evidence from teachers' everyday experiences of observing and listening to children and collecting samples of their work" (Chittenden & Jones, 1999, p. 110).

Documentation can occur in a variety of ways. Because they do not have the luxury of writing observations throughout the day, every day, teachers cannot record all the kinds of thinking that take place in the classroom. Teachers can be effective by (1) taking the time to write running records on each child at regular intervals, (2) being alert for actions and dialogue that display a child's thinking in

> *Documentation involves using a variety of approaches to record and display the learning of a child or group of children.*

When taking dictation the teacher can learn from listening to the child.

the inquiry process, and (3) gathering documentation of the child's work periodically and often.

As children are actively making sense of their world, the teacher strives to recognize their quest for cognitive understanding. The skills that you apply to understanding other aspects of development are also used to determine children's thinking. What are they paying attention to? What is their focus? What do they do with the materials? Children will be considering many thoughts and ideas in their play and exploration. Ideas that they pay attention to or return to are worthy to note. Children will "tell you" their thinking if you observe and listen closely.

STANDARDS

Candidates know about and understand the goals, benefits, and uses of assessment. They know about and use systematic observations, documentation, and other effective assessment strategies in a responsible way, in partnership with families and other professionals, to positively influence children's development and learning.

Standard 3. Reprinted with permission from National Association for the Education of Young Children. NAEYC standards for early childhood professional preparation: Initial licensure programs. (2003). In *Preparing early childhood professionals: NAEYC's standards for programs,* M. Hyson (Ed.). Washington, DC: Author (p. 29).

Portfolios

Portfolio is a collection of a child's work, which shows growth in areas of development.

Another important source of information is through documentation of the child's work. A **portfolio** of the child's work includes drawings, dictated stories and photos, or simple line drawings of three-dimensional work accomplished in the block area, in woodworking, or in other constructions. The child can help decide the work that will go into the portfolio. In addition to showing the child's growing abilities in art, language, and social skills over time, these collections will show current thinking and focus.

Using Photography for Authentic Assessment

Technology can play a pivotal role in helping children and adults focus on the processing of children's ideas. Using instant playback features of video or still digital cameras, the child and the adult can focus on what the child has just done. The video camera, as a "tool of the mind," allows the child to review the details of actions on the videotape. The video replays the physical detail. The child is now free to think about what his actions mean (Forman, 1999).

> ## ANECDOTE
>
> George Forman has just videotaped Derrick moving a truck he has made of Lego-like elements. He writes in his research article on Instant Video Revisiting, "I find a reason to ask Derrick why he is being so careful in the way he moved his truck. . . . He drives the truck over the cliff very carefully."
>
> **Mr. Forman:**   Look at that [*both look at replay*]. You started to just push it over and then you slowed it down.
>
> **Mr. Forman:**   [*rewinds to show that segment again*] Watch this. See. Did you see how you just let it go reall slowww. Why did you go real slow?
>
> **Derrick:**   'Cause I didn't want to break it.
>
> **Mr. Forman:**   You didn't want to break it, yeah, 'cause if you just let it go, that's kind of a drop from way up there. (Forman, 1999, paragraph 9)

Like the video camera, the digital camera can be an effective tool in assessment (see Chapter 11). As Cynthia Hoisington recalls, the children in her class were missing something as they built with blocks. "Children would build one thing one day, something different the next; they didn't seem to be making any connections between their various building experiences" (Hoisington, 2002, p. 26). Here Hoisington found that children who reviewed their work recorded on camera could better solve construction problems because they could see the problem in new ways (Hoisington, 2002).

Zone of Proximal Development in Assessment

Another assessment tool is to ascertain where the child is in learning a particular skill using the ZPD. By being aware when a child attempts to master something new, a teacher considers how to scaffold this developing skill. This can be achieved by

1. structuring the task and the surrounding environment so that the demands on the child at any given time are at an appropriately challenging level
2. constantly adjusting the amount of adult intervention to the child's current needs and abilities (Berk & Winsler, 1995, p. 29).

Scaffolding can be a usable tool in authentic assessment.

Discussion Used in Assessment

Group discussions are effective in determining children's current understandings of a topic that they are concerned about. Children may show a high interest in the suggested topic, may move their interest to a related topic, or may show little interest in following the topic further. In addressing an interest, teachers may review a previous discussion using the words and phrasing they have recorded directly from the children. Through reflecting children's evolving ideas back to the group, teachers make their discussion and ideas more significant.

The "exploration into the understandings of a community of learners can provide insight into the prior knowledge and experiences that students bring to learning environments" (Chittenden & Jones, 1999, p. 109). This kind of discussion can pave the way to topics important for the group. From there, teachers and children can process decisions for curriculum together.

ASSESSMENT GUIDES CURRICULUM

In using any of the aforementioned assessment tools, teachers have a base of information derived from individuals and the group. The decisions for teaching are derived from a broad base of knowledge of the children because assessment is based on a collection of patterns of behavior and thinking over time. Thus assessment drives the teaching (Meisels, Harrington, McMahon, Dichtelmiller, & Jablon, 2002).

Teachers consider a focus for curriculum from assessment, from discussions, and from noting children's evolving interests. Then decisions are made to take an idea further. In using authentic assessment, not all curriculum is derived this way, yet classrooms often incorporate what children are concerned about into projects, in-depth study, or, at times, short-term ideas. Different kinds of ideas can emerge from involvement of one, a few, or all children (Table 4–1).

TABLE 4–1   Curriculum Possibilities Based on Assessment

Area of Interest	Topic Observed	Curriculum Study
Play themes	Mothers and babies	Study of newborn babies, children's growth from babyhood
Books	From *It Looked Like Spilt Milk* children imagine all kinds of shapes	Focus on clouds, including types, shapes
Events in classroom	Fish added to existing aquarium	Comparing fish, kinds of fish
Events outside	Ladybugs are found in playground	Study of ladybugs
Events in a child's life	Family on vacation flies in airplane	Study of airplanes
Materials used/how used	Children make ramps for matchbox cars	Construct ramps, study uses of ramps
Materials used/how used	Children focus on mixing paint colors	Mixing paint colors, making substances of various colors

PREOPERATIONAL THOUGHT PROCESSES IN DISCUSSIONS

Because a group of young children can process the thinking that occurs in preoperational thought, this social process of dialogue is an important step in inquiry. Here children explore ideas and concepts at their level without considering adult logic. This discourse may not move them to concrete thinking, but often this challenges some unfounded belief structures that naturally occur because of intuitive thinking. In this kind of discussion the thinking of children is not static; it is moving and changing. In *Apprenticeship in Thinking*, Barbara Rogoff (1990) highlights the meaning of this social discourse.

As children listen to the views and understanding of others and stretch their concepts to find a common ground; as they collaborate and argue with others, consider new alternatives, and recast their ideas to communicate or to convince, they advance their ideas in the process of participation. It is a matter of social engagement that leaves the individual changed. (pp. 195–196)

ANECDOTE

Fish Observation from Donna Erickson, a Philadelphia kindergarten teacher. While I was reading *The Rainbow Fish* to the class, a child asked what "scales" were. A few days later I bought a fish at the supermarket and brought it to the class. Sitting in a circle, I showed the children how to feel the scales and invited them to tell us anything else that they noticed about the fish. Their discussion follows.

Darryl: You got to scrape the scales off and then cook it.

Kate: Was the other fish bigger in the book? [*Class thought the book fish was bigger.*]

Blair: I had a fish that die.

Jennifer: Fish will swim in the water.

Sarah: I love to eat fish. . . .

Frank: It reminds me of my alive fish. This one's alive. No. It's dead. I see the blood (around the eye).

Earl: It's wet. I can feel its scales. I think it's alive.

John: I think it's dead.

Teacher: Why?

John: I don't know.

Mickey: It smells bad. I think it's dead because I see blood.

Richard: It's dead.

Teacher: Why do you think so?

Richard: Because fishes always die?

Shelby: I like fish. I think it's alive?

Teacher: Why do you think it's alive?

Donovan: I like fish.

Ashley: It feels like my cousin's fish. It's dead 'cause it ain't movin'.

Danielle: It's not movin'. It's dead.

Daryl: [*Jumps up and yells.*] No! Fishes swim in the water. You gotta' put it in water! [*Many students agree.*]

Zoe: It's dead.

I got a plastic shoebox and filled it with water and put the fish in and set it before the children. . . . I told the class I'd put the fish on the table and they could keep their eyes on it. Kids went over throughout the day to check it out. Once there were screams of "It's moving! It's moving!" but then someone said, "No, it's not. You just bumped the table and the water's movin'." By the end of the day when I asked the class about the fish, they all agreed that it was dead because it never moved.

Reprinted with permission from the American Association for the Advancement of Science (AAAS) (1999). American Association for the Advancement of Science (pp. 111–112).

Often young children's ideas do not flow logically or sequentially, so by staying open to hearing their processes you can learn a lot from them. The adult's role is to be a participant in this thinking and guide it along the ways children carry it along. "This . . . requires an attitude of listening, of asking questions in an open way, and of attending to unanticipated answers" (Chittenden & Jones, 1999, p. 109).

The teacher listens intently to follow children's ideas.

CO-CONSTRUCTION OF KNOWLEDGE

With this process of working with the children's ideas through ongoing discussion, teachers and children build a **co-construction** of knowledge. In working closely with children over a period of time, teachers form important relationships. In these supportive relationships, the teacher can provoke "occasions of discovery through a kind of alert, inspired listening and stimulation of children's dialogue, co-action and co-construction of knowledge" (Edwards, 1998, pp. 182–183). In this social process, adults watch the process of the children's dialogue, listen for their ideas, and take note of the thoughts that take the children to a deeper level. Edwards (1998) uses the word *spiraling* to describe the way ideas circle among the group and are built to new levels. As these thinking processes of children and teachers develop, the work of assessment flows into the process of inquiry.

Co-construction is the process of two or more people who construct concepts together beyond what the individual can accomplish.

SUMMARY

Teachers assess what makes sense in building curriculum using both individual and group knowledge. Knowing that authentic assessment can drive curriculum, you will develop ongoing curriculum in all areas of learning. Listening and responding to children will be useful tools to guide you in facilitating thoughtful discussions. You can incorporate observation, documentation, and questioning in implementing the steps of inquiry that will be built in the following chapters. In the next chapter you will encounter exploring as the first step in inquiry.

TO FURTHER YOUR THINKING

1. By taking the opportunity to observe each time you are around children, you have the opportunity to learn about these particular children, and therefore, children in general. In places where you see a child or children (your home, your place of work, on public transportation, in the park), take the time to observe what a child is doing, thinking of the actions from the child's perspective. Share your thoughts with a colleague.
2. Do you remember a child saying something that seemed unrealistic? Consider this chapter's opening quotes and apply your understanding of cognitive development. Can you set aside your perspectives to grasp why a child might think this?

3. Look up one of the assessment systems available on line, either Creative Curriculum, www.CreativeCurriculum.net, or The Work Sampling, at www.pearsonearlylearning.com. In the assessment system that you find, look for the categories listed that relate to cognitive development of young children. How does one collect information about the child for the system you selected?

4. Using the Fish Observation of Donna Erickson (pages 67–68), consider the possible ways the social interaction prompted an increased understanding of what the children were observing. How did the social interactions influence the line of thinking followed among the children? How did the teacher's decisions influence the thinking of the group?

5. What does the phrase *assessment drives curriculum* mean? What kinds of assessment tools can be used for this process?

6. From Table 4–1, select one of the areas of interest in the left-hand column. Using the topics observed, begin a list of other kinds of incidents that you would look for as evidence of interest in this topic. What assessment tools would you use to identify them? What curriculum study could result from this?

7. Define co-construction of knowledge to a colleague. How can co-construction of knowledge develop in dialogue among children and teachers?

REFERENCES

Berk, L. E., and Winsler, A. (1995). *Scaffolding children's learning: Vygotsky and early childhood education.* Washington, DC: National Association for the Education of Young Children.

Bredekamp, S., and Rosegrant, R. (Eds.). (1992). *Reaching potentials: Appropriate curriculum and assessment for young children.* Vol. 1. Washington, DC: National Association for the Education of Young Children.

Chittenden, E., and Jones, J. (1999). Science assessment in early childhood programs. In American Association for the Advancement of Science, *Dialogue on early childhood science, mathematics, and technology education* (pp. 106–114). Washington, DC: Author.

Edwards, C. (1998). Partner, nurturer, and guide: The roles of the teacher. In C. Edwards, L. Gandini, and G. Forman (Eds.), *The hundred languages of children: The Reggio Emilia approach to early childhood education* (pp. 179–199). Norwood, NJ: Ablex.

Elkind, D. (1999). Educating young children in math, science, and technology. In American Association for the Advancement of Science, *Dialogue on early childhood science, mathematics, and technology education* (pp. 62–70). Washington, DC: Author.

Forman, G. E. (1999). Instant video revisiting: The video camera as a "tool of the mind" for young children [Electronic version]. *Early Childhood Research and Practice*, 1(2), 1–8. www.ecrp.uiuc.edu

Hoisington, C. (2002, September). Using photographs to support children's science inquiry. *Young Children, 57*(5), 26–32.

Meisels, S. J., Harrington, H. L., McMahon, P., Dichtelmiller, M. L., and Jablon, J. R. (2002). *Thinking like a teacher: Using observational assessment to improve teaching and learning.* Boston: Allyn & Bacon.

Mindes, G., Ireton, H., and Mardell-Czudnowski, C. (1996). *Assessing young children.* Clifton Park, NY: Thomson Delmar Learning.

National Association for the Education of Young Children. (2003). NAEYC standards for early childhood professional preparation: Initial licensure programs. In M. Hyson (Ed.), *Preparing early childhood professionals: NAEYC's standards for programs* (pp. 17–63). Washington DC: Author.

Pfister, M. (1992). *The rainbow fish.* New York: North-South Books.

Rogoff, B. (1990). *Apprenticeship in thinking.* New York: Oxford University Press.

Shaw, C. G. (1999). *It looked like spilt milk.* New York: Celebration Press.

ADDITIONAL RESOURCES

Beaty, J. J. (2002). *Observing development of the young child* (5th ed.). Upper Saddle River, NJ: Pearson Education. This text contains a practical approach to observing children.

McAfee, O., and Bodrova, E. (2004). *Basics of assessment: A primer for early childhood educators.* Washington DC: National Association for the Education of Young Children. This basic assessment tool for students and teachers provides newcomers to an overview of its concepts, approaches, and challenges. www.naeyc.org

Videos

Observing young children: Learning to look, looking to learn [Video]. Washington, DC: Teaching Strategies, Inc. Practical tool from The Creative Curriculum for learning to use individual observations of children. www.TeachingStrategies.com

Observation of young children I: The eyes have it [Video]. Crystal Lake, IL: Magna Systems, Inc. Teachers complete observations and use these for authentic assessment and individualizing instruction. www.magnasystems.org

Web Sites

www.CreativeCurriculum.net On-line version of the Creative Curriculum assessment and outcomes reporting tools.

www.pearsonearlylearning.com This is one of several Web sites on the Work Sampling System, developed as a performance-based assessment system by Meisels and colleagues (2002). This can be accessed by following the prompts to Rebus at the listed site.

Chapter 5
Exploring

OBJECTIVES Through the process of discovery in this chapter, you will be able to:

1. Describe the ways young children take in information through their senses.

2. Explain brain development related to sensory input in the cerebral cortex.

3. Compare sensory learning of the sensorimotor and preoperational child.

4. Compare the language used as descriptors of sensory experiences with the importance adults place on sensory modalities.

5. Describe ways young children learn through exploring by observing, handling, investigating, manipulating, and trying out their ideas.

6. Identify exploring in functional play.

7. Describe ways adults foster the child's exploration.

8. Plan for safe and healthy guidelines to follow for exploring.

9. Describe a plan for children to taste in food experiences.

10. Discuss materials for and organization of a discovery area.

IDEAS TO PONDER

- How do children learn through their senses?
- How can teachers expand children's use of their senses?
- How do children explore?
- How does play enhance the process of exploration?
- How can teachers talk with children to enhance exploration?
- How can teachers plan food experiences to emphasize using the senses?
- How can teachers plan for ongoing exploring in the classroom?

In the morning in the Head Start classroom, Felicia, one of the teachers, notices Hector moving hesitantly to the sand table. With his hands grasping the edge of the sandbox, he peers inside. Then he lets his hands slide down to the sand. Gently he lifts a handful, holding it next to the straight side of the box. He moves it up slowly almost to the top of the box and lets it gradually flow out of his hand. Felicia watches this and quietly moves to the sand box, facing him. She uses her hand to do the same action, commenting, "That feels so smooth when the sand flows out of my hand." Hector looks at her and smiles shyly. He repeats the action, this time with more energy and a broad smile.
(Author)

SENSORY LEARNING

Kinesthetic is the sense of movement felt in the body.

In the feel of the sand running through his fingers, Hector was learning through the sense of touch. Other senses the young child relies on are sight, hearing, taste, smell, and **kinesthetic.** From infancy on, the child is taking in information about his world through sensory experiences. Since the young child continues learning from sensory experiences, sand, water, homemade play dough, xylophones and tambourines, simple food experiences, and activities exploring movement are ever present in classrooms for young children. Thus sensory learning contributes to exploratory learning, the first step of inquiry.

SENSORY DEVELOPMENT IN THE BRAIN CORTEX

Sensory processing is making sense of the intake from all senses and registering the input in a particular part of the brain.

Although there are many areas of the brain that process sensory information, one primary area where **sensory processing** takes place is the outer layer (cerebral cortex) about midway back from the forehead. Before birth this area is already well organized, delineating a specific area that deals with the exact location and type of sensory input. One area is visual, and other areas process sound, taste, smell, pain, temperature, and touch (Eliot, 1999).

In the area of the brain that processes sensations through touch, some sections take up much more area than others. So, for example, the portion dedicated to the mouth is much larger than what is allotted many of the other areas of the body, such as the back. For the mouth area, this section includes the tongue, gums, and the upper and lower lip (Eliot, 1999). No wonder the infant is intent on putting everything in her mouth!

SENSORY LEARNING OF THE SENSORIMOTOR AND PREOPERATIONAL CHILD

For the sensorimotor child, much of the learning is directly related to the sensory input. So as the infant goes about putting edible and nonedible material in the mouth, sensory learning is about how the cracker tastes, smells, feels, and changes in texture as it is mashed on the gums. In comparison, the infant senses how the rattle tastes, smells, feels, and does not change in texture no matter how long it is mashed on the gums. As the motor skills increase, the baby will try out other actions on the same materials. Shaking and banging the rattle will bring out interesting sounds, but the same action on the cracker brings little or no sound. The infant continues with varied actions that build up a store of knowledge in sensory processing (Gonzalez-Mena & Eyer, 2001).

The preoperational child does not abandon sensory learning in handling materials. Watching a three-year-old washing hands, you see the sensory action of feeling the water flowing from the faucet over outstretched hands. Then he consciously explores covering the hands with soap and extends the sensory exploration into more depth. He will find more ways to smooth the tiny bubbles on fingers and hands and then extend soapsuds up the forearms, or perhaps to the face. Later on, at the water table this same child may continue by seeming to ask, "What will happen if I try this?" Once the child has extensive sensory experiences, he can expand his knowledge into a trial-and-error process of seeing how things work.

The young child uses all senses in gaining information to understand her surroundings. From there the child includes sensory input as a springboard for further exploration. The sensory information is adapted to explore intuitively, then construct, and, finally, decide what it represents, as the child explores materials such as homemade play dough.

Sensory experiences of soap suds leads to exploration.

Exploring homemade play dough can lead to forming objects.

ANECDOTE

Terrance, three years old, finds that the soft pliable homemade play dough keeps his thumb imprint, and, when sticking his thumb through the soft mound, the hole he makes remains. With this new understanding of homemade play dough, he leans over and focuses on making more holes. Terrance quickly gathers up the pieces and deliberately forms a round ball, pounds it to flatten it—and sticks his thumb through it. A few minutes later, Terrance holds up the flattened circle with three holes in it and announces to his teacher, "Holey cheese."

ADULT USE OF DESCRIPTORS WITH THE SENSES

In using sensory input, no doubt there is a store of pleasant associations for most adults with certain aromas, tastes, sounds, and the kinesthetic sense. The smell of Brut™ cologne may remind a person of her father. The aroma of a dinner cooking may conjure images of the warm kitchen of one's home as a child. The lap of waves on the beach may bring a fond memory of a relaxing vacation at the seashore. And seeing children run at full speed may remind a person of the joy of running with friends as a child. These are senses that remain very operative, but these are the ones least relied on during adult life.

An awareness of these senses may sometimes filter into spoken communication, but usually this is limited to general comments. One may praise the cook for the wonderful aromas he has produced from the dinner being served. Yet it is difficult, almost impossible, to explain that aroma with specific **descriptors.** Words are much easier to use in describing something seen, such as a recently purchased sweater. Even though all the senses are in continual use, adults rely on sight more than the other senses, and language parallels this emphasis on sight.

A descriptor is a word or phrase that describes sensory input.

DESCRIPTORS OF SENSES

Children will be more aware than adults of information from all the senses. As you communicate with children on what they explore using different senses, you will sustain this continued overall use of sensory input. In addition to hearing what the homemade play dough looks like with its holes, Terrance will also respond to descriptors of touch and smell.

STANDARDS

Abilities necessary to do scientific inquiry: In the early years of school, students can investigate earth materials, organisms, and properties of common objects.

Content Standard: A1. Reprinted with permission from *National science education standards.* (1996). The National Academy of Sciences, courtesy of the National Academies Press, Washington, DC (p. 105).

EXPLORATION IN FUNCTIONAL PLAY

Functional play may seem to carry little purpose to the casual observer (for example, running hands through the sand or dripping small rocks onto the ground). Yet it is in this play that children gain a basic knowledge of the characteristics of materials. To the adult the feel of water is a common experience, but to the child this is a fascinating exploration of its properties. When a new material, such as water-based clay, is presented to the preschool child, she explores its characteristics before attempting to make items from it. With an understanding gained from sensory learning the child can then move into constructive play.

LEARNING THROUGH EXPLORING

In preschool and, to some extent in kindergarten, large blocks of time are planned for exploring, through observing, handling, investigating, and manipulating. As children act on materials, the teacher's involvement facilitates sensory learning.

ANECDOTE

Several children eagerly bury their hands in the new sand just poured into the indoor sandbox on a summer day. Shannon, their teacher, joins them by burying her hands. "My goodness, this sand is soft." Children continue burying and moving their hands under the sand.

"The sand feels cool because it was stored in the basement. It's cooler there than in our classroom," Shannon comments.

As Javier is actively using his fingers to smooth the sand away from one spot, Shannon notices his work. "You are making a hole, Javier. What kind of animal would live there?"

Javier answers with emphasis, "It looks like something, sounds like a big dinosaur!"

Shannon suggests, "You might find a big dinosaur on the shelf over there." Javier leaves to search the nearby shelves. As Shannon watches him, he stays at the shelves, examining several animals.

"Did you find one?" She goes to check on him. "No?" Pause. "You have the tiger."

Javier replies strongly, "He bites." He returns to the sand, and using the tiger he scratches the sand away from the corner of the sandbox. Then he packs the sand over the tiger, pressing hard with intense interest. He brings the tiger out of the sand, brushes it off quickly, and buries it again.

Shannon asks, "You are making the tiger disappear and then reappear."

"Yeah, he gets lost and comes back."

These sensory experiences and exploratory actions supply Javier information about the sand before he moves to pretending. Sensations of coolness, softness, and resistance are felt through his exploratory touch. As he understands the sensory information, Javier contemplates other questions: What happens when I press my hand hard on the sand? And what happens when I cover up the tiger and press hard on it? In his inquiry Javier may be contemplating: What is the material like? What does it do? What can I do with it?

TEACHER'S ROLE IN EXPLORING

When focusing on the exploration of a child, the teacher's comments serve to highlight the child's exploratory learning, like Shannon's conversations with Javier. Just as in an adult's attempt to describe the aroma of dinner cooking, often the young child does not have the vocabulary to describe his explorations.

To focus on exploring and provide descriptive vocabulary, the teacher can describe what is experienced in sensory exploration. Sometimes the adult may

The child's exploration is supported by the teacher.

mirror the child's experience (as in this chapter's opening quote). Some open questioning can provide children an opportunity to describe their sensory learning, but a barrage of questions may turn off children.

In beginning an interaction, the teacher often directs a comment that focuses on the child's explorations. By trying out a question, the teacher can watch and listen to the child's response to gauge the direction of the conversation, whether to continue using comments or questions.

Small group work with ample time for play will facilitate exploratory learning. With a small group the teacher can oversee and facilitate this learning through adjusting the space, organization, materials, as well as provide focus with each child. With ample time, the child can spend as much effort as he wants in exploring. To support exploring the teacher can manage to be involved with each child.

SAFEGUARDING SAFETY AND HEALTH

In the classroom materials presented will be safe for children to handle and not expose them to potential disease or harm. Teachers are careful in selecting and preparing materials incorporating current knowledge of safety and health hazards. Extreme caution is required at all times.

1. Since we know that the easiest way to transfer pathogens for disease is through the hands, thorough hand washing must take place before and after handling water-based materials, especially when these materials are shared.

This guideline is even more important when young children tend to taste materials, which is expected until at least three years of age. So care is taken when children share homemade play dough, manipulate wet sand, and engage in water play together. If children tend to put materials in their mouth, materials can be planned for individual use, such as planning for each child to have an individual container of water or lump of homemade play dough.

2. Since standing water and wet or moist materials harbor growth of bacteria, the water table must be drained after use and the container washed with an approved disinfectant. Wet sand used indoors must be allowed to dry. If homemade play dough will be reused, it can be refrigerated, which can be effective in slowing bacterial growth.

3. All materials handled by children must be nontoxic; and when individuals tend put things in their mouths, the materials used in exploring are edible.

4. As noted in the packaging recommendations for toys used by young children, items with small parts are not to be used by children three and under. In addition, follow this guideline if any child tends to put things in his mouth. This includes items where small parts can be pulled out, unscrewed, or broken off. (Aronson, 2002; Marotz, Cross, & Rush, 2004).

PLAN FOR CHILDREN TO TASTE

Food experience is a planned experience where children prepare a food for tasting and eating.

Because children enjoy tasting experiences they will want to taste all ingredients in a **food experience.** How would they know the difference between salt and sugar, lemons and oranges, except through taste? After washing hands, tasting naturally occurs as food preparation gets underway. By putting out individual teaspoons and a small plate or bowl for each child, children can safely taste following the necessary health precautions. A tablespoon is used to serve "tasting bits" into individual small bowls. Be sure to plan enough ingredients for tasting. During tasting children can discuss and compare taste, texture, appearance, smell, and touch. After cooking, children will compare the raw ingredients with the finished product.

FOOD EXPERIENCE OF COOKING APPLESAUCE

The experience of cooking apples is rich in many sensory experiences. All the steps of cooking can be completed with older children. Younger ones will need assistance in cutting and peeling, but all will enjoy the tasting of this familiar fruit uncooked and cooked (Fig. 5–1).

Wash apples, and, if you opt to not strain the cooked apples, peel four apples with a vegetable peeler or plastic knife. (It is not necessary to have this done completely since the skin will be soft when cooked.) With an apple slicer, cut all six apples into sections. Allow children to taste some sections of the peeled and unpeeled apples. Put aside some apple slices to compare with applesauce when done. Cook the remaining apples in water over low heat until soft, stirring occasionally and adding more water if necessary. The cooked applesauce can be strained or put

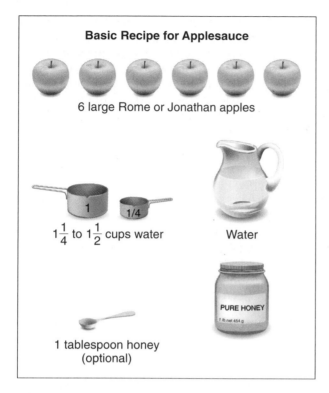

Basic Recipe for Applesauce

6 large Rome or Jonathan apples

$1\frac{1}{4}$ to $1\frac{1}{2}$ cups water

Water

1 tablespoon honey
(optional)

Figure 5–1 A simple recipe for tasting.

through a blender. Or it can be served as is with a small amount of honey (optional) (Goodwin & Pollen, 1980).

For this food experience, children have ample opportunity for exploring through their senses and using terminology about these explorations. Allow children to handle the whole apples and talk about how the fruit looks, feels, and smells. Ask children how the raw apples taste, smell, and feel in their mouth and hands. Compare skin and flesh. Cut an apple and examine the seeds, stem, and core. Plan to have children watch the cooking of the apples. Ask how the apples look while cooking (include the beginning, middle, and end of cooking time). One way to involve the children in experiencing the change during cooking is to place the pan wrapped in a Turkish towel on a low table at intermittent times during cooking. Children will need to be reminded that the hot pan cannot be touched. After the cooked applesauce has cooled, children can smell, touch, and taste the warm applesauce. Comparisons can be made with raw and cooked apples using all the senses: taste, smell, touch, sight, sound (crunchiness), and kinesthetic (in the feel of moving the mouth when eating). Enjoy.

For tasting and cooking it is essential that children experience all aspects of preparing, tasting, and comparing. All children can accomplish this in a small group. Often food experiences are popular, so it is hard to limit the number of young cooks. There are several ways to accomplish this, such as planning the cooking experience to be repeated on that day or several days or planning a variety of cooking experiences often. Food preparation can be presented the same as any other classroom activity. For example, in a kindergarten classroom the tools and ingredients for the carrot and raisin salad are placed on a low table for a small group. As some children finish the task, others come to prepare the food. The total number of children at one time is limited to four.

THE DISCOVERY AREA

A discovery area is a table or other area in the classroom where children can explore materials.

To enhance discovery through exploration, the classroom contains an interesting and current **discovery area.** In a noticeable space in the classroom teachers plan a place for "messing around" with materials. This space can be a table near a bright window, shelves with many alternatives, or a rug area with space for investigating. Since all areas of science can be a source for continued exploration, ideas are endless: an old wind-up clock, a flashlight, ramps and pendulums, a bit of earth collected from the garden, weed seeds, fall leaves, the leftover jack-o-lantern, an evergreen branch or branch with new leaf buds in spring, seeds sprouting, growing plants, the aquarium with fish, or a terrarium for small animals, fresh snow, first flowers. The list could go on.

The discovery area provides space and materials for exploration.

The plan for the discovery area includes considerations for both safety and sustained interest:

1. Materials must be safe to explore, nontoxic, and items children will not tend to put in their mouth (see the previous discussion).
2. Exploratory materials relate in some way to ongoing classroom experiences.
3. Materials are updated and/or changed often according to the interests of the children.
4. Various containers or trays facilitate handling and sorting of materials.
5. Balance scales, magnifiers, and simple microscopes can support close inspection of materials.
6. Materials are collected by children for the discovery area and can be part of their ongoing experiences. In addition, families can become involved in contributing various items to the area.

An attractive arrangement of materials and a simple arrangement for handling materials invite children to investigate. For example, for children four to six years of age, several ears of field corn are placed in a tray on the discovery table. In addition, magnifiers, measuring cups, a mortar and pestle, and a large rectangle dish lined with white paper are available. These tools invite exploration, such as investigating the husk, the corn, the silk, and the cob. Children shell the corn into the dish and look at the results. To extend these experiences the shelled corn could be examined in the magnifier or measured. Also, the shelled corn can be cut with a paring knife (teacher does this). And corn can be ground with a mortar and pestle. No doubt children will be touching, listening, smelling, shelling, and grinding—even tasting the ground corn.

In reality children's discoveries go far beyond a table in one area of the classroom, as their exploration will be in all the sensory experiences they encounter in art, **manipulatives,** block play, music and rhythm instruments, movement, and the many learning discoveries outdoors. Wherever inviting experiences "just happen," the teacher's role is to observe the children's focus, then bring the focus to the event or materials with a group of children. Or, if it is the adult who first notices, bring the discovery to the attention of the children.

Manipulatives are various kinds of materials that children use to create their constructions.

SUMMARY

As we allow for children to handle, observe, touch, take apart, and manipulate, the use of senses furthers their understanding of the world. As you work along with the children you will be easily moving from exploring to identifying along with the other steps of inquiry. In the next chapter you will see how simple exploratory experiences can evolve into identifying materials and processes.

TO FURTHER YOUR THINKING

1. To explore sensations around the mouth, you can relate to your own experiences. How are you drawn to sensory input, such as the taste of a decadent piece of chocolate or the refreshing appeal of a smooth piece of spearmint chewing gum? While deep in thought, many of us will unconsciously entertain sensations felt around the mouth, such as chewing on a pencil or touching the lower lip.

2. Plan to describe to a parent of a three-year-old child what the child gains through exploring. Consider that this parent is concerned that the child continues to "get into everything" at home. What would you want the parent to know, and how would you support the parent in her concern?

3. Take a moment to conjure the delicious aromas of your favorite dinner, and then attempt to put into words the descriptors that specifically label the smells. Saying it is "like the most succulent barbecue ribs ever" will not suffice. For this exercise the words you choose must directly describe the characteristics of what you smell. Now describe your favorite sweater, using descriptors of sight. Is this possible? You may also opt to describe a newly purchased sweater using descriptors of touch. Do those words come easily?

4. Imagine you have just received a camera as a gift. What do you do first? You might take it apart, read the directions, or load it and snap a picture. Which of your choices is exploring? How does exploring help you learn about the camera and its operation?

5. Observe a child at play in a home or school. What does the child do to explore? What senses are you aware of him using?

REFERENCES

Aronson, S. S. (Ed.). (2002). *Healthy young children: A manual for programs,* (4th ed.). Washington, DC: National Association for the Education of Young Children.
Eliot, L. (1999). *What's going on in there? How the brain and mind develop in the first five years of life.* New York: Bantam.

Gonzalez-Mena, J., and Eyer, D. W. (2001). *Infants, toddlers, and caregivers* (5th ed.). Mountain, View, CA: Mayfield.

Goodwin, M. T., and Pollen, G. (1980). *Creative food experiences for children.* Washington, DC: Center for Science in the Public Interest.

Marotz, L. R., Rush, J. M., and Cross, M. Z. (2004). *Health, Safety, and Nutrition for the Young Child* (6th ed.). Clifton Park, NY: Thomson Delmar Learning.

National Academy of Science. (1996). *National science education standards* [Book version, on-line]. Washington, DC: National Academies Press. www. nap.edu

ADDITIONAL RESOURCES

Feeney, S., Christensen, D., and Moravcik, E. (2001). *Who am I in the lives of children?,* (6th ed). Upper Saddle River, NJ: Prentice Hall. Two chapters are of particular note on exploring: Chapter 7, "A Caring Place," emphasizes safe environments and Chapter 10, "The Curriculum," has an informative column on curriculum for sensory development.

Hendrick, J. (2001). *The whole child: Developmental education for the early years,* (7th ed.). Upper Saddle River, NJ: Prentice Hall. Chapter 2, "What Makes a Good Day," is an overview of good practice where exploring is involved.

Kasson, M., and Henderson, A. (1994). *Pretend soup and other real recipes: A cookbook for preschoolers and up.* Berkely, CA: Tricycle Press. Very young cooks can read the pictured recipes.

Lakeshore Learning Materials (n.d.). *Multicultural cooking with kids.* Carson, CA: Lakeshore Equipment Co. Plastic-coated pages offer recipes from a wide variety of cultures. www.lakeshorelearning.com

Children's Books

Carle, E. (1997). *From head to toe.* New York: HarperCollins. This book engages the child in imitating the animals.

dePaola, T. (1978). *Pancakes for breakfast.* New York: Harcourt Brace Jovanovich. In this wordless book a woman goes about making pancakes.

Hoban, R. (1993). *Bread and jam for Frances* (reprint ed.). New York: Harper-Collins. Frances refuses to eat a variety of foods.

Hoban, R. (1997). *No other foods will do for Frances*. New York: HarperCollins. Frances again prefers certain food.

Turkle, B. (1987). *Deep in the forest* (reprint ed.). London, UK: Puffin. A wordless book. A bear experiences tasting and trying out a family's furniture.

Web Sites

www.cookingwithkids.com One of many Web sites on cooking with kids. This one features recipes from *Cooking with kids for dummies* by Kate Heyhoe.

www.jurassicsand.com This sand product for classrooms is clean and allergy free.

www.kaplanco.com Kaplan has a wide assortment of sand/water tables and sand and water play materials. Some of the featured small water tables can be helpful in preventing the spread of infection.

Chapter 6
Identifying Materials and Processes

Photo courtesy: Patrick Clark

OBJECTIVES Through the process of discovery in this chapter, you will be able to:

1. Explain the role of social knowledge in identifying.

2. Discuss ways young children learn extended vocabulary.

3. Demonstrate naming objects, materials, and processes in conversations with children.

4. Explain using the following skills of supporting language in identifying:
   Parallel talk
   Language expansion
   I wonder statements
   Pondering questions

5. Recognize the respect for what children think through listening and reflecting.

6. Discuss the disposition of supporting children's thinking in groups.

IDEAS TO PONDER

- How can I expand the child's ability in communicating?

- How do I converse with a child about what he is doing?

- How does communication support identifying materials and processes?

- What does it mean to respect the child's ideas?

- How do I follow children's ideas in inquiry?

During group time in an urban Head Start program, Shannon is introducing a large thermometer. She introduces this three-foot-long thermometer by talking about how to make the red line move up or down. Christiana, who is sitting next to her, says, "We can turn it this way [she demonstrates with her hands to flip it over, top to bottom] to see if the red line will go down."

Shannon says to the class, "Christiana thinks that the red line will go down if we turn it over. What do you think?" Shannon flips the thermometer over and passes it first to Christiana, who looks quickly at the red line and shakes her head. "Christiana, what do you think?"

Christiana, looking at the line again, says, "It doesn't go down."
(Author)

LANGUAGE AND IDENTIFYING

Language becomes the means to express both process and labeling in identifying. In the opening quotes, Christiana is able to formulate her idea that leads to exploring a simple act of turning the thermometer upside down. She observes, then quickly sees that this action will not change the red line, and states her conclusion.

Identifying what is experienced is expressed through words. In finding the words to name the objects and materials, ponder questions, and describe processes taking place, the child and adult voice these in the common language. Identifying is communicating social knowledge which, as noted earlier, is learned from others.

As a child experiences the different aspects of the inquiry process, the teacher can label these as they occur. An adult can state the experience of the child as she

Feels the sponginess of the newly made play dough

Looks at how bubbles pop right before her eyes

Picks up a small leaf and stacks it on top of leaves that are just like it

Guesses "this one" when asked which she can blow away, the feather or the rock

Points to the ramp to indicate raising the end of it higher

After hearing the teacher's labels, the child may begin to use some of these words, and thus she is identifying materials and processes herself.

Talk is important for children to communicate their ideas as they observe, explore, and investigate their world. Science can be thought of as "a method of asking, investigating, and responding to questions about the world around us" (Owens, 1999). This language of inquiry is limited in the early years yet becomes a more important component as children master science inquiry later. This social component of communicating through dialogue is crucial in inquiry for preschoolers and older children.

Fast mapping is a process of quickly increasing vocabulary by relating a new word to a similar word already known.

Expanding Vocabulary

Children's use of "big words" will expand if included in language they hear. Many times young children do **fast mapping**, which is a quick method of adding new words to their usage after hearing a word only once. From the way they hear the word used, they make sense of it by relating it to a similar word. For example, when his father refers to his neighbor's dog as a collie, Sean quickly grasps that "Collie is one kind of dog." Yet this rapid increase in vocabulary is limited in comprehension. That is, Sean has only a rudimentary idea of the word meaning from hearing the word *collie* only once. Sean can assume that a collie is a rather big dog but does not know if it only refers to this dog or many big dogs or some brown big dogs.

A recent longitudinal study on language used at home highlights significant differences in vocabulary of preschool children. In their book *Meaningful Differences,* Betty Hart and Todd R. Risley (2002) report this extensive study on recording the language used by parents with their children from the ages of 10 to 36 months. Their conclusion was that, although children of all socioeconomic status (SES) levels heard the same kind of talk from their parents and other in-home caregivers, the amount of talk varied with the SES level of the family. If the children came from a lower SES, by the time children entered school at three they had heard, on average, much less rich talk. The researchers found that the lesser amount of talk heard in the first three years was comparable to the smaller vocabulary these same children used in preschool.

Quoting from the jacket cover of the book, the authors summarize that by "giving children positive interactions and experiences with adults who take the time to just talk to them, children will get the vocabulary, oral language, and emergent literacy concepts to have a better chance to succeed at school and in the workplace" (Hart & Risley, 2002).

Naming Objects and Materials

Even commonplace objects may not be called by name by young children. They may ask for objects using general referents *that* or *this.* To teach names of objects, shapes, colors, or other distinctions of objects, the adult describes and names in conversation as a child handles these objects. For example, the child who hears the name of the object *funnel* as she or other children use it in water play will have the basis for both understanding and using the word when referring to it. Thus, when the child is using the object or material, this becomes the opportune time for her to learn its name and salient characteristics. She is learning about a **substance in context.**

Naming Processes

When teachers use the language by identifying the very things that children are doing, children's vocabulary expands. This talk puts into words the actions or thought processes that children are experiencing at the moment. This talk provides the structure of children's emerging cognitive processes, whether exploring, trial and error, questioning, magical thinking, or cause and effect (see Chapter 2). For example, while children are mixing substances together in making homemade play dough, the adult comments on their actions by saying, "you are stirring the water into the salt and flour."

Substance in context is the knowledge of a material or object in relation to the actual use of these materials.

Parallel Talk

Parallel talk is commentary that follows what the child is doing.

One way of using language with young children is the use of **parallel talk.** Once you have observed the child long enough to understand what he is about, begin by describing in simple but exact words what you see the child doing. In the following anecdote Carlos gradually becomes a participant even though he is in the process of acquiring English.

ANECDOTE

Bertha watches Carlos as Carlos is picking out animals that belong in the barn.

Teacher: Oh, now you have a sheep. You find where the sheep goes.

Teacher: Oh the sheep belongs there. You put the sheep up there. [*Teacher points to the door on the second level of the barn.*] You are putting the animals in.

Carlos: Look, Miss Bertha.

Carlos responds to hearing parallel talk.

Teacher: I see you are putting those animals here, too. [*She points to the first floor of the barn.*]

Teacher: You are taking him out and putting him in that place.

Carlos: Look Miss Bertha . . .

Teacher: I see you put it inside.

Carlos: Look, Miss Bertha, I have . . . [*He shows her the sheep.*]

Teacher: Oh, the sheep belongs there. You put the sheep up there. I see many animals are now in the barn.

Teacher: You are finished. Now you are putting them away. You are putting everything away.

Parallel talk is simply a running commentary. There will be no questioning and no requirement for the child to say anything. From this talk the child knows you are paying attention to what he is doing, which may serve to sustain his play. Also, parallel talk expands vocabulary, as discussed previously. A more expanded vocabulary is chosen if child is fluent, or a simpler language for less fluent speakers. This kind of talk is particularly helpful for children learning a second language. Nonverbal cues support beginning or second-language learners. For parallel talk, by all means focus on the child, get down to his level, and make eye contact if possible (*Good Talking with You,* 1987).

Language Expansion

Once the child decides to talk to the adult about what he is doing, the adult can easily reflect back what the child says. Because the child initiates at this point, he feels an equal partner in the conversation.

ANECDOTE

As Diamonte arranges pairs of animals on long blocks, the teacher watches intently.

Diamonte: The horse too big. [*He looks up.*]

Teacher: The horse is too big to fit with the pig.

Diamonte: So the pig by itself.

Teacher: Oh, since the horse is too big you put the pig by itself. I was wondering why you put the pig by itself.

Diamonte considers his plan of arranging animals two-by-two.

The teacher replies using a reflective response, keeping the same information as Diamonte states. These comments model the complete sentence structure and expand the thought. After using **language expansion,** as in the preceding example, the teacher will wait a moment before replying to see if the child will continue expanding on his thoughts. With these kinds of responses to the child's talk, the child responds to the interest in his ideas, and often, though not always, will continue the conversation expressing more complex ideas.

Language expansion is responding to what a child says by expanding the word, phrase, or sentence using a complete sentence or a more complex one.

I Wonder Statements

As a child works with materials and you sense the focus of his work, you can wonder with the child in many ways, such as wonder why something is working, wonder why something won't work, or pose another possibility.

In the preceding anecdote, the teacher could ask, "I wonder if there is a way to make another animal fit next to the pig." Note that in this case the adult does not have an answer in mind but wonders to open up possibilities. In hearing the phrase, "I wonder . . ." the child can choose whether or not to consider the possibility. While striving to match a child's intent through observation of his work, you will not always be accurate in knowing his purpose. A child can easily ignore these **I wonder statements** when the statements do not match the child's intent.

The I wonder statement can also be used to reflect what a group of children are considering. Following are two conversations about children's ideas, one during an activity and one in a discussion group.

I wonder statements phrase an extension of an idea or suggest possibilities to consider in response to children's ideas.

ANECDOTE

Two children are focused on gluing four tubes from paper towel rolls together side by side at the art table. Their intent is to build a wall around a large block building for their "wild animals." After liberally applying the glue between each tube, Terrence holds the four rolls out in front of him as he hurriedly walks to the block enclosure. He deftly places them in a standing position, and as he lets go, the two end ones flop to the floor. Running over to catch the tubes, Elena wails "Ohhh," as she reaches for them. Her face turns into a scowl.

Ms. A. quickly moves from the art table, stops next to the blocks, and looks at Terrence and Elena a moment. "The tubes did not stay together like you wanted. I wonder what would work."

ANECDOTE

A group of five children have just finished hearing the book *The Giving Tree* read by Ms. A. Mario goes to the discovery table and brings back a big leaf and holds it while gently flipping it over and over on the teacher's lap. Ms. A. suggests, "When we went to see our tree in the park we found these huge maple leaves. And Mario, you saw . . . "

"Branches, lots of 'em."

Other children add their ideas.

"They were broke from the tree."

"That must a' hurt!"

"The tree must've cried."

"Why do you think the tree cried?" Ms. A. asks.

"It hurt him."

"It must hurt to lose a branch. You are thinking of how the tree feels when it loses branches." Ms. A. pauses, then adds, "I wonder what it would be like to pretend to be that tree when it loses a branch."

Pondering Questions

Pondering questions pose ideas that children can choose to think about.

Pondering questions have a similar purpose to I wonder statements but are more direct. Inherent in this kind of questioning is the belief that children do think about their intent and ideas of how and why things happen. Teachers can share their interest in discussing things with children through these questions. As children begin to share their ideas, the teacher can remain on the sidelines allowing the children to converse among themselves (Cadwell, 1997).

Open-Ended Questions in Inquiry

Guidelines for Documenting Science Discussions

1. Discussion begins with open-ended questions, such as
   "What are some things made of paper?"
   "What do you know about water?"
   "What have you noticed lately about our caterpillars?"
2. Children shape the agenda of the discussion,
3. Participation by all children is encouraged.
4. Records are made of each child's statements (Chittenden & Jones, 1999, pp. 110–111. Reprinted with permission from the American Association for the Advancement of Science (AAAS). Copyright 1999 American Association for the Advancement of Science.

An open-ended question is a type of question that stimulates thoughtful responses and does not have one specific answer.

As children follow up with their ideas, the teacher can support their ideas by adding a comment or another question. An example from the preceding discussion is, "Why do you think the tree cried?"

Teachers return to the recorded conversation to look for the questions and interests of the participants. Sometimes the group is carried easily into a topic; other times teachers find questions to guide the children from this review.

All of these pondering questions are **open-ended questions** which often serve to stimulate the thoughts of the children. As children become accustomed to being asked these questions, they will respond readily. And they will propagate their own ideas without prompting when they realize that their ideas are heard.

> ### STANDARDS
>
> Nurture collaboration among students. Structure and facilitate ongoing formal and informal discussion based on a shared understanding of rules of scientific discourse.
>
> Teaching Standard E. Reprinted with permission from *National science education standards.* (1996). The National Academy of Sciences, courtesy of the National Academies Press, Washington, DC (p. 50).

CONSIDERATIONS IN QUESTIONING

Questioning is an important process in inquiry. Further investigation is opened up through questioning. As children explore on their own, they are asking their own questions as they handle, explore, and act on materials. A higher level of inquiry takes place when the question is verbalized and shared with others. With the support of the teacher, a child poses a question that sets the group in motion for a search to find answers. The resulting investigation often leads to in-depth exploration.

Unfortunately, children researching their own questions are usually not taken seriously in the social context. Often the adult takes it upon himself to answer the child's questions with information the adult knows. The result is filling up the child with information. This information given is treated as social knowledge, not physical or logicomathematical knowledge as it truly is (Kamii & DeVries, 1993). The child accepts this information from the adult without question and thus the child believes that the adult is the "container" of knowledge. In believing that all learning stems from the adult, the child abandons his reliance on his own emerging thought processes. This kind of thinking may lead to the lack of autonomous learning (Kamii, 1982).

Louise Boyd Cadwell (1997), who shared her learning of the **Reggio approach** in *Bringing Reggio Home,* says,

> The teacher's role is to ask good, open-ended questions that stimulate children's thinking and provoke discussion . . . so that children consider the matter at hand with all their attention and interests. In these conversations the teacher does not fish for right answers or impart information. This is clearly a departure from the traditional idea of the teacher's role. (p. 70)

The Reggio approach is the pedagogy of schools for young children in Reggio Emilia, Italy, and is based on the co-construction of knowledge and collaboration of children, teachers, and parents.

> ### ANECDOTE
>
> I had the privilege of visiting the now-famous schools of Reggio Emilia, Italy, through an education seminar. As I visited classrooms, I experienced firsthand the profound respect for the thinking of the young child. Conversations, questions, and ideas of children were taken so seriously that sometimes children's ideas evolved into a study that lasted many months.

In the Diana School of Reggio Emilia, a small group of children commented on the walls of the enclosed patio inside the school. These six boys said that the leaves covered the wall during the summer, but that the leaves would die in the fall, leaving the walls bare. Observant teachers began looking at those leaves with the children. Together they studied them, played in them, drew them, and discussed them. As the study progressed the children made leaves out of clay, fired them, and then restudied the formation of their leaf sculptures. They critiqued their work together and went back to work forming more leaves. During the year the group of five-year-olds had moved on from forming leaves to making insects in clay. As they revisited their work of their insect forms, the children realized they appeared flat. They decided to bring in real insects, and the resulting clay work then took on a three-dimensional shape.

When my colleagues and I visited the school in late May, these same children were working on building salamanders in clay. These realistic forms with a swirling tail were very much like the forms of lizards they saw in a well-illustrated book. For the close of the school in June, children were planning that some would take their clay-fired sculptures home, while other selected products would be arranged by the same six original children on the wall of the indoor patio, according to their early discussion last fall. In the seriousness of listening to the expressed thoughts of children the class developed a full year of study of the original problem and progressed into related areas of interest.

(Author)

Learning to Ask and Listen

Adults are often at a loss when considering the skill of questioning. As seen in Chapter 4, by taking the time to observe the way the child explores a material the teacher can begin to understand her thinking. It is from there that the adult may capture the particular comments and questions that stem from the child's interests.

ANECDOTE

In one chapter from *Reflections on the Reggio Emilia Approach,* Brenda Fyfe (1994) writes of the experience of early childhood teachers from St. Louis who became involved in developing the Reggio approach. As these teachers take the time to "closely observe, listen and engage in dialogue with children . . . they are learning to enter the child's world without disrupting or diverting the flow of a child's work or intentions" (p. 25).

The author relates the reflections of Dorris, a teacher of three-year-olds, who observed painting by children recording what she saw. After a short time the children became curious about what their teacher was doing. As a result of sharing her observations, children became involved in talking with her about "what effect their actions had on the painting" (Fyfe, 1994, p. 25). The children were aware of her keen interest in their painting and she learned much about their thinking as she watched them and followed their ideas as they painstakingly explained all this to her (Fyfe, 1994).

Posing Questions

As you pose questions to a group, be observant of the group, their interests, and what is considered in the conversation. In planning the size of a group for discussions, in the beginning work with a group of two, three, or four children. Usually teachers hold successful discussions with five to eight children. By keeping the group small it is much easier to both involve all the children and follow children's ideas. On occasion, discussions can involve a larger group up to fifteen, but usually the more exuberant children will carry the ideas. Beyond a gathering of eight, the teacher will need to provide some structure for fuller cooperation among all participants.

Since beginning teachers may not be used to starting good conversations with children, you may expect to try things out, falter, and thus learn more about posing questions along the way. When talking with children, use a tape recorder, ask another adult to record, or plan to record their comments as you move along. After each of these conversations, review the records to look for the kinds of queries that brought thoughtful comments from the children (Cadwell, 1997).

Carefully selected questions follow the children's thought.

Ingredients for Good Conversations

The project approach is a curriculum approach that uses a project for the focus of an in-depth investigation of a topic.

When focusing with a child or a small group of children, let go of expectations that planned questions will lead the group along a certain path. The process may bring out a similar topic that a teacher had in mind or evolve into a different one. In bringing an idea to a group of young children within the **project approach,** teachers often ask children what they already know and what they would like to know about a topic. Over time the teacher constructs with the children the ideas on where the project will go. Once children's interests are followed, the project takes on a depth of exploration because children are truly involved in finding out (Helm & Beneke, 2003; Helm & Katz, 2001).

DEVELOPING SKILLS IN LANGUAGE

Through the use of all these language skills you will be supporting children's thinking. Children do learn language when they have opportunities to use these skills in authentic situations. Teachers can support children as they acquire and practice these new, increasingly sophisticated skills. "To speak, children must translate their own mental representation in linguistic output that can be shared with others. In listening, they create mental representations based on someone else's language" (Conezio & French, 2002, pp. 16–17). These are awesome skills for preschoolers and kindergarteners, but when they are integrated in talking and listening and the actual experiences where children gain firsthand information from their actions on materials, these skills become a powerful tool.

SUMMARY

In the act of communication with children, skills in language can be expanded, whether talking about what children are doing, listening and reflecting, posing questions, or deciding plans. Each plays a roll in expanding the language of children by helping them scaffold their ideas and thought processes.

The language of identifying and the probing of questions lie at the center of the inquiry process. It is through language that the communication process brings forward the child's thinking on a topic and becomes the medium of interchange for the child to understand her ideas and be challenged by others. Communication is central to identifying. It is also pivotal in the other steps of inquiry. In the next chapter the processes of classifying, comparing, and contrasting will be explored.

TO FURTHER YOUR THINKING

1. Find the list of experiences of the child in the inquiry process under the heading "Language and Identifying" in the beginning of this chapter. For each experience write a statement that you, as a teacher, could say to the child who does that action. Compare your statements with a colleague.

2. Take a moment to remember your thinking processes as a child. As you questioned something or figured out some phenomenon in math or science, were you able to state your thoughts to an adult? How did you express this? How was that idea or question received? How did the adult response affect what you communicated in math or science ideas from that time forward?

3. Think of describing a natural phenomenon or explaining how something works, such as the sound from a guitar or the mechanics of an on/off switch of a lamp. State your ideas clearly or write them down in exact detail. How easy or difficult is it to state this? Now describe or write a social event such as greeting a good friend after a year apart. Compare the ease of describing the social versus the scientific event. If you find a difference, what could have made one harder to explain? What aspects in the social context could be influencing this?

4. Do you remember reading about a new sport or hobby and not understanding the vocabulary of the process or the materials used for this? For example, in order to learn to knit, at the outset you may know the identity of knitting needles from general knowledge, but you would need to learn the meaning and technique of knit and purl. How would you learn this from others—from a book, a class, or learning from a family member?

5. Select a "big word" to introduce to a young child or a group of children. Select a word within a topic in which you know the child has an interest, such as *tyrannosaurus*. Use the word as you or the young person handles the object. Continue use of the word over several days. Then casually ask a question that would prompt the child to use this word in conversation. How well does the child understand the meaning of the word in these few days?

6. What are your concerns about using running commentary and/or posing questions to a young child? Bring out these concerns in a discussion with a colleague or the class.

7. From the Guidelines for Documenting Science Discussions (page 94), decide on some opening questions for the following topics: observing shadows and collecting fall leaves. Work with a colleague to make these open-ended questions. If you have the opportunity, try out your questions with a young child or two.

8. Scan the chapter for examples of comments and questions teachers use. Read each example and suggest an example of a child's response. Which comments or questions seem reasonable choices for you in talking with a child or a small group?

REFERENCES

Cadwell, L. B. (1997). *Bringing Reggio Emilia home.* New York: Teachers College Press.

Chittenden, E., and Jones, J. (1999). Science assessment in early childhood programs. In American Association for the Advancement of Science, *Dialogue on early childhood science, mathematics, and technology education* (pp. 106–114). Washington, DC: Author.

Conezio, K., and French, L. (2002, September). Science in the preschool classroom: Capitalizing on children's fascination with the everyday world to foster language and literacy development. *Young Children, 57*(5), 12–118.

Fyfe, B. (1994). Images from the United States: Using ideas from the Reggio Emilia experience with American educators. In L. G. Katz & B. Cesarone, *Reflections on the Reggio Emilia Approach.* Urbana IL: ERIC.

Good talking with you: Language acquisition through conversation. (1987). Let's talk: First steps to conversation. Viewer's guide. Educational Productions. Portland, OR.

Hart, B., and Risley, T. R. (2002). *Meaningful differences in the everyday experiences of young American children.* Baltimore, MD: Paul H. Brookes.

Helm, J. H., and Beneke, S. (Eds.). (2003). *The power of projects: Meeting contemporary challenges in early childhood classrooms—Strategies and solutions.* New York: Teachers College Press.

Helm, J. H., and Katz, L. (2001). *Young investigators: The project approach in the early years.* New York: Teachers College Press.

Kamii, C. (1982). *Number in preschool and kindergarten.* Washington, DC: National Association for the Education of Young Children.

Kamii, C., and DeVries, R. (1993). *Physical knowledge in preschool education.* New York: Teachers College Press.

National Academy of Science. (1996). *National science education standards* [Book version, on line]. Washington, DC: National Academy Press. www.nap.edu

National Association for the Education of Young Children. (2003). NAEYC standards for early childhood professional preparation: Initial licensure programs. In M. Hyson (Ed.), *Preparing early childhood professionals: NAEYC's standards for programs* (pp. 17–63). Washington DC: Author.

Owens, C. V. (1999, September). Conversational science 101A: Talking it up! *Young Children, 54*(5), 4–9. Washington DC: National Association for the Education of Young Children.

Silverstein, S. (1964). *The giving tree.* New York: HarperCollins.

ADDITIONAL RESOURCES

Fassler, R. (2003). *Room for talk: Teaching and learning in a multilingual kinder-garten.* New York: Teachers College Press. This evolution of discourse develops shared meaning among children's talk that comes from peer scaffolding, and helps dual language speakers adopt a form of speaking together.

Gable, S. (2002, July). Teacher–child relationships throughout the day. *Young Children, 57*(4), 42–46. Healthy interactions support relationships, and by fostering a caring community, teachers acknowledge the thinking of young children.

Koralek, D. G. (2003). *Spotlight on young children and oral language.* Washington, DC: National Association for the Education of Young Children. This compilation of articles from *Young Children* presents ways to promote oral language throughout the early childhood curriculum.

Paley, V. G. (1997). *The girl with the brown crayon.* Cambridge, MA: Harvard University Press. A story of Paley's classroom where children's thoughts and ideas are valued.

Routman, R. (2000). *Conversations: Strategies for teaching, learning and evaluating.* Portsmouth NH: Heinemann. This comprehensive text emphasizes literacy, dialogue and inquiry. Includes vast resources for quality teaching in K-12.

Weitzman, E., and Greenberg, J. (2000). *Learning language and loving it.* Washington, DC: National Association for the Education of Young Children. This resource presents interactive strategies for supporting language learning for children in all levels of language development.

Children's Books

Fleming, D. (1998). *In the small, small pond.* New York: Henry Holt & Co.

Mayer, M. (1977). *The monster word book.* New York: Golden Press. Monster characters demonstrate the words and actions.

Hoban, T. (1997). *Exactly the opposite.* New York: HarperTrophy.

Hutchinson, O. (1971). *Changes.* New York: Macmillan. A wordless book with different situations.

Silverstein, S. (1964). *The giving tree.* New York: HarperCollins.

Wood, A. (1984). *The napping house.* New York: Harcourt.

Web Sites

www.edpro.com Educational Productions has an excellent selection of training videos for educators and parents on supporting language.

www.scholastic.com Scholastic has a large source of appropriate books for young children in both Spanish and English.

Chapter 7

Classifying, Comparing, and Contrasting

OBJECTIVES Through the process of discovery in this chapter, you will be able to:

1. Describe ways the young child uses each of these basic math skills:
   a. Classifying
   b. Comparing
   c. Contrasting
   d. Seriating
   e. Creating sets

2. Hone skills for observing basic math in everyday circumstances.

3. Identify basic math skills used in inquiry.

4. Describe young children's use of symbols and signs.

5. Identify three stages of graphing in young children.

IDEAS TO PONDER

- How do young children learn basic math skills?
- What is most important in math learning for the young years?
- Where, when, and how does math occur in the early childhood classroom?
- What concepts do young children learn from graphing?
- How can young children work with graphing?

At the Duplos® table, all four preschoolers concentrate on their own structure. Soon all the rectangle Duplos are being used. Alison wants more. She finds two square pieces and holds these together and fits them exactly over the top rectangle of her structure. When she finds an

even bigger Duplo piece, she discards that. As Divonti is also missing the same size rectangle pieces for his construction, he notices Alison's placement of two squares, looks down at his own, and copies her idea.
(Author)

BASIC MATH SKILLS

As children use materials in constructing, whether clay, blocks, or Duplos, they naturally employ classifying, comparing, and contrasting as tools to use. In addition, young children will use seriation and creating sets. When they use cognitive tools such as these, it is math. The very basic tool of one-to-one correspondence is also exercised in all these math skills. All these logicomathematical skills progress as children manipulate the materials on their own. In using various materials they are using **basic math** to see objects in all kinds of relationships (Kamii & DeVries 1993).

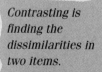

Basic math is using skills of classifying, comparing, contrasting, seriating, and making sets.

Classify, Compare, and Contrast

Both Alison and Divonti **classify** as they seek out the rectangle Duplos for their building. The two children put one square Duplo next to another square, matching the two. Then as they added them to the structure, they also classified these as "pieces I can use to build."

Classifying is putting like objects in groups.

Both Alison and Divonti **compare** Duplos each time they look for a rectangle piece to match the same as the rectangle ones they are already using. Seeing that the two squares together match the rectangle, Alison finds a useful comparison to continue building.

To determine the differences when comparing, Divonti looks at Alison's building, then his, and sees that hers continues with doubles of squares on the top. So he figures out that he can do the same and continues his building by adopting what he learns through **contrasting** his with hers.

Comparing is the act of examining two objects to determine if they are the same or different.

Contrasting is finding the dissimilarities in two items.

Duplo constructions involve classifying, comparing, and contrasting.

CLASSIFICATION BY YOUNG CHILDREN

Younger three-year-olds sometimes start a collection of like objects, then lose their first intention of the kind of objects. For example, this younger child would begin to line up the cars, then change by adding little people figures to the line. By three-and one-half years of age, most children can sort according to simple characteristics, such as type or shape.

The older preschooler and kindergartener become capable in classifying objects according to one of several obvious characteristics, such as type, color, or size. Sometimes this older child can use flexible thinking when he sees that a group of objects can first be classified by one characteristic and then regrouped another way. He can first sort according to type and shape, then regroup items according to color.

The young child can also classify according to other attributes, such as a general category or purpose. For example, the child can select a group of clothes worn by a baby or clothes worn in winter. Yet before the age of seven she cannot see how items can belong to more than one group, such as baby's mittens belonging to both baby clothes and winter clothes.

At age three, the class of "his family" is not established enough to know that he belongs no matter what his sister claims.

Classification of water toys occurs during cleanup.

Classification sets apart a group of objects to be used in play. In similar fashion, the concept of seriation gradually develops.

SERIATION

Seriation is the ordering in sequence of some characteristics like size, or weight, or volume. Seriation is going up (or down) the tones of the musical scale. The number system uses seriation: Two is one more than one, three is one more than two, and so on.

Children accomplish seriation using three or more objects that differ in gradients, such as the sizes of bowls as in *Goldilocks and the Three Bears*. In the young years, the child typically applies seriation this way. He sets out two items, such as a long and a short straw, then picks a third and, through comparing, finds out

> *Seriation is ordering according to a known characteristic.*

Ashley arranged the hearts in seriation.

if the third straw should go between the two or before or after the two. He continues to work this through, comparing each piece. As a kindergartener he will more easily see the whole picture in seriating. He may start with the longer piece, then search for the next in order, and the next. This process takes less steps than what he did a year ago.

A set is a group of objects with certain characteristics.

CREATING SETS

In the process of classifying, a person decides on making a **set,** a group of objects with certain characteristics. A set can contain any amount of two or more. Its characteristics can be broadly based, such as winter clothing, or specific, such as shapes or color of wood pieces (Fig. 7–1).

Figure 7–1 Sets of wood pieces are placed within yarn circles.

Sets of different sizes of wooden spheres are lined up.

As a child works with a set of objects, he can move them around, line them up, or stack them. As he reworks the arrangement of pieces many times, he can begin to observe that this set of objects does not change in amount.

The young child can use two sets to compare the amount in each and, there-fore, use the concepts *more* and *less*. When the amount in each set is five or less and the size of the objects in each set is similar, the child can see the difference in amount (Baroody & Wilkins, 1999). With over five items the child can use other skills to determine *same, more,* or *less,* such as lining up each set side by side. In

STANDARDS

Recognize "how many" in sets of objects.

Chapter 4: Number and Operations Standard for Grades Pre-K–2.

this way, using one-to-one correspondence, the child can clearly contrast the size of each group. One-to-one correspondence is crucial here as well as in many aspects of number (Kamii, 1982). If the child has developed a concept of number and can count correctly, the child has another way of comparing numbers in sets. The concept of number will necessarily be securely based before the child will use number to determine the amount in a set. This number sense will be examined in Chapter 10.

HONING SKILLS FOR OBSERVING BASIC MATH

As children become involved in sand play, you can observe their actions and listen for their comments to see their work of classifying, comparing, contrasting, seriating, and making sets in their play.

ANECDOTE

Miguel presses a round mold into the sand, lifts it off, looks at the sand, then presses it into the sand next to the first result. He lifts the mold and pats both small mounds of sand until they become flat.

Angie lifts a cup of sand and pours it quickly. She repeats this but lets it fall slowly, watching the sand leave the cup.

Raul scoops up some sand in a small plastic bottle top and holds it high while letting it pour out. "It goes like water," he comments softly.

Raul looks at the cup Angie is using, puts his bottle top down, and reaches for the cup in Angie's hand. "I want that one." Angie moves the cup away from Raul.

Raul refills the plastic bottle top and places it on a clean spot on the bottom of the sandbox. He reaches for a small cup, fills it with sand, and places it next to the bottle top. Now that Angie has left the sandbox, Raul grabs the cup Angie left behind. He places that filled cup next to the small cup. "For baby bear, mama bear and papa bear!" he exclaims as he points to each one.

Miguel looks at Raul. "That's food for the three bears."

When visiting an early childhood classroom you will find that children use basic math concepts in many areas of the room as they explore, construct, and play dramatic play themes. Once you are familiar with these concepts, you will observe them in many interest areas.

WHEN IS IT MATH? WHEN IS IT SCIENCE?

The math concepts in this chapter are presented as part of the inquiry process. Because these math concepts occur in inquiry, they are naturally a part of science. Yet mathematical thinking also occurs outside of science. As children play

---

ANECDOTE

Classifying: It's wet.
   I think it's dead.
   It smells bad.
   It's dead.
   Because fishes always die.
Comparing: Was the other fish bigger in the book?
   I had a fish that die.
Contrasting: It reminds me of my alive fish. This one's alive. No. It's dead.
   I see the blood.
   It's moving! It's moving!
   No, it's not. You just bumped the table and the water's movin'.

Adapted from Chittenden & Jones, 1999, p. 111. Reprinted with permission from the American Association for the Advancement of Science (AAAS). Copyright 1999 American Association for the Advancement of Science.

---

a lotto game where pictures are matched to pictures on a card, or children sort toy cars by size, the math concepts they use stand alone. With this explanation you can see the meaning of the phrase, "You can take the science out of math, but you can't take the math out of science."

⌈Sometimes math will stand on its own and at other times it is integral to the inquiry process.⌋ It is math only when children are comparing sizes of coins to create sets of each kind, or collecting all the buttons having one particular attribute such as those with four holes. Other times math will be an integral part of the inquiry process, such as seen from the comments in the following discussion.

In the kindergartners' discussion of the dead fish (see Chapter 4), they were using math concepts in trying to comprehend their question of whether the fish was alive or dead.

In reviewing this incident, you can categorize the children's comments into the math concepts of classifying, comparing, and contrasting. They classified according

---

STANDARDS

Sort and classify objects according to their attributes and organize data about the objects.

Chapter 4: Data Analysis and Probability Standard for Grades Pre-K–2.
Reprinted with permission from *Principles and Standards for School Mathematics,* Copyright 2000 by the National Council of Teachers of Mathematics (p. 109). All rights reserved.

Tally is using marks to represent the number of objects in a set.

to what they knew and observed. They compared and contrasted with previous experiences. In the last set of comments one child exclaimed that the fish was moving, as he used his immediate sense of seeing the water moving. The other child compared the events with his previous experiences to conclude the cause of the movement.

USING SIGNS AND SYMBOLS

Symbols are marks used to represent a number ○○○, ✔✔✔, ■■■ (Kamii, 1982).

As children work with basic math, they will at some time want to represent these in a different form. Akin to the emergence of literacy is the emerging representation in math. Children may represent objects pictorially or try out other marks to represent something, such as **tallying.**

This emergence of **symbols** sometimes appears naturally in drawing. Symbols have a direct relation to the object, even to the point of a drawing of the object as seen in playing cards of hearts, diamonds, spades, and clubs. **Signs** are the verbal or written form of the numeral. Because signs are a systemized set of words and representation in a language, these are necessarily learned through social knowledge (Kamii, 1982). Teachers can represent the numbers of things by using symbols of the object before expecting that children use signs. When children in a group vary in ability to recognize signs, teacher-made or computer-generated cards can show both the sign (3) and symbol (○○○).

Signs are the spoken word or the written numeral in the number system.

STANDARDS

Create and use representations to organize, record, and communicate mathematical ideas.

Chapter 4: Representation Standard for Grades Pre-K–2.
Reprinted with permission from *Principles and Standards for School Mathematics,* Copyright 2000 by the National Council of Teachers of Mathematics (p. 136). All rights reserved.

GRAPHS

A graph is a systematic representation of data usually shown two dimensionally.

Young children can advance into making **graphs** through experiences with basic math concepts. The class construction of simple graphs enables children to grapple with observing, classifying and making sets, comparing sets, contrasting information in graph form, as well as ordering and one-to-one correspondence. When the children actually make graphs to show their understanding, they are communicating in exact ways. The kind of thinking involved in displaying and organizing data involves analysis and probability.

Children age three to six are in the process of developing an understanding of representation. This can evolve into an understanding of simple graphs, from a realistic graph to one using symbols. These can be categorized in three stages.

Realistic Graph

For the first stage, a group of children can first represent ideas in a real way by ordering real people or real objects into a human or object graph. For example, children choose their favorite kind of apple: red delicious or golden delicious. After tasting apples, they choose their favorite by joining the teacher holding the apple of their choice. At this early stage of graphing usually children consider only two contrasting items, such as which is preferred, red or golden delicious. After the groups are formed, each group of children forms a line adjacent to the other. They form partners by reaching across to the opposite group and holding hands. By using this one-to-one correspondence, children can compare which group has more (Fig. 7–2).

Representative Graph

In the second stage, the group can work with pictures of the objects such as drawings or an outline of the object that represents the objects on the graph (Smith, 2001). Also, when the children see each person's act of contributing to the graph, this is another way of processing from the real to representation of the real object, such as drawing their choice on a sticky note and placing it on the graph.

Figure 7–2 Children show the vote of their favorite kind of apple through a human graph.

Later in this second stage more objects could be added to a graph, such as categories of three or more choices (Fig. 7–3).

Bar Graph

In the third stage, children understand a bar graph, where a block or a square represents the object. Bar graphs do not contain a direct representation of the object but use a square as a symbol of the object (Smith, 2001). Some children at five and six years may be able to move to this stage after many opportunities to create the first two (Charlesworth & Lind, 2003) (Fig. 7–4). You will find more examples of graphs in Appendix C.

ANECDOTE

The four-year-old group is discussing the name for their new fish soon to be added to the aquarium. Mrs. D. listens closely to their ideas and hears two names mentioned, Samantha and Swimmy. Since there seems to be high interest in both names, she asks, "How can we decide?" Children excitedly chime in their ideas.

"Let everybody who wants the name Swimmy to vote."

"And the others?"

"They can vote, too."

"Everybody who wants Swimmy, stand up."

"And those who want Samantha . . . ?" Asks Mrs. D.

"They can stand up next."

The group tries this, and one is chosen to count. The vote is pretty equal and the child counting does not count herself.

"We still don't know," one child says.

Mrs. D. suggests, "Each one could put their vote in by selecting the one they want. That way we can see which has more. The one with more votes will be the name of our fish." Mrs. D. reaches for a can of clothespins and goes on to explain. "Each one will have one clothespin to place on the name he or she wants." Children are quiet with the new idea; then John says, "Yeah, a real vote." They seem to agree with this new concept. Ms. D. continues, "We can set this graph here during work time. And you can vote before lunch." Later, a board with the question and the two names are placed at the story rug, and as children go to wash hands for lunch they each pick out a clothespin and place it under "Swimmy" or "Samantha." After lunch they gather around the voting board eagerly anticipating the outcome. Mrs. D. leads in counting the clothespins under each name with the group. She announces three for "Samantha" and seven for "Swimmy."

"Oh phooey," says John, who realizes that "Swimmy" has more. "Oh well, that's okay. We'll have a Swimmy fish."

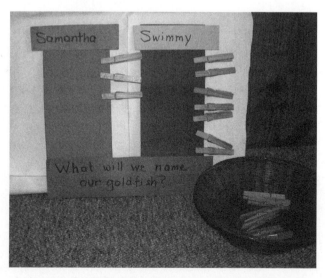

On this symbolic graph each child placed one clothespin as a vote for the name that he wanted.

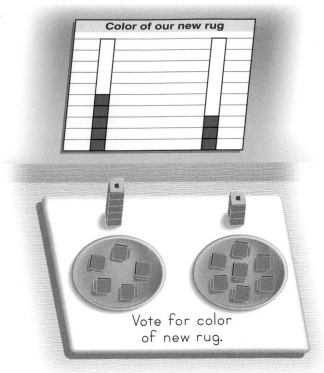

Figure 7–3 By using two stacks of Unifix® Cubes and then a bar graph, children can grasp both a representative and a bar graph.

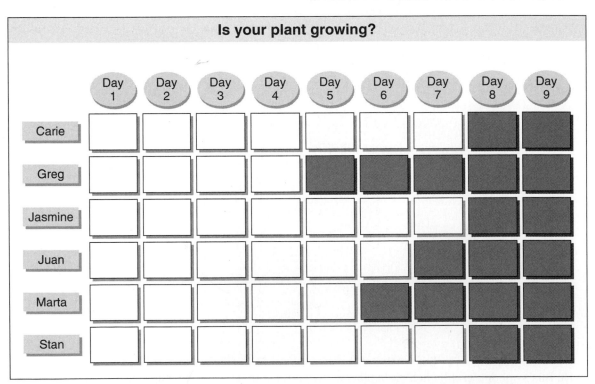

Figure 7–4 A computer-generated bar graph displays the days each child observed the sprout of the seed he planted.

SUMMARY

With the introduction of the basic math processes discussed in this chapter, you have an idea of how children process these tools in math and in the inquiry process. You can see how graphs are a natural extension of basic math. Children can use what they know in basic math to understand science in their lives. With this understanding of classifying, comparing, and contrasting, you will move on to the next step of the inquiry process, hypothesizing and generalizing, which you will find in the next chapter. In Chapters 10, 14, and 15, you will examine young children's number sense and gain further insight into curriculum planning using early math.

TO FURTHER YOUR THINKING

1. Observe children from ages three to six at play. Ask yourself what basic math concepts they are using in their play. Discuss your findings with a classmate. Together find another activity that would follow the same math concept that was seen in one of your observations.

2. In what ways do you use the following in your daily lives: classifying, comparing, contrasting, seriating, and making sets? How many of these skills do you use without using the number system?

3. Look at the anecdote on sand play (page 108). How would you classify these actions and statements of children according to basic math concepts?

4. Take some time to explore materials typically found in a preschool or kindergarten classroom and list or discuss the math concepts inherent in them. Limit your discussion to classifying, comparing/contrasting, seriating, and making sets. Look for blocks, dramatic play materials, manipulatives, lotto games, simple board games, puzzles, scales, graduated cups (sand and water play), musical instruments, and magnifiers.

5. Explain the meaning of the phrase, "You can take the science out of math, but you can't take the math out of science."

6. Does your understanding of basic math skills match your expectations about math at the beginning of the course? Does this seem hard or easy compared to your initial expectations?

7. Explain the three stages of graphing. Give an example of each.

REFERENCES

Aylesworth, J. (2003). *Goldilocks and the three bears.* New York: Scholastic.

Baroody, A. J., and Wilkins, J. L. M. (1999). The development of informal counting, number and arithmetic skills and concepts. In J. V. Copley (Ed.), *Mathematics in the early years.* Reston, VA: National Council of Teachers of Mathematics.

Charlesworth, R., and Lind, K. (2003). *Math and science for young children* (4th ed.). Clifton Park, NY: Thomson Delmar Learning. Thorough resource on math understanding of young children and math activities throughout early childhood.

Chittenden, E., and Jones, J. (1999). Science assessment in early childhood programs. In American Association for the Advancement of Science, *Dialogue on early childhood science, mathematics, and technology education* (pp. 106–114). Washington, DC: Author.

Kamii, C. (1982). *Number in preschool and kindergarten.* Washington, DC: National Association for the Education of Young Children.

Kamii, C., and DeVries, R. (1993). *Physical knowledge in preschool education.* New York: Teachers College Press.

National Council of Teachers of Mathematics. (2000). *Principles and standards for school mathematics.* Reston, VA: Author.

Smith, S. S. (2001). *Early childhood mathematics* (2nd ed.). Boston, MA: Allyn & Bacon.

ADDITIONAL RESOURCES

Baroody, A. (2000). Does mathematics instruction for three- to five-year-olds really make sense? *Young Children, 55*(4), 61–67. This article focuses on teaching basic math.

Copley, J. V. (Ed.). (1999). *Mathematics in the early years.* Reston, VA: National Council of Teachers of Mathematics. A compilation of research on early math conceptual development and instructional approaches. Available **www.nctm.org** and **www.naeyc.org**

Whiten, P., and Whiten, D. J. (2003, January). Developing mathematical under-standing along the yellow brick road. *Young Children, 58*(1), 36–40. Washington, DC: National Association for the Education of Young Children. Kindergarteners experience graphing resulting in in-depth math learning.

Web Sites

www.nctm.org National Council of Teachers of Mathematics has resources for classrooms (for K–12) and the Principles and Standards for School Mathematics on line.

www.naeyc.org Access *Young Children* articles on mathematics on line.

Chapter 8

Hypothesizing and Generalizing

OBJECTIVES Through the process of discovery in this chapter, you will be able to:

1. Define hypothesizing and generalizing and give examples of this thinking in young children.

2. Name essential features of the National Science Education Standards that involve hypothesizing and generalizing.

3. Discuss the limits and capabilities of young children to hypothesize and generalize.

4. Describe the processes of following children's intent, intersubjectivity, co-construction, and collaboration to process children's ideas as a group.

5. Discuss how to develop a hypothesis with a group of children.

6. Discuss how to reach a generalization with young children.

7. Describe inquiry as a circular process, not a linear one.

IDEAS TO PONDER

- How can young children accomplish hypothesizing and generalizing?

- How can children whose thought processes are intuitive come together to work on problem solving?

- What is the teacher's role in co-construction? In leading collaboration of a group?

- How can the teacher assist children in developing processes to hypothesize and generalize?

Before Valentine's Day there was plenty of white and red paint at the easel. One morning Tara looks up from her concentrated focus on painting and says to Ms. A., "Look, I made pink!"

"How did you do that?"
"I had a lot of red here, and I added white to it—and it is pink."
"You added the white to the red. I wonder what would happen if you added red to that bit of white paint up there."
Tara takes a minute to try out this new idea. Then she looks up, "Look, again I got pink."
"So adding white to red, and red to white, both make pink. So if you want to make pink you can . . ."
"Put one on top of the other."
"Which colors?"
"White and red."
"You know that white and red make pink either way."
(Author)

HYPOTHESIZING AND GENERALIZING BY YOUNG CHILDREN

Sometimes the hypothesis and generalization is from a brief encounter like in the preceding example, when Tara came upon her first discovery of pink. The teacher led her to find out what would happen by joining the colors in a different way (hypothesize). Tara does not necessarily know that if she always puts one of those colors on the other she will get pink. The teacher led her to generalize. Tara now has the power to determine how to make this color when she wants to make it. Yet the two inquiry processes of hypothesizing and generalizing indicate thinking at a level beyond the stage of preoperational thinking.

Jacqueline Johnson suggests that current early childhood practices encourage children to get "stuck" and then help them to discover ways to get them "unstuck." "Within this framework," she continues, "children are encouraged to handle objects, observe and predict results, hear and use language, and collaborate with adults and older children to develop ideas" (Johnson, 1999, p. 20).

In the processes of working through their ideas as a group, young children can get to the point of making guesses of why something works, or predicting what will happen (hypothesize). The next step is action, to try out their hypothesis. When the group senses that it has have reached some conclusion, the children with their teacher use the information they have discovered to collectively state something they now know in their world (generalize).

STEPS OF INQUIRY IN THE NATIONAL SCIENCE EDUCATION STANDARDS

From a list of Essential Features of Classroom Inquiry as proposed by the National Science Education Standards (National Research Council, 2000), hypothesizing and generalizing are incorporated into two of the five essential features of inquiry for K–12 learners. Both of these include hypothesizing, and the second one includes generalizing.

STANDARDS

- Learners formulate explanations from evidence to address scientifically oriented questions.
- Learners evaluate their explanations in light of alternative explanation, particularly those reflecting scientific understanding.

(National Research Council, 2000, pp. 26–27)

FOLLOW INTENT IN CHILDREN'S THINKING

On their own preschool and kindergarten children do not necessarily reach hypothesizing and generalizing. Yet when the adult follows the children's line of thinking, the adult can make sense of, and also validate, the children's system of inquiry through continuing their **intent.** It is from this place that adults can be helpful in forming questions of hypothesis and statements of generalization.

Intent is the focus or direction of thought and action.

It is all too easy to lose the focus of the children because of adult goals in science experiences. Teachers should not let their own motivations get in the way of the children's developing ideas in inquiry. In the following anecdotes, the outcomes of two very similar physical science experiences show children responding differently.

The first group of students was satisfied with their outcome. But they had not grappled with the children's thoughts and ideas. The second group was frustrated

To follow the intent of the child, the adult focuses on the child's actions and words.

ANECDOTES

PHYSICAL SCIENCE EXPERIENCES

Two groups of college students in my science and math class developed a physical science experience in which children added small cubes to a boat to see how many cubes would make the boat sink in water.

a. The first group set up this process to engage interested children one by one. Individually, each child was asked to predict how many and then an adult recorded that number on a chart. The child would then drop the wood cubes into the boat until the boat sank. With an adult she then counted and compared this to her first prediction. After this, each child quickly left to find another interest center in the classroom.

b. In another area of the same classroom the activity was presented by a second group. Four children sat around the table experimenting with the boats and the cubes in them. As children took the cubes out and put them in again, water spilled all over the table. At first the four children followed the students' questions and answered them. Then they seemed to find their own sense of what they wanted. The cubes became "the captain and the crew" of the boats. In this pretend mode the crew answered to the "boss." The boats were capsized, not because of too many cubes but because of imagined occurrences of the captain and crew. Children stayed interested in this playful experience for the entire free choice time.

(Author)

---

because the children did not follow their plan. Yet they seemed a step closer to understanding children's intent because they allowed the project to flow with the children. This second group of students could have followed the children's ideas more closely about what the captain and crew do and what made the boat capsize. In this way the students would have captured the intent of the children's play and followed with questions about what the children were doing and thinking. To discover children's intent teachers must step outside their own process, follow children's thoughts, and reflect on them.

HIGHER-ORDER THOUGHT PROCESSES

In considering the capabilities of young children, review their preoperational capabilities and limitations (see Chapter 2). Between three and six years old, children are preoperational, which often does not naturally lead to the higher-level processes of hypothesizing and generalizing.

Co-Construction

Yet, when a group of children use co-construction in thinking, the group can reach aspects of more advanced thought. In thinking through ideas as part of a group, the children can reach conclusions that take them beyond their preoperational thinking.

Intersubjectivity

Intersubjectivity is the process of two people adjusting to be within the same intent.

An important quality of Vygotskian view is that of **intersubjectivity,** a concept introduced by Newson and Newson (1975) (as cited in Berk & Winslow, 1995). This concept looks closely at the interactive relationship between a child and teacher (a parent, peer, or other adult). It is important that those involved in an activity are working toward the same goal. During a learning activity they work to adjust to each other's ideas. The adult puts her understanding into a process that can be comprehended by the child (Berk & Winslow, 1995). And the child tries to communicate her ideas—so there is a commonly shared intent. This is shown clearly as Tara and her teacher discuss how to make the color pink.

Intersubjectivity can be accomplished as teachers work with a group, co-constructing ideas. This necessitates that teachers listen closely to the children's ideas, seeing the links and beginning concepts as they are expressed. In this process of following and reflecting children's thoughts, teachers can take the children deeper in inquiry and, sometimes, embrace hypothesis and generalization.

Collaboration

Collaboration is the collective work of actively listening and developing ideas.

Collaboration is an important part of group functioning. In discussing Vygotsky theory, Laura Berk and Adam Winslow explain that "through cooperative dialogues with more knowledgeable members of society . . . children learn to think and behave in ways that reflect the community's culture" (Berk & Winsler, 1995, p. 19). Both adults and peers can and do offer guidance that leads to more mature thinking. In a group experience the adult can take the role of guiding and supporting the group thinking process as it unfolds.

SCIENCE CONCEPTS BEYOND THE YOUNG CHILD

Especially in the preschool and kindergarten years, because of the constraints of preoperational thinking, some science phenomena are beyond the child's ability (Lind, 1999). For example, consider understanding the rotation of the earth on its axis, or fertilization in mammals. If the child asks, "What makes night?" or "How did I get in Mommy's tummy?" how do you answer? Scientific explanations will only confound the young child. Instead you can find out what the child is thinking about and answer from that perspective. If you ask, "What do you think?" this just might be the opportunity he wants to tell you what he has thought out. Or his answer can provide more information to indicate the kind of answer he is searching for. So, depending on what more the child says, answers may be something like, "When the sun goes down, it brings on the night," or "It must have been that your mommy and daddy were wanting you." Because you follow the child's thinking process, as Elkind states, "Such answers are not really 'wrong,' and they accomplish the important goal of encouraging further questioning while providing a wonderful sense of being understood" (Elkind, 1999, p. 67).

PROCESSING THINKING WITH CHILDREN

By accepting that the thinking of young children is logical for them, teachers can more easily process that thinking along with them. The educators in Reggio Emilia schools believe that animism is not negative, or merely a stage of childhood thought, but rather an approach to the world that offers a way to enter into a relationship with that which is considered different than we are (Cadwell, 1997). Yet the children's thinking is intuitive, not logical and not linear. Their thoughts may lead them to use thought processes including realism, animism, artificialism, lack of cause and effect, and transductive thinking.

"If we accept this way in which children see the world as their own special intelligence instead of thinking it is cute and/or incorrect, we have much to learn from the children we listen to" (Cadwell, 1997, p. 66). This thinking means that young children may not progress to looking at a hypothesis or generalization on their own. By joining in with the discussion involving their ideas, teachers follow children's intent wherever that may go. At some point, teachers may see the link to hypothesizing and generalizing. Then thoughtful questions, incorporating the last steps of inquiry, may lead to further study.

Co-Constructing with Children's Ideas

The key is to follow the intent of the children whether or not it follows a logical path. As a group follows up on a beginning **study** together, the path may meander from a logical idea to imaginative reasoning. The child may give human characteristics to plants and animals, or turn a water experiment into dramatic play (as in the preceding example). This is their way of viewing the world, and by catching this and staying with their thoughts you choose to become a part of it (intersubjectivity). The following conversation that Louise Cadwell captured in the Diana school in Reggio Emilia follows the ideas of the children.

With the children's focus on the feelings of plants, it is important to follow this intent and, therefore, reach this part of inquiry. In earlier chapters you have followed exploring, identifying, classifying, and comparing and contrasting. As a result you can see children actively involved with materials. With involvement in their ideas and further questioning, young children can continue to develop their line of thought, which can take them through exploring a question to evolving new ideas.

A study is a process of learning that children and teachers involve themselves through discussion, design, and representation of a topic.

ANECDOTE

When children had returned the plants to the classroom after they had cared for them in their homes during summer vacation, their teacher, Marina, asked, "Do you think these plants are happier here at school or at your houses?"

Ale: Mine is happier at home because I give it food. But it is also happy here.

Marina: Why is that?

Ale: Because it's happy when you come near because it thinks you are going to give it water. If you don't come near it would think that you aren't a friend anymore.

Maria: I think the plants are happy here because now we're here.

Marina: So when we all go home, how do you think the plants feel?

Ale: They are better off when we're here, because we're their owners and we give them water and food. (Cadwell, 1997, p. 41)

Questions for Hypothesizing

By carefully following children's expressions, adults pick up the questions children have or ask others that follow their intent. Then teachers can collaborate with children to develop or restate the questions that can lead to the involvement of a project of study.

There are prime times when children are considering ideas; at such times a question can be posed that follows these ideas. The following are examples of posing questions:

"What do you think will happen if . . ."

"How would we do that?"

"What will happen next?"

"How long do you think it will take for the mold to grow?"

"What do the seeds need to grow?"

Thoughtful answers to these questions can form the hypothesis. So the next step is to suggest,

"Shall we try it? What should we do first?"

"How do you think we can find out?"

"How shall we keep track?"

"I hear you say that it will grow if we put it in the sun."

Then the process is to try it out.

Children examine the strawberry to look for mold. They can use this information to understand the graph on "How many days will it take for the food to mold?"

Questions for Generalizing

Sometimes children try the hypothesis and learn from the result. Because of pre-operational thinking, children may see this result yet may not combine this understanding with other similar understandings. When sensing what the children do grasp in their inquiry the adult can question or restate what they discovered and relate this to other events of a similar nature.

"What did we find out? Do you think if we did it again it would happen the same way?"

"Is this the same as we found out with growing the marigold seeds?"

"So when we put the water in the higher end of the hose, it poured out the other end. So when you want to have water go from one place to another, make the end that you put the water in higher, and the place you want it to come out lower."

"Let's look at what we did . . . . What happened when we . . . ? What will happen if we do that again?"

This kind of discussion carries the collaboration beyond finding the answer to the particular question. Often young children need guidance to see that this also applies to similar instances. Kindergartners are beginning to apply one result to other similar circumstances. Gradually children become involved in the process of generalizing.

Circular process occurs when the stages of inquiry move from one step to another and return to an earlier step.

The Circular Process of Inquiry

The processes of hypothesizing and generalizing described in this chapter may happen at any point in the inquiry process. Children may develop one hypothesis and then move on to another one. In actuality, for the younger ages in inquiry it is often a **circular process,** not linear. Children may explore one idea, come up with some understanding, or test a hypothesis, and then move on to something similar.

SUMMARY

In inquiry children may not move through all the steps, and these last two steps (hypothesizing and generalizing) are the ones most likely to be skipped. Yet teachers who actively collaborate with young children find that they can cue into their thinking and co-construct the hypothesis and generalization with a group. In the following chapter, you will see the finalization of inquiry in documentation of the experience. Documentation will take many forms in recording work of the individual child and a group or class.

TO FURTHER YOUR THINKING

1. Review the experience of Tara mixing red and white paint. Identify each step of the inquiry process you see in this experience. Describe whether some steps were missed or glossed over. If so, indicate what more the teacher could do to pinpoint those steps with Tara.

2. Review an elementary science text or look up Internet resources for the inquiry process in the elementary years. Identify the four steps of this process as used in this text. For other terms used, describe how they do or do not parallel the four steps used in this text.

3. In the two activities of cubes in the boats set up by students (page 121) which group of children was more involved in inquiry? Which group "owned" the thinking process? Why do you think this is important for young children?

4. Why is it difficult for the young child to accomplish hypothesizing and generalizing? Use your knowledge of preoperational thought to verify your answer.

5. How is it possible for young children to accomplish hypothesizing and generalizing? Use your knowledge of their thinking and theories you have learned to verify your answer.

6. Discuss with a partner how you respond to children discussing the feelings of plants as presented in the anecdote (page 124) in this chapter. How does this fit with the goals of inquiry for young children?

7. Discuss with a partner a list of questions and comments you could use as the children discuss the feelings of plants. What questions lead to hypothesizing? As you consider one question that leads to hypothesizing, decide what you and the children could do with this? What might the children find out? What generalization could come out of this? How would you discuss this with the children?

REFERENCES

Berk, L. E., and Winsler, A. (1995). *Scaffolding children's learning: Vygotsky and early childhood education.* Washington DC: National Association for the Education of Young Children.

Cadwell, L. B. (1997). *Bringing Reggio Emilia home.* New York: Teachers College Press.

Elkind, D. (1999). Educating young children in math, science, and technology. In American Association for the Advancement of Science, *Dialogue on early childhood science, mathematics, and technology education* (pp. 62–70). Washington, DC: Author.

Johnson, J. R. (1999). The forum on early childhood science, mathematics, and technology education. In American Association for the Advancement of Science, *Dialogue on early childhood science, mathematics, and technology education* (pp. 14–25). Washington, DC: Author.

Lind, K. K. (1999). Science in early childhood: Developing and acquiring fundamental concepts and skills. In American Association for the Advancement of
Science, *Dialogue on early childhood science, mathematics, and technology
education* (pp. 73–83). Washington, DC: Author.

National Research Council. (2000). *Inquiry and the National Science Education
Standards: A guide for teaching and learning.* Washington, DC: National Academies Press.

ADDITIONAL RESOURCES

Fu, V. R., Stremmel, A. U., and Hill, L. T. (2004). *Teaching as inquiry: Rethinking
early childhood education.* Upper Saddle River, NJ: Pearson Education. A look
at inquiry in early childhood education.

Helm, J. H., and Katz, L. (2001). *Young investigators: The project approach in the
early years.* New York: Teachers College Press. These authors introduce involvement in projects.

Helm, J. H., and Beneke S. (Ed.). (2003). *The power of projects: Meeting contemporary challenges in early childhood classrooms—Strategies and solutions.*
New York: Teachers College Press. This book compiles the success stories of
projects in many classrooms.

Cadwell, L. B. (2003). *The Reggio approach: Bringing learning to life.* New York:
Teachers College Press. This text in a journal style relates the implementation
of the Reggio approach in the United States.

Rogoff, B. (1990). *Apprenticeship in thinking: Cognitive development in social
context.* New York: Oxford University Press. Barbara Rogoff's research relates
the cognitive abilities gained within the cultural context.

Web Sites

http://ecrp.uiuc.edu Listservs can bring you into conversation with early childhood education teachers who want to communicate their ideas and questions
about Reggio Emilia or Project Approach. You can access either group through
the listed Web site. Under search enter REGGIO-L or PROJECT-L for information on how to join.

www.exploratorium.edu This site contains a description of inquiry, inquiry in
kindergarten, and facilitating inquiry investigations among its choices. From
the exploratorium in San Francisco's Palace of Fine Arts.

www.inquiry.uiuc.edu The University of Illinois–Urbana has a page of topics on
the inquiry process.

Chapter 9
Communicating Results

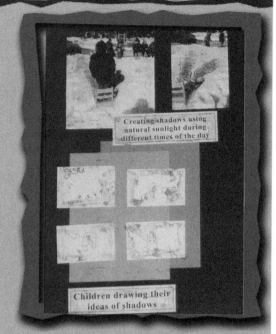

Creating shadows using natural sunlight during different times of the day

Children drawing their ideas of shadows

OBJECTIVES Through the process of discovery in this chapter, you will be able to:

1. List ways of communicating results of a study for the individual child and group.

2. Describe the purpose and process of documentation of a study.

3. Explain the organization of portfolios.

4. Discuss outcomes of communicating results for children, teachers, parents, and visitors.

5. Describe what can be included in documentation.

6. Determine effective methods to develop documentation.

7. Discuss the process of finalizing a study.

IDEAS TO PONDER

- What do nonliterate children gain from documentation?

- What can teachers do to develop documentation during a process of study?

- What can children do to help develop the documentation?

- How do teachers determine when a process of study is complete?

- How can a group end a study?

One can see the path from whence one came with a good map.
(Author)

Taking children's work seriously in this way [documentation] encourages in them the disposition to approach their work responsibly, with energy, and commitment, showing both delight and satisfaction in the processes and results. (Katz & Chard, 1996, p. 1)

DEFINING DOCUMENTATION

The process of a study can be recorded so children and staff can see from whence they came. This documentation can serve to communicate this process to others. The documentation can take the form of a book of photos and dictation, a single poster telling the children's story, or several panels displaying graphic representations and print. Whatever form it takes, all participants in the early childhood program can come to know the children's experiences through documentation. This process accomplishes the goal of making visible the ways children learn (Fu, Stremmel, & Hill, 2002).

Documentation can be any of the following:

- drawing
- sculpting
- writing
- journals of child or adult
- graphing
- individual and group dictation
- questions
- webs
- lists
- plans
- observations
- anecdotes
- photographs
- videos
- audio recordings
- group projects

Documentation can be the map that marks the way a group proceeds in a study and notes the significant changes and turns as the group moves along. Even though at the beginning the final steps are not clearly determined, as the group discusses and plans, the path leading to the final destination becomes clear.

Although this chapter on communicating results comes at the end of the steps of the inquiry process, the recording in the classroom occurs from the very first discussion. As children and teachers question and problem solve along the way, the group can use the recorded steps for further clarification and memory of what has occurred. This can provide direction for future steps.

PORTFOLIOS

A portfolio is a collection of the individual child's work that shows his growth through the year (see Chapter 4). What goes in the file is both the individual work, comprising such items as art, dictation, and writing, and the work done as part of a group, as in the preceding list. In addition, observations, anecdotes, and assessment profiles are recorded here (see "Additional Resources" in Chapter 4 for assessment systems).

The following is an example of math accomplishment recorded for the child's portfolio:

ANECDOTE

Anthony agrees to play this math game. I make a circle on paper and count nine buttons placed around the circle. I asked Anthony to do the same. He slowly drew a circle and then carefully placed counters, one by one, counting them.

T.   Are they the same?

A.   Yes.

T.   How do you know?

A.   Because I saw how you did the circle and how you counted. (B. Johnson, personal communication, May 15, 2003)

OUTCOMES OF DOCUMENTATION

Communication about findings is one of the standards emphasized in the Content Standards for Science as Inquiry in the National Science Education Standards.

STANDARDS

Communicate investigations and explanations.

Content Standard: K–4a.
Reprinted with permission from *National science education standards*. (1996). The National Academy of Sciences, courtesy of the National Academies Press, Washington, DC (p. 105).

STANDARDS

Scientists make the results of their investigations public, they describe the investigations in ways that enable others to repeat the investigations.

Content Standard: K–4a.
Reprinted with permission from *National science education standards*. (1996). The National Academy of Sciences, courtesy of the National Academies Press, Washington, DC (p. 105).

While in preschool and kindergarten, children can begin to document in collaboration with peers and teachers, and as their skills increase they can accomplish more in communicating their results.

Assets for Children

Of what gain is documentation for the young child who is a nonreader? The young child is in the process of understanding symbols that are meaningful. Of course, some children will be making sense of the different kinds of representations while others only understand that what is being recorded are the words or work of the individual or group. Wherever they are on this continuum, they see the worth of what is placed in the document. They understand that language in print is "talk written down" while other types of documentation (such as drawings from the group or perhaps their very own art work) holds the same merit as it is shown alongside the printed word.

Because children share the creation of the recorded work, they know the meaning of the message and they are invested in it. As they revisit the documentation at a later date, they can revisit the study through memory.

As the children and their teacher review a document from an ongoing study or one done earlier in the year, the steps of the process can be viewed as the map record. The process of preparing and reviewing the work provides opportunities for new understandings that can be clarified, deepened, and strengthened (Katz & Chard, 1996). Children will see the progression from start to the present point, or finished if completed in the past. As they revisit, the clear thoughts, questions, realistic representations, actions, and direction of their work are given validity. Yes, we really experienced it! We did this!

ANECDOTE

After a study of worms, a group of preschool children dictated their understandings to teachers:

WORMS

Worms live in dirt.
I know 'cause I saw them.
They have no feet.
They have a tail.
They have big tails.
I don't think they have a head.
Their names are Savanna and Wormy.
Do they walk?
No, they slither.

By Irene Orozco and Cynthia Stevens

Mercedes points to the contribution she made to the class bulletin board.

In addition, as others show interest in the documentation, the children see that their work is taken seriously. From parents to strangers, others who want to look at the record seem to say, "I am interested in what you think, do and record."

Because individual work and communication become a part of the documentation, the individual realizes her part in this process. As Mercedes finds the quote that she contributed on the bulletin board, she sees herself as a contributing member of her kindergarten group, and one that has worth.

The child's portfolio is also available for the child to peruse. The child can view her portfolio items to remind her of a particular work, or compare changes that are evident from her work collected over time. Her teacher may read some of the anecdotes or observations to share her development.

Assets for Teachers

Teachers benefit from recordings of discussions in class. As a study is in process, they will look back on these recordings to assess the focus of the group, to question the way the group is proceeding, and to give direction to the next step in the process. By reviewing the teachers may pick up a thread that appears to be pertinent to the children. This thread could become a significant step in the study.

Teachers also confer with each other on their process of co-construction with the child or the group. Has the focus paralleled the intent of the children? Was the direction given by teachers sensitive to what the children were thinking? Could teachers have gone further? Deeper? Selected a similar choice? Did teachers miss a strand that was left hanging? Are there questions that have not been addressed? Is there an idea for a future study? When teachers reflect together following the current documentation, they can learn more about their processes as teachers in the venture.

Assets for Parents

Parents also learn about the learning taking place of which their child is a part. Sallee Beneke believes, "Documentation helps parents begin to see the learning that is taking place as children engage in the activities. . . . They begin to see the products of the child's learning, such as drawings and constructions, as signs of emerging understanding" (Beneke, 1998, p. 69).

As parents and their children review documentation together, this shared time can highlight the children's school experience. Children and parents can learn from each other about these events with the documents in front of them. Children need these kinds of reminders to talk about their activities, and parents will see the learning as it is documented.

Demonstration of School Purpose

Documentation that displays past events may tie the past with the present activities that visitors see in the classroom. As visitors can use both the present scene of children in a study and the recorded history, they can build a base of knowledge about the process of learning in the classroom. With this documentation visitors can better understand the educational philosophy of the school.

TYPES OF DOCUMENTATION

In a group, documentation is the process of telling the story of the children working on a project. The kind of documentation that develops from this depends on the topic of the inquiry, the form of the study that evolves from the collaboration of children and teachers, the preferences of teachers, and the ideas and capabilities of children.

The purpose of the documentation will also determine the format and the way it is addressed. Documentation displayed in the classroom in a current study will be displayed at a level where children can easily view it, and the children's involvement is shown through the direct comments and activities. A display of the work over time provides a history through narrative and pictorial records for parents and the school community. A display inviting adults to explore the school's philosophy may include slide shows, videos, and actual projects of the children.

Figure 9–1 Web showing types of documentation.

[Reprinted by permission of the publisher from Helm, J., et al., *Windows on Learning* (New York: Teachers College Press, © 1998 by Teachers College, Columbia University. All rights reserved.), p. 36]

The documentation web (Fig. 9–1) provides a view of a wide array of methods to make these recordings. This figure was first developed by Helm and Beneke for educators in the Valeska Hinton Early Childhood Education Center. As the teachers worked at documentation in their classrooms, this web was expanded to what is represented here. This web displays the many directions in which recording can go, but documentation is not limited to what is shown here (Helm, Beneke, & Steinheimer, 1998).

Some of the items on this web are discussed here.

Recorded Conversations From the first interests to problem solving, discussions on the topic are recorded in some way. In addition to the recording for documentation, teachers are interested in reviewing the discussions as they progress through the study.

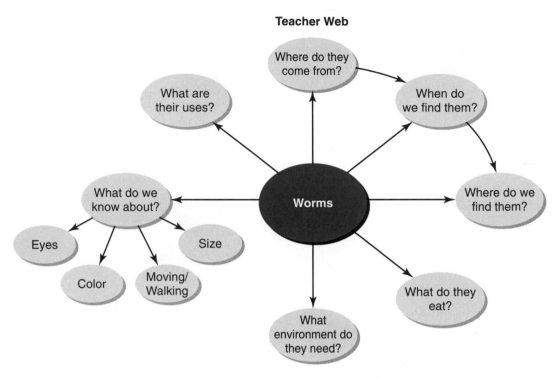

Figure 9–2 A teacher web is used to initiate planning for the study of worms. By Irene Orozco, Cynthia Stevens, and Norbella Valadez. (Kidspiration™ Inspiration Software, Inc.)

The web is a diagram depicting ideas or information on a particular topic and showing connections and relationships of concepts.

Webbing Teachers create **webs** as they consider a topic. This is helpful to determine if the topic is suitable for the group and to understand the possibilities of the topic (Fig. 9–2). After some initial discussion about a new topic, children may be asked to web the topic. The result of webbing together can set the direction for this topic (Helm & Katz, 2001; Workman & Anziano, 1993).

At any time in a study, webbing by children or by teachers may further define the direction the study will take. In the discussion this web can bring the group to a more definitive idea of the group's focus and therefore set the direction of the study.

Lists Lists are another way a group can focus on an aspect of a study. For example, lists made at the beginning may be, "What we know about vegetables" or "What we would like to know about vegetables." Lists can develop along specific lines as the topic develops. Some other list topics are, "What different things we noticed on our tree," "What we found on our walk under the trees," and "Plans for a parent event." Lists can be made and later added onto as children uncover more ideas (Fig. 9–3).

Project Narratives Children can tell a part of the story through recorded narratives. Individuals or groups can tell what they want to know, what they try, or what they discover.

What the children know about worms:	What the children want to learn:
Carlos—They go underground and they come out.	Aaliyah—Ant.
Michael—Ants.	Carlos—Ants and worms.
Kearra—Worm.	Kearra—Worms.
Taylor—Worms help plants.	Taylor—How they live underground and how they help the plants.
Kiana—Worms are happy in the ground.	Kiana—How they live underground.
Harold—Worms dig in the ground.	Harold—Why they dig in the ground?
Nathan—A bug.	Nathan—Why do they sleep in the ground?
Veronika—Bug.	Isaly—Why worms eat dirt.
Isaly—Worms eat dirt.	Diego—Why worms are no sister.
	Samantha—Uh, uh, they go inside the dirt.
	Julian—Why worms eat dirt.

Figure 9–3 The lists show what children know and want to know. By Thamara Estrada and June Brown.

ANECDOTE

Chloe is pouring water through a transparent curved tube in the water table. "I pour it in here and it comes out here. See? And if I don't want it to come out I put the bottom of it up—and it stops!"

Chloe intently watches what happens to the water in the tube.

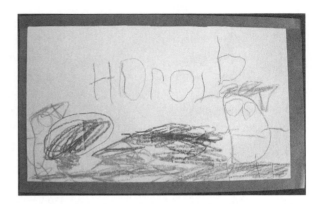

Harold

    We were going on the walk to find the worm.
Ms. June turned over the rock to look for worms and
then Ms. Thamara turned over the other rock and
picked up a worm.

Harold tells his story through drawing and dictation.

Teachers can use their journal writing to record events in the development of a topic of inquiry. They may use a narrative style to tell the story of inquiry in the documentation.

Individual and Group Dictation Children's ideas in story form or their recording of events add to the understanding from their point of view. **Dictation** can be

Dictation is the process of recording a child's thoughts or story so it can be saved for others to read.

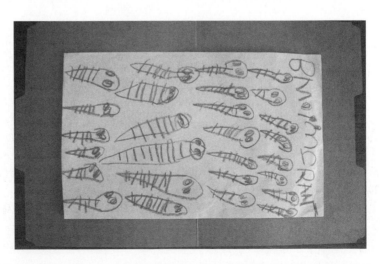

Maria shows her understanding at this time that worms have eyes.

The children represent what they know in clay.

gathered at any point during the study. For these the child or adult can request that the adult take dictation handwritten or keyed directly into the computer.

Drawings, Sculpture, and Other Representations The representations can be presented in the current form or photos can be made of the work. These representations are often selected to show the children's ideas as they emerge in the long-term study, not just the end product that documents its completion.

Photos and Videos Large photos and close-up videos can show the children at work in the various steps of the process. With digital capability, enlarged clear

Photos and drawings record this study of shadows.

reproductions that focus on the process add a wonderful dimension to the record. Videos can be shared with a group and become part of a demonstration display.

Group Projects Along the way children may build representations of what they are studying or completing a **group project** that represents the culmination of the work. At the end of the project this can be displayed along with the documentation.

> *A group project is a representation of the object of study.*

HOW TO DEVELOP DOCUMENTATION

During their first documentations, beginning teachers may be reluctant to tackle the work of recording the events in the classroom that relate to a topic of study. Recording does require an investment of time. When teachers see how the documentation guides them through a study as well as it easily portrays its completion, it does not seem so burdensome.

As mentioned before, the classroom discussions are recorded because teachers refer to them for understanding and direction. These can be audiotaped and transcribed, or the teacher can record for the group as the discussion takes place, or another adult can record conversations.

Yet not all has to be written down. As shown previously, there are many ways of documenting. Some preplanning will help teachers focus on particular types of documentation at certain places and times. A particular event does not need to be documented in several ways. So it will save time and effort when the teachers can decide ahead of time that a walk will be videotaped, or the children's drawings of plant growth will become the record of what they observe.

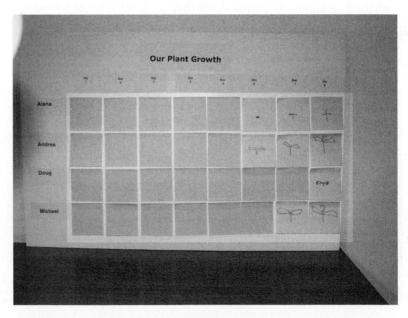

Children record what they observe in growth of their plants.

If the record is to be written by teachers, teachers can transcribe the dialogue directly into the computer as soon as possible. Teachers often print this out in a draft form to review and discuss among themselves or to revisit ideas with children. Later, when preparing the print for documentation, the print is carefully and correctly printed in **manuscript** form or computer-generated print. The print portrayed in any display will serve as a model for children as they practice beginning writing (Seefeldt, 2002).

Manuscript is the accepted form of print in letter size and formation for early childhood classrooms.

As selections are made of children's work, there are many reasons to choose among all their items. One may represent an earlier grasp of the topic, another a more advanced one. While the content and representation may guide the selection at the particular time, be sure the work of each child is portrayed. Each child is shown as having a part in the class's work, and no single child's work is exhibited more than others overall. In some cases a small group of children may help with the selection of the work.

Involve the children in planning and organizing the documentation. The more children are involved, the more they own this step of the work as well as understand documentation as a process. Sallee Beneke explains her rationale for preparing charts for documentation by involving the children.

> Children benefit from opportunities to see adults model the organization and production of charts and graphs designed to record the results of investigation. Children also need the opportunity to participate in the production of such charts and graphs so that they can understand their usefulness and eventually learn to produce them independently. (Beneke, 1998, p. 33)

Present the documentation clearly and completely, as a story that unfolds in the classroom. The details presented in story, narration, photos, and projects document the depth of children's learning.

Finally, the documentation should have a professional look. With a clear message, a title, the words in computer print, and presented in a neat and balanced design, this documentation will carry the message that what the children have accomplished is worthy. The record of children's work deserves the attention of an artfully designed communication.

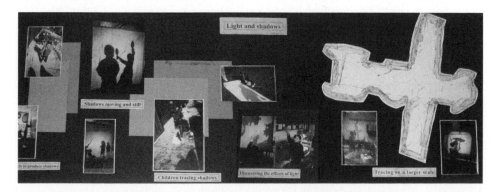

Documentation on shadows displays many stages of children's work.

In the classroom, especially, documentation will show the current or recent story of learning displayed in spaces where the children can easily view it. Since schools value these records of children's learning, each class will save these through the year. At the close of a year these will be placed in safekeeping as each documentation becomes a part of the ongoing history of the school. Teachers will want to review them in order to review the growth of the children and their own professional growth.

FINALIZING A STUDY

Finalizing a study is the culmination of a long-term project.

At some point the group will be **finalizing a study.** The children (and perhaps the adults, too) are not so enthused anymore; interest is waning. There is little investment in working with the concepts, and new processes do not emerge. So children and teachers come together to decide how to end the work on this topic. What would be a meaningful way to close it?

The following is a journal entry of a student teacher:

One logical outcome of the study is to plan a way to communicate the results. The planning of the documentation can become the focus of the ending point. The work of showing others what was accomplished can be in the document for the walls, or a book to share with parents, or the display of a joint project by the group.

Another way to end a study is to invite another group to celebrate the completion of the project. The class may choose to invite parents or other members of the school who relate to the project. One class of three-year-olds and four-year-olds completed "Our Mail Project" by inviting the students in a neighboring classroom who happened to be their Pen Pals in the project. (Helm, Beneke, & Steinheimer, 1998).

ANECDOTE

Since January, our children in the kindergarten room had been immersed in space travel. The group built a space station which continued to draw all the boys in ongoing dramatic play, but recently there were no new ideas. I think all of us [teachers] were ready to move on, but we saw that the children were reluctant to leave their prized space station. We noticed how involved they were in dramatizing radio transmissions in the space ship. In order to capture this interest in communicating, we decided to continue on to communication systems. At group time we broke the news and suggested the new topic. First they were disappointed, but they began to discuss what they knew about modern communication in two-way radio and satellite stations. Ms. C. started searching on the Internet for a classroom that would be interested in sharing a common interest. Luckily she found a first-grade classroom in Orlando, Florida. The children took more photos of their space station, and e-mails were exchanged with the Orlando class including sending photos on space back and forth. And our new topic has begun! (T. Johnson, personal communication, March 3, 2001)

The ending of a study only needs to be a fitting finale mutually agreed upon. It can be a mini-review or a big event. The children can join with the teachers in deciding and completing plans for this event.

SUMMARY

Communicating results is an integral part of inquiry, and young children can be involved in communicating the thoughts, work, and conclusions that the group shares. As the other parts of the inquiry process are circular, so is the communication throughout the study. In the end the document created becomes a part of classroom history to be shared with the school community.

The next chapter will explore thoroughly the number sense of math so you can see this process as children gain logicomathematical knowledge for themselves and incorporate that knowledge in the inquiry process.

TO FURTHER YOUR THINKING

1. Select a few anecdotes of individuals or groups from Chapters 2, 5, 6, 7, and 8 and decide if they could be entered as an area of either science or math domain in a portfolio for an individual child.
2. Select a book highlighting projects from the References and Additional Resources at the end of the chapter. In this book find webs and lists made with children during the start of the project. What kinds of information are in these lists and webs? How can they help direct the involvement in inquiry?
3. Using the same book as in question 2, discuss the process of documenting what children inquire and what they find out. How is this shown in a document?
4. Refer to the "To Further Your Thinking" sections in Chapters 5 through 8 to find activities that you did that included one or more steps of the inquiry process. With fellow students generate ideas for documentation of each of those.
5. What are the difficulties in recording discussions with children? List three or more ways to record ongoing discussions. Then brainstorm ideas to make the recording easier to accomplish.

REFERENCES

Beneke, S. (1998). *Rearview Mirror: Reflections on a preschool car project.* Urbana, IL: ERIC.

Fu, V. R., Stremmel, A. J., and Hill, L. T. (2002). *Teaching and learning: Collaborative exploration of the Reggio Emilia approach.* Upper Saddle River, NJ: Pearson Education.

Helm, J. H., Beneke, S., and Steinheimer, K. (1998). *Windows on learning: Documenting young children's work.* New York: Teachers College Press.

Helm, J. H., and Katz, L. (2001). *Young investigators: The project approach in the early years.* New York: Teachers College Press.

Katz, L., and Chard, S. C. (1996, April). *The contribution of documentation to the quality of early childhood education.* Champaign, IL: Eric Digest. #Edo-PS-96-2.

National Academy of Science. (1996). *National science education standards* [book version, on line]. Washington, DC: National Academies Press. www.nap.edu

Workman, S., and Anziano, M. C. (1993, January). Curriculum webs: Weaving connections from children to teachers. *Young Children 48*(2), 4–9.

Seefeldt, C. (2002). *Creating rooms of wonder: Valuing and displaying children's work to enhance the learning process.* Beltsville, MD: Gryphon House.

ADDITIONAL RESOURCES

Fraser, S., and Gestwicki, C. (2002). *Authentic childhood: Exploring Reggio Emilia in the classroom.* Clifton Park, NY: Thomson Delmar Learning. A section describing documentation, its pluses and pitfalls follow this chapter.

Meisels, S. J., Harrington, H. L., McMahon, P., Dichtelmiller, M. L., and Jablon, J. R. (2002). *Thinking like a teacher: Using observational assessment to improve teaching and learning.* Boston: Allyn and Bacon. Prepares the teacher for the Work Sampling System.

Videos

Connecting content, teaching and learning (Rev. Ed.) [Video]. Washington, DC: Teaching Strategies, Inc. Introduces the Creative Curriculum Developmental Continuum with content areas for preschool.

Observation of young children II: Making the connection [Video]. Crystal Lake, IL: Magna Systems, Inc. Teachers and education coordinators demonstrate kinds of data collected for portfolio systems and use of computers to collate the data. www.magnasystems.org

Windows on learning: A framework for making decisions. [Video]. Center for the Best Practices in Early Childhood. 1996. Follows the theme of the book, *Windows on learning.* Available from www.naeyc.org and www.tcpress.com

Web Sites

www.ecap.crc.uiuc.edu This Web site has resources in early childhood education, including Reggio Emilia education and the Project Approach.

www.ericfacility.net Educational Resources Information Center (ERIC) has a database of educational articles.

www.cdacouncil.org The Council for Professional Recognition has an on-line bookstore (paid publications) with resources and videos on Reggio Emilia documentation.

Chapter 10

Number Sense in Math

Photo courtesy Patrick Clark

OBJECTIVES Through the process of discovery in this chapter, you will be able to:

1. Explain the understanding of number involved in counting.
2. Based on examples, identify the number sense children use, including ordinal and cardinal numbers.
3. Compare social knowledge and logicomathematical knowledge in understanding number sense.
4. Identify five principles of counting for children.
5. Based on informal research, determine skills children use when asked to make a set of objects following a model.
6. Describe decomposing of small numbers and its mathematical purpose for number operations.
7. Use assessment of math skills to determine appropriate activities in counting.
8. Describe the processes of teaching social knowledge in number sense.
9. Support logicomathematical learning in counting.
10. Use counting books for both social knowledge and logicomathematical knowledge with young children.
11. Explain the relationship of number sense to inquiry.

IDEAS TO PONDER

- What does the child need to understand before he is able to count objects? Understand the amount?
- How does the child learn the social knowledge in number sense?
- How can assessment be used to determine levels of math activities?
- What is the teacher's role in children learning number sense?
- What kinds of books and activities can teachers use for developing the number sense?

Ms. T. counts the children lined up to go outside. She places her hand on Samantha's shoulder saying, "Three."
"I'm not three. I'm four."
Ms. T. laughs as if it is a joke, but Samantha is serious.
(Author)

"I know my numbers. I can count to twenty," says Jake. He counts very rapidly, but correctly to twenty.
(Author)

"You are number one. You are number two. You are number three," Juan announces at the beginning of a bowling game he is organizing in the Head Start classroom.
(Author)

Marianna counts out the tortillas she has made with play dough. "One, two, three, four-r-r-r, five, eight." She points to the pieces randomly as she counts but the rhythm of the counting does not match the movement of her finger. "One, two, three, four, five—, six," she repeats, changing it slightly. She rearranges the tiny tortillas neatly in a line and quickly counts again, "One, two, three, four, five, six, seven," confidently this time.
(Author)

"We need three purses and three babies or we can't go shopping together," Sue Lin announces as she puts a long skirt over her shorts. Cherise and Tanya nod their heads. Sue Lin digs out three huge purses and three small dolls from the mess of clothes on the floor of the house-keeping area. She hands one each to the other girls and they walk around together swinging their purses and holding their babies.
(Author)

Ong, in kindergarten, arranges Unifix cubes in three rows of six each. He separates the cubes in each row to show the combinations of 5 + 1, 4 + 2, and 3 + 3. "See, there are these ways to make six."
(Author)

USES OF NUMBER

When children work with number they are actually confused by its different uses. Each of these vignettes shows a different use of number:

- Samantha shows that her understanding of number is part of her, telling how old she is. This social knowledge comes from others, not from the child's own experience. Her family told Samantha she was four at her last birthday; she cannot relate this to the fact that she has lived for four years, or even remember four birthday parties.
- Jake certainly knows **rote counting.** This skill is also learned from others. He knows the names of numbers in correct sequence, similar to singing the alphabet song or naming all his robot people.

Rote counting is saying the numbers in order with no reference to counting objects.

Ordinal number is the label of the position of an object in a series.

Concept of number is understanding the total amount of items in a set by applying one or more processes.

Decompose is to take apart a number and arrange it in one or more subsets.

- Juan is using number to determine the position or order. He is working out this concept of **ordinal number.**
- Marianna counts by using the number names to count, but she is inconsistent in matching the number name with each object and using the correct name for the number in the series, so the last number in the series is different each time.
- Sue Lin understands that the set of three children need three items. **Concept of number** is a known entity she actively uses in making decisions and communicating to her peers in play.
- Ong experiments with the concept that six items can be **decomposed** into a variety of arrangements that still total six. This will build on his concept of number.

SOCIAL KNOWLEDGE IN COUNTING

Social knowledge is using a particular name for a marker, such as the English terms *one, two,* and *three.* Along with the number names the child learns these names in order. As Marianna counts tortillas, she shows she is practicing using number names in specific order. These two aspects of social knowledge in counting are both practiced by the child and learned from the modeling of peers and adults.

Rote counting is where children learn the order of counting without relating to objects, usually done very fast. Rote counting is an exhibition of the social knowledge of counting.

PRINCIPLES OF COUNTING

Five principles of counting must be adhered to for success in counting:

1. The **one-to-one rule.** In counting only one counting word is used for each object.
2. The **stable order rule.** Counting words (1, 2, 3, . . .) must be used consistently and in the same order.
3. The **cardinal principle.** The final number counted equals the total number in the set.
4. The **abstraction rule.** Dissimilar objects can be counted in a set (i.e., knives, forks, and spoons can all be included).
5. The **order irrelevant principle.** This is the rule that a group of objects can be counted in any order as long as each item is counted only once (Bjorklund, 1995, p. 350; Gelman & Gallistel, 1978).

LOGICOMATHEMATICAL KNOWLEDGE IN COUNTING

Most of these principles of counting are developed through logicomathematical thinking. The processes are understood through the child developing her own constructs, as described next.

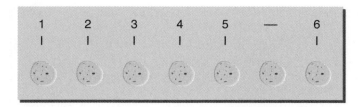

Figure 10–1 Matching one-to-one is sometimes missed.

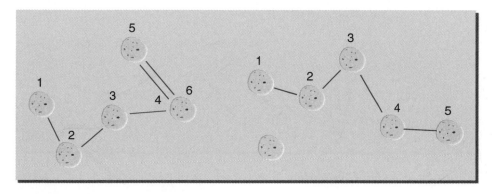

Figure 10–2 A counter may be counted twice or skipped.

One-to-One Principle

One-to-one correspondence is applied to counting objects as the child matches the number name to the object being counted. In counting a group of six to seven counters, the child does not at first always match one number name to one object, as seen when Marianna first counted six tortillas (Fig. 10–1). Or the child may move randomly from counter to counter so some may be counted more than once—or even skipped (Fig. 10–2).

Stable Order Rule

First the child learns the social knowledge of the order of the number names (often in stages of 1 to 6, 1 to 10, and then 1 to 20). The child gradually learns through the many trials and errors in counting that the order of the number names is to be used consistently in stable order.

Cardinal Number

The relationship of counting and quantity is based on the concept that the total is equal to the last number name given (Fig. 10–3). Two is in the relationship of being together. Separate they are not two. But they will always be

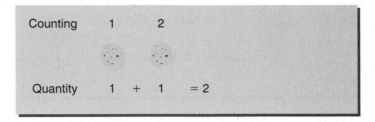

Figure 10–3 The cardinal principle is that the total is equal to the last number counted.

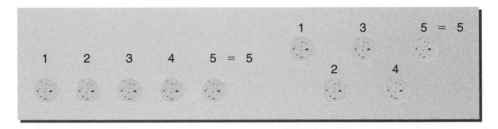

Figure 10–4 A set of five objects in any order are in relationship.

two when only they are put into relationship (Kamii, 1982). This is true with any set of numbers in any order (Fig. 10–4).

To understand the cardinality of number, the child must realize that the last number counted represents the whole group counted. It would be fairly easy to teach this, but in knowing this "math fact" alone the child does not realize the concept of "five-ness" that is inherent in the group of objects.

Order Irrelevant Principle

At first the child may believe that she is applying a name to an object, that for the present that number name belongs to that object, like the age of four "belongs" to Samantha for the year. Next the child will grasp that in using the number name she is putting the object in relationship to other objects so the number is not inherent within the object itself. As she counts objects several times and moves them around in the process, the number name given to each counter may change each time. This is irrelevant order.

Abstraction Rule

The child will gradually understand that a group of dissimilar objects can be counted as a group, such as beads of different colors and shapes. Groups of items that are more dissimilar can also be counted as one group, such as all the items of clothing that are hung up after play in the housekeeping area. Here the child understands the abstraction rule.

DEVELOPING NUMBER SENSE

Most children in the preschool years are already exposed to number. Since the age of two, children have been using numbers in conversation and play. On the surface it appears that for many preschoolers understanding of number is already in place. In reality the full development of number sense depends on knowing the meaning of number. But that is an advanced skill, as you will see from the research discussed in the following section.

Number sense is the understanding of how numbers work.

What Counts in Counting

If the child has developed a concept of number and can count correctly, the child has another way of comparing numbers in sets. Yet the concept of number will be securely based before the child will use number to determine the amount in a set. Research by Meljac (as cited in Kamii, 1982) shows different levels used to answer the question of making equal sets (Table 10–1).

The concept of number is knowing the total amount in a set.

TABLE 10–1 Relationship Between Age and Level on Quantification Task Reported by Meljac (1979). (Cited in Kamii, 1982)

Age Group	Number of Children	LEVEL			
		0	I	II	III
4.0 to 4.6	20	3	13	4	
5.0 to 5.6	22	4	8	4	6 (27%)
6.0 to 6.6	32	2	5	10	15 (47%)
7 years	11			5	6 (55%)
Total	85	9	26	23	27

Reprinted by permission of the author, C. Kamii, from *Number in Preschool & Kindergarten,* ©1982 National Association for the Education of Young Children (p. 34).

In the research shown in Table 10–1, nine chips are arranged in a circle and children are asked to put out the same number as the researcher. The four levels reported in Table10–1 are

Level 0: Inability even to understand the adult's request

Level I: Rough, visual estimation or copy of the spatial configuration

Level II: Methodical one-to-one correspondence

Level III: Counting

Reprinted with permission of the author, C. Kamii, from *Number in Preschool and Kindergarten,* © 1982 National Association for the Education of Young Children (p. 35).

It is not until age six or seven when even half of the children in the study used counting as a reliable tool. Meljac further found out that children under six did not reliably count out nine objects when asked to do so. It seems these children know they could not use counting reliably and so depended on other means (Kamii, 1982).

The names and number order do need to be taught, as these are social knowledge. The signs for numbers (e.g., 1, 5, and 11) and saying them in the correct order (one, two, three . . .) are simple skills for the child to learn when he is ready.

> Studies [are] suggesting that pushing baby to learn words, numbers, colors, and shapes too early forces the child to use lower-level thinking processes, rather than develop learning ability. It's like a pony trick at the circus: When the pony paws the ground to "count" to three, it's not counting: it's simply performing a stunt. Such "tricks" are not only not helpful to baby's learning process, they are potentially harmful. Putting pressure on a child to learn information sends the message that he needs to "perform" to gain acceptance, and it can dampen natural curiosity. (Lipari, 2000)

According to Constance Kamii, "It is good for children to learn to count and to read and write numerals, but a more important objective is for the child to construct the mental structure of number. If a child has constructed this structure, he will be able to assimilate signs into it with the greatest of ease" (Kamii, 1982, p. 25). Using all the tools in early math, including the five principles of counting, can lead children to higher-order thinking in math and inquiry. Our emphasis needs to remain on that, not on counting and learning numbers.

In looking at the following two anecdotes, consider the message of what is important in learning.

ANECDOTE

COUNTING VERSUS BASIC MATHEMATICAL CONCEPTS

On one of my visits to preschool classrooms in the inner city I observed children in one three-year-old classroom counting as they worked with manipulatives. Whatever materials children were using, the teacher asked them to count the objects, "1, 2, 3, 4, 5." They were correct. Whether the children would do this on cue or on their own, they always received much praise from the teacher nearby. I sensed that the teachers formed the social construct of what was important in this classroom. (They thought it was important!) And the children responded. Nothing else was included in conversations with children.

On another visit to an inner-city classroom, where I was working closely with the teachers, there was not much to do outside on a summer's day. There was only sparse grass—and dandelions. We picked those dandelions, ordered them according to the length of their stems, picked off the flower petals to find the beginnings of seeds, and blew the seeds with their individual "kites" to see them fly away. Children brought a large collection of what they found inside, where they grouped dandelions according to bud, flower, or seed. With a teacher's help, they put in order the beginning bud to empty stalk. They had no resources to look up dandelions, but a creative teacher drew the steps from bud to seed on pieces of typing paper. Teachers then mounted these drawings on construction paper. Of course the dandelions wilted that day, but the children used the seriation game made from the teacher's drawings over and over.

(Author)

Advancing Number Concepts

In Ong's experience of arranging Unifix cubes in different arrangements of six, he decomposes one number into parts that make up the whole. Called **part-part-whole,** this ability involves exploring a number as a series of subsets that equal the whole. Using manipulatives, Ong will see that each number from 4 through 12 can be divided into subsets (Smith, 2001, pp. 122–23). These part-part-whole arrangements serve as a precursor to number operations.

Part-part-whole is the ability to decompose a number or an object into subsets and recompose it into a whole.

STANDARDS

Develop a sense of whole numbers and represent and use them in flexible ways, including relating, composing, and decomposing numbers.

Chapter 4: Number and Operations Standard for Grades Pre-K–2, (Reprinted with permission from *Principles and Standards for School Mathematics,* copyright 2000 by the National Council of Teachers of Mathematics, 2000, p. 78). All rights reserved.

The six-year-old child also has a wonderful fascination with large numbers. The number system will begin to make sense as she explores larger numbers.

ANECDOTE

From the back seat of the car, Alana, at age six, gaily counted as they drove along. At the number nineteen, she stopped. "Twenty," said her mom. Alana went through the twenties, but stopped at 29, to wait for the next number. She continued in this way up to 80.

Additional skills are needed in counting past 19, including the transition (20 after 19). As Alana moved along to 29, 39, 49, she needed to hear each number used in the transition (Baroody & Wilkins, 1999).

One more advance in cognition will help her grasp the concept of number. When she knows that the amount or number will not change when things are moved around, she will know the consistency of amount, or conservation. This is not fully developed until the child is seven, and seven is the age to introduce mathematical processes of adding, subtracting, multiplying, and dividing. Until then the young child will continue to have a different concept of number than adults.

ASSESSMENT OF COUNTING SKILLS

Using assessment provides a guide (Chapter 4) for selection of math activities for a child or the group. Through observing a child count and recount objects, one can assess for all five principles of counting. Assess the first two principles by observing for one-to-one in counting and stable order, and then assess for all principles. With assessment teachers plan for the child to handle activities that challenge her as well as utilize concepts she knows. When a teachers is clear about what a child knows and recognizes the next stage in math, "teaching and assessing become one and the same" (Richardson & Salkeld, 1995, p. 29).

Math activities are offered to individuals and small groups, and different math questions and problems are posed to challenge a group. In these situations the responses of some will stretch the thinking of others.

ANECDOTE

In a small group activity Ms. S. turns the game to Marianna by asking her to give her four teddy bear counters. Marianna selects four without actually counting, placing them in a group in front of Ms. S. When asked for five, and then six counters, Marianna gives Ms. S. more than the amount requested.

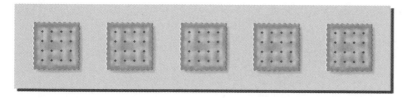

Figure 10–5 Ms. S. makes a set of five crackers.

To help Marianna grasp the concept of numbers greater than four, Ms. S. asks Marianna to help set up snack. Ms. S. makes sets on **index cards** for Marianna to model (Fig. 10–5). Ms. S. can indicate sets of five or more items for snack. In setting out snack, Marianna can use whatever skills she needs to make the set.

Marianna knew the concept of four more from the sight of the set than from counting. As she attempts to make a set of five crackers, she can accomplish this using more than one math skill. It is most important for her to figure out this process herself. Over time she will gain the concept of cardinality.

Supporting Logicomathematical Concepts

Most principles of counting are developed by the young child through logicomathematical thinking. The child understands through developing his own constructs of math. This is why the wise teacher allows the child to work at these skills while allowing mistakes (see the discussion of scaffolding math in Chapter 3, page 44). Cardinality is inherent in relationships of these materials, so the child can self-correct and gradually "owns" these principles. Correctness is not as important as his motivation to use number in meaningful ways. If the adult corrects, it becomes social knowledge—the fact comes from another person, not what the child sees in the logicomathematical relationship. In other words, the child needs to see how a particular construct he develops does not fit so he can discard that one and try another.

The social knowledge of number names and order of numbers can be learned through counting in groups and from listening to others count. Modeling serves as a better teaching tool than correcting. Group activities of counting and making decisions about number are part of day-to-day classroom activities.

MODELING NUMBER NAME AND ORDER

Number can be integral in large group experiences. Use counting books and fingerplays in group time. Count items together. Count children in a small group. Count items that children in a small group need. "Let's see if you each have a glue bottle for your collage. Let's see how many children at the table. How many glue bottles are here?" "For each pot we need four marigold seeds. Let's count them" (Fig. 10–6).

Figure 10–6 Counting marigold seeds.

COUNTING THROUGH THE DAY

It is effective to use counting in meaningful ways in the classroom day. As the group gains more abilities in number sense, the difficulty can be increased by the amount of items counted. Because the abilities vary, include tasks that are a challenge for those beginning as well as the more advanced. When math problems are tackled by a group of children, the ones who are more advanced in this thinking will lead others in peer learning.

When a classroom project involves counting, children can use tallying. The child decides on a symbol that stands for the real thing, such as a truck, a car, and a bicycle seen on a walk. The mark or picture symbol will represent the set of items they are looking for. Each child can tally one choice or one can keep the tally for the whole group. Small clipboards can be used with a primer pencil tied to the clipboard (Fig. 10–7).

Counting Games, Books and Activities

A simple game can help with number names and order as well as one-to-one correspondence.

Figure 10–7 Tallying on a clipboard.

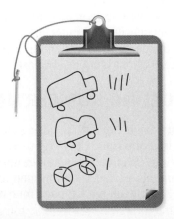

```
                        ANECDOTE
```

COUNTING WITH DUCK, DUCK, GOOSE

A version of Duck, Duck, Goose can be played with a small group. One child walks behind the circle of children, touching each child's shoulder in turn, saying the name of each child. At the completion of the circle he again touches the shoulder of the child counted first. At this signal, this second child moves quickly to take that child's place and continues around the circle. One goal of this game is to match the rhythm of the child's walking step. The rest of the group can clap that rhythm along with the child naming. After this process is accomplished in the game, change the process to counting words. In this version all the children can join in the counting.

Counting books that delight young readers can assist several levels of learning numbers from first learning the number names to actually counting objects up to 20. With books read to the group, number name and order are modeled. Books are chosen that employ the total number that challenges the group in counting (Dickinson, 2003).

Individual children can enjoy counting on their own with such books as *Anno's Counting Book* (Anno, 1992). This wordless book provides many small pictures to develop counting skills by highlighting the months of the year. Some activities that closely follow this book are:

1. Along with the book, use manipulatives for counting. Arrange materials in baskets or bowls with small flannel boards or placemats as a space for counting. For early counters keep the numbers under six. For older children supply 10 to 20 counters.
2. Using a clipboard, ask the children to draw the symbol of the item they choose to count and then tally the items.
3. In a kindergarten classroom, ask children to take inventory of manipulatives. Records of inventory are kept to track the totals (and children's developing skills) through the year.
4. For older preschoolers or kindergarteners ask the group to develop its own counting books in the same style as *Anno's Counting Book*. A child takes on the project of designing a page through her own drawings or through computer-generated pictures and stamps.

NUMBER SENSE AND INQUIRY

In addition to classifying, comparing, and contrasting, number is involved in inquiry. Number sense can be found in measurement and in estimation, as one of the outcomes of graphing, and for counting in real world situations (Basile, 1999). For example, in a study of leaves the children may classify them by shape, measure them by Unifix cubes, graph the types in the classifications they choose, and compare amounts through counting the leaves. "Separating mathematics from science seems to go against this natural thinking process. . . . Especially for young children, it would be beneficial to integrate disciplines in order to enhance cognitive processes" (Basile, 1999, p. 157).

SUMMARY

Because of the explanation of learning the number sense, when you observe a child actively using counting, you will see the process from his point of view. You will be better able to scaffold children's emerging concepts of number whether this counting is used in the inquiry process or in math skills. In the next chapter you will draw useful and meaningful ways to adapt the technology to augment mathematics and science learning in the classroom. You will find more activities in basic math and number in Chapter 14.

TO FURTHER YOUR THINKING

1. From everyday experiences in math give examples of ordinal and cardinal number.

2. Describe the difference between social knowledge and logicomathematical knowledge in this chapter's opening quotes.

3. To a parent of a two-year-old who is rote counting to 12, explain what kinds of math experiences the parent can try with his child to develop an early understanding of number.

4. Observe children of different ages as they count objects. Using the five principles of counting, what do you see present as they count both correctly and incorrectly?

5. What is your memory of using the times tables? Was this first learned by rote or by understanding math concepts, including the relationships of adding, subtracting, multiplying, and dividing? If learned by rote, how did you learn the basis of these math concepts?

6. Using pennies or other counters, role-play ways that a child could accomplish each of the four levels of counting described for Table 10–1. What would you look for in the way a child would accomplish the task at each level?

7. Compare the two math anecdotes of the author's visits to two preschools (pages 152–53). What math is emphasized in each anecdote? How much is each anecdote related to real-world experiences?

8. In the task of placing a set of crackers on the plate for snack, decide three ways Marianna could use the index card with the set of five crackers (Fig. 10–5) to accomplish the task.

9. Select two or three counting books for preschool and kindergarten children (Dickinson, 2003). Try using one or more of these to teach social knowledge and one or more for a child to work on counting on his own. What other materials would support either use of these books?

REFERENCES

Anno, M. (1992). *Anno's counting book.* New York: HarperCollins.

Baroody, A., and Wilkins, J. L. M. (1999). The development of informal counting, number, and arithmetic skills and concepts. In J. V. Copley (Ed.), *Mathematics in the early years* (pp. 48–65). Reston, VA: National Council of Teachers of Mathematics.

Basile, C. G. (1999). The outdoors as a context for mathematics in the early years. In J. V. Copley (Ed.), *Mathematics in the early years* (pp. 156–61). Reston, VA: National Council of Teachers of Mathematics.

Bjorklund, D. F. (1995). *Children's thinking: Developmental function and individual differences* (2nd ed.). Pacific Grove, CA: Brooks Cole.

Dickinson, P. (2003). Choosing books you can count on. In D. Koralek (Ed.), *Spotlight on young children and math* (pp. 32–34). Washington, DC: National Association for the Education of Young Children.

Gelman, R., and Gallistel, R. (1978). *The child's understanding of number.* Cambridge, MA: Harvard University Press.

Kamii, C. (1982). *Number in preschool and kindergarten.* Washington, DC: National Association for the Education of Young Children.

Lipari, J. (2000). Bonding with baby: New thinking about newborns changes the way we look at parenting. *Chicago Tribune,* 3 Sept. 2000, Leisure section.

National Council of Teachers of Mathematics (2000). *Principles and standards for school mathematics.* Reston, VA: Author.

Richardson, K., and Salkeld, L. (1995). Transforming mathematics curriculum. In S. Bredekamp and T. Rosegrant (Eds.), *Reaching potentials: Transforming early childhood curriculum and assessment,* Volume 2 (pp. 23–42). Washington, DC: National Association for the Education of Young Children.

Smith, S. S. (2001). *Early childhood mathematics* (2nd ed). Boston, MA: Allyn & Bacon.

ADDITIONAL RESOURCES

Copley, J. V. (2000). *The young child and mathematics.* Washington, DC: National Association for the Education of Young Children. Math makes sense in early childhood classrooms. Available from www.nctm.org and www.naeyc.org

Early Childhood Mathematics: Promoting Good Beginnings. A joint position statement of NAEYC and NCTM. (2003, January). Learning paths and teaching strategies in early mathematics. *Young Children, 58*(1), 41–43. Using math content areas, this graph explains development of math skills. www.naeyc.org

Sophian, C. (1999). Children's ways of knowing: Lessons from cognitive development research. In J. V. Copley (Ed.), *Mathematics in the early years* (pp. 11–20). Reston, VA: National Council of Teachers of Mathematics. This research shows children use of number and transferability from one situation to another. Available from www.nctm.org and www.naeyc.org

Unglaub, K. W. (1997, May). What counts in learning to count? *Young Children, 52*(4), 48–50. A clear and simple explanation of children's growing abilities in counting.

Warfield, J., and Yttri, M. (1999). Cognitively guided instruction in one kindergarten classroom. In J. V. Copley (Ed.), *Mathematics in the early years* (pp. 103–111). Reston, VA: National Council of Teachers of Mathematics. For readers who want to look at problem solving with number, look at the results of this project which relies on children's thinking. Available from www.nctm.org and www.naeyc.org

Web Sites

www.mathperspectives.com Mathematical Perspectives Teacher Center presents K–3 math tools and reflections of teachers.

www.naeyc.org Early Childhood Mathematics: Promoting Good Beginnings, a joint position statement of NAEYC and NCTM. On the site, select Position Statements & Improving Program Practices.

www.discountschoolsupply.com This mail-order company has a large selection of all kinds of counters and Unifix cubes.

Chapter 11

Technology in the Classroom*

Photo courtesy Patrick Clark

OBJECTIVES Through the process of discovery in this chapter, you will be able to:

1. Describe technology use as a tool for inquiry curriculum.

2. Describe the young child's approach to computer use.

3. Discuss the selection of developmentally appropriate software.

4. Describe technology use for young children in comparison to the goals of constructivist education.

5. Describe the use of software whereby children can communicate ideas in print and drawing.

6. Describe ways that classrooms communicate with others through the Internet.

7. Discuss accessing information for inquiry through Web sites and software technology.

8. Discuss recording for inquiry through the digital camera, video camera, and audiocassette.

9. Describe the use of photocopiers, scanners, magnifiers, and microscopes.

10. Describe the use of the transparency projector and light table to study materials in different perspectives.

11. Integrate technology and software into the curriculum.

12. Describe one's developing skills to advance classroom technology.

IDEAS TO PONDER

• What are appropriate uses of the computer in classrooms?

• How can worthwhile information for young children be found on Web sites and software?

*This chapter was co-written with Warren Buckleitner.

161

- How can young children who are not literate use e-mail?
- How can cameras, video cameras, and audio recorders augment children's inquiry?

- How can I learn the new technology to use in the classroom?

There is now no doubt that computers and good software have earned a valued position in every early childhood classroom. Keep in mind, however, that no technology can accelerate a child's development or teach a concept that a child is not ready for.
(Buckleitner, personal communication, June 18, 2003)

"They get this wonderful 'I have figured it out!' look in their eyes as they really begin to understand both the science of nature and the science of magnification," states Yvonne Carlisle as she describes preschoolers' reaction to the microscope computer add-on.
(Buckleitner, 2002, May, p. 6)

TECHNOLOGY AS A TOOL FOR LEARNING

A smart toy is one with a computer chip that is programmed to perform certain activities for the child.

With today's choices in technology, teachers can select a **"smart toy"** at a very low cost (Buckleitner, 2001, January) or invest in a computer center with an extensive support system, including printer, scanner, digital camera, and projection screen (Buckleitner, 2003, May). These basic or extensive sets of tools can support inquiry and expand curriculum when used in thoughtful and creative ways. With thorough knowledge of how to select and put these tools to use in appropriate ways, these technology tools work to your advantage (Table 11–1).

APPROPRIATE TECHNOLOGY

Software is a computer program made for a particular purpose that can become portable by storing on a CD.

In the past twenty years, microprocessor-based technology has evolved at an incredible rate. Today, there are 1200 early childhood **software** titles available to a typical early childhood teacher, as well as a new generation of smart toys with powerful microprocessors (Buckleitner, 2001, January). Today's teacher can use technology to support her choices of learning theories. There is now no doubt that when technology is used in developmentally appropriate ways, it can have dramatic impacts on learning (Haugland, 1997). However, like any other classroom material, the effectiveness of a technology-based activity in an early childhood classroom depends on the quality of the activity, as determined by your views on how children learn (Buckleitner, 2002, April).

With the vast selection on the market today, sound choices can be made. The NAEYC "Position Statement: Technology and Young Children—Ages Three through Eight" promotes that "professional judgment by the teacher is required to determine if a specific use of technology is age appropriate, individually appropriate, and culturally appropriate" (NAEYC, 1996, p. 11). The software in use in one

TABLE 11–1   Possibilities with Technology

Just imagine:

With technology children can draw and dictate or write their thoughts and ideas. Curriculum webs (see Chapter 9) can be designed as a group in a software program. Children can identify what they know or what they want to explore. And these early communications can be recorded, copied, displayed on a screen, or sent to others . . . .

With technology children can view things in their world from different perspectives. The tools can be put in their hands so they can record images from their perspective and show others. Through the digital camera, or a microscope attachment to the computer, children can view close-ups or enlarged views of plant or animal life (Buckleitner, 2003, April). Here they can compare and contrast what they know . . . .

With technology teachers, along with the children, can find more information and view pictures on practically any topic. A wide array of suitable Web sites is accessible, and complete encyclopedias are available as software programs (Buckleitner, 2003, April). With these children can examine plant and animal life from the pictures and compare with what they know from their real-life experiences . . . .

With technology children can problem solve a variety of situations, build places such as a zoo or playground (Buckleitner, 2003, January/February), or make sand castles. These problem-solving situations available in software are usually designed for a variety of levels for the young child. With these different mediums children can experiment and hypothesize outcomes.

classroom may not be appropriate for a classroom next door—or across the country. When teachers are knowledgeable about ways children learn, about guidelines to appropriate software, and about what is available on the current market, they can make the best selections in children's software.

STANDARDS

Rather than being merely an enrichment or add-on to the curriculum, technology has taken a central place in early childhood programs. Candidates demonstrate sound knowledge and skills in using technology as a teaching and learning tool. . . . Candidates demonstrate knowledge about how to combine appropriate software with other teaching tools to integrate and reinforce learning.

Standard 4b. Reprinted with permission from National Association for the Education of Young Children. NAEYC standards for early childhood professional preparation: Initial licensure programs. (2003). In *Preparing early childhood professionals: NAEYC's standards for programs,* M. Hyson (Ed.). Washington, DC: Author, (pp. 38–39).

YOUNG CHILDREN AND COMPUTERS

The preschool years are the first real years of independent computer use. In these years children love to explore, pretend, and figure things out. Good software for preschoolers helps develop these emerging characteristics by putting young children "in control" (Buckleitner, 2002, April). Ease of use is critical—the best programs are intuitive to use and give children a sense of accomplishment and mastery. In addition, good software grows in dimension with the child, enabling her to find new challenges as she becomes more proficient.

Kindergartners at the computer can easily accomplish the basic skills for using software. They can use pull-down menus to launch programs themselves. They can also use the computer for simulations, creativity, and even for reference. With adult help, they can go onto the Internet to research a topic of interest. This is the time to begin computer activities that build more computer skills. Programs that are open ended encourage exploration and creativity. Children's software can also involve problem solving, number concepts, and science exploration (Buckleitner, 2002, April).

Young children latch on quickly to new technology. Because their world already includes the remote control for the television and the controls for PlayStation 2® they eagerly reach for new challenges rather than being threatened by new skills required for using a program.

Open-ended software is a type of program where children learn through discovering rather than being told right or wrong.

Children Are Active Learners

The spirit of play is never stronger than the early years of childhood. That's why the best software taps a child's urge to experiment. New concepts can be tried out in a variety of ways, giving children a chance to choose activities compatible with their own interests and abilities. The best programs often provide opportunities for children to incorporate their ideas into the software experience. **Open-ended software** gives children the opportunity to explore and discover, make choices, and then find out the impact of their decisions. For instance, they decide what to create in a draw program, how to end a story, or in what direction to take an exploration. "Open-ended software encourages wondering and hypothesizing, problem solving, collaboration, motivation, and a more positive attitude toward learning" (Northwest Educational Technology Consortium, n.d.).

Drill-and-practice software presents an academic task for the child, provides feedback, and takes the child to the next higher level.

This does not mean that structured software—even **drill-and-practice software**—should never be on the menu. Because children new to computer use may be more confident with a structured program, this may be the place to start. It just means that to further the competencies of constructing their experience, the menu will feature open-ended programs. Still, children feel most comfortable when there is a goal or end result that they are searching for, not just exploratory programs. Children will communicate their thoughts and ideas when they choose to illustrate a story or represent what they have made with blocks on the software Kid Pix® (see Appendix B).

SELECTING TECHNOLOGY

Most teachers are inexperienced in selection of technology and software for the classroom. Fortunately, there are guides to selection, yet this process requires thorough investigation of software to make good decisions. There are simulations, open-ended creativity tools, structured activities, puzzles, tutorials, and reference titles, made by over 700 publishers. With all these options, the job of selecting software can seem overwhelming.

In evaluating software teachers can look at questions on ease of use, responsivity (to a child's actions), learning potential, and entertainment value. In Appendix B you will find a helpful checklist for evaluating software from *Children's Software Revue*. When using this checklist, keep in mind that not all guidelines are applicable for every type of software. This is a generic list of attributes for a typical early childhood computer activity such as Millie's Math House™ (see Appendix B).

Because the software experience is an interactive and multidimensional one, the evaluator of a children's interactive media activity must consider the educational theory reflected in the product design and decide if it supports or undermines his or her own early childhood curricula (Buckleitner, 2002, April).

CONSTRUCTIVIST EDUCATION GOALS IN TECHNOLOGY USE

When applying constructivist education goals (see Chapter 1) to technology for young children, this pedagogy can define the appropriateness of all aspects of technology use for early childhood classrooms. To review, "constructivist education takes its name from Piaget's research showing that children actively interpret their experiences in the physical and social worlds and thus construct their own knowledge" (DeVries, Zan, Hildebrandt, Edmiaston, & Sales, 2002, p. 35).

Questions are used to identify what constitutes constructivist classrooms and applied to selecting various technology in the early childhood classroom. Choices range from computer software to transparency projectors (Table 11–2).

In applying constructivist goals, teachers can look at the full range of technology presented in this chapter. One can see that software that supports drawing and emerging literacy would fall into the constructivist category. In using the **Internet** to research information on a topic and communicating through **e-mail,** Internet use can promote constructivist theory. Using the still camera or video camera to enhance curriculum and share ideas also would promote constructivist thinking.

From this application of theory, the kinds of children's software programs that are educational games or activities are the most difficult to evaluate. By using the evaluation tool shown in Table 11–2 and The Software Evaluation in Appendix B, teachers can review each software program according to the educational outcomes they prefer.

The Internet is a system of interconnected computers that provide easy access to a vast amount of data and material from any connected site in the world.

E-mail is a process of sending messages usually in typed form to be received by a user on another computer through the Internet.

TABLE 11–2   Applying Constructivist Education Goals to Technology

Constructivist Education Goals	Goals of Technology Use
1. Does the activity promote open inquiry?	Does the use of this technology open up inquiry? Is there a process of discovery that is led by the child or group?
2. Is the activity appropriate to the intellectual abilities of the children?	Does the use of this technology challenge children through its design and levels of mastery? Does the topic build on something children know and spark their interest in finding out? Each time the child uses this technology, does it follow new paths or are the same actions repeated? (NAEYC, 1996) Does the program have flexibility in levels of difficulty? Does the child maintain control of the program? (Buckleitner, 2002, April)
3. Does the activity allow for a wide range of possible responses?	Does it promote children's creativity? Does the technology allow for children to select different choices to follow?
4. Will the activity lead to new insights and awareness?	Does the technology only hold momentary interest? Does it deepen understanding or is it mindless curriculum that does not have abiding value? (Bredekamp & Copple, 1997)
5. Will the activity provoke the child's curiosity, engage their attention, and sustain interest?	Does the activity lead to new insights and awareness? Does it take the child into deeper understanding of phenomena? Of learning in one or more areas?
6. Does the activity allow the children to do most of the thinking?	Are the situations open ended without right or wrong answers? Or does the program mainly entertain, presenting actions for children without involving their thinking at a meaningful level?
(DeVries, Zan, Hildebrandt, Edmiaston & Sales, 2002)	Does the technology promote collaboration among children and with teachers?

EXAMINING THE TECHNOLOGY

A wide range of technology is flooding the market; in the coming years this will expand exponentially. The decisions on choosing appropriate technology for young ages will be even more challenging. The guidelines presented in this text can help teachers use knowledge about technology and pedagogy to make informed decisions.

Software for Drawing and Print

With extensive software, the sky is the limit as to what children can create in picture and print. Important for the preschool and kindergarten level is a program that simplifies tools so painting and early writing can be handled by young hands.

Kid Pix or other drawing programs can be used to draw freely. Stamps, fill-in colors, and other picture-making tasks are handled easily. Teachers can take dictation and put the story in print immediately on the computer-generated picture. By seeing her work printed out, the child can feel a sense of accomplishment.

When planning curriculum with children, webs and lists (see Chapter 9) can be accomplished on the computer using Kidspiration with graphics, print, or both combined. As children continue to build on their ideas, webs or lists can be updated.

Communication with Others Near and Far

E-mail can be a useful tool for individuals and groups of children to communicate with others. A computer-drawn picture can be attached to an e-mail and sent to a parent with a note written by the teacher in the e-mail.

ANECDOTE

When three-year-old Zac finally mastered the draw program, he drew a picture that he wanted to send to his dad. Ms. Ester copied his drawing into an attachment and, for the body of the e-mail, she took the following dictated words from Zac: "To my daddy, I drawed this worm."

In one hour his father answered his e-mail with, "Dear Zac, I was so surprised to find the picture you drew for me! I printed out the picture and have it on my desk. Thank you! Love, Dad." Of course, Ms. Ester printed out his father's response and Zac carried that e-mail with him all day.

A Web site is a particular place accessed through the Internet with its own code (address) where particular information and images can be viewed.

Words and ideas can be communicated through dictated messages on e-mail. Individuals may want to send important messages to family members or friends. A group or a class can communicate requests and thank you's to people working with them on projects. As children are experiencing the meaning of print, the impact of sending and receiving communication underlines its importance (Fig. 11–1).

School **Web sites** can be an important link between school and family and others interested in the child's school life—even grandparents who live across the state. Using simple programs for educators, the school can create a Web site for

Dear Mr. Maxwell,

We are sending our thanks to you for our visit to the bakery.
All enjoyed seeing fresh bread being made and baked today.

The children have these things to tell you:

"I loved the bread."
"I didn't know it got so big in the oven."
"It smelled so good."
"You do a wonderful thing in making all that bread."
"Yum, yum."
"Thank you, Mr. Maxwell!"

The A Classroom at the Child Development Center

Figure 11–1 A class says thank you through an e-mail.

posting ongoing information from each classroom (Buckleitner, 2002, October; 2003, May). Schools may decide to limit postings to children's writing and work, and eliminate children's photos.

ANECDOTE

The children returned from their short trip to visit "their class tree" in December.

During naptime Ms. Jonel added the current photo to the ones taken in late July and October. When children saw the new photo, some said, "The tree's dead." "It's too cold now." Ms. Jonel posted the photo and their comments on the class Web page.

As Renee's mother arrived later in the afternoon, she saw the Web page on the classroom computer. With this current information, she talked to Renee about the changes in the tree while on the way home. On the home computer, Renee's mother viewed the "classroom tree" with her. By the next morning Renee's mother found a suggestion on the school Web page for them to do at home which she shared with Renee. With this suggestion Renee looked at the tree outside their window and described it, and Renee's mother sent an e-mail with Renee's comments for Ms. Jonel to find on Monday morning.

Information on the Internet

As individuals or groups of children become interested in particular topics, access of information is available on the Web. Often the Internet can easily provide an answer to a child's question. Once when Warren was teaching, one of his children found a mysterious, beautiful dead moth on the playground. Warren and the child had no idea what kind they had found and had to wait until Warren could make it to the library (which he never did) (Buckleitner, 2002, May).

Today, it is easy to visit any **search engine** and type in "butterfly" quickly and easily identify a butterfly or moth. The best search site is Google (www.google.com), considered the fastest and the best, but make sure the **safe search filter** is active, just in case. For encyclopedia reference try www.encarta.msn.com. Before accessing a particular site for the first time with children, sites must be previewed for their reliability and usability (Buckleitner, 2002, May). With Internet access the teacher can access an approved site, search with children, and read the materials found. In addition, software stores of information can be purchased in the form of encyclopedias, such as Encarta. From any source, pertinent information and pictures can be downloaded for classroom use.

A search engine is a tool used to find Web sites containing information on a given topic.

Digital Cameras, Camcorders, and Audiocassettes

Technology extends beyond the computer center. Combined with the computer, the **digital camera** becomes a very flexible tool. Children can use a simple camera, and adults can record the processes of children at work. The results of photos taken can be seen immediately on the camera and almost instantly can be shown on the computer screen or television monitor. And these photos can be printed in any size, shared through e-mail, or posted on the school's own Web site. With the computer you can alter pictures to your liking, store thousands of photos for later use, and erase those not wanted. After you have snapped a few hundred pictures without using any film, you'll wonder how you ever got along without one.

Safe search filter is a program that limits access to the Internet to include only Web sites that are deemed appropriate for young viewers.

By putting the camera into the hands of the child, you will view the world from the mind of the child. The photos you and the child want to keep can be put into the child's computer portfolio. Also for the child's portfolio, use the camera to record the child's work as documentation. A photo of a construction or an art project is a concise way to build these records. When recording a group project, the image can be inserted into the portfolio of each child working on the project.

The digital camera uses digital imaging, which can be transferred and viewed on the computer.

Consider the camera as the "third eye" that can retain the images of children learning. If the camera is kept handy, it can catch scenes of importance throughout the day. The group may look at these photos to remember events, observe something in close range, review their steps, or decide the next step of a project (Table 11–3).

Photography to Support Inquiry Digital cameras bring many advantages into the classroom: The instant imaging, the ability to select from a large amount of photos, and the ability to enlarge and crop bring the image close to the viewer. With these advantages, the immediacy of viewing close-up images of their work or their excursions provides children with visual reminders of their recent experiences so that they can reflect further on what occurred (Entz & Galarza, 2000; Fraser & Gestwicki, 2002).

Photographs of children's work in progress can pinpoint the construction and view the work from a different perspective.

Camcorder A powerful tool for documentation is the camcorder, with its ability to record events in action, in an instant, and over time. The video can be shown immediately on a television monitor and stored for later use in a VCR/DVD format.

TABLE 11–3 Suggested Uses of the Camera in the Classroom

- Capture close-ups of items of interest on a field site visit.
- Take full-length individual photos of children at the same spot and distance throughout the year to see their growth.
- Capture the visiting insect on camera before it is let free.
- Take photos of the changes in emergence of the butterfly from the chrysalis or of the frog from the tadpole. (Children can compare these stages through the photos, but they still won't believe it.)
- Record the growth of the newborn gerbil from the first viewing to full grown.
- Keep a record of the planted bean seed from black dirt to new sprout and plant. (This can be data for the plant graph.)
- Keep a step-by-step record of blocks under construction.
- Record on camera a scene of beauty so it can be enjoyed and savored.
- Record the planning of a mural, then the steps to create it.
- Keep a record of places visited and things seen.
- Use close-ups of an item of interest so children can examine details more closely and learn about how it works.
- Record an item of interest from different perspectives so the child can see it from several views. By seeing the camera's perspective, the child can enlarge her own.
- Record in increments of time the steps of a project—whether in hours or days or weeks—so children can review their steps and revisit or revise their process.
- Record the culminating events of children's work as celebrations of their lives (see Chapter 9).

ANECDOTE

Cynthia Hoisington writes of using digital photos of block building to revisit and extend children's investigations.

The next day at circle time I shared this photo showing a detailed shot of Christine building towers with cylinder blocks. Christine responded with what she was doing, "Building with fat round blocks and skinny round blocks."

The following day Christine took out one of the hard plastic boards . . . and used it as a base. She carefully placed an additional block, using both hands. "I notice you are placing that block very carefully," I said.

"I don't want it to fall down!" she answered. . . . Christine's unit block tower was much taller than she was . . .

"Fat round blocks make the biggest towers!" Christine exclaimed happily. (Hoisington, 2002, pp. 26, 28)

Through photographs Christine was able to revisit earlier building and apply this to her emerging block building skills.
(Photo courtesy Cynthia Hoisington.)

From this building project with Christine and other children, Cynthia Hoisington concludes, "I knew that helping children to generalize about why certain materials and certain strategies were more successful for making strong buildings was a gradual process. . . . They were beginning to see patterns and make connections between their own explorations and discoveries

> and what we observed outside in the world. . . . Photos had been instrumental in helping them to do this. Several new, unplanned uses of photography emerged: to help children revisit and extend their investigations, to reflect on their building experiences and articulate the strategies employed, and to analyze and synthesize these building strategies" (Hoisington, 2002, pp. 26–32).

The video camera can be kept accessible to record children tracking the path of the pendulum or digging in the soil. It can also capture children's reactions to the sights and sounds of spontaneous events like that very first snowstorm or the bloom on the narcissus. After capturing classroom events, the video can be studied immediately to remember the details or reviewed later to compare what children have learned (Buckleitner, 2001, April; 2001, May/June).

George E. Forman completed research on use of video as a memory machine that would provide instant replay on classroom events. "Used in this way, the video camera could become a modern 'tool of the mind,' a staple in the classroom. . . . [Using] a special type of video camera—the 8mm video camera with a foldout screen allows children to watch their activities immediately after they happen" (Forman, 1999, p. 1). This opens up new uses for the video camera as a quick review or reflection on past events by an individual or group.

The video can capture ongoing discussion by a large or small group. The children's words can be captured in writing on computer later. The video format can be reviewed through the television monitor and teachers can bring back the exact quotes from the written form. Bringing the ideas back to the children helps them refine and build on ideas generated in these earlier discussions as they instigate a project.

Audiocassette Recorder   The audiocassette recorder has valuable uses in the classroom. With one of the small portable voice recorders carried in a pocket, it is easy to record a group discussion, keep notes on what a child does, or record what he says about his drawing. The tape of a group discussion can be played back to be transcribed, as with videos (Buckleitner, 2001, May/June).

Photocopiers and Scanners

The underutilized photocopiers have many assessment possibilities, including making "quick and dirty" copies of a child's artwork or a copy of a dictated story for storage in a portfolio. If collecting items for two-dimensional portfolios, copy photos and art into cost-saving black and white images for records (Buckleitner, 2001, March; 2001, May/June).

A scanner is a device that inputs an image into the computer to be saved or processed.

Sometimes the downloaded images from the Internet are small. These can be enlarged on the photocopier or scanner.

The **scanner** operates something like a photocopier, except the pictures end up on the computer screen first instead of on a sheet of paper. Scanners are useful for scanning and saving work samples in each child's folder on the computer desktop. You can store her work in an electronic portfolio as well as making photo quality copies. A child would love to see her work as it is being scanned, slowly appearing on the computer screen (Buckleitner, 2001, March; 2001, May/June).

ANECDOTE

While searching for images to use for an earthworm project, the pictures I found were small. On the photocopier these were enlarged to match the actual sizes of the earthworms and these enlargements were covered in plastic sleeves. Once the children were comfortable holding the worms, they would place the wiggling worms on an image to match the size and attempt to match them in "wiggles" as well.

(Author)

Most any object can be scanned and copied, such as leaves, shells, or found collections. Teachers can make images of small (nonflying) insects or a worm to make memories of those many creatures that visit the classroom and then are let free (Buckleitner, 2001, March).

Microscopes and Magnifiers

An acrylic magnifying lens on a frame with a handle or mounted on a tripod easily magnifies three or four times the size of the object. For capturing insects to view before releasing them, use magnifying bug viewers. Microscopes for the classroom can magnify 5× to 50× or 100×. These come with prepared slides of common objects and have the ability to magnify and view objects found by the children. A computer add-on microscope will put this on the computer screen for a group of children to view together (Fig. 11–2).

Figure 11–2 Microscope attachment for computer.

ANECDOTE

EXAMINE CLOSELY

Yvonne Carlisle of COMPUTERTOTS also uses technology to bring nature indoors, with a computer microscope (see Appendix B).

> We took the children out on a nature walk to find interesting things to examine under the microscope. We found some dead flies, some live insects and spiders and a few plant samples. When the children got back to the computer, we began looking at our specimens. While everything was very interesting the most wonderful thing happened when we began looking at one of the green leaves a child had collected. From the top, it was just a leaf (very interesting on its own!) but when we turned it over there happened to be baby aphids on the leaf that were invisible to the naked eye! The kids got so excited and they would look at the leaf and see nothing and then look at it under magnification and see the baby aphids. Wow! It was incredible to see them "discover" what magnification was! (Buckleitner, 2002, May; Carlisle, personal communication, June 18, 2003)

Transparency Projectors and Light Tables

The light table has a tabletop that projects a diffused light through a translucent surface where children can explore materials.

These two items use a source of light to illuminate items in a different perspective (see Appendix B). The **light table** can be purchased or refashioned from a standard sand/water table by wiring the inside with fluorescent lights and fitting a new top with translucent Plexiglas. The **transparency projector** can be on an audiovisual (AV) cart or anchored on a low table and the light projected on a light-colored wall. Both use light to show items in different perspectives. A wide variety of translucent items can be arranged and transformed in arrays of pattern, color, light, and dark. The beauties of nature such as rose petals can be examined in light; and drawings of these on tracing paper over the light are enhanced in vivid color.

The transparency projector projects a transparent image onto a wall or other vertical surface.

For project work (Helm & Katz, 2001), color or black and white photos can be copied into transparencies (by some photocopiers) and projected with the overhead onto a wall so children can revisit a field site or compare earlier work. Color transparencies can also be made of the children's drawings so they can be discussed as part of planning and then placed into a mural. Children can also draw directly on transparencies with markers for projection.

INTEGRATING TECHNOLOGY INTO CURRICULUM

Technology can be integrated into the curriculum using a selected application to enhance the goals of learning. The technology application shall follow the curriculum, not the other way around. With an openness to what technology can do, these uses will naturally expand curriculum.

Support Scientific Inquiry with Technology

From this chapter you have many applications of technology that are easily used as tools in inquiry. The following two activities show some possibilities.

Guess That Sound Take your classroom tape recorder on a walk around the school, and tape record various sounds. Ask the children for ideas as to what to record (make sure to incorporate their ideas). The next day, sharpen their auditory skills by listening to the tape and asking what they think they hear. After the second or third time hearing it, record their answers over the sound. Many shorter "sound bites" work better, followed by the verbal answer to confirm the guess. Put the tape in the listening center to extend the activity.

Graph the Results Take small groups of children, each with a clipboard and primary pencil, to view and make records of what they find on short trips around the school, such as recording the litter found on the playground. This research can follow any topic of interest. Each child will select a category to keep track of and record findings in his own way. Make transparencies of each child's record and, using the transparency projector, ask each child to explain his findings to the group. Ask children how the ideas could be represented on one paper (or one transparency), and work with their ideas toward representing and/or graphing what they found. Follow their ideas. Videotape or audiotape these discussions and replay them to reintroduce the discussion at another time.

Software Integrated into Curriculum

Curriculum can successfully integrate children's software in classroom experiences. Here are three examples.

Math: Pairing and Comparing and Millie's Math House *Materials:* Ten pairs of shoes of different sizes (from baby shoes to large men's shoes), a computer with a monitor within eye-shot of the children, and Millie's Math House software program.

Large or small group activities: To start, dump all the shoes in the middle of a circle. Ask the children to sort them into pairs (one-to-one correspondence) and then according to size. Trying to put the shoes on their own feet adds another comparison and aids in sorting the shoes into groups of little, middle, and big.

Next, call children's attention to the computer screen, where you have the activity shown, and tell them, "Here's some more shoes to sort, but this time on the computer screen." Leave the program on the computer for a while so that all the children have a chance to sort in the abstract (Buckleitner, 2002, March).

Children can decide what to do with the shoes they used in the group activity: Continue sorting, use them for dress-up, or design a shoe store with shoes categorized according to size—or type—or for which person: baby, child, or adult.

Later come back and compare the real experience with the abstract one. For discussion you can ask,

"Were those shoes in Millie's Math House real? How were the shapes and sizes different than the shoes in our classroom?"

A child selects pairs of shoes in Millie's Math House. [Millie's Math House, Edmark (Riverdeep), 1995.]

"Was this easier or harder in Millie's Math House? Why do you think that?"

"What can you do to show a classmate who has not done this on computer? In real life?"

"What else can we do both on the computer and in real life? How can we do this?"

Children and teachers may be able to see other ways to match software activities with real events in the classroom.

Sand, Virtual Sand, and More Sand   *Materials:* Sand box or sand area outdoors, sand play tools, water, dress-up clothes for summer at the beach along with beach play tools and picnic basket to herald dramatic play at the beach, software program of Just Grandma and Me™.

Large or small group activities: Using water and sand, indoors or out, allow children to build sand castles and take photos of the sand constructions children build over many days. Next to the photos write the dictation you take on their sand constructions. When you have a collection of different kinds of these constructions, bring a small group to the computer program Just Grandma and Me and ask if children can make something similar with this software. Print out the computer-generated sand castles and compare with the photos of the children's work.

Children can compare a computer-generated sand castle and one constructed in the sandbox.

(Just Grandma and Me, The Learning Company, 1997)

Discuss going to the beach and introduce the dress-up clothes, beach play, and picnic materials for dramatic play. After children implement this kind of dramatic play, discuss the story on Grandma and Me and ask them to dictate stories on "Going to the Beach." The dictated stories can be written on computer, printed, and read. The group may decide to act out these stories at group time.

The culminating activity can be a trip to the beach. Together determine what they will do at the beach, what they will need, and how they will get there. Children can draw what they predict the beach will be like. Take photos at the beach of similar activities predicted by children.

Back in the classroom, make transparencies of drawings and photos and compare these using the transparency projector. With these same transparencies children can plan and build a mural of the beach.

Sorting and Representing

Materials: Small paper bags, outdoor area for collecting, trays, large sheets of paper, markers, Kidspiration software, digital camera, computer software for printing pictures, printer, index cards, glue, and yarn.

Large or small group activities: As children become interested in looking closely at their surroundings, get them involved in making a collection. Give the children small paper bags, and take them on a mini field trip to a nearby playground or park. Ask them to collect interesting items to bring back to their classroom. Supervise them closely as they collect items.

Once your children have their collection, its time to start sorting. Ask each child to dump the collection into a plastic tray or pan and then sort, compare, classify, and/or seriate. Have paper and markers on hand so that they can trace and label their collections. With the computer, use a program like Kidspiration to take this representation to another level, using the program's rich library of "stickers" to represent each item. With a label (computer generated or traced) children can sort and classify objects found onto labeled sheets of paper. The Kidspiration program makes it easy to break the collection into groups, sorting by attributes like living and nonliving, shape, color, or size (Buckleitner, 2003, April).

"I Spy" bulletin board activity: Start with a photo of each child's collection, and make a large print of each. For each picture, print out copies of the poem shown in Figure 11–3. Ask each child to identify one object that shows in his picture for the "I Spy" poem. For the clues to the object, write what the child dictates on the second line (color, shape, size, its use). Paste the poem on one side of an index card. On the back of the card the child can draw a picture of it and print its name (Fig. 11–3).

On the bulletin board hang an "I Spy" card on each photo with a short piece of yarn. Under the display place a hand magnifier for children to use to examine photos closely. The child who created the label for his particular photo can take a friend to view the photo, "read" the poem, and ask the friend to guess the "I Spy" item (Buckleitner, 2003, April).

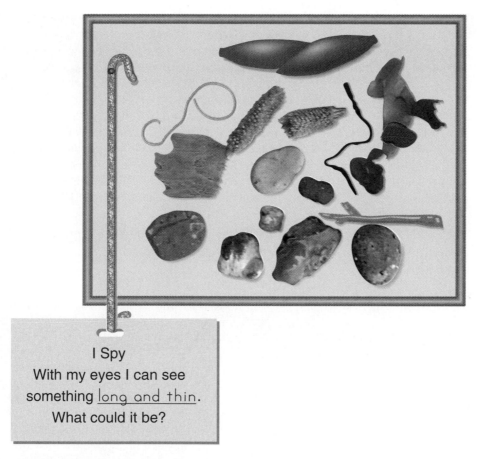

I Spy
With my eyes I can see
something <u>long and thin</u>.
What could it be?

Figure 11–3 The child completes the "I Spy" riddle for his photo of collected items.

YOU AND TECHNOLOGY

To make these curriculum ideas come alive in your classroom, the first step is to become familiar with the technology and use it. By hands-on learning you will know each tool and can support children in the process. Share technology expertise you have as you also learn from others. Do not wait until you are expert, as children will appreciate that you are on a learning curve as well. Continue to extend the learning to new techniques, and be open to learning along with the children. They will learn a valuable lesson from your openness to embrace the new and unfamiliar. Karen Muschasic (2003) sees this facilitation as ways to support children exploring further as they navigate choices, problem solve, and find new information.

SUMMARY

With new technology becoming more specific in use, user friendly, and available, it is edifying to grasp its profound potential in the classroom. Whatever the medium, you can facilitate its use in order to challenge young minds. With guidelines for selecting the technology tools and appropriate implementation, you can effectively use technology to augment children's learning at a deeper level. In the next chapter you will learn about inquiry in various types of curriculum. You will find expanded possibilities of technology use in the Inquiry Topics in Chapters 14 to 19.

TO FURTHER YOUR THINKING

1. Shop for information at computer stores, camera shops, and school catalogs for types of technology and software suitable for young children. Explore each piece of equipment and/or read the details to get an idea of how each technology item is operated. Ask yourself what you would need to learn to be able to use this equipment. For software, list titles available in the 3- to 6-year age range to add to the list you develop in number 3.

2. Make a graph depicting your skills in use of each of the following: using the computer as word processor, installing software, printing, using the Internet, using e-mail, taking pictures with a digital camera, downloading digital photos on the computer, editing and printing digital photos, photocopying, scanning, using a video camera, showing video on a television monitor, transcribing from video camera to VCR/DVD, using an audiocassette recorder, using a simple microscope or microscope attachment to a computer, and using a transparency projector and a light table.
On the graph determine whether you are expert or novice (or somewhere in between) in using this technology. If not an expert, what would you need to do to have a working knowledge of this tool? (You may be surprised at your working knowledge of technology.) You can opt to advance your skills in one new area.

3. If you have the opportunity, ask a young child you know to show you the children's software she likes. Using the Software Evaluation in Appendix A, check off the points you observe while the child shows you the software program. In

class, compare your evaluation to other students' reports of software programs for young children. Keep a list of software programs you would select for classroom use.

4. Go on line to review the latest children's software. You can access reviews at www.childrenssoftware.com and www.childrenandcomputers.com. Compare with the recommendations in Appendix B and with a child's favorites. Continue a list of children's software you would select.

5. Select a science subject you are interested in and use a Web browser to see what you can find out. For a search engine try www.google.com and for on-line encyclopedia and references to extensive Web sites, try www.encarta.msn.com.

6. Take an idea for curriculum from one of the chapters (you can go back to Chapter 10 or peek ahead). Decide a unique way to integrate technology into this curriculum idea. Make a list of possibilities generated from the class for your future use.

REFERENCES

Bredekamp, S., and Copple, C. (Eds.). (1997). *Developmentally appropriate practice in early childhood programs.* Washington, DC: National Association for the Education of Young Children.

Buckleitner, W. (2001, January). Getting smart about smart toys. *Scholastic Early Childhood Today, 15*(4), 9.

Buckleitner, W. (2001, March). Scan it! *Scholastic Early Childhood Today, 15*(6), 6–7.

Buckleitner, W. (2001, April). Lights! Camera! Action! *Scholastic Early Childhood Today, 15*(7), 10–11.

Buckleitner, W. (2001, May/June). Great gadgets for assessment. *Scholastic Early Childhood Today, 15*(8), 6–7.

Buckleitner, W. (2002, March). Make math as easy as 123! *Scholastic Early Childhood Today, 16*(5), 5–6.

Buckleitner, W. (2002, April). Children, computer chips and creativity. *Scholastic Early Childhood Today, 16*(16), 4–5.

Buckleitner, W. (2002, May). Tech makes science sizzle. *Scholastic Early Childhood Today, 16*(7), 6–7.

Buckleitner, W. (2002, September). Take a good look. *Scholastic Early Childhood Today, 17*(1), 5–6.

Buckleitner, W. (2002, October). Parents and teacher—A winning team! *Scholastic Early Childhood Today, 17*(2), 8–9.

Buckleitner, W. (2003, January/February). Liven up your math program—With a touch of tech! *Scholastic Early Childhood Today, 17*(4), 10–11.

Buckleitner, W. (2003, April). Turning collections into curriculum—Technically speaking! *Scholastic Early Childhood Today, 17*(6), 6–7.

Buckleitner, W., Orr, A., and Wolock, E. (2002). *Complete sourcebook on children's interactive media.* Farmington, NJ: Active Learning Associates, Inc.

Cadwell, L. B. (2003). *Bringing learning to life: The Reggio approach to early childhood education.* New York: Teachers College Press.

DeVries, R., Zan, B., Hildebrandt, C., Edmiaston, R., and Sales, C. (2002). *Developing constructivist early childhood curriculum: Practical principles and activities.* New York: Teachers College Press.

Entz, S., and Galarza, S. L. (2000). *Picture this: Digital and instant photography activities for early childhood learning.* Thousand Oaks, CA: Corwin Press. This idea book proposes camera use to create innovative learning tools.

Forman, G. E. (1999). Instant video revisiting: The video camera as a "tool of the mind" for young children [On line]. *Early Childhood Research and Practice, 1*(2), 1–8. www.ecrp.uiuc.edu

Fraser, S., and Gestwicki, C. (2002). *Authentic childhood: Exploring Reggio Emelia in the classroom.* Clifton Park, NY: Thomson Delmar Learning.

Haugland, S. W. (n.d.). *Selecting developmentally appropriate software and Web site.* [On line]. Children and Computers. www.childrenandcomputers.com.

Haugland, S. W., and Wright, J. L. (1997). *Young children and technology: A world of discovery.* Boston: Allyn & Bacon.

Helm, J., and Katz, L. (2001). *Young investigators: The project approach in the early years.* New York: Teachers College Press.

Hoisington, C. (2002, September). Using photographs to support children's science inquiry. *Young Children, 57*(5), 26–32.

Muchasic, K. (2003). *Enhancing learning at computers: The powerful role of adult interaction* [On line]. www.childrenandcomputers.com.

National Association for the Education of Young Children. (1996, September). NAEYC position statement: Technology and young children—Ages three through eight [On line]. *Young Children 51*(5), 11–16. www.naeyc.org.

National Association for the Education of Young Children. (2003). NAEYC standards for early childhood professional preparation: Initial licensure programs. In M. Hyson (Ed.), *Preparing early childhood professionals: NAEYC's standards for programs* (pp. 17–63). Washington, DC: Author.

Northwest Educational Technology Consortium (2001). Technology in early childhood education: Finding the balance. [On line] Author. www.netc.org/earlyconnections.

ADDITIONAL RESOURCES

Buckleitner, W., Orr, A., and Wolock, E. (2002). *Complete sourcebook on children's interactive media.* Farmington, NJ: Active Learning Associates, Inc. For a complete review of all interactive media for children, use this review: Find them on the Web at www.childrenssoftware.com.

Children and Computers sponsored by K.I.D.S. & Computers, Inc, Denver Public School Department of Curriculum and Instruction and Metropolitan State college of Denver. You can find more information on children and computers, software program awards and articles. www.childrenandcomputers.com

Entz, S., and Galarza, S. L. (2000). *Picture this: Digital and instant photography activities for early childhood learning.* Thousand Oaks, CA: Corwin Press. This idea book uses the camera to create innovative learning tools.

Haugland, S. W., and Wright, J. L. (1997). *Young children and technology: A world of discovery.* Boston: Allyn & Bacon. This text follows developmentally appropriate guidelines in discussion of technology use.

Helm, J., and Katz, L. (2001). *Young investigators: The project approach in the early years.* New York: Teachers College Press. A section in Chapter 6 describes the utilization of technology in projects. Available also at www.naeyc.org.

Murphy K. L., DePasquale, R., and McNamara, E. (2003, November). Meaningful connections: Using technology in primary classrooms. *Young Children, 58*(6), 12–18. This article promotes technology as a tool that is selected because it supports learning. Available at www.naeyc.org.

Woods, C. S. (2000, September). A picture is worth a thousand words—Using photographs in the classroom. *Young Children, 55*(5), 82–84. With a camera, a teacher can use photos of the children to create many activities and displays for children's active involvement.

Web Sites

www.compuvisor.com An add-on microscope for computers can be found for the Digital Blue QX3™ + Computer Microscope.

www.eNasco.com The Nasco On-line Catalog has microscopes and magnifiers for young children, including a small two-way microscope for individual viewing. Also the overhead (transparency) projector.

www.insectlore.com Insect Lore has resources on line for microscopes and magnifiers.

www.naeyc.org Salmon, M., and Akaran, S. E. (2001, July). Enrich your kindergarten program with a cross-cultural connection. *Young Children, 56*(4), 30–32. This article shares a story of a rich cultural exchange through e-mail.

www.netc.org/earlyconnections Northwest Educational Technology Consortium. Early Connections: Technology in Early Childhood Education. Developmentally appropriate statements integrating technology use with thoughtful curriculum planning.

www.techandyoungchildren.org NAEYC Teachers and Young Children Interest Forum promotes discussion and sharing information on best practices regarding technology.

Chapter 12
Approaches to Curriculum

OBJECTIVES Through the process of discovery in this chapter, you will be able to:

1. Discuss curriculum choices that enhance the inquiry process.

2. Recognize elements of developmentally appropriate practice that support inquiry.

3. Discuss the integration of curriculum areas with science and math curriculum.

4. List interest areas in a classroom and describe the fluid use of these areas and their space to enhance inquiry.

5. Describe two ways that play supports the topic of study.

6. List sources for the choice of a classroom topic.

7. Describe ways of transforming thematic curriculum into one that embraces inquiry.

8. Describe elements of the following curricula for inquiry:
   a. Constructivist curriculum
   b. Reggio approach
   c. Project approach

9. Discuss using a curriculum framework to advance intellectual dispositions.

10. Discuss the investment of a teacher in implementing curriculum.

IDEAS TO PONDER

- How do I choose curriculum for an early childhood classroom?

- What elements of curricula must be present to support inquiry?

- How is play effectively woven into curriculum?

- What is my investment in the curriculum in my classroom?

If we are able to read and give voice to children's intent, perhaps children will learn that others are interested in what they think. Perhaps they will not learn to hunt for what adults want them to say, but will use that energy to give voice to their own theories. Perhaps they will learn to set problems for themselves and come to teachers less for approval than for support in their investigation. And perhaps they will be more inclined to develop a disposition toward co-constructing theory, a disposition toward investigation, and an inclination to represent in order to learn.

In the process, children's understanding of the topic goes deeper, and when children remain engaged long enough to go deep into an idea, they are likely to progress from magical thinking to more logical thinking. (Oken-Wright & Gravett, 2002, p. 218)

CHOICES IN CURRICULUM

Emergent curriculum is an in-depth study for learning that develops out of children's and teachers' interests and questions.

In the United States, as well as in other countries, there are many choices of curriculum for preschool and kindergarten. Whatever choice is made in curriculum, teachers can support children in voicing their intent, probing their questions, and making their discoveries so they can experience being autonomous thinkers. In the school where you teach, you can make a curriculum choice that fits with the teaching style of you and your colleagues and the goals of the school, and match this with the culture found in the families and community you serve.

Three approaches to curriculum are described in this chapter: the constructivist approach, the Reggio approach, and the project approach. Inquiry is naturally an integral part of these approaches because of the process of discovery by children. In addition, other curricula that involve inquiry are worthy of mention. In the Additional Resources at the end of the chapter you will find excellent descriptions of **emergent curriculum** (Jones & Nimmo, 1994; Jones, Evans & Rencken, 2001) and the study (Dodge, Colker, & Heroman, 2002).

Thematic planning is curriculum on a topic that is preplanned by teachers.

In the more traditional curriculum of **thematic planning,** teachers can also involve children in the inquiry process by selecting the topics that are ripe for discovery and focus on children acting on materials to discover concepts. This process is described later in this chapter.

DEVELOPMENTALLY APPROPRIATE CURRICULUM

Developmentally appropriate practice is a set of principles and guidelines that follow the way children develop and learn in programs for children from birth through age eight.

For curriculum one can draw from the extensive work on **developmentally appropriate practice** (DAP) developed by the National Association for the Education of Young Children. First, curriculum must follow what teachers know about how children develop and learn. In DAP the emphasis is on being developmentally appropriate for the particular group of children, for age, geographic location, and culture. In addition, the curriculum is appropriate for the individual as well. When following DAP, teachers will be aware of the uniqueness of individual programs. When seen in different places across the country, curriculum does not look the same. When seen in the same classroom from year to year, curriculum does not look the same. And within the same classroom the experiences from child to child do not look the same (Bredekamp & Copple, 1997).

Additionally, DAP states that curriculum is child centered, **meaning centered,** and integrated across areas of learning. Under the DAP guidelines, teachers base decisions in teaching on needs, abilities and interests of children, and the ways young children learn.

According to Bredekamp and Rosegrant (1992) and DeVries and Kohlberg (1987), the learning process is a cycle in which knowledge is constructed using awareness, exploration, and inquiry. For the young child, learning involves a hands-on approach, investment into exploration, and communication about what is learned with others.

Some pertinent curriculum questions can help teachers base decisions on needs, abilities, and interests of children, and the ways young children learn.

Meaning-centered curriculum focuses on a worthwhile topic that advances learning in depth.

- What are children's current interests?
- What do children in the group need or need to know?
- What do they know about a topic?
- What are they capable of in investigation?
- What is worth investigating for this group?
- What can they learn from investigations in their school and community? (Bredekamp & Rosegrant, 1992; Helm & Katz, 2001)

MEANING-CENTERED VERSUS MINDLESS CURRICULUM

Teachers select activities and goals following intellectual integrity, not a **mindless curriculum.** Curriculum ideas that are mindless will not increase understanding of a selected concept. Some examples of mindless curriculum are coloring a copy of a rabbit or growing watercress in eggshells with faces drawn on them so the tiny plants represent hair. Examples of mindless curriculum are prevalent in activity books and magazines written for teachers.

Mindless curriculum involves activities of children that do not involve them in understanding more about their world through inquiry and investigation.

Ideas could be selected that relate to the topic of study but only carry a relationship on the surface level and are not relevant to the underlying concepts of the topic. Helm and Katz (2001) discuss mindless curriculum as not being harmful in itself or even being beneficial in a few ways but lacking sufficient intellectual depth to support intellectual dispositions. For example, in a study of cars, children use matchbox cars to make lines in paint by running the cars in small puddles of paint placed on paper.

In the meaning-centered approach, the curriculum decisions advance the learning on the selected topic in depth (Bredekamp & Rosegrant, 1992). For an example of in-depth study on cars, the children examine the inside and outside of a car, focusing on how parts of it work. The process of this study can further thinking toward intellectual dispositions.

Integrated curriculum is curriculum that encompasses many areas of learning no matter what the topic.

INTEGRATED CURRICULUM

For a particular science or math topic the learning process allows for an **integrated curriculum** across traditional subject-matter divisions (Bredekamp &

Rosegrant, 1992). As a topic develops, all areas of learning are integrated: science and math, language, emergent literacy, social studies, the creative arts of music and art, technology use, motor activities, and advances in the concept of self and social abilities. In the integrated approach, there are not any distinct lines where solely one area of learning is featured. Even though in this text topics in math and science predominate, integrated curriculum embraces the development of the whole child in all areas of learning (Bredekamp & Rosegrant, 1992).

STANDARDS

Candidates use their own knowledge and other resources to design, implement, and evaluate meaningful, challenging curriculum that promotes comprehensive developmental and learning outcomes for all young children.

Standard 4d. Reprinted with permission from National Association for the Education of Young Children. NAEYC standards for early childhood professional preparation: Initial licensure programs (2003). In *Preparing early childhood professionals: NAEYC's standards for programs*. M. Hyson (Ed.). Washington, DC: Author, (p. 29).

INTEREST AREAS

Interest areas are well-planned spaces for particular kinds of activities to take place in an early childhood classroom.

In the early childhood classroom, **interest areas** are commonly used to organize spaces for play, learning, and interaction. No matter what the curriculum choice, these areas provide places where play and inquiry can take place.

Interest centers will vary with the goals of the program, yet the following interest areas are commonly found in programs for preschool and kindergarten.

- Blocks
- Dramatic play
- Manipulatives
- Art
- Music and movement
- Library
- Writing
- Math
- Science
- Water and sand
- Technology
- Gross motor (in classroom, gym, and/or outdoors)

FLUIDITY OF INTEREST AREAS AND SPACE

Within this plan of interest areas, fluidity and openness will support the process of inquiry. Children and teachers will approach learning and problem solving creatively if there is a sense that materials from one area can be used in another. Examples of fluidity in practice are as follows:

ANECDOTE

In a preschool classroom that was exploring aspects of Reggio Emilia, the teacher placed a vase containing blooming narcissus bulbs in the middle of the art table. Children eagerly used the soft charcoal pencils to draw their perceptions of the bulb and emerging flowers.

At clean-up time some five-year-olds who had built a barn for a variety of animals in the block area ran to the writing area to write a sign they taped on their block structure, "SAF FOR THE AMIMLS." (Save for the animals.)

With concentration, Selena attempted to roll a small car down a long block that she held on an incline. Mario watched her repeated attempts to start the car and keep it on the block during its descent. "I have an idea," he exclaimed. Then he selected a large piece of construction paper from the art area and helped her tape the paper so it encompassed the block on three sides like a trough. Then Mario joined Selena and eventually they found success in rolling the car down the block for its full length.

Teachers and children will foster thinking "outside the box" when the concept of the interest area is fluid. To accomplish this, an interest area can be made larger or smaller, added to, or combined with another.

ANECDOTE

When the group of children in housekeeping becomes involved with "moving," they want to load the "truck" made from hollow blocks. Instead of holding to the rule of "blocks belong in the block corner," the teacher helps them open up the house area so the moving can take place.

When Carlina and Marianne start a process of making sets of similarly shaped objects from the many small pieces in the bins of manipulative area, the teacher talks to the two and, with their input, they design a floor space with large sheets of paper so they (along with three others who become interested in the project) can effectively classify all the shapes they find.

PLAY IN CURRICULUM

Since play is known as a strong medium for learning in the years from three to six, play is central in curriculum. The interest areas tend to promote play, whether this is dramatic play in the housekeeping area, constructive play in the block and manipulative areas, or functional and constructive play in sand and water.

The child elaborates his ideas in constructive play.

Outdoor playgrounds are planned as areas for play. Some of the types of play indoors can be expanded outdoors, such as dramatic play themes. Planned spaces in large areas outdoors can provide space for expansive investigation in water, sand, and mud. Motor activities are planned in areas for climbing and movement. These expand the knowledge of what children can accomplish with their bodies as well as through exploring materials outdoors.

As teachers observe play, they will be able to see what children have incorporated in their learning. This is one way they can obtain feedback on the inquiry topic in math and science. Children often play out what they know or what they are attempting to understand. The math concepts they are working on may appear as children work out fair sharing of materials. As physical science exploration with water is part of the curriculum, children may pretend to use water in similar ways, showing their current understanding of water. Seen in these ways, play may be a gauge of what children understand.

Teachers can involve additional ways for play to incorporate the topic of study. In the following ways, play involves learning:

1. As the concepts within a topic emerge, children are able to work out their beginning concepts through play. In pretending they may try out new possibilities and apply their understanding to further ideas along the lines that the topic of study is taking.
2. If the objects and materials that follow the topic are supplied for use in play, children may be handling and investigating these materials and therefore continue to learn through exploring.

The following example of these two ways of learning through play follows children's play during an ongoing project of planting.

ANECDOTE

After the group of three-year-olds plant their own seeds in soil, plastic flowers and plant stems along with plastic gardening tools and empty seed packets are added to the sand table. Using the plastic gardening tools, Juanito and Misty both bury a small rock and pat sand over it. Misty pretends to water it and moves back, waiting. Juanito takes a plastic plant stem and straightens it above the place where he placed his "seed." Misty first inserts a plant stem, then quickly replaces it with a flower, saying, "Mine made a flower." Together they pick up their plants and gently pull on leaves and flower, investigating the different parts. Misty leans over to Juanito and exclaims, "They ain't got no roots!"

CONTENT VERSUS PROCESS

In inquiry the focus is on **process.** In order to have a subject to study, a topic that involves process must also include content. Children become involved in process through acting on their ideas, developing questions, exploring, comparing, hypothesizing, and generalizing. **Content** is a part of the process as children and teachers name objects, describe processes, seek more information, and communicate various statements of hypotheses and generalization. Both process and content are necessarily set in the framework of the curriculum even though in inquiry process is emphasized over content.

Process is how children learn, such as exploring or experimenting.

DECIDING ON TOPICS

Children's interests provide a prevalent source for the topics chosen for a group to study. Yet the selection of a topic is not limited to children's interests. There are many considerations for topics. All choices of topics are based on a particular classroom for a given time.

Teachers observe and listen to children to gather ideas of their interests. Children may show their interests through play or through discussions with teachers and with groups of children. Teachers can question children about what they know and what they want to learn. The interest level on a particular topic can be gauged in these discussions.

Teachers become aware of incidents and resources within the community or ongoing projects around the school that could evolve into a study. When there is an accessible location in the community to study a particular topic, this provides concrete and real materials to investigate.

Content is what children learn in identification of objects and processes, such as names of flowers or stages of growth.

Usually topics lead to long-term study and in-depth learning about a topic that children are interested in learning about. It is a topic that can be invested further than surface knowledge. Children should be able to understand the concepts that evolve.

Sometimes an event in a child's life will spark interest, especially if it is significant to the child. When a child brings in photos or an object or talks excitedly about it, this event may herald a study. Or the child may introduce the event through play. Through contact with parents, teachers may become aware of family events that will be important for that child and others.

Teachers may contribute the topic idea following their own interests or knowledge. Teachers' investment of learning more about a topic can promote a study in depth (Helm & Katz, 2001; Jones & Nimmo, 1994).

Lilian Katz discusses the unworthiness of involving time in the children's lives to work with commercial elements or trivial topics (Helm & Katz, 2001). In itself, a commercial topic from a current movie, television cartoon characters, or other well-known theme does not deepen inquiry. Yet sometimes a worthwhile topic can develop from this initial interest. For example, one group of children was interested in how Ferris wheels worked after many of the families had taken their children to theme parks during the summer months. In this instance, a commercial topic developed into a worthy topic of study.

THEMATIC PLANNING

For the past twenty to thirty years, the most common approach to curriculum has been thematic planning. Typically this curriculum is teacher decided and teacher directed. The lesson plan is prepared two or three weeks ahead of time or perhaps for the whole school year. With this advanced planning by the teachers, the theme selected may actually have no bearing on the life of the classroom.

With a shift in focus, thematic planning can incorporate an inquiry approach, emphasize process over content, and follow children's evolving interests. To accomplish this, teachers continually observe the activities in the classroom to note what the children are exploring. These notes will be incorporated into deciding the theme. So instead of typically using spring flowers as a theme, teachers discuss the interest of some of the children in making toy boats sink or float in the water table. With this kind of input, decisions on the theme are not made through long range planning but are often realized one or two weeks in advance.

The focus of thematic planning can center on process over content. Teachers devise goals and objectives based on the process of learning rather than on content. For example, instead of identifying objects that float or sink, the goal may be to question what will happen to different objects in water, or what the child can do to change what happens. These goals will be written as steps of inquiry, questions, or processes developed for children's actions.

For thematic curriculum to follow inquiry, it remains flexible so teachers can adapt to the flow of individual children or groups (Bredekamp & Rosegrant, 1992). As processes are explored, the focus of the theme may shift to a concurrent idea or perhaps evolve into a new investigation. For example, in the goal of processing what happens to objects in water, children show interest in building small boats to carry objects in the water. When this occurs teachers facilitate the experimentation to follow this related concept. For the thematic approach to be based on inquiry, teachers can work flexibly within an existing system of curriculum planning.

CONSTRUCTIVIST CURRICULUM

The **constructivist curriculum** is based on children building theory as they work to understand how phenomena in the world work. Teachers develop curriculum from the questions of children, either ones they are asking as they explore materials or ones that teachers envision children asking (DeVries, Zan, Hildebrandt, Edmiaston, & Sales, 2002).

In the classroom are varied materials with which children can experiment and investigate varying processes. These materials are carefully planned by teachers to engage children in asking questions of what they can do to make something happen. In-depth experiences and many ongoing opportunities to work through ideas help children make connections. Children come to know through constructing their own theories (DeVries, Zan, Hildebrandt, Edmiaston, & Sales, 2002).

In a constructivist classroom one would see many choices of activities. The classroom may have many choices of manipulating materials in a physical science investigation. Teachers, along with their careful observation of children,

Constructivist curriculum is a framework for children to construct their knowledge about how the world works through active engagement in meaningful inquiry.

The teacher supports the child's process of discovery.

prepare materials for children to explore "big ideas." In physical science, for example, water flow or the inclined plane may be explored. As children actively explore ideas, teachers help children focus on their own questions and support their process of drawing conclusions.

Principles of teaching include providing a challenge to children. As children work through finding answers to their questions, teachers may challenge them with materials that pose a contrast to their first discoveries. The overriding purpose is to promote reasoning in the quest of understanding their world. DeVries and others conclude that teachers flexibly create activities that follow children's interests as in-depth engagement, and they modify their interventions in terms of insights into children's thinking obtained through careful observation of children's actions (DeVries, Zan, Hildebrandt, Edmiaston, & Sales, 2002).

THE REGGIO APPROACH

The Reggio approach is based on a city-wide program in the city of Reggio Emilia in northern Italy, with an established educational program for children from four months to six years of age. As early childhood educators in the United States became interested in this program, teachers and educators of these programs in Italy and the United States have continued an ongoing exchange. Many programs have been established in the United States that incorporate the Reggio approach and adapt components to integrate the culture of the school and community here.

This curriculum "emerges from the interests and ideas of the children, but [educators] also believe that there should be negotiation between all those involved in the development of the curriculum and in the planning and projects as they unfold. This perspective of curriculum is based on the theory that children co-construct knowledge within their social group" (Fraser & Gestwicki, 2002, p. 168).

In the Reggio approach, teachers use close observations and discussions with the children for decision making regarding the topic and the direction in which it will flow. Teachers spend time together discussing the content of what children are telling them. Decisions on curriculum choices are based on the children's interest and the underlying questions that emerge. As the curriculum develops, teachers continue to note the children's thought processes, which drive development of the curriculum along these lines of interest. Curriculum is negotiated and flexibly adjusted accordingly through the continuous dialogue among teachers and with children.

All through these processes children have ample opportunities to represent their ideas in the art media. Whether drawing, sculpture, or painting, art becomes one of the ways of communicating ideas. Representations become part of the discourse as children learn from each other, revise concepts, and deepen their understanding of concepts. These representations may also become the beginning of an idea or a blueprint for further work.

With carefully considered questions and opportunities to represent thoughts, the interactions go beyond discussions. Teachers use the recorded conversations to plan the next phase of a project. They take the ideas they have learned from the children to decide on possible next steps. This collaboration of children, of teachers and children, of teachers together, and of parents and teachers leads to decisions about the project.

During a project, documentation is both an integral part of the teaching process and a record of the events of a project. In using documentation, teachers may revisit earlier discussions with children, and this builds the process of discourse along the way. With completion of the project, the documentation is the record of the group's process from beginning to end. This documentation is often mounted artistically on a presentation board for all participants to see.

Long-term projects often progress from these plans. The project may be as short as two days or extend through most of the school year. Sometimes extensive projects develop as teachers reintroduce an invested study from the year before. Whatever the project is, it follows intent of the children. Through discourse, children integrate the ideas of other children and grow in understanding. This is co-construction at work (Fraser & Gestwicki, 2002).

THE PROJECT APPROACH

In this curriculum a project is an in-depth investigation of a topic worth learning more about. The investigation is usually undertaken by a group of children within a class, and sometimes by a whole class (Katz, 1994). The topic of study is something that children are invested in, and it emerges from observations and listening to children. Teachers take the ideas that they learn from the children and decide if those ideas are worthy of a long-term study. Or teachers introduce an idea that relates to ongoing events in the school community or choose a study that they think will be of interest to the children.

Using the project approach, teachers understand that some topics are worthy of study. These are more successful if they are more concrete than abstract and can involve firsthand, direct experiences. These are more successful if there are related sites where children can revisit the topic as they gain more information and where they can research with minimal assistance from the adult. These are more successful if children can represent what they know through group constructions and representative art media and when the materials they construct or organize provide settings for dramatic play (Helm & Katz, 2001).

Beginning the Project

After project selection, teachers bring children into the process by finding out their interests, their prior knowledge, and their experiences related to the topic. In this phase teachers help children clarify the focus and the questions they have about the topic. Sometimes in the discussions about the topic, lists or graphs are formed; sometimes teachers and children develop a web on the topic.

Developing the Project

From the information gained from the children, the teachers use curriculum webs or lists to develop the next phase. This phase focuses on information gathering about the questions children have. The children, usually working in small groups on subtopics related to the main topic under investigation, take initiative and responsibility for data gathering. Children use books, people, and other sources to gather information. Often there are field trips, revisiting the same location more than once. Using the information gathered, children work on representing what they know through making constructions, drawing charts, and using art media to show their findings (Helm & Katz, 2001).

During this phase teachers reconsider the progress, the new knowledge of the children, and other relevant questions that emerge as they learn new information. Children may decide on new investigations as their interests continue.

Concluding the Project

At some point teachers become aware of waning interests in the topic. With the guidance of the teacher, the children plan and conduct a culminating activity through which the story of the investigation and its findings are summarized and shared (Helm & Katz, 2001).

STRENGTHEN INTELLECTUAL DISPOSITIONS

Within a curriculum that supports inquiry, children develop intellectual dispositions more than content of a topic. Also, the learning of academic skills of reading, writing, and mathematics develops through the activities children do. When guiding the inquiry process with children, it is important to provide ample opportunities for children to develop intellectual dispositions through inquiry. Intellectual dispositions grow as children predict and check predictions, speculate about cause and effect, seek solutions to problems, and find things out. They will be making sense of their experiences at a very young age (Helm & Katz, 2001).

Any of the curricula reviewed in this chapter can engender these intellectual dispositions in young children. The particular topic studied provides a focus. As teachers and children are engaged on that topic, there is ample opportunity for intellectual dispositions to develop.

INVESTMENT IN INQUIRY CURRICULUM

In any of the curriculum choices that include inquiry, teachers necessarily will be involved in the inquiry themselves. As they observe the processes of the children, they will participate in the exploring, the discussions, and the planning for the next steps. As children divulge their processes through words and actions, teachers move along with them to develop the materials and plans as together they take the ideas further. This will take invention, creativity, and the ability to actuate the process as it develops.

This is not an easy task; it takes an investment and requires support through fellow teachers and the space and time to develop new ideas. The result is a classroom teeming with excitement, as children take great strides in learning.

SUMMARY

Within a variety of curriculum choices, involvement of inquiry can be imbedded in a framework where learning is integrated. Even though the experiences detailed in later chapters (14 through 19) are presented as a particular inquiry experience, you will see these naturally come together as integrated curriculum, connecting science and math with reading, writing, discussions, art, technology use, physical skills, emotional and social development. In the next chapter you will envision carefully planned environments for supporting inquiry in an integrated curriculum.

TO FURTHER YOUR THINKING

1. What do you value in the inquiry process for young learners? As you think of young children learning, what are the important processes that you believe children should experience? Discuss this with your colleagues or journal about your choices.

2. Explain to a colleague three premises of developmentally appropriate practice as described in this chapter. List an example for each premise. Then look up the examples of DAP in the book of that title (Bredekamp & Copple, 1997).

3. Reflect on an occasion when your process of inquiry was supported or not supported by teachers or other adults. What was your motivation to search for understanding? How did you respond to the adult's action with you? What did you do because of or in spite of that response?

4. Compare meaning-centered and mindless curriculum. Discuss whether the intellectual dispositions given at the end of this chapter (p. 196) would be involved in each.

5. Reread the anecdote on gardening play in the sand (page 191) and discuss how learning occurs in two ways in that play.

6. Briefly explain each of following curricula listed in the chapter: thematic planning, constructivist, Reggio approach, and project approach. Using the Additional Resources at the end of the chapter, look up emergent curriculum (Jones & Nimmo, 1994; Jones, Evans & Rencken, 2001) and the study (Dodge, Colker, & Heroman, 2002). Look for similarities across all these curricula.

REFERENCES

Bredekamp, S., and Copple, C. (Eds.). (1997). *Developmentally appropriate practice in early childhood programs.* Washington, DC: National Association for the Education of Young Children.

Bredekamp, S., and Rosegrant, R. (Eds.). (1992). *Reaching potentials: Appropriate curriculum and assessment for young children.* Vol. 1. Washington, DC: National Association for the Education of Young Children.

Bredekamp, S., and Rosegrant R. (Eds.). (1995). *Reaching potentials: Transforming early childhood curriculum and assessment.* Vol. 2. Washington, DC: National Association for the Education of Young Children.

Fu, V. R., Stremmel, A. J., and Hill, L. T. (2002). *Teaching and learning: Collaborative exploration of the Reggio Emilia Approach.* Upper Saddle River, NJ: Pearson Education.

Fraser, S., and Gestwicki, C. (2002). *Authentic childhood: Exploring Reggio Emilia in the classroom.* Clifton Park, NY: Thomson Delmar Learning.

DeVries, R., and Kohlberg, L. (1987). *Constructivist early education: Overview and comparison with other programs.* Washington, DC: National Association for the Education of Young Children.

DeVries, R., Zan, B., Hildebrandt, C., Edmiaston, R., and Sales, C. (2002). *Developing constructivist early childhood curriculum: Practical principles and activities.* New York: Teachers College Press.

Helm, J. H., and Beneke, S. (Eds.). (2003). *The power of projects: Meeting contemporary challenges in early childhood classrooms—Strategies and solutions.* New York: Teachers College Press.

Helm, J. H., and Katz, L. (2001). *Young investigators: The project approach in the early years.* New York: Teachers College Press.

Jones, E., and Nimmo, J. (1994). *Emergent curriculum.* Washington, DC: National Association for the Education of Young Children.

Katz, L. (1994). *The project approach.* Champaign, IL: ERIC Clearinghouse on Elementary and Early Childhood Education.

National Association for the Education of Young Children. (2003). NAEYC standards for early childhood professional preparation: Initial licensure programs. In M. Hyson (Ed.), *Preparing early childhood professionals: NAEYC's standards for programs* (pp. 17–63). Washington, DC: Author.

Oken-Wright, P., and Gravett, M. (2002). Big ideas and the essence of intent. In Fu, V. R., Stremmel, A. J., and Hill, L. T. (Eds.), *Teaching and learning: Collaborative exploration of the Reggio Emilia approach* (pp. 197–220). Upper Saddle River, NJ: Pearson Education.

ADDITIONAL RESOURCES

Cadwell, L. B. (1997). *Bringing Reggio Emilia home.* New York: Teachers College Press. This and the following journal both tell the story of learning Reggio Emilia in Italy and developing a similar program in the United States.

Cadwell, L. B. (2002). *The Reggio Approach to early children education: Bringing learning to life.* New York: Teachers College Press.

Chaillé, C., and Britain, L. (2003). *The young child as scientist: A constructivist approach to early childhood science education* (3rd ed.). Boston: Allyn & Bacon. The authors develop the premise for the constructivist approach to curriculum.

Davidson, J. (1996). *Emergent literacy and dramatic play in early education.* Clifton Park, NY: Thomson Delmar Learning. This easily read book exemplifies how literacy can develop in play.

Dodge, D. T., Colker, L. J., and Heroman, C. (2002). *The creative curriculum for preschool* (4th ed.). Washington, DC: Teaching Strategies. Chapter 4 contains excellent questions on selecting a topic for study and steps in planning a study. www.TeachingStrategies.com

Edwards, C., Gandini, L., and Forman, G. (Eds.). (1998). *The hundred languages of children: The Reggio Emilia approach—Advanced reflections.* Westport, CT: Ablex. Many contributors tell the story of Reggio Emilia in Italy and the United States. Fascinating stories of projects can be found in Part III and Part IV. Note especially the photo essay in Chapter 13.

Helm, J. H., and Beneke, S. (Eds.). (2003). *The power of projects: Meeting contemporary challenges in early childhood classrooms—Strategies and solutions.* New York: Teachers College Press. Also available from NAEYC. www.naeyc.org

Jones, E., Evans, K., and Rencken, K. S. (2001). The lively kindergarten: Emergent curriculum in action. Washington, DC: National Association for the Education of Young Children. The process of developing emergent curriculum in kindergartens and how they work. www.naeyc.org

Jones, E., and Reynolds, G. (1997). *Master players: Learning from children at play.* New York: Teachers College Press. Learning comes alive from the anecdotes of children at play.

Videos

Teaching the whole child in kindergarten [Video]. Developed by Stephanie Feeney, McInerny Foundation. This video captures the elements of appropriate teaching and assessment in two kindergartens. Available from www.naeyc.org.

The creative curriculum for preschool [Video]. Washington, DC: Teaching Strategies. www.teachingstrategies.com

Room arrangement as a teaching strategy [Video]. Washington, DC: Teaching Strategies. www.teachingstrategies.com

Web Sites

www.ecap.crc.uiuc.edu ERIC. Early Childhood Education. This Web site has resources on Reggio Emilia education in the United States. These resources can be accessed at the Early Childhood and Parenting Collaborative (ECAP) Web site Information Center.

www.ecap.crc.uiuc.edu The Project Approach, Popular Topic Web site can be accessed here.

www.mpi.wayne.edu Reggio Children promotes Reggio Emilia education in the United States through its office at the Merrill-Palmer Institute, Wayne State University.

Chapter 13
Environments

All of us [children, teachers, and parents] have the right to spend our days in school surrounded by places and spaces that will enhance our lives, support our growth, and hold us in respectful ways. (Cadwell, 2003, p. 117)

The principle of active learning requires that the classroom have a stimulating environment that offers children many choices, provokes them to engage in many activities, and encourages them to explore a wide variety of materials. (Fraser & Gestwicki, 2002, p. 109)

LABORATORY FOR INQUIRY

Aesthetic is relating to beauty in the environment, either natural or planned.

The preceding quotes help frame the quality of environments for young children and adults from the perspective of the Reggio approach. These quotes embrace the essence of **aesthetic** and inviting places for young children to learn and for teachers and parents to enjoy. Both indoor and outdoor spaces are planned for investigation, creative expression, and play. The respect for the child's work shows in the careful organization of space, the detail of placement of materials, and the documentation of what occurs in these spaces.

In explaining use of space in Reggio Emilia programs, Lella Gandini (1998, p. 177) declares, "The environment is seen here as educating the child; in fact it is considered as 'the third educator' along with the team of two teachers." While focusing on redesigning the environment for children, a group of teachers began by asking themselves about the use of space in the classrooms.

1. How well does the room reflect the values we have identified as important to us?
2. What overall messages will the room convey to children, parents, and other visitors to the classroom?
3. How will the environment mirror an image of the child that is rich, powerful, and competent?
4. How well does the arrangement of the room reflect our respect for children, families, and the community? (Fraser & Gestwicki, 2002, p. 106)

With respect to those whose space it is, especially the children, the classroom arena takes on new significance. Teachers can look at a classroom focusing on these values of learning:

- Children are participants in planning and using space.
- Space is created as the laboratory for investigative work.
- The classroom is a beautiful setting for all who live and learn in it.

Since children are full players in the space, they can become co-constructors in it. As children participate in the changes in their school environment, children feel an ownership of their own space and appreciate it more. A small group can organize a collection of materials, or the class can decide on placement of an object being added to the classroom. When children jointly create and share, they tend to care for their space more.

SERIOUS WORK AND BEAUTY REFLECTED IN CLASSROOM SPACE

By carefully carving out space for investigative work, children understand from their teachers that exploring and experimenting are taken seriously. Children will find space to dig for worms outdoors, create a new challenge with pendulums, build a structure taller than themselves, or use ample time to apply tempera paint to Plexiglas easels. When children want to save their work for further examination, space is arranged so children can keep the work for revisiting again. The participants in ongoing inquiry create the space and materials to explore their ideas as far as teachers and children decide to go.

The space can be a place where children and adults feel the existing beauty. Since the school experience is alive with actions and enjoyment, spaces and objects change as the people using the space grow and change. Decisions necessarily include an eye for aesthetic arrangement. "A beautiful environment informs children how to behave and interact with others. Surrounded by beauty, children are motivated to create beauty themselves" (Seefeldt, 2002, p. 97). Some ways of highlighting this beauty are the simple clean lines and occasional splashes of color in the children's work. For a thoughtful array of materials in areas of the classroom, an artistic display may include combinations or careful sorting in baskets or clear containers. Sometimes there are baskets of assorted pine cones set out with clay, a collection of rocks set next to the balance scales, or a flashlight placed with a collection of shiny collage materials. Sometimes an item is displayed attractively

An organized and attractive classroom with attention to detail invites children and adults into the space.

in an interest area, such as fresh flowers placed to catch the light in the art area or tiny bright red and blue blocks arranged on a tray on the shelf above unit blocks. This attention to detail in an organized space brings out the awareness of qualities that arouse pleasure in those who view and use the classroom.

The National Science Education Standards articulate aspects of an organized environment for science inquiry.

STANDARDS

Teachers of science design and manage learning environments that provide students with the time, space, and resources needed for learning science. In doing this, teachers

- Structure the time available so that students are able to engage in extended investigations.
- Create a setting for student work that is flexible and supportive of science inquiry.
- Ensure a safe working environment.
- Make available science tools, materials, media, and technological resources accessible to students.
- Identify and use resources outside the school.
- Engage students in designing the learning environment.

Teaching Standard D. Reprinted with permission from *National science education standards.* (1996). The National Academy of Sciences, courtesy of the National Academies Press, Washington, DC (p. 43).

SPACE AND FLEXIBILITY

Some particular topics of study may take a small space, others a large section of the classroom or space outdoors. While some activities can have a "home" in a particular interest area, often these will go beyond an area into other, more spacious areas of the classroom. Teachers will think flexibly to consider expanding to bigger areas or choosing alternate areas for projects. For example, the study of construction to new heights naturally would start in the block area. As children try to construct taller structures, their ideas lead to building at the woodworking bench. As teachers see the potential for building even a taller structure, this leads to outdoor space. So as projects grow, the area or the location may grow and flow from one area to another.

MATERIALS FOR EXPLORATION

As teachers respond to children's interests, in one or more phases they will gather materials for the exploration and study. Some will be found in storage, yet teachers will need to reach out to the community to find to others. For example, with the study of earthworms, containers for the worms and potting soil will be needed. Since during the spring and summer worms can easily be found outdoors, tools for digging will be supplied. When a large container for the earthworm **habitat** will be needed, teachers make requests to families, find a recyclable item, or make a purchase.

As the classroom is a laboratory, a wide variety of tools and materials will be available for study of a particular topic. As materials are introduced, these are thoughtfully presented in inviting ways. The room will take on a different appearance as children focus on a new topic.

Habitat is a natural or planned environment where a particular plant or animal will thrive.

ATTRACTIVE ORGANIZED STORAGE

As projects grow, so does the supply of materials. Careful attention to the ways these are stored and presented has a tremendous impact on how materials are used. Materials must be accessible by children and adults. Louise Cadwell (2003) describes the detailed storage in the schools of the St. Louis-Reggio.

> On the low shelves transparent jars of shells, buttons, beads, wires, tiny pine cones, dried rose petals, sequins in the shape of flowers, and spiral shavings from colored pencils reflect the light and reveal their enticing contents to both children and adults. Children know where things are and can find them. So do the teachers and so do the parents. The environment is useful and plentiful and organized. What is here is being used and loved. (pp. 117–18)

Adults, along with children, often take a fresh look at materials to keep them up-to-date. As items lose their appeal, the children's interest wanes.

Organized storage of art materials makes them easily accessible.

ANECDOTE

In one Reggio-inspired Head Start classroom of Chicago Commons in Chicago, teachers and children asked parents to bring in recycled materials for their study. Huge garbage bags of materials appeared. Children started going through them, and they had many ideas of what to do with this "beautiful junk." Interesting projects emerged, but as interest waned, the piles children had sorted looked even junkier. The teachers asked the children what to do next. Children wanted to put the recycled plastic plates and cups in the housekeeping, and teachers wanted the large pop bottles for terrariums, but the rest was put in the proper recycle bins. It was time to start new.

DISPLAY AREAS

Display of children's work, photos of recent activities, and documentation (Chapter 9) have a place in the classroom and in the spaces leading to the classroom. As to where to place these, first consider their purpose and who will view them. If the parents and visitors will be the main viewers, the placement will be where adults enter the school or classroom. If the display is to promote review and revisiting for the children, it will be placed low in classroom spaces where children can easily view it.

In organization of wall displays, consider the impact of the amount of materials shown. Carol Seefeldt (2002) explains, "When walls are filled with work, children have no way to focus on a display and reflect on their past experiences or extend their current work. The clutter distracts their eyes and their brains become overloaded with things to think about, so they turn away, avoiding the cacophony they see on the walls" (p. 100). Wall space will contain attractive exhibits as well as open space.

OUTDOOR ENVIRONMENTS: A LABORATORY OF EXPLORATION

The purpose of the outdoor play space is to expend energy, run, climb, and ride, all of which cannot be done to the same degree indoors. Outdoor space also provides places to examine nature, experiment with physical science, and explore earth science. In all this children's creative and dramatic play naturally occur.

Regarding the space used for playgrounds, it is helpful to divide the area into these four kinds of spaces:

1. A smooth-surfaced area
2. Climbing and physical activity areas

3. Sand area
4. Nature area

Because of the amount of space in a playground and its location—urban or rural—it is difficult to prescribe space allotment for each of these areas. For the topic of outdoor space, this chapter focuses on the rich possibilities for inquiry in each type of space. For teachers using an already designed space, the information here can be used to expand current uses. When encountering new design options for outdoor space, these ideas can be incorporated into a design for inquiry to obtain the utmost use for this from the space available (see Additional Resources).

A Smooth-Surfaced Area

A smooth surface of cement or asphalt is necessary for wheeled toys and the physical movement of children's bodies. As they gain skills in using their body, children also experience physical science as they maneuver the tricycles, pull wagons, and run freely. For these activities it is best to have an elliptical or round area, as this follows the natural path of the wheeled toys. In addition, a more expansive smooth surface allows for block building with the larger hollow blocks and boards. This constructive play with blocks and boards can lead to dramatic play by adding simple props. This space also lends itself to the creative arts by adding easel, table, and art supplies. With the proper equipment and close supervision, woodworking works well outdoors away from traffic areas. Additionally, on the hard surface water play can be added as weather permits, with equipment like the sprinkler and water table with plastic pipe and connectors and other water flow materials (see Fig. 17–1).

Climbing and Physical Activity Areas

On climbing structures children can "develop their bodies and experience basic physics—gravity, pendulums, inertia, the optics of being upside down" (Rivkin, 1995, p. 22). These structures can be simple with one activity in mind, such as a tire swing, or an integrated structure with such items as stairs, tunnels, bridges, slides, and lofts that challenge various locomotor abilities. Structures can also feature spaces that foster imagination. Inventive playground design can incorporate structures representing the community into places of play, such as the boat when the town sits at the water's edge. Other play structures for physical activity can be a grassy hill for climbing, a log for rolling, or a large sewer pipe big enough to crawl through or stand inside.

Sand Area

For sand play a large area can serve as several play spaces for children, featuring different tools for various sand areas. Or a small area can serve this same purpose by having the materials change to follow children's interests. A beginning list of materials to extend inquiry in sand play includes:

- Boards and boxes and blocks
- Pails and shovels and troughs
- A pulley system to move buckets of sand across or up to a higher level
- Transportation toys
- Props for dramatic play

When weather permits, the combination of water with the sand changes its consistency. Children can then mold the sand and, with addition of boards and plastic, create "ponds and streams" in sand. Water and sand together provide a rich medium for the creation of dioramas and for creativity and dramatic play.

For sand areas outdoors, special precautions are needed to keep animals out of this area for health reasons. This often means covering the sandbox when not in use.

Nature Area

In small city spaces the area for plants and small animal life may be shortchanged. With careful planning even small playgrounds can have this presence. When planned with a careful eye to combining various plants and closed and open areas, the nature area of any playground can be a rich garden for forays of exploration.

A small garden along the playground fence can provide ongoing beauty and study.

Vegetation can become an aesthetically pleasing landscape. Perhaps it only skirts the yard with some varieties of shrubs, trees, bulbs, and **perennials.** The presence of shade from one or more trees is welcome in the summer sun. With perennials blooming at different times, teachers and children can anticipate their blooms and incorporate them into curriculum as appropriate.

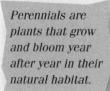

Perennials are plants that grow and bloom year after year in their natural habitat.

When there is enough area for variety, plant tall grasses and design paths through the grass for children to explore. For urban children there is even more need for these places where they can explore islands of nature. Inside these natural spaces children can find "long grass to crawl through; bushes to hide in and to pick leaves from for play food; and sticks to make . . . spoons, signs, and other creations" (Moore, 1990) (as cited in Rivkin, 1995, p. 24).

Vegetation will support animal life. When small insects—such as ants and sow bugs—butterflies, robins, and squirrels inhabit the outdoor space, children can observe them firsthand. When the time comes to capture a worm or insect for an hour or two, they can be viewed easily indoors or outdoors and then let free in their habitat. By planning the vegetation to support a butterfly habitat or importing insects to live in the natural arena within the playground, teachers can strengthen children's firsthand knowledge of these friendly creatures.

Planning a Butterfly Garden Inviting butterflies (and moths) into your outdoor space is as easy as growing flowers. Both will probably find the flowers in your playground no matter what kinds of flowers are there, but planning a **butterfly garden** will make sure they'll flit in your direction.

A butterfly garden is an area planned with the kinds of plants and environment that attracts butterflies.

First, you need some sun. Butterflies can feed in shade, but they must have sun to charge their energy batteries. On cool mornings, have you noticed how butterflies stand around, slowly opening and closing their wings? (They also won't fly away when the young child goes to inspect them.) This inactivity is called *basking,* and it's how cold-blooded butterflies gather solar energy. For this you can put some flat, dark colored stones in a spot that gets morning sun and watch the butterflies use the sun-warmed stones as their warm-up room.

An easy way to attract butterflies is through planting flowers they like.
Photo courtesy Patrick Clark.

To attract the greatest number of butterflies and have them as residents, you will need to have plants that serve the needs of all their life stages. They need a place to lay eggs, form a chrysalis, and have plenty of nectar sources for the adult. Usually butterflies lay their eggs on the same plant that the larva and caterpillars will eat. The milkweed is the choice of the Monarch.

For the adults of these different species, grow flowers that produce nectar. Give butterflies what they need by growing what they like. This will make it impossible for them to stay away. Plants that are native to your region not only are more likely to grow and survive but also provide the specific foods that native butterflies and moths rely on. As long as your garden includes plenty of flowers, preferably the nectar-rich types with fewer petals (single flowers), you will still see plenty of butterflies (Krischik, n.d.; Bailey n.d.). Use a search engine (search "butterfly garden") to find information on the plants and butterflies native to your area.

Gardening and Digging Each classroom needs a place to plant. For some, there will be an individual plot of ground for each class. For others, there will be **planter boxes**, perhaps starting these on a classroom windowsill and later moving them outdoors to get full sunlight.

Children need a place to dig—a place that will not disturb any plantings. Small shovels and containers and a board to sit on will support their digging. A planned barrier to separate this area can be formed from shrubs or smooth rocks.

Planter boxes are containers for small plants for indoor or outdoor use.

MATERIALS FOR INQUIRY OUTDOORS

To support inquiry, teachers can have materials on hand that promote it. Teachers can arrange to store items in sturdy Ziploc® bags and to place these bags on hooks in the storage area. If there is no outdoor storage, a prepacked book bag can contain these same items and be carried out to the playground. Either way children and teachers can obtain these easily for investigation.

This list of instruments and supplies can start the process of gathering the tools to support exploring outdoors. As children investigate more, additional tools may be needed.

1. For looking closely at plants, animals, and earth, have an assortment of bug catchers—some have a magnifying glass built in—additional magnifying glasses, dirt sifters or a colander to sift dirt and sand, small Ziploc bags, and plastic containers to store leaves and other found treasures.
2. For earth science, have on hand a rain gauge, prisms, mirrors, color paddles, and small containers to collect rain, snow, and ice.
3. To help budding mechanics assist with examination or small repairs, simple tools such as a screw driver, a tack hammer, a pair of pliers, lubricating oil, a flashlight, and sand paper can be used with close supervision.
4. For discoveries of outdoor phenomena, children can record their findings through drawing, recording, and graphing on small clipboards with notepads and primary pencils.

SAFETY IN AND OUT OF THE CLASSROOM

Because the materials for inquiry curriculum go beyond the usual list of what is available in an early childhood classroom, safety of use is an issue. When planning activities and materials, these five guidelines can help keep children safe indoors and outside:

1. Carefully look over materials coming into the classroom or materials found outdoors. They should be free of harmful materials, sharp edges, and breakable objects.

    Examples: Wood that is used for projects will not have splinters.

    Recycled materials that come from a collection from homes or outdoors will be washed.

2. Teach yourself to recognize and label harmful plants, parts of plants, and animal life. Use reliable resources to become knowledgeable.

    Examples: Black locust seeds (in a large brown pod) that children may find on walks can be harmful if ingested.

    Green or spoiled potatoes if eaten may cause vomiting.

    Common philodendron, a house plant, can be very dangerous if any part is ingested (Moore, 2002; Starbuck, Olthof, & Midden, 2002).

    In the spider family, most are not poisonous but some do bite. Best to handle (carefully) only the harmless daddy longlegs. (Starbuck, Olthof, & Midden, 2002).

3. Teach children how to use all materials safely. This does not take the place of supervision, as it is the adult who is ultimately responsible.

    Examples: Teach children to hold boards or 2 × 4's low as they move them around.

    Teach children to examine their building structure to see if it is secure by testing it with their hands before attempting to walk on it.

    Teach children to wash hands after handling a living being and after using water (in play) that other children share.

4. Try out handling new materials yourself before bringing these into the project so you can anticipate unsafe uses. Then observe children using new materials to note unsafe uses. Alter the materials and teach children safe use.

    Examples: Before offering a new woodworking tool, use it yourself to understand safe use.

    As children try out a pendulum hung from the ceiling, anticipate the arc of the pendulum swing. Change the material or length of the pendulum.

    Require safety goggles for children handling tools and materials that could cause eye injury.

5. Supervise, supervise, supervise.

    a. Whatever the children are exploring, the adult must be aware of their activity and the materials they find.

    Example: Teach children to show you the different things they may find outdoors.

b. The adult must be constantly present and focused on children as they use tools and appliances such as sharp tools or cooking appliances.

Examples: On the playground children turn over the wagon and, with tools, "work on" the mechanical aspects of the underside of the wagon. One teacher constantly watches the children as they work with tools.

While using an electric skillet to cook eggs, the teacher shows how to use the spatula and keep hands from the hot surface. During cooking the teacher always remains seated with a small group. When the activity is stopped the skillet is placed away from the children.

Sometimes there is fine line between children being safe and the natural urge of children to explore and construct with materials themselves. Teaching safety will help children develop skills in using materials in safe ways. This teaching will emphasize that children will only use particular tools and materials in the presence of an adult at home or in school. Safety will always be in the consciousness of the teachers. Teachers will err on the side of keeping children safe.

SUMMARY

There is beauty in materials, in their arrangement, and in displays of children's work. The ways these are displayed brings this beauty into the lives of all who enjoy the indoor and outdoor space. These spaces become the laboratory for active inquiry. Care in the organization of space and selection of materials will enhance children's investigations, not limit them. Once understanding this organization of space, you will be more able to plan curriculum, whether for a long-term study or one single experience. This chapter completes Part 1, "Theory and Inquiry." The seven chapters that follow in Part 2, "Inquiry Curriculum," emphasize enabling powerful inquiry curriculum, first in math and then in science.

TO FURTHER YOUR THINKING

1. Consider a room in a home or a familiar building in which you feel a sense of beauty. In your mind picture yourself in that space and sense the spaces all around you. What makes that place attractive to you? Share this sense of

beauty with your colleagues. What comparisons can you make with each of your mind pictures?

2. In teams, stroll around your campus or building to find an attractive wall arrangement or a beautiful space. Compare with your team about which basics of design attract you to this: color, line, texture, and/or composition. What aspects of these would you apply in a classroom to create "Islands of Beauty"? For more on this discussion, see Chapter 2 in *Creating Rooms of Wonder* by Seefeldt (2002).

3. What message does an arrangement or display in a classroom that is aesthetically designed say to children, parents, and other adults who view it?

4. Visit a playground designed for young children. Draw a simple diagram and identify any of the four kinds of spaces you observe in the playground.
   - Smooth-surfaced area
   - Climbing and physical activity areas
   - Sand area
   - Nature area

5. If children are present in the playground you visit, what spaces are they using? Label the number of children in each play area at a given point in time. What kinds of spaces do the children prefer?

6. What natural materials do you recall either playing with or observing children using in play, such at pebbles, sticks, or dandelions? What were you taught about using these or what did you convey to children using these? What safety concerns are there in using any of these materials?

7. Recall some of your early experiences playing outdoors or visiting natural areas such as a park. What were you attracted to in nature? What did you learn about plants and animals?

REFERENCES

Cadwell, L. B. (2003). *Bringing learning to life: The Reggio approach to early childhood education.* New York: Teacher's College Press.

Fraser, S., and Gestwicki, C. (2002). *Authentic childhood: Exploring Reggio Emilia in the classroom.* Clifton Park, NY: Thomson Delmar Learning.

Gandini, L. (1998). Educational and caring spaces. In Edwards, C., Gandini, L., and Forman G. (Eds.). *The hundred languages of children: The Reggio Emilia approach—Advanced reflections* (2nd ed.) (pp. 161–78). Westport, CT: Ablex.

Krischik, V. (n.d.). *Creating a butterfly garden* [Online]. www.extension.umn.edu

Bailey, S. (n.d.). *How to make butterfly gardens* [Online]. Entomology/Agriculture, University of Kentucky. www.uky.edu

Moore, R. C. (2002). *Plants for play: A plant selection guide for children's outdoor environments.* Berkeley, CA: MIG Communications.

National Academy of Science. (1996). *National science education standards* [Book version, online]. Washington, DC: National Academies Press. www.nap.edu

Rivkin, M. S. (1995). *The great outdoors: Restoring children's right to play outside.* Washington, DC: National Association for the Education of Young Children.

Seefeldt, C. (2002). *Creating rooms of wonder: Valuing and displaying children's work to enhance the learning process.* Beltsville, MD: Gryphon House.

Starbuck, S., Olthof, M., and Midden, K. (2002). *Hollyhocks and honeybees: Garden projects for young children.* St. Paul, MN: Redleaf Press.

ADDITIONAL RESOURCES

Althouse, R., Johnson, M. H., and Mitchell, S. T. (2003). *The colors of learning: Integrating the visual arts into the early childhood curriculum.* New York: Teachers College Press. This bright and alive book combines the children's experiences in art with the whole curriculum, including science, and points the way that the curriculum can be displayed through the children's art work. Also available through www.naeyc.org.

Estes, Y. B. (1993, May). Environmental education: Bringing children and nature together. *Phi Delta Kappan* 74: Special report. This account describes the creation of an elementary school environment that supports plants and animals that the children, community, and staff work together to maintain.

Moore, R. C. (2002). *Plants for play: A plant selection guide for children's outdoor environments.* Berkeley, CA: MIG Communications. This extensive description and charts of plants for playgrounds describes purposes according to children. Includes list of poisonous plants and pesticides according to the amount of toxicity. www.migcom.com

Moore, R. C., Goltsman. S. M., and Iacofano, D. S. (Eds.). (1992). *Play for all: Guidelines. Planning, design and management of outdoor play settings for all children* (2nd ed.). Berkeley, CA: MIG Communications. This book takes the reader on a thorough tour of plans for playgrounds, incorporating inviting approaches for play and including detailed plans for inclusion. www.migcom.com

Seefeldt, C. (2002). *Creating rooms of wonder: Valuing and displaying children's work to enhance the learning process.* Beltsville, MD: Gryphon House. This handy book is an excellent source of practical suggestions to build in the beauty that comes from children's work and creating environments that highlight their learning. www.gryphonhouse.com

Starbuck, S., Olthof, M., and Midden, K. (2002). *Hollyhocks and honeybees: Garden projects for young children.* St. Paul, MN: Redleaf Press. Thorough text on planting with children. Lists insects and animals that could be harmful as well as a chart on poisonous plants. www.redleafpress.org

Titman, W. (1994). *Special places, special people: The hidden curriculum of school grounds.* Surrey, UK: Wild World Fund for Nature/Learning through Landscapes Trust. This book exemplifies the ways playgrounds can support nature study.

Web Sites

www.ansci.cornell.edu/plants and www.health.ucsd.edu/poison These two sites have information on poisonous plants and plant parts.

www.cdacouncil.org The Council for Professional Recognition's on-line bookstore (paid publications) features this book, *Children's spaces and relations: Metaproject for an environment for young children.* This thorough discussion of the project is from the Reggio approach.

www.extension.umn.edu Krischik, V. (n.d.). *Creating a butterfly garden.* This helpful resource was found under "butterfly garden" on the Web.

www.gardensalive.com This is one supply for beneficial insects for the garden.

www.kidsgardening.com This helpful site has information on children's gardens and grants to support children's gardens.

www.reeusda.gov Access this site to find your state community gardening coordinator for information on plants right for your area.

www.uky.edu Bailey, S. (n.d.). *How to make a butterfly garden.* This resource is published through Entomology department of University of Kentucky.

Part Two

Inquiry Curriculum

Chapter 14

Exploring Basic Math and Number Sense

OBJECTIVES Through the process of discovery in this chapter, you will be able to:

1. Develop math experiences using basic math and the number sense in the daily classroom life.
   a. Taking attendance
   b. Setting the table
   c. Preparing for snack
   d. Selecting activities
   e. Cleaning up
   f. Organizing materials and making plans

2. Discuss involving children in problem solving using divergent thinking with math.

3. Recognize how organization of materials and containers can promote development of basic math and number skills.

4. Describe planning a range of math materials to match the developing skills in young children.

5. Use simple board games to advance math skills in one-to-one correspondence, comparing, classifying, making sets, and using numbers.

6. Identify three stages of graphing that extend learning in basic math and number sense.

7. Recognize issues of equity in selecting subjects for graphing.

8. Use estimation of reasonable amounts for data analysis and probability.

9. Discuss developing an inquiry topic to promote basic math and number sense.

10. Discuss involvement of math in inquiry topics.

IDEAS TO PONDER

- What daily classroom activities can involve math?

- What kinds of activities and materials promote basic math and number sense?

- How do children understand graphing?
- How can board games promote understanding in basic math and number sense?

- How can children develop realistic estimation?
- How can an inquiry topic promote math?

Children engage in all sorts of everyday activities that involve mathematics and, as a result, develop a considerable body of informal knowledge. (Barody & Wilkins, 1999, p. 49)

Children actively construct meaningful mathematical knowledge. . . . [It] is an active problem solving process in that children try to make sense of personally important tasks and devise solutions for them. It entails reorganizing our thinking—broadening our perspective. (Baroody & Wilkins, 1999, p. 50)

Adults can foster children's mathematical development by providing environments rich in language, where thinking is encouraged, uniqueness is valued, and exploration is supported. Play is children's work. Adults support young children's diligence and mathematical development when they direct attention to the mathematics children use in their play, challenge them to solve problems, and encourage their persistence. (National Council of Teachers of Mathematics, Standards for grades Pre-K–2)

EXPLORING MEANINGFUL MATH

The current evidence underlines the belief that math is meaningful to young children when used in their daily lives, when appropriate materials are used often, and when problem solving entails math concepts. Informally, as young children encounter math ideas in their play, they often solve problems that relate directly to their emerging math skills.

Tasks and decision making should not become routine, as the goal here is to bring about flexibility in thinking. Questions for children will change as teachers respond to the children's abilities and interests. A new way to approach a task or decision will help children approach math in different ways.

STANDARDS

Apply and adapt a variety of appropriate strategies to solve problems.

MATH IN DAILY ACTIVITIES

For both basic math and the number sense, concepts are integral in many aspects of classroom living. These concepts can be interwoven into the structure of the day and ongoing learning opportunities. In following the developing concepts through the year, these activities do not stay static but evolve as skills develop. The following descriptions of math in everyday activities are intended to be fluid. Table 14–1 shows the fluidity of learning within these everyday experiences.

Taking Attendance

With the various ways to take attendance, children work with different levels of basic math or number sense. At a small group time, where the children are assigned to a particular small group, one child can use a child-friendly (duplicated) daily attendance form to take the attendance of those in his group. He simply highlights the name of each child who is present. The attendance charts of each group are put on the bulletin board. Later, in large group, the teacher can ask questions that compare the small group attendance charts, such as, Which groups have everyone here? Which group has the most, the least, the same number of children? In this method, children use their immediate experience to compare small numbers of children.

Another type of attendance is handled as children enter in the morning. Each child finds her name card printed in manuscript form. She prints her name on a sheet of paper the same size as her name card, each to her own ability, and places her completed card into a pocket on a large pocket chart for daily attendance. Two children are selected daily to monitor the chart. These two monitors find anyone present who has not signed in. Then they make a separate chart using

TABLE 14–1   Math in Daily Activities

Daily Activity	Math Concepts Used: Basic Math/Number Sense
Morning meeting	An individual or group takes attendance and obtains information for the daily weather chart. The group makes decisions on daily jobs and work/play choices. The group makes decisions about classroom plans.
Cleanup time	The group can decide the number of children to complete a task and organize where and how items are stored.
Preparing for snack	A menu card will indicate how many snack items for each or the server decides the number of items served.
Setting the table for lunch	Children select the amount needed for each table setting at the table they are preparing. They can match one to one, make sets, or count.
Cleaning up after lunch	Tableware can be sorted in tubs, such as plates, dishes, glasses, silverware, and discarded items.

the name cards of absent children. During group time they report to the group the absent children. The teacher asks questions appropriate to the group's understanding of more and less and compares numbers of children absent and present. Looking at the classification of present and absent children, children can compare and contrast differences from the charts. As children grow in number ability, the differences in number can also be compared.

Daily counts of children will engage children's growing ability in number. In counting a group the counter will need to realize that she includes herself in the count. At first, the child counts children in a small group and, as counting skills increase, the group size counted is increased to include all the class plus the adults.

Setting the Table

When an individual child or a few selected children set tables, they can work with many math concepts depending on the child's ability. A child can begin with an attendance chart for each table or a set of name cards placed on each table. Or the adult can place the number of chairs at a table indicating the total number who will eat there (including the teacher). The child figures out her own method to get all the items in the table setting to match the set of children at that table. The child can choose the math—from one-to-one correspondence to counting—to accomplish the task.

In order for the child to develop in her own logicomathematical thinking, the teacher does not point out errors. The child can be asked if each place setting has all it needs. If there are still missing items, this may be discovered after children come to the table to eat. Then the child in charge is asked to obtain the missing items.

Preparing Snack

Many math decisions can be a part of snack preparation. Whether children enjoy snack in small groups at a self-selected time or as a large group, math can be built in. One process is for two children to take on the task of snack preparation. Questions about the plan for snack can include, How many items are to be placed on the serving tray or basket? How many will each child have to eat? For some items, it may be one (cracker, apple slice, cheese slice) or one glass (milk, juice). Other items might vary in number (grapes, fish crackers, orange sections).

Using representation, the two children can develop a menu card that lists how many of the snack items each child may select. At first the teacher writes the menu

STANDARDS

Create and use representations to organize, record, and communicate mathematical ideas.

card with the children. As children get the idea, then the teacher writes the words and numbers and child draws the symbols of each food, indicating the amount, such as three cheese cubes or six fish crackers. Later in the year a pair of children can design the snack menu themselves. Most can write the whole menu card although they can always ask an adult or another child for help (Merriweather, 1997).

Selecting Activities

In selecting an interest area for play, teachers often organize self-selection by limiting the number of children who can play in an interest area at one time (so it will not be overcrowded). A chart can show each interest area in the classroom. On each area there is a set of symbols (such as stick figures of children) that indicate the total number who may play in that area. When selecting activities or an interest area for play, each child indicates a choice by placing her name or photo over one of these symbols to indicate her area of choice. When the number of children selecting a particular interest area equals the predetermined number for that area, the child must choose another area.

Cleaning Up

For cleaning up the classroom after play, daily decisions can be made about matching the task with the number of children who will complete cleanup in a particular interest area. For an area that requires a lot of work, the group will allot more children for cleaning up than an area that has only few materials to put away. If the messy work areas change daily, children will be challenged with decisions of dividing the tasks among all the group members.

Within each interest area, the labels of materials on the container match with a label on the shelf. Outlines of shapes, such as the unit blocks and utensils in the housekeeping area, match the particular item. These outlines are helpful so children can figure out by matching where an object or container of materials is stored.

Organizing Materials

Children can be involved in decisions about planning and reorganizing storage of materials in the classroom. When teachers embrace such opportunities for problem solving, they will be using math processes that will enhance flexible thinking. By bringing children into solving real, ongoing decisions, teachers meet Constance Kamii's first principle of teaching, "encourage the child to be alert and to put all kinds of objects, events, and actions into all kinds of relationships" (Kamii, 1982, p. 27).

For example, after a clean-up time when materials are placed haphazardly in a shelf or corner, the teacher can bring this event to the group for discussion. The teacher can ask how the class can organize these materials so putting them away flows smoothly. Children present their ideas and teachers record them. Then the group discusses these suggestions and one or more of their ideas are decided on. Following this, the teacher arranges for a small group to carry out the organizational decision. While reorganizing storage in the room the group becomes involved in flexible thinking through listening to ideas and rethinking the classification of items.

In another example, when materials are all jumbled together, the teacher can ask a small group of children to help sort out the materials during play time. Using extra containers to facilitate sorting, children decide on the sets and sort all the items. Then these children can decide on another way to organize these materials.

Making Plans

As children look forward to a special event, such as a parent's day in their classroom, the total group can develop steps for preparation of the event. Children can take on tasks to prepare for and lead the class and visitors through the event. For example, children can help prepare by dictating invitations, making centerpieces for the snack table, and preparing the food, and, at the event, individuals can lead by greeting the parents, taking parents on tours of their classroom, and inviting them for snack. Mathematical problems the group may encounter in planning include how many items to buy for the snack or finding enough chairs to seat everyone.

Making Fair Decisions

Teachers can involve children in classroom situations that involve fairness for all members. Challenges include deciding on making a new class activity fair to all, or discussing a situation when several children all want the same materials. Involvement with the children in solving everyday situations recognizes their growing ability to be equitable to all.

ANECDOTE

HOW MANY MORE RAISINS FOR EACH?

During snack the small group of children were finishing all the raisins in the bowl. Kayla, the server for that day, said, "There are more raisins." Several children chimed in, "I want more." With the teacher's approval, Kayla poured the rest of the raisins from the package into the bowl.

"How many can we take?"

Kayla shrugged her shoulders.

"What can we do so all can have some?" queried the teacher.

"Each take a bunch."

"How about each take five?"

"Or ten."

"So you suggest each take a bunch, or five, or ten. What is your estimate of how many would be fair for all?" the teacher asked.

"Maybe five." . . . Others nodded. So each child counted out five more raisins and there were only four left in the bowl. All seemed to be satisfied with their solution. "You worked out a solution so everyone had five more raisins."

ANECDOTE

HOW CAN THIS BE FAIR?

When a new math game is made available for free choice time, all the kindergartners clamor to the table.

"I think we need to make a plan so everyone will have an opportunity to try the game. What do you think we should do?" suggests Allan, their teacher.

"Give everyone five minutes" (the usual time for new things).

"But the game may take longer!"

"Shall we see how long it takes?" Allan asks.

Two children play the game while three others alternately start three-minute hour-glass timers when the preceding one is finished. The game is soon finished. "That's three times!" "Each one [timer] makes three minutes."

One child makes tally marks on a piece of paper: three marks in each row. He ends at three rows, then goes back to count his tallies. "Nine minutes for the game. That's a loooong time."

Allan agrees, "That is a long time."

Jeanmarie counts on her fingers, "1–2–3–4–5, for the five-minute timer." And she continues on her other hand, "6–7–8–9. Uhh, we don't have a four-minute timer."

"And three would be too short. Not nine."

"What if we used two fives?" Allan posed the thought.

"No, too long. It's already nine and we want time for everybody."

"I want to play today."

"Me, too."

"We just have to take turns into tomorrow, and maybe tomorrow again."

"Yeah, cause I don't want to stop in the middle."

"We could try ten."

Allan helped them settle it by saying, "Try ten until everybody has a chance to play. Then we can discuss it again."

Divergent thinking is using information to develop different ways of tackling a problem.

The teacher helped them use emerging counting skills as well as **divergent thinking** in learning skills for living equitably.

DEVELOPING MATH MATERIALS FOR DIFFERING ABILITIES

Collections of items form the basis of materials for basic math concepts and for number sense. In any classroom children will be working at a variety of levels in basic math and number sense. Since children will be moving through differing abilities, it is practical to make materials that stretch from simple to more complex. For this, the number of materials can be from three to twenty-five and move from simple classification to making sets of ten.

In addition to planning flexibility in the design, the containers and the materials need to be sturdy and reusable. The storage box, such as a clear plastic shoebox-size container, will be well labeled and stored on a shelf that is also labeled. This will make selection and the return of materials easy. Appendix C, Table C–1, provides a full description of planning materials and the containers for them.

For example, store a collection of assorted large buttons or plastic bottle caps of various sizes and colors (30 to 50) in a clear box. Collect trays and containers for the arrangement of buttons as follows: Muffin tins, ice cube trays, and clear plastic egg cartons can be containers for children to lay out items one to one or by matching. Individual flannel boards and placemats (such as Scoot–Guard tableware from marine suppliers) can provide surfaces for classification and making sets (Appendix C, Table C–1).

For a second example, store a collection of aquarium glass (silver dollar size) or large, similarly shaped rocks in a clear container. Children can make their own arrangements of these items on a table top. Use circles of heavy yarn for children to make sets of the objects. For counting, supply index cards with the numeral (sign) and dots to indicate the amount in symbols. Children can choose the card they want to follow and make a set of that number (Fig. 14–1). The teacher can predetermine which cards to make available. When ready for more challenge,

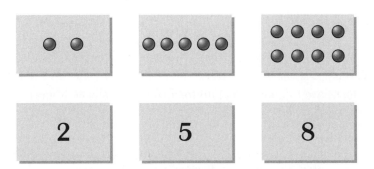

Figure 14–1 Index cards show the number in both sign and symbol.

An inviting selection of materials for basic math.

cards with higher numbers are presented (Appendix C, Table C–1, provides a full description of planning materials and the containers for them).

GAMES

Commercial board games, Dominoes, and a deck of cards provide a wealth of experiences for gaining basic math as well as the number sense. With a regular deck of cards one game that advances number sense is the game War. The face cards in the deck are always put aside. For the remaining cards, the adult can determine the numbers children know, such as from 1 to 6 or 1 to 10. Since the cards have both the number sign and the symbols (like three hearts or seven diamonds), children can use either the signs or the symbols to determine which card has the larger amount. In this game, children often select the strategy that fits for the moment, such as counting the symbols or even comparing one to one when the answer is close.

Dominoes is another familiar material useful for number sense. Children will enjoy making a long line around the table matching Domino tiles end to end or standing the tiles in a line. Turn taking provides an order that will be used in board games. Dominoes can also be used as a form of concentration, where one of the ends of the tiles matches the end of a second tile to form a pair.

Board Games

Candyland, Hi-Ho Cherry-O®, and Chutes and Ladders are classic board games for young children. Lotto games and simple Bingo engage the younger child whose first task may be following the sequence of turn taking in a game. By playing or watching one of these games being played, the adult can easily identify the basic math skills in these.

Designing Board Games

A variety of games can be made that emphasize one or more basic math or number skills. Board games have one-to-one correspondence as playing pieces are moved along a path. Die, spinners, or cards can use dots as symbols, numerals, or color matching that give the directions for moves in the board game. In this way the challenge in the game can be matching colors, matching symbols (such as an animal picture on a card matches a place on the path), matching sets, or counting.

A circular path game is the organization of a noncompetitive board game with a circular path for players to follow.

Since competitive games are sometimes difficult for young children, a **circular path game** can be used. In this process, the players move pieces around an oval path on the game board. All participants contribute to a goal, making the game noncompetitive. The player is asked to do a task when landing the playing piece on a specific square, such as collecting tiles that match the kind of flower on the square. These specific pieces can be drawn, made with purchased stickers, or made with computer clip art (Moomaw & Hieronymus, 1999).

With careful planning, a generic board can provide the basis for games with different directions to add interest and challenge that fits a group of children (Charlesworth & Lind, 2003). Directions and playing pieces for each game can be stored in Ziploc bags with the name of the game and its own logo on a card and with printed directions on the back. Directions for three games using one game board are given in Appendix C, Table C–2. Many resources at the end of this chapter give specific directions for games, suggestions for games following favorite books, and other types of appropriate board games for young children.

GRAPHING WITH CHILDREN

Teachers can develop three stages of graphing with young children through applying what children are finding out and representing it in one or more stages of graphing (see Chapter 7). Possibilities of the wide variety of things to be graphed can easily be integrated into the curriculum. Appendix C, Table C–3, has directions for all three types of graphs.

Development of Graphs

The orientation of the graph can be either from left to right (horizontal) or bottom to top (vertical). Over time both orientations can be introduced. A picture of the item is at the left side or the bottom of the column. For these labels, use representations that are not the same as those on the graph itself. Otherwise children will tend to include this item in "reading" the representative graph.

Preparation of the graph can be done ahead of time, but entering the data onto the graph is done with the children. Because children act on their environment in order to understand it, it is important that they participate in placing the data.

Questions Used in Graphing

In the classroom experiences where children use graphing, questioning can lead to further understanding of math concepts. As children think through what they have done in constructing a graph, teachers use appropriate comparing and contrasting questions such as the following:

Which group has more?

Which group has fewer?

How do you know this?

How could we make these two the same size?

What group is this? Why are these children in this group?

What would happen if we added two more of . . . Would that change the result?

Listening to children's responses can help teachers see what they comprehend. Because children are still preoperational thinkers in the preschool years, expectations are simple and ideas are discussed several times. Both preschool and kindergarten children will not be basing answers on the understanding that the amount of items remain constant. Also, children may grasp an understanding of a situation in one instance but not adapt that understanding to a new situation.

EQUITY IN CLASSROOM ACTIVITIES

Carefully chosen activities can eliminate comparisons between boys and girls, ethnic backgrounds, and socioeconomic differences among children in the classroom so children sense the equitable treatment of all. In research on gender-fair curriculum, Wilbur (1991) offers an equation of a gender-fair curriculum as one that

- Acknowledges and affirms variation, that is, similarities and differences among and within groups of people;
- Is inclusive, allowing both females and males to find and identify positively with messages about themselves; and

- Is integrated, weaving together the experiences, needs, and interests of both males and females (as cited in Marshall, Robeson, & Keefe, 1999, p. 12).

What Wilbur says along gender lines is also true of ethnicity and socioeconomic status. For example, ways of getting to school might be decided along socioeconomic lines, such as whether a family has a car or has a parent at home during the day. In some situations, the types of shoes or coats children wear could be decided along gender or economic lines. Teachers will need to analyze carefully the children and the families they represent so the subjects chosen do not arbitrarily sort children.

One goal in early education is for each child to be autonomous; yet children want to be "normal" and often vote for the most popular choice. For example, a child may not want to be seen as the shortest in the room or be the only one who likes vanilla ice cream.

A show of hands in voting promotes popular voting as well as the problem that the child may not grasp that voting only once is fair. Instead, as part of a transitional activity children can vote by placing a block in a basket labeled "Yes" or "No." Or a pair can poll classmates during a free choice activity and tally the answers.

By using a mystery bag that has a selection of cubes or teddy bear counters, materials for a graph can be selected by classmates through chance rather than choice (Smith, 2001). When using materials that each child finds by chance, teachers will stay clear of equity issues. In continuing graphing, teachers can carefully select other choices that are equitable.

ESTIMATION

Estimation is providing a rough guess.

Estimation of possibilities is an important math concept. Experiences that build on what children know can be used for estimation. Estimation should be based on a grouping of items children know something about. For numbers over 10 and guesses with items that are unfamiliar to them, estimation becomes a guess that has little meaning. As children join in an estimation activity, all of the children's predictions need to be accepted equally (Lang, 1999). Between five and six years of age, children have a better sense of estimation over 10.

To gain experiences in estimations of small amounts, the following game can be played. First create a 10-strip row of cells, 1 inch square. This can be computer generated. One child scoops a handful of unshelled nuts (or other manipulatives) from a bowl and estimates the number. The second child places the nuts on the 10-strip. They both count the number and compare with the estimate (Smith, 2001) (Fig. 14–2).

After children have experiences in scooping unshelled nuts and placing them on a 10-strip, they can place them into a small clear jar or arrange counters in a plastic lid. Then they can be asked to estimate what number items that will fill the container. For this activity the estimates are recorded without the child's name (Smith, 2001). After the estimations are recorded, children have more time to work with

Figure 14–2 A pair of children check their estimate of nuts using a 10-strip graph.

the material. After their play, the group can count the numbers needed to fill the container. Then children can be asked what they can do to estimate without counting. Children can be given further opportunities to estimate the same materials. The goal is for children to use their knowledge of the material and space it takes in the container to estimate reasonably close answers rather than relying on wild guesses. This skill in estimation relates to **data analysis** and **probability** in math (Fig. 14–3).

Data analysis is collecting data, organizing, and representing it.

Probability is exploring the concept of chance.

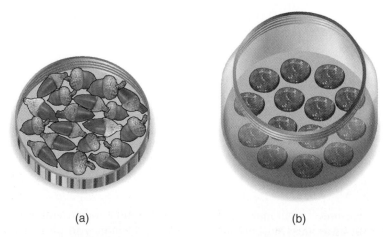

(a)   (b)

Figure 14–3 Estimation relates to data analysis and probability.

INQUIRY TOPICS

Inquiry topics can involve basic math and number as a part of studying a topic in depth. Mathematics for young children is used naturally in understanding how the world works. Math is not differentiated from the study of science both from the way young children approach learning and from scientists at work. In Chapters 15 through 19, the inquiry topics involve math in various ways.

In order to build a basis for math, teachers can develop topics with children to practice in play what is meaningful to them. The math topic of shopping can center on children's interests in shopping for particular categories and follow their developing math skills. Since children will have varying abilities in the math involved, planning will stretch the capabilities of advanced thinkers and help others to gain skills as they encounter the play materials. Children will advance through the scaffolding from peers who can accomplish certain aspects of the math within these activities. Within this broad topic a wide range of choices allows for building curriculum that follows children's abilities and interests.

Inquiry Topic on Exploring Basic Math and Number

INQUIRY TOPIC

SHOPPING

Purpose

Children will apply their knowledge of basic math and number sense to the dramatic play theme of shopping in roles of merchants and customers. Children will relate to the real world through planning and purchasing items during a field trip to a selected store.

Teachers Prepare

Questions   What math skills are children most focused on at this time? What awareness do they have about use of money to purchase goods?

What do they understand about the value of coins? What is their ability to cooperate, take roles, organize, and carry out projects?

Study   Neighborhood store or stores that would welcome class visits.

Gather materials   Determine resources for materials to fill inventory of store, containers, shelving, play money, cash register, make replica of computer scanner, old computer, boxes, scales.

After determining with the children the type of store, decide on the method to obtain inventory.

Recipes   If selected, plan for children to create bead bracelets and display them for sale in the store (for 5–6 year olds) (Appendix C, Table C–4).

Children' Books

Market Day by Ehlert

Pigs Will Be Pigs: Fun with Math and Money by Axelrod

Pigs Go to Market: Fun with Math and Shopping by Axelrod

Use technology   Photograph sections of the community store and use in planning the play store. With care in selecting sites, surf the Internet for items to sell in the store and note categories and prices. Some pictures of items can be downloaded. Or find circulars of advertisements from similar stores. Use the computer to make labels and price tags.

Using Kidspiration, or other word processing programs, generate advertisements of items in the store. Add pictures of items from the Internet and prices the children determine.

In Experiences About This Inquiry Topic, Children Will

Explore   Children will explore the materials that make up the inventory, the play money, and the cash register. Children will observe customers and merchants at a store to determine these roles.

Classify and Match   As merchants, children will organize the categories of materials for sale and decide how materials will be organized on shelves. They will place money in the cash register classified by sizes or values of coins and dollars. They will classify items of similar size and match items to fit the size of a storage box. With quantity items, group materials into sets. Match price tag to item. Distribute money to customers for shopping. As customers, children will decide a category to purchase, make personal shopping lists, and classify money they have.

Compare and Contrast   Children visit a community store and compare the display of merchandise and the checkout area with plans for their play store. Photograph areas of the community store and use this to develop plans for the play store.

As merchants, children compare size of item to appropriate box and match size of set of items to storage shelves or containers. Children will match empty spaces on shelves with items that need restocking. At the checkout counter, the checker will list prices of items and provide a total (without accuracy).

As customers, children will compare items with advertised items or items on personal shopping list. Compare money they have with price of item purchased. Match total bill with money they give to checker (without accuracy).

Problem solve   Decide roles of children in dramatic play of store, dictate or write lists, make tallies of items for record keeping.

Hypothesize   How much money will an item cost? How do I purchase something? What does a merchant do to sell goods? How do we plan a purchase at a store?

Generalize   If I want . . . I use play money at the class' store. If I want . . . I take real money to the actual store. To plan a purchase at a store we need to know exactly what we want, find out how much it costs, and determine if we have the money to purchase it.

Extended experiences   Make plans to purchase an item at the community store, deciding what is needed and the cost of item and obtaining the money.

SUMMARY

Using your knowledge of how young children learn math, the daily experiences in the classroom will bring math into children's real and ongoing problem solving. Organizing math experiences with materials and containers supports activities for a wide range of abilities. Math knowledge is extended through graphing and basic board games. All these experiences promote learning in basic math and number and can be blended into all areas of curriculum. In the next chapter other important math skills are introduced with extended experiences for children's learning.

TO FURTHER YOUR THINKING

1. Using the classroom activity ideas for math in daily activities, write out the kinds of basic math thinking in each activity. What possibilities in math thinking emerge in these tasks? For example, in the different ways of setting the table, how can one-to-one correspondence, making sets, comparing, and counting be used by the way the child approaches the task?

2. Discuss one way of taking attendance (see pages 221–222 in this chapter). Identify the basic math skills used in this example. What other ways could a class take attendance to use these and other math skills?

3. Using the activity of children writing snack menus, write (on an index card) a menu for a healthy children's snack in a home or school. What (few) words, signs, and symbols to signify each item and amounts of items would you use? What is required of a child to understand your snack menu? Compare your results with other classmates.

4. Using the anecdotes on dividing the extra raisins in the snack and the timing of turns with a new board game (pp. 224–225), decide the math skills used by the children involved.

5. What estimation skills do you use in daily life? Is estimation helpful in solving everyday problems?

6. Play Dominoes or War. Discuss the math concepts used in playing the game. Using the cards or Dominoes, play with these materials to develop other simple games young children could play.

7. Play a commercial board game designed for three- to six-year-olds, such as Candyland or Chutes and Ladders. Play with a young child. What are the easier and harder math skills in this game?

REFERENCES

Axelrod, A. (1997a). *Pigs will be pigs: Fun with math and money.* Glenview, IL: Scott Foresman.

Axelrod, A. (1997b). *Pigs go to market: Fun with math and shopping.* Glenview, IL: Scott Foresman.

Baroody, A., and Wilkins, J. L. M. (1999). The development of informal counting, number, and arithmetic skills and concepts. In J. V. Copley, (Ed.). *Mathematics in the early years* (pp. 47–65). Reston, VA: National Council of Teachers of Mathematics.

Charlesworth, R., and Lind, K. (2003). *Math and science for young children* (4th ed.). Clifton Park, NY: Delmar Learning.

Ehlert, L. (2002). *Market day.* San Diego, CA: Harcourt.

Kamii, C. (1982). *Number in preschool and kindergarten.* Washington, DC: National Association for the Education of Young Children.

Lang, F. K. (1999, July). What is a "Good guess" anyway? Teaching quantity and measurement estimation. *Young Children, 54*(4), 78–81.

Marshall, N. L., Robeson, W. W., and Keefe, N. (1999, July). Gender equity in early childhood education. *Young Children, 54*(4), 9–13.

Meriwether, L. (1997, September). Math at the snack table. *Young Children, 52*(5), 69–73.

Moomaw, S., and Hieronymus, B. (1999). *Much more than counting: More math activities for preschool and kindergarten.* St. Paul, MN: Redleaf.

National Council of Teachers of Mathematics. (2000). *Principles and standards for school mathematics.* Reston, VA: Author.

Smith, S. S. (2001). *Early childhood mathematics* (2nd ed). Boston, MA: Allyn & Bacon.

Taylor-Cox, J. (2003, January). Algebra in early years? Yes. *Young Children, 58*(1), 14–21.

ADDITIONAL RESOURCES

Copley, J. V. (Ed.). (2004). *Showcasing mathematics for the young child: Activities for three-, four-, and five-year-olds.* Reston, VA: National Council of Teachers of Mathematics.

Cuyler, K. M., Gilkerson, D., Parrott, S., and Bowne, M. T. (2003, January). Developing math games based on children's literature. *Young Children, 58*(1), 22–27. There are two versions on line, one is on line only. The articles contain math board games based on well-known children's books. **www.naeyc.org**

Dickinson, P. (2003). Choosing books you can count on. In D. Koralek (Ed.), *Spotlight on young children and math* (pp. 32–34). Washington, DC: National Association for the Education of Young Children. **www.naeyc.org**

Martin L., and Miller, M. (1999). *Great graphing.* New York: Scholastic. Graphing ideas for children in grades 1–4; can spur ideas for adaptations for young children.

Moomaw, S., and Hieronymus, B. (1995). *More than counting: Whole math activities for preschool and kindergarten.* St. Paul, MN: Redleaf. Clear explanations of theory with instructions to simple math activities. Includes math games from children's songs.

Polonsky, L. (Ed.). (2000). *Math for the very young: A handbook of activities for parents and teachers.* New York: John Wiley & Sons. Written by teachers in a math project, this book presents teaching in all math areas.

Seefeldt, C., and Galper, A. (2004). *Active experiences for active children: Mathematics.* Upper Saddle River, NJ: Pearson Education. An insightful and practical portrayal of mathematics in all areas of curriculum.

Waite-Stupiansky, S., and Stupiansky, N. G. (1992). *Learning through play math: A practical guide for teaching children.* New York: Scholastic. A collection of math activities for the younger child that focuses on basic math.

Whitin, D. J. and Whitin, P. (2003, November). Talk counts: Discussing graphs with young children. Teaching Children Mathematics,*10*(3): 142–149. Divergent questioning used as kindergartners discussed their graph.

Videos

Path to math: Sets & classification; seriation (Ordering) [Video]. Magna Systems, Inc. www.magnasystems.com

Path to math: Number & counting; numerals [Video]. Magna Systems, Inc. www.magnasystems.com

Children's Books

Aker, S. *What comes in 2's, 3's & 4's.* New York: Simon & Schuster. Sets of small numbers for two- and three-year-olds.

Anno, M. (1992). *Anno's counting book.* New York: HarperCollins. Small illustrations that invite counting are best when shared with one preschool child. (See Chapter 10).

Axelrod, A. (1997a). *Pigs go to market: Fun with math and shopping.* Glenview, IL: Scott Foresman. Silly and fun shopping at Halloween for primary years.

Axelrod, A. (1997b). *Pigs will be pigs: Fun with math and money.* Glenview, IL: Scott Foresman. Silly and fun story for primary years.

Brusca, M. C., and Wilson, T. (1995). *Three friends, tres amigos.* New York: Henry Holt & Co. Counting in English and Spanish.

Crews, D. (1986). *Ten black dots.* New York: Greenwillow Books. Outstanding clear black dots stand out in amounts from one to ten for preschool years.

Crowther, R. (1999). *Robert Crowther's most amazing hide-and-seek numbers book.* Cambridge, MA: Candlewick. A lift-the-flaps book for numbers from one to twenty; then the book takes counting by 10s up to 1000 for primary years.

Ehlert, L. (2002). *Market day.* San Diego CA: Harcourt. Folk art forms a beautiful backdrop for this simple story.

Hamm, D. J. (1994). *How many feet in the bed?* New York: Simon & Schuster. Lovely and loving family show pairs of feet that come and leave the bed. For preschool years.

Hutchins, P. (1986). *The doorbell rang.* New York: Mulberry. A delightful book for all, this cumulative family tale presents the idea for older children to represent what happens mathematically.

McCloskey, R. (1976). *Blueberries for Sal.* New York: Viking. This classic book on picking blueberries is delightful for all.

Reid, M. S. (1995). *The button box.* Glenview, IL: Scott Foresman. Also, *La caja de los botones.* Simple beautiful text and illustrations focus on Grandma's button box. For preschool years.

Web Sites

www.childcraft.com Childcraft is one source of a solar-powered play cash register and shopping cart with grocery items.

www.gse.buffalo.edu A site for building blocks is funded to create mathematics materials for young children. One can also access Web site sources for mathematics standards for early childhood.

www.mathperspectives.com The Mathematical Perspectives Teacher Center provides math tools, strategies, and assessments for pre-K to grade six.

Chapter 15

Exploring Math in Shape, Space, and Time

OBJECTIVES Through the process of discovery in this chapter, you will be able to:

1. Extend the study of math for young children to include
   a. Patterns
   b. Part–whole relationships
   c. Symmetry
   d. Shape
   e. Space
   f. Measurement
   g. Time

2. Explain classroom activities using patterns and part–whole relationships.

3. Describe materials, activities, and discussions that promote knowledge of two- and three-dimensional shapes.

4. Identify classroom materials and develop materials that promote knowledge of space.

5. Apply a beginning understanding of measurement using nonspecific and specific units with children in length, volume, and weight.

6. Describe appropriate ways to work with children in time increments: daily schedule, passage of time, and the weekly calendar.

7. Discuss measurement as an inquiry topic and the possibility of studying shape, space, and time in other inquiry topics.

IDEAS TO PONDER

- How do shape, space, and time relate to the study of math?

- How do I involve young children in working with patterns and part–whole relationships?

- What can be planned for children to work with shape and space?

- How can young children measure?

- How can young children understand the calendar?

- How do I plan a math topic?

Kayla and Shavonti gaily approached Ms. Jonel, their teacher. "We want to move that table into our house so we have more room."

"Show me," Ms. Jonel responded, and she followed the two girls with their bobbing braids as they danced to the housekeeping area. After they pointed to a space between furniture, Ms. Jonel asked, "Do you think the bigger table will fit?"

The girls looked at each other, shrugged their shoulders.

"How do you think we can find out?"

"Move the table and see," offered Shavonti.

"Is there another way to tell besides moving the table?"

The girls were quiet.

"What about measuring?"

"Yeah, like we measured how big we are." Shavonti smiled excitedly.

"Yes, try the long blocks." Ms. Jonel returned the smile.

The girls worked together to get four double-unit blocks and measured the length of the table and the width of the space on the floor where they wanted the table. Since the space was much smaller, they decided to measure the width of the table. They found that it would just fit and proceeded to put the table in its new place for their play.
(Author)

BEYOND BASIC MATH AND NUMBERS

Math is more than comparing and counting. "At the heart of mathematics is the search for sense and meaning, patterns and relationships, order and predictability" (Richardson & Salkeld, 1995, p. 23). Young children begin to realize this meaning through working with patterns, part–whole relationships, shape, space, time, and measurement. As Ms. Jonel brought measurement into solving a problem, these areas of math can be integrated into classroom life through real, related activities and problem solving.

STANDARDS

Recognize and apply mathematics in contexts outside of mathematics.

Chapter 4: Connections Standard for Grades Pre-K–2. Reprinted with permission from *Principles and Standards for School Mathematics,* Copyright 2000 by the National Council of Teachers of Mathematics (p. 132). All rights reserved.

PATTERNS

Children experience repeated **patterns** in their world and create patterns with materials and manipulatives. The teacher who observes the child in the creation of a pattern can capitalize on this by commenting on this creation. Of the child's work, the teacher can say, "I see red, blue, green, red, blue. What will be next?"

Also, the teacher can create an alternating pattern and ask the child what will be next. It is most common to see this using two colors. Patterns can also be made with shapes, two objects, orientation of a shape, or alternating shapes (Fig. 15–1).

Once children have an understanding of predicting from a pattern of two alternating objects, three objects can be used to form a pattern. So children advance from ab ab ab to abc abc abc. While this is not a difficult concept for the young child, it is helpful to point out what the child is seeing in the pattern. The next step is for the child to predict what will happen next when two- or three-object patterns are begun. A pattern can be given, abc, and the beginning of the repeat is added, abca, so the child has the necessary information in order to predict the next element.

There are four levels of exploring patterns: Recognize a pattern; describe a pattern; extend a pattern; create a pattern (Smith, 2001). Preschoolers readily recognize a simple pattern and can often extend it. As the adult describes the pattern in simple words, he supports the child's discoveries by adding the language to describe it. After the child has experienced describing and extending, he can create his own pattern.

In their school years children will use patterns in understanding the number system. For example, the odd, even sequence or counting by fives are ways patterns are seen in the number system. Looking for patterns is a logical form of

> *Patterns are the result of repeating elements in a regular fashion.*

STANDARDS

Recognize, describe, and extend patterns such as sequences of sounds and shapes or simple numeric patterns and translate from one representation to another.

Chapter 4: Algebra Standard for Grades Pre-K–2. Reprinted with permission from *Principles and Standards for School Mathematics,* Copyright 2000 by the National Council of Teachers of Mathematics (p. 92). All rights reserved.

Figure 15–1　A pattern is made with alternating shapes of blocks.

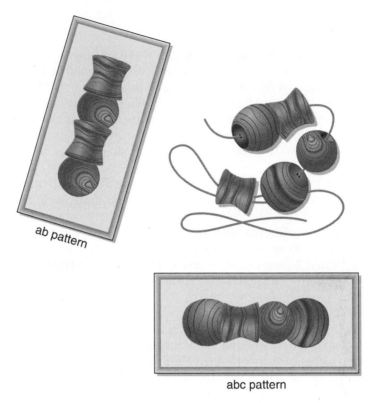

Figure 15–2 Stringing beads can continue an abc pattern.

problem solving and estimating small numbers. Once into algebra in later years, predictability is extended to solving the missing function. In its simplest form, if $1 + 1 = 2$, then $2 + 1 = 3$, $3 + (\ ) = 4$, and the numbers go on and on (Copley, 1999; Smith, 2001; Taylor-Cox, 2003).

One pattern activity is done through arranging stringing of beads (see the recipe for beads in Appendix C). In this recipe kindergartners can make patterns and draw their pattern on small cards (Fig. 15–2). Patterns can be made from all kinds of materials: buttons, blocks, shoes, pine cones, buckeyes, and acorns.

Patterns can be explored in different modalities as well. Rhythms in hand clapping are repeated patterns that children easily recognize and repeat. With experience children can create their own hand patterns for a group to copy, such as clap, clap, patsch, clap, clap, patsch. Rhythmic patterns in movement can be expressed as step, step, hop, hop, step, step, hop, hop. Follow-the-leader games can emerge from hand and movement patterns.

Musical notes can be repeated for developing patterns. Words can be added, such us pronouncing and repeating the child's names in syllables (i.e., Su-san, Su-san) or repeating two names in two tones (Fig. 15–3).

By using xylophones equipped for **Orff instrumentation,** which have tuned tone bars, children can play a well-tuned instrument for patterning. On these, the

Orff instrumentation uses instruments such as xylophones with removable tone bars.

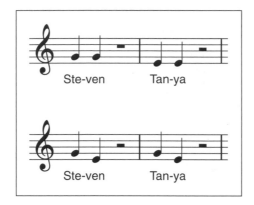

Figure 15–3 Repeating musical patterns use children's names.

tone bars not used are removed. This allows the child to use instruments with accuracy. The child can first follow a musical pattern and later create her own with these instruments.

PART–WHOLE RELATIONSHIPS

A particular concept that the young child actively develops is seeing something as whole and then seeing it divided into parts. In **part–whole relationships,** younger preschoolers cannot both see the object divided into parts and returned to the whole. Inlaid puzzles demonstrate this concept as the child repeatedly assembles and disassembles them. A full understanding of the part–whole relationship follows the onset of reversibility at about age seven.

In food preparation children naturally organize food as whole, then break it into parts. As a child breaks the graham cracker into four sections or cuts a piece of bread into two halves, she can process looking at the food item as both whole and in parts. Apples and oranges can be sectioned or cut in fourths and can be shown put back as a whole again.

This concept builds into the understanding that the whole number can be divided into parts (decomposing); those parts add up to the whole. One can take the

Part–whole relationships are seeing objects as whole and subdivided into parts.

STANDARDS

Develop a sense of whole numbers and represent and use them in flexible ways, including relating, composing, and decomposing numbers.

Chapter 4: Number and Operations Standard for Grades Pre-K–2. Reprinted with permission from *Principles and Standards for School Mathematics,* Copyright 2000 by the National Council of Teachers of Mathematics (p. 79). All rights reserved.

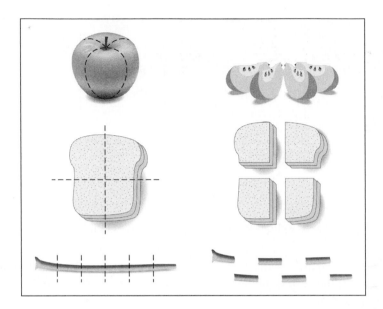

Figure 15–4 Wholes can be cut into pieces and arranged as wholes again.

whole number and divide it several ways, as Ong (see the opening quotes of Chapter 10), realized that six could be decomposed in three ways. The total will always equal the whole. Equality is the concept that will develop over time and be used in mathematics and algebra. Fractions are another area of math that is drawn from the part–whole definition. The manipulation of objects into parts and wholes helps lay these foundations to be used symbolically later (Copley, 2000; Smith, 2001; Taylor-Cox, 2003).

To plan for part–whole arrangements, with preparing food for snacks, children can cut apples or celery sticks, or make sandwiches by cutting bread in halves or quarters. As children make the pieces, ask them to arrange the item back the way it was before. Can it be one whole? Can it be four pieces (Fig. 15–4)?

In addition to the part–whole arrangements of snacks, pictures or drawings can be created as whole units that can be divided into parts. First, show the child a plan by explaining how he can select (or make) a picture that he can cut apart and put back together. Cut the original picture to fit inside a shallow box or a shoebox lid so that the cut pieces can be shown as one whole fitting inside the box frame. Glue the picture to tag board. By cutting the drawing in equal fourths or thirds at first, children can see the part–whole connections. As children continue this concept, they may create their own part–whole arrangements that fit as pieces inside the box.

SYMMETRY

Symmetry is regularity of form.

Equality can also be seen in working with manipulatives and unit blocks. Two square Duplos equals a long rectangle Duplo and four half-unit blocks equal a double-unit block. Patterns that have **symmetry** relate to the concept of equality.

Symmetry is displayed in children's block building.

Two equal sides make a whole. Simple symmetry is found in designs representing items in nature, such as a flower or a butterfly. Children construct block buildings that show symmetry in their simple or complex structures.

STANDARDS

Recognize and create shapes that have symmetry.

Chapter 4: Geometry Standard for Grades Pre-K–2. Reprinted with permission from *Principles and Standards for School Mathematics,* Copyright 2000 by the National Council of Teachers of Mathematics (p. 97). All rights reserved.

SHAPE

As children work with blocks, attribute blocks, and other manipulatives with basic shapes, they learn how these shapes relate to each other. The unit blocks are designed to show these relationships. Two triangle shapes make a square, two squares make a rectangle, and so on (Fig. 15–5).

Figure 15–5 Two half-unit blocks equal one unit block.

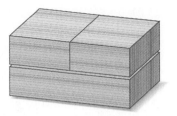

Early in the preschool years, children recognize differences in shapes and work to manipulate different shapes to accomplish their objectives in building, drawing, making collages, and putting puzzles together.

In the process of constructing with blocks and manipulatives, children will intentionally place two pieces together to form a new shape (see the opening quotes, Chapter 7). Wood pattern blocks and tangrams (sets of geometric shapes) provide opportunities to create all kinds of shape patterns and designs. As they create designs, children will see relationships of shape and the formation of a shape from putting two together.

STANDARDS

Investigate and predict the results of putting together and taking apart two- and three-dimensional shapes.

Chapter 4: Geometry Standard for Grades Pre-K–2. Reprinted with permission from *Principles and Standards for School Mathematics,* Copyright 2000 by the National Council of Teachers of Mathematics (p. 97). All rights reserved.

A sphere is a three-dimensional shape of a ball or orb.

A rectangular prism is a three–dimensional form containing right angles.

A rhombus is a two-dimensional diamond shape.

An ellipse is a two-dimensional compressed sphere.

Promote Knowledge of Shape

Often teachers provide the names of these shapes as children build. Running commentaries help with this. With this background children begin to use shape names in conversations themselves. "The ideal time for children to learn about shapes is between three and six" (Clements, 1999, p. 71). "The main point is that children's ideas about shapes do not come from passive looking. Instead, they come as children's bodies, hands, eyes . . . and minds . . . engage in action. In addition . . . children need to explore shapes extensively to understand them fully. Merely seeing and naming pictures is insufficient. Finally, they have to explore the parts and attributes of shapes" (Clements, 1999, p. 67). Play is the mode for this learning.

While children often learn the names of basic shapes, especially using two-dimensional terms such as *circle, square, triangle, rectangle,* they often do not know the definable names in the three dimensions: *pyramids, cones, cubes,* **spheres,** *cylinders,* **rectangular prism,** and *triangular prism.* Also, to round out the terminology of the two-dimensional terms, **rhombus** and **ellipse** can be added. All of these can routinely be used in conversation about children's work, especially with blocks and other manipulatives of geometric forms (Fig. 15–7).

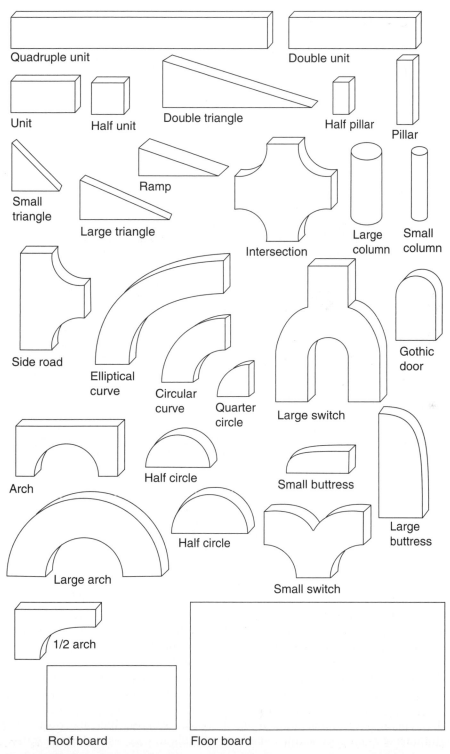

Figure 15–6 Unit block shapes and their labels (*Source:* Wellhousen & Kieff, 2001).

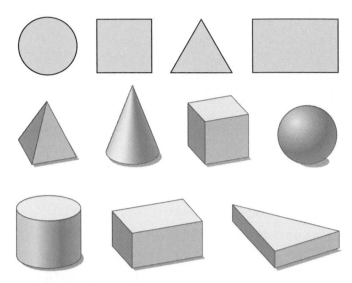

Figure 15–7 Children can know many two-dimensional and three-dimensional shapes and forms.

STANDARDS

Recognize, name, build, draw, compare, and sort two- and three-dimensional shapes.

Chapter 4: Geometry Standard for Grades Pre-K–2. Reprinted with permission from *Principles and Standards for School Mathematics,* Copyright 2000 by the National Council of Teachers of Mathematics (p. 97). All rights reserved.

According to research by Hannibal (1999) (as cited in Smith, 2001, Clements, 1999, and Clements & Sarama, 2000), children learn to apply a name to one kind of shape, such as an equilateral triangle, and do not include other kinds of triangles in their recognition of that shape. Children have difficulty distinguishing a square from a rectangle and, in addition, do not realize that a square is also a rectangle. Both the two-dimensional and three-dimensional geometric shapes *of all kinds* should be available in the classroom. The terminology should be in conversations about all types of these shapes so children do understand that rectangles, rectangular prisms, triangles, cones, and pyramids have many different shapes within each type. In addition, the identity of the square and cube include the definitions as a rectangle and rectangular prism (Fig. 15–8).

Geoboards, either homemade or obtained commercially, provide the backdrop for children making their own two-dimensional shapes with varying arrangements in space (Fig. 15–9).

If a teacher determines that a group of five- and six-year-olds is ready for using definitions of geometric shapes, she can add this to discussions of the different

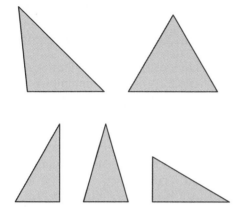

Figure 15–8 Triangles vary in shape.

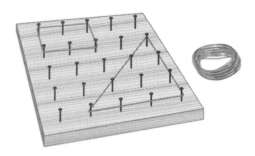

Figure 15–9 Children can experiment with shapes on the geoboard.

shapes. When this definitive language is introduced, use specific terms, such as *side, corner,* and *point.* This terminology will help children use the definition of shapes in exact terms in later years. Most three- to five-year-olds can learn to say the definition of a triangle, "A triangle has three sides and three points," but cannot yet use this information in identifying a triangle (Clements, 1999). There is a gap between saying the definition and using it in identifying a shape. Kindergartners can begin to apply the definitions of shape. Children can apply the shape names in the following game.

In the classroom children will enjoy the game of finding representations of different shapes. To be sure that children develop the concept that shapes appear different, such as long thin triangles or rectangles, they will find examples of these shapes in different areas of the classroom.

ANECDOTE

Mr. Conan begins a new shape game with the kindergarten class by placing five three-dimensional shapes on the table and naming each shape so children can use these terms in the game. He covers the shapes and repeats a magical chant. "Geo-jutsu, mix-you-escape-you; Geomagic returns to confuse you; now what eludes you?" The cloth over the shapes is swept away and Mr. Conan exclaims, "Voila! What have we here? Is something missing . . . let's see, I see a pyramid, a cylinder, a cube, a cone . . . but what is not here?" After several times, he gives Max the lead. Max repeats the magic chant (approximately) and removes a shape, hiding it under his shirt. Anna volunteers to identify the pyramid, cylinder, rectangular prism, and cone. Some children knowingly say, "The cube! The cube's gone." And Max beams as he brings it out from under his shirt. And so the game goes.

ANECDOTE

In the pre-kindergarten classroom, children have worked with identifying two-dimensional shapes. Ms. Jonel plans a shape walk in the community. In preparation, pairs of children select a shape and share a clipboard and primer pencil. On the walk each pair studiously tallies the number of items seen that contain that shape. Some of the children draw the shape each time they see one. Others place a tally mark on the paper. Upon return Ms. Jonel asks them to count their tallies, and they record their findings through a dictated report from each group and recording the tallies on a large sheet. Ms. Jonel asks the class, "How can we make another way to show the shapes you found? I wonder what would show this clearly."

After a few moments, Clair pipes up, "We could take a picture of each kind of shape and put that on the big paper."

"And put our tallies next to the shape."

"Or make a picture of the shape."

"Make lines up and down and across and put one mark in the place for each tally."

Ms. Jonel reviews their ideas with them for the graph, and she plans with them to go back to photograph an example of each shape.

SPACE

Space is a concept related to shape. Shapes fill space. A combination of shapes, or many shapes that are the same, fills the space in different ways. Large shapes fill up the space more quickly. As children use the various kinds of blocks and manipulatives in the classroom, they experience these concepts.

Young children can work together to completely cover two-dimensional rectangle space with geometric shapes. They will try to cover the entire rug with the large hollow blocks and will be challenged to cover a small area where a large block will not fit.

When four-year olds decided to make a multicolored quilt for their wall they started with covering a 12" × 18" sheet of paper with pre-cut smaller rectangle shapes. Children used general phrases or used their hands to describe the shape and size of the rectangle shapes they wanted. Problem solving occurred as children completed their individual tasks and as they came together to join their individual projects onto one large project of the class quilt (Copley et al., 2004).

Space is also conceived from how the child relates to space. Do I fill up a space or not (while in hiding in the empty kitchen cabinet at home or inside a block structure at school)? Children feel how their bodies take up space. They relate to the spaces that are familiar to them: my living room, my classroom, and the path from the classroom to the school bathroom.

Children use their bodies to understand the space they occupy. They relate to objects close to their bodies. Because young children learn by actively involving their bodies, climbing in and out of spaces, going under and over and beside objects, climbing high and sliding down are examples of active involvement. Words describing their actions (running commentary) provide the vocabulary for the orientation in space. Large appliance boxes, laundry baskets, and blankets over a block building make wonderful inside spaces for play. Obstacle courses that include the movement of their bodies in space are inviting challenges for children. Along with the active play in, out, and around these obstacles, directions are given. These can be done both orally and by using symbols and printed directions.

STANDARDS

Find and name locations with simple relationships such as "near to" and in coordinate systems such as maps.

Chapter 4: Measurement Standard for Grades Pre-K–2. Reprinted with permission from *Principles and Standards for School Mathematics,* Copyright 2000 by the National Council of Teachers of Mathematics (p. 97). All rights reserved.

Practical problems relating to space can be solved in their daily lives as in moving play furniture.

ANECDOTE

PROBLEM SOLVING IN USE OF SPACE

Ms. Smith asked three girls in the Head Start class to help her move the large dollhouse from a neighboring classroom to their room. With three children on one end and Ms. Smith on the other, they carried the dollhouse on a large flat frame to the classroom doorway. As they tried to go through, it was obvious that the frame for the dollhouse was wider than the doorway. "What shall we do?" Ms. Smith asked the girls. She waited while they suggested some ideas. One girl pushed the long side of the frame up almost as high as her head. As Ms. Smith was watching, she moved the corresponding side from her end up, also, making the frame almost vertical. They moved it through the doorway. "Well," she told the girls, "we had success. You solved that problem."

MEASUREMENT

Young children are comparing sizes and amounts in many ways. Their actions may be imprecise and do not describe the comparison accurately. Children can learn more about these comparisons through informal measurements.

The English system using length developed out of informal measurements. Originally in measuring length, an inch was three barley corns, a foot was the length of a man's foot, a yard was the length from a person's nose to the end of his finger on his outstretched arm (Smith, 2001). These informal measurements gradually became formalized through use of a ruler and yard stick.

Similar to the early development of the English system, informal units of measure can help with determining size. As children discuss which block tower is taller, the height of a teacher or a child can form the basis for comparison. Unit blocks make a good comparison for length. How many double-unit blocks can fit along this side of the table? How many cubes fit on a piece of paper? How many glasses of water will fill a pitcher?

Questions can direct children to thinking about measurement:

- Where will the cage for our new gerbil fit?
- You are out of double-unit blocks. What else could you use?
- How much did the narcissus grow over the weekend?
- Which pitcher holds more juice? How can you tell?
- Which weighs more, the bag of groceries or the bag of apples?

Measuring Length

As children begin to explore the kinds of comparative questions in measurement of length that appear in the daily classroom life, informal tools for measurements can be used. An adult can use her foot to determine space on the floor or floor tiles can be counted. A piece of yarn can be used to compare the space for an item with the length of the item. Paper clips can be made into a chain to measure height. Blocks can be brought over to determine lengths of other items.

To measure how many blocks long a table is, bring enough unit blocks to cover the length of the table. In order for children to see the concept of how many blocks

STANDARDS

Understand how to measure using nonstandard and standard units. Measure with multiple copies of units of the same size, such as paper clips laid end to end.

Chapter 4: Measurement Standard for Grades Pre-K–2. Reprinted with permission from *Principles and Standards for School Mathematics,* Copyright 2000 by the National Council of Teachers of Mathematics (p. 103). All rights reserved.

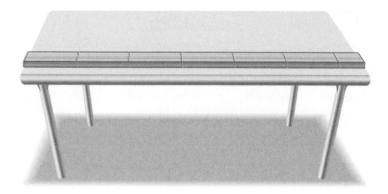

Figure 15–10 Measurement of a tabletop results in six unit blocks plus one half-unit block.

represent the length of the table, the unit blocks are laid out end to end and then counted. Children will not grasp the concept visually if the length is measured by moving one block along and counting the moves. If the measurement is "six blocks plus a little bit more," children can discuss how much more, perhaps placing a half-unit in the space left over. Then the measurement is recorded as six unit blocks and one half-unit block (Fig. 15–10).

The same measuring process can be applied to the length of the children as they lay down in the block area. Each measurement is recorded and then these can be compared in terms of the number of unit blocks.

At some point 20–centimeter or one foot rulers can be used. For clear under-standing, use centimeter sticks or rulers that are exactly 20 centimeters or 12 inches long. These can be made from tag board without the markings of indi-vidual units. Again, as in using unit blocks, the measurement is taken by placing the rulers end to end and counting them. Most children will count the total rulers used (Fig. 15–11).

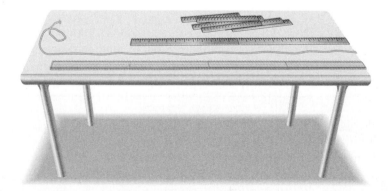

Figure 15–11 Standard forms of measurement are done with 20-centimeter or one foot rulers placed end to end and then counted.

Measuring Volume

For volume, containers of any shape and size can be used to compare amounts. As with use of rulers, the cup measure can be introduced as a measure other people use. Use cup measures that equal 1 cup when filled to the top or graduated cup measures ($\frac{1}{4}$ cup, $\frac{1}{2}$ cup). In order to compare volume, the measure must be filled to the top. As children make play dough, the full cup can be discussed. To measure three cups of flour and one cup of water for the standard recipe for homemade play dough, have enough one-cup measures for the total number of cups of ingredients (as in this case, four). In order for children to begin to use volume measures independently, make recipe cards for standard homemade play dough, allowing pairs of children to make fresh play dough often (Fig. 15–12).

Measuring Weight

For weights of items, children can begin by holding items and estimating which is heavier. A good balance scale can then be used. Have a number of identical-size weights so children can physically see that placing a 1-oz weight on each pan will make it balance. When comparing weights, begin with items that are obviously different in weight. This way the child can use the sense of weight kinesthetically to determine what is light and heavy (Fig. 15–13).

TIME

Time concepts are difficult for young children. Yet as children experience time elements in their daily lives, time does make sense to them. At home the preschooler

Homemade Play Dough Recipe

3 cups flour

$\frac{1}{4}$ cup salt

1 cup water

3 drops food coloring

1 tablespoon oil

Flour

Salt

Water

Oil

Figure 15–12 Children can follow an illustrated recipe for homemade play dough.

knows that when the digital clock reads 8:30 A.M. it is time to go to school, or that at 4:00 PM her favorite television program is on. Analog clocks are helpful in understanding the passage of hours and minutes, but children are not ready for this concept until the primary years.

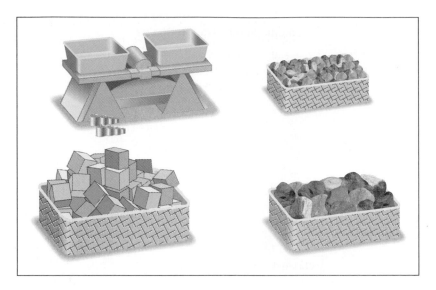

Figure 15–13 Children can compare weights of items on the balance scale.

Time in Minutes

For time increments of minutes, use a timer in the classroom to help with taking turns for favorite activities, and announcing minutes until clean-up time. As teachers talk about time increments, be accurate (the teacher can use the timer for this) or use general time responses, such as, "I will be over to see your block structure as soon as I get Tara started with her painting." Children learn about time from the ways other people talk about time. If the phrase "five minutes to clean-up time" stretches to 20 minutes on some days, children do not gain an accurate concept of time.

Today, Tomorrow, and Yesterday

Tomorrow in a sense never arrives, because then it is today. Young children are working on reference to present, past, and future because this reference always changes. With the group of children, talk about what happens next in the day, and help them anticipate special events. "Tomorrow is Thursday, and Thursday is the day we go to the library, return books, and borrow new books for our room." Also talk about yesterday's and today's events, so children will gradually understand these time relationships.

Daily schedule is the general organization of a classroom day into time periods.

Daily Schedule

A **daily schedule** that shows main events in the classroom day is helpful. A chart that allows highlighting the event of the moment can help children understand the passage of time in regular events. Children are very aware of this. For example,

Steve, after one week of being at day care, cried when someone else's father walked through the door after nap. He had learned that the appearance of his father coincided with the events of the classroom, including the appearance of other parents. Because another father arrived earlier than usual, Steve's emerging concept of time about his father's arrival was disturbed.

Weekly Calendar

Many classrooms follow an elementary school practice of using the monthly calendar in daily group time. Children are asked the day of the week and today's date. The response to the name of the day of the week is often incorrect; the monthly date may be correct only if it is a single digit number. While some worthwhile concepts can be practiced in this way of handling the calendar, this is not the way young children understand time. Children do not relate to the 30 or 31 days in a month, because it is too long in measuring days, and, from their point of view, it appears arbitrarily determined. So this kind of calendar contains little meaning until the primary years. Young children can relate to the daily occurrence of school days and nonschool days that make up a week. To the young child, the week starts on the first day of the school week, on Monday, and ends with the two nonschool days, Saturday and Sunday.

The more the **weekly calendar** can be tied to the events the children experience, the more it will be understood. This can be done in the following way: On each school day, a selected child draws a symbol that relates to some event of that day and places her drawing on the chart under the day of the week. On Friday, children talk about the upcoming weekend and note that they will not be at school for two days. On Monday, events of children during the weekend are discussed before the new calendar for the week is introduced. To mark this as a timeline from week to week, the weekly calendar can be displayed end to end with the last week's calendar (Fig. 15–14).

For each calendar, the days of the week, beginning with Monday, are placed on the wall near the group time area. Color coding can divide the school days from nonschool days. Other workable ideas for the weekly calendar can be found in Appendix C, Table C–5.

> *The weekly calendar is representation of days into the period of a week.*

This Week Calendar

Figure 15–14 Young children can relate the weekly calendar to patterns of days in their lives.

INQUIRY TOPICS

As children become involved in inquiry topics in the following chapters, some math concepts relating to space, shape, and time will naturally emerge. With the understanding of how children approach these concepts, teachers can draw on problem-solving experiences within these topics to expand the math. You can also use the general outline of the inquiry topic of measurement below to expand any of the math concepts. Measurement can be implemented when there is interest in knowing the measurement of something relevant to the classroom life. It also can be initiated through one of several books listed below.

Inquiry Topic on Exploring Measurement

INQUIRY TOPIC

MEASURING LENGTH

Purpose

Children will develop skills in measuring length through applying standard and nonstandard measurement and chart their results through representing the measurement realistically and through graphing. Children will decide on a purchase of cloth for their room (such as material for a tablecloth for the housekeeping area), decide on standard measurements, and purchase the item.

Teachers Prepare

Study　History of English and metric system. Explore various nonstandard measurements to compare with standard ones. Investigate a field trip to a yard goods store to purchase cloth.

Questions　What interests do children show in measurement? What do they understand in measuring using nonstandard units? Using standard units? What do they understand in graphing?

Gather materials　Yarn or string, tape, markers, boards of 2-foot lengths, centimeter sticks, rulers, yard sticks, measuring tape, unit blocks, white butcher paper from a roll, poster board for graphs.

Recipe　Draw the outline of each child on butcher paper and tape each outline on the wall around the room with the feet in each drawing just touching the floor. Outline the teachers as well.

Children's Books

How Big Is a Foot? by Myller

Inch by Inch by Lionni

Is It Larger? Is It Smaller? by Hoban

Use technology   Using Inspiration software, list the teachers and children and graph their height in units that children decide on.

In Experiences About This Inquiry Topic, Children Will

Explore   Children will explore nonstandard and standard measuring materials by trying these out with the outlines of class members and teachers. Experiment with different sizes of cloth to find what fits on the housekeeping table. They can also try measuring various classroom items with measuring tools.

Classify, Compare, and Contrast   Children can become involved in finding things both bigger and smaller than they are. At first this can be accomplished by standing (or lying down) next to items. Make a list of things bigger and smaller.

Then add comparing the adult size to the list and find out if these same things are bigger or smaller than an adult.

Record data   Discuss how they can measure the length of their bodies. Try out different measuring tools on themselves. Decide on a way of measuring everyone in the class. Then proceed measuring each child and record the data on a posterboard chart or a computer generated chart. This chart can be referred to later in the year using the same measuring tool; children can determine if individual class members have grown. The exactness of the data may also be seen to affect making these determinations.

Use a measuring tape or a long piece of yarn to obtain a record of each child's height. Mark each child's tape or yarn with his name. These tapes can be arranged vertically on a wall with the lower end of the tape touching the floor. If there is interest, go back to the list of things bigger and smaller and compare them with their own tape measures. Or take tapes outdoors and compare the child's tape with smaller and larger items in the playground. Ask children how they can decide how tall each item is. Individuals can try different materials to measure. Compare teacher's and children's height. Compare with heights of items in the room: shorter than the door, same height as the easel, taller than the sandbox.

Identify   Talk about the process of measuring length, height, and use measurement terms when using nonstandard or standard measurement. Practice using exact terminology whether using standard or nonstandard units: This table top is eight unit blocks and one half-unit block long. Use dimensions and space relationships: The table is in front of the aquarium; the table top is longer than it is wide.

Hypothesize   Predict the length of different items. Is it larger or smaller than me? How can we find out how much cloth to purchase? How do we tell the store clerk how much to give us?

Generalize   Some items will be larger and others are smaller than themselves, and this can be determined through measuring and through making lists, classifying items smaller and larger than themselves. If you want to know how big something is, you can measure it. Measuring will need to be accurate in order to use and understand recorded data and communicate measurement to others. Standard measurement tools are needed to communicate information. We can measure the length of cloth wanted in standard units to tell the store clerk how much.

SUMMARY

With the description of young children learning in the mathematical areas of shape, space, and time, one can see the experiences that are appropriate to the thinking in young children. By knowing abilities of the children, teachers can expand and solidify the children's thinking through what they study. This is helpful in bringing math into everyday experiences and incorporating math into all areas of curriculum. As you encounter the science areas in succeeding chapters, you will be able to incorporate some of these aspects of math. In Chapter 16 you will apply physical knowledge criteria to various physical science topics.

TO FURTHER YOUR THINKING

1. What kinds of patterns do you experience in your daily life? Working with a colleague, create some repeating patterns using one or more mediums found in manipulatives, found objects, music, rhythm, or movement. How complex a pattern can be remembered in the modes you chose?

2. Explain to a colleague the relationship of patterns to the numeric and algebraic system. Were these concepts already familiar to you?

3. Take apart and assemble an inlaid puzzle yourself or observe a child putting one together. What comments from you could direct a child to look at the pieces (parts) as well as the whole picture of the completed puzzle?

4. Use a set of unit blocks and name the units (Fig. 15–6). Find units that can be doubled to equal other units and write these findings as equations. Build a small structure that has symmetry and describe this to a partner.

5. Using the shape names in the text, compare these with the names that are common to you. From Figure 15–7, practice using the names and describing them using the terms *side, corner,* and *point.* Using two- or three-dimensional shapes, ask a young child to find a shape identical to the one you are holding. Then using the shape names, ask the child to find the shape as you name it. What did you learn about this child's understanding of shape?

6. Play the shape game in the anecdote on page 249 with several preschoolers or with a colleague. If with children, how long did it take them to begin using the shape names that were new to them? If you played this with a colleague, discuss what children learn from the game.

7. Use some of the materials suggested in the text to make informal measurements of items around you. Then measure these same items with conventional measurement tools, both English and metric. What different results do you get from using the different measuring tools? Would these differences have an effect on what children could learn from the informal and formal measurements?

8. Discuss with a colleague the use of the metric system. What parts of it do you understand? What would be needed to incorporate the metric system into our daily lives? What can we do to enable children to use both systems equally?

9. Select one of the models of the weekly calendar and try this out with a group of young children. What do they understand from their use of it for more than a week? What difficulties do you see in using this kind of calendar in the classroom?

REFERENCES

Clements, D. H. (1999). Geometric and spatial thinking in young children. In J. V. Copley (Ed.), *Mathematics in the early years* (pp. 66–79). Reston, VA: National Council of Teachers of Mathematics.

Clements, D. H., and Sarama, J. (2000) Young children's ideas about geometric shapes [On line]. www.gse.buffalo.edu

Copley, J. V. (1999). *The young child and mathematics.* Washington, DC: National Association for the Education of Young Children.

Copley, J. V., Glass, K., Nix, L., Faseler, A., De Jesus, M., and Tanksley, S. (2004, February). Measuring experiences for young children. *Teaching children mathematics 10*(6). 314–319.

Hoban, T. (1985). *Is it larger? Is it smaller?* New York: Greenwillow.

Lionni, L. (1960). *Inch by inch.* New York: Astor-Honor.

Myller, R. (1990). *How big is a foot?* New York: Random House.

National Council of Teachers of Mathematics. (2000). *Principles and standards for school mathematics.* Reston, VA: Author.

Richardson, K., and Salkeld, L. (1995). Transforming mathematics curriculum. In S. Bredekamp and T. Rosegrant (Eds.), *Reaching potentials: Transforming early childhood curriculum and assessment* Vol. 2 (pp. 23–42). Washington, DC: National Association for the Education of Young Children.

Smith, S. S. (2001). *Early childhood mathematics* (2nd ed.). Boston, MA: Allyn & Bacon.

Taylor-Cox, J. (2003, January). Algebra in early years? Yes. *Young Children, 58*(1), 14–21.

Wellhousen, K., and Kieff, J. (2001). *A constructivist approach to block play in early childhood.* Clifton Park, NY: Thomson Delmar Learning.

ADDITIONAL RESOURCES

Hirsch, E. S. (1996). *The block book.* Washington, DC: National Association for the Education of Young Children. A classic on block building with unit and hollow blocks. www.naeyc.org

Seefeldt, C., and Galper, A. (2000). *Active experiences for active children: Social studies.* Upper Saddle River, NJ: Prentice Hall. Chapter 5. "The Past is Present" presents interesting and appropriate experiences on measuring time.

Smith, R. R. (2002, November). Cooperation and Consumerism: Lessons learned at a kindergarten mini-mall. *Teaching children mathematics. 9*(3), 179–183. Explains the extensive learning from this ongoing math project.

Worsley, M., Beneke, S., and Helm, J. H. (2003). The pizza project: Planning and integrating math standards in project work. In D. Koralek (Ed.), *Spotlight on young children and math* (pp. 35–42). Washington, DC: National Association for the Education of Young Children. In using the project approach math is involved in in-depth study. www.naeyc.org

Video

Path to math: Shapes; parts and wholes [Video]. Magna Systems, Inc. www.magnasystems.com

Path to math: Space; measurement [Video]. Magna Systems, Inc. www.magnasystems.com

Children's Books

Archambault, J. (1997). *Knots on a counting rope.* New York: Owlet. Sensitively written Native American story of child's life. The knots represent passage of time. Written for primary years.

Dodds, D. A. (1998). *Shape of things.* Glenview, IL: Scott Foresman. These illustrations take the young reader from shape to seeing shapes in houses and other composites of shapes for all young ages.

Hoban, T. (1985). *Is it larger? Is it smaller?* New York: Greenwillow. Tana Hoban's sharp detailed photography lends itself to exploring size for preschool years.

Hoban, T. (1998). *So many squares. So many circles.* New York: Greenwillow. Artful display of shapes leads to exploring more in the child's world. For preschool years.

Lionni, L. (1968). *The biggest house in the world.* New York: Pantheon. Story carries the reader along in looking at size. For preschool years.

Lionni, L. (1960). *Inch by inch.* New York: Astor-Honor. This little inchworm measures big things. For preschool years.

Myller, R. (1990). *How big is a foot?* New York: Random House. Simple story explains the need for standard measurements. A good explanation for primary years.

Web Sites

www.communityplaythings.com Community Playthings has fine block sets. The catalog has an excellent description and diagrams of unit blocks.

www.etacuisenaire.com ETA Cuisenaire on-line catalog has a variety of materials for measurement and shape. Examples are GeoSolid® sets of three-dimensional shapes, geoboards, floor size pattern blocks, digital timer, inch and centimeter rulers, and even a centiworm and inchworm ruler that follows the story of *Inch by Inch*.

www.gse.buffalo.edu Foundations for Mathematical Thinking explains math learning research and curriculum for early childhood.

www.naeyc.org Joint Position Statement by NAEYC and NCTM (National Council of Teachers of Mathematics). (2002). *Early childhood mathematics: Promoting good beginnings.*

Chapter 16

Exploring Physical Science

Photo courtesy Patrick Clark

OBJECTIVES Through the process of discovery in this chapter, you will be able to:

1. Describe the extensive learning experiences inherent in the physical science activities that most closely match the four physical knowledge criteria.

2. Given four examples of physical science activities, decide the applicability of each to the physical knowledge criteria.

3. Discuss application of the physical knowledge criteria to biological science experiences.

4. Discuss the applicability of physical science activities in which electricity, magnetism, density, and chemical change are explored.

5. Describe physical science experiences in ramps, pendulums, pulleys, and blocks.

6. Describe inquiry topics in tinkering, woodworking, and water flow.

IDEAS TO PONDER

• How do I determine what physical science activities are best?

• How can physical science experiences enhance physical knowledge?

• How can I implement physical science experiences?

• What physical science experiences are not appropriate for young children?

• How can physical science experiences be implemented when they do not meet all of the physical knowledge criteria?

The learner is actively constructing knowledge rather than passively taking in information. . . . Learners do not acquire *knowledge that is transmitted to them; rather, they* construct *knowledge through their intellectual activity and make it their own.* (Chaillé & Britain, 2003, p. 10)

PHYSICAL KNOWLEDGE CRITERIA APPLIED TO SCIENCE

For the young child to construct knowledge in physical science, he must actively engage with the materials to make it his own. The type of knowledge that Kamii and DeVries (1993) call physical knowledge is gained most thoroughly from the child acting on the object. There are many kinds of physical science, ranging from balancing a block to chemical reactions. Only some of these allow the child to directly act on objects to experience the results.

The four criteria for activities that promote physical knowledge can be applied to various kinds of physical science experiences. Table 16–1 indicates the four criteria originally presented in Chapter 2.

These four criteria can be applied to the following four examples. You can see how each activity matches the physical knowledge criteria.

> *An inclined plane is a slanted surface of varying degrees from the horizontal.*

A. Two children can choose from balls or wooden cars for the **inclined plane** experiment. They can make the inclined plane higher or lower and watch the speed of the cars or balls roll down it. With the teacher's guidance, they mark how far each item rolls (Fig. 16–1).

B. After children have had many experiences making homemade play dough in class, the teacher puts out a set of the following materials for each child: small amounts of flour and salt in plastic containers with $\frac{1}{8}$ cup measures, plus water with a $\frac{1}{4}$ cup measure and food coloring in a small squeeze bottle. There is a small amount of vegetable oil in a plastic squeeze bottle. Each child can make his own play dough in small mixing bowls. Each can select ingredients, decide on amounts, and add more as long as the ingredients last (Fig. 16–2).

> *An electrical board is a system of electrical devices, wires, and battery that can be arranged to turn on and off the devices.*

C. An **electrical board** with a lantern battery is placed for two children to work with. On the top of electrical board are a small noisy motor, an electric bulb, and a doorbell. On the bottom are an electrical on/off switch, a simple switch, and a button switch. Each of these six items can be connected using

---

TABLE 16–1　Physical Knowledge Criteria Applied to Science

Physical Knowledge Criteria Applied to Science Activities	Activity A	Activity B	Activity C	Activity D
1. Child produces the movement by her actions.				
2. Child can vary his actions to affect outcome.				
3. Child can observe the action of the object.				
4. Child can immediately experience the effect.				

(*Sources:* Chaillé & Brittain, 2003, pp. 68, 69; Kamii & DeVries, 1993, pp. 8, 9)

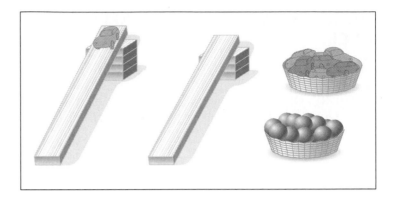

Figure 16–1 Inclined plane.

an insulated electrical wire. For example, a child can (1) connect two wires from the battery to the light; or (2) connect first to a switch, then to the light, and return to the battery (Fig. 16–3).

D. The teacher directs children to make a large cone of clay with a hole in the top for a "volcano." She fits an empty frozen juice can inside the cone. To make the volcano work, she explains that she will mix ingredients found in the kitchen, baking soda and vinegar. She pours a spoonful of baking soda in the juice can, then asks children to step back from the table and adds a spoon of vinegar. After viewing the reaction, the teacher says, "There, we have a volcano" (Figs. 16–4 and 16–5).

Lump of play dough

Figure 16–2 Making homemade play dough.

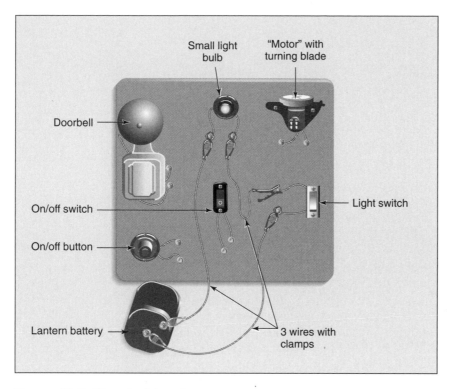

Figure 16–3 Electrical board.

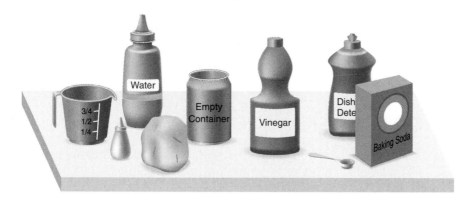

Figure 16–4 Volcano experiment.

You will need

1 empty frozen juice can (6-oz size) or a small jar

A mound of clay

2 tablespoons of baking soda

3–4 drops of red food coloring

$\frac{1}{4}$ cup dishwashing liquid

$\frac{1}{3}$ cup plus 1 tablespoon vinegar

$\frac{1}{2}$ cup water

Make a cone of clay by forming it around the can or jar in the shape of a volcano, and allow it to dry overnight. Put the baking soda in the can or jar. Mix the last four ingredients in a small dish. Slowly pour this solution into the can or jar. Watch the bubbles form, slowly rise, and overflow over the top of the "volcano."

Figure 16–5 Recipe for making a volcano.

You can see that there are differences in the preceding four activities when they are compared with the physical knowledge criteria in Table 16–1.

From this you know that some kinds of physical science activities will meet all criteria and some will not. The science experiences that meet all four of the criteria will best support young children's learning in physical knowledge.

The variety of materials that children can act on directly include the inclined plane, play dough and other manipulative materials, pulleys and pendulums, building blocks and woodworking construction, and experiences with sand and water. Ongoing opportunities to build and experiment with these materials in the classroom provide the raw materials through which children can see the results of their actions and try changing them to meet their goals. These physical science experiences are the best choices for building young children's understanding of cause and effect.

CHOICES IN PHYSICAL SCIENCE

One does not need to stop at this point. There are countless materials to explore where children cannot observe the force on the object (no. 3 in Table 16–1). Young children cannot yet grasp the concepts that explain the **intervening force,** such as the force of magnetism. Where the other three categories of physical knowledge criteria for science can be met, children can act on the materials directly (employing the intervening force) and vary results and observe them. Here children can experience the result of the intervening force.

The common sink-and-float activity is a prime example where the concept is not understood. In their handling of objects from boats to bolts, children explore the materials in water. They find that some float, some sink. Yet they cannot yet understand the complexity of **density.** (Otherwise why would a steel tanker

Intervening force is a phenomenon that is not caused directly by the child acting on it and is usually not observable by the child.

Density is the mass of a substance per unit volume.

float?) They cannot predict with accuracy what will float and sink, but they can explore and comment on what they find out.

Forces and energy that young children cannot explain include **magnetism,** electricity, or even the working of a computer. Yet children use these everyday. When simple materials using force or electricity can be explored, children can recognize that there is an intervening force that causes actions. For example, they feel the force of the magnet and see the result of the electricity in a circuit. In this technological world they will continue to adapt to the ensuing advances that they experience without blinking an eye.

Magnetism is the force exhibited in magnets and other phenomena.

But as in the "explosion" (vinegar and baking soda) when the result is magic to children, thay are simply observers of a **chemical change** (Chaillé & Britain, 2003). In this case although they immediately see the reaction, the reaction is outside their understanding and control. The actual change is not seen, only the end result (the fizzing). Also, since the chemical reaction is not usually seen in their daily lives, it does not lead to further understanding their world. Additionally, labeling this chemical reaction as a volcano misinforms children because a volcano is not caused by the combination of baking soda and vinegar. In junior high, as children learn about chemical structure and change, the vinegar and baking soda combination is a safe one to try. When older children can understand the CO_2 as a gas given off in that chemical reaction, then this can be related to the fizz in their drink and the corn bread rising in the oven.

Chemical change is a change in the composition of materials.

There are many kinds of activities like this that are best left to the science lab in junior high school. Additional examples of these include growing crystals and repelling talcum powder suspended in water by the addition of soap.

APPLYING PHYSICAL KNOWLEDGE CRITERIA TO BIOLOGICAL SCIENCE

In biological science children observe the change from caterpillar to butterfly and the sprout of the tiny grass seed as something beyond their comprehension. The four physical knowledge criteria are not all met in many biological science activities. Yet in experiencing these phenomena of metamorphosis and germination over time children generalize that these fascinating changes do take place. In their wonderment they can see the purpose of growth and change, as they sense their own bodies changing.

PHYSICAL SCIENCE EXPERIENCES

Fortunately, there are many physical science materials that meet the criteria for physical knowledge. In choosing these, teachers provide a wide range of constructivist learning tools. This is the main focus of physical science in preschool and kindergarten.

STANDARDS

As a result of the activities in grades K–4, all students should develop an understanding of

■ Properties of objects and materials

■ Position and motion of objects

■ Light, heat, electricity, and magnetism.

Content Standard: K–4. B. Reprinted with permission from *National science education standards* (1996). The National Academy of Sciences, courtesy of the National Academies Press, Washington, DC (p. 106).

The classroom can be set up for ample ongoing opportunities for processing cause and effect. Children will explore materials they can actively manipulate to create a variety of results.

Activities with Inclined Planes

Inclined Plane 1 The inclined plane can be made with cardboard tubes from wrapping paper, clear tubes, long boards, and blocks. The height of the inclined plane is varied by the number of blocks used. Materials to roll on the inclined plane are balls of various sizes, cylinder blocks, or cars. Larger, well-constructed cars are best so the car will "track" in a straight line. Plan for children to vary only one variable at a time, such as the height of the clear tube (see Fig. 16–1).

Organize the inclined plane experience by selecting an area of the classroom that has ample space. A barrier made out of unit blocks limit the balls or cars rolling out of the area, or they can be stopped by directing them to a wall. If children are ready to track the distance reached by the moving object, provide different colors of tape to match different colors of cars or balls so the distance an object travels can be marked (Kamii & DeVries, 1993).

Inclined Plane 2 Children often roll objects down ramps they have constructed in the course of everyday block building. After the children have gained informal experience with ramps, you could help them set up a ramp experiment. For example, three children could build ramps of different heights, all starting from a line marked on the floor. They could decide to roll a ball or a car down their ramps to compare which rolls the farthest. Before they actually begin, the children could predict how far they think their objects will roll, mark that spot with a color of tape, and then check to see how far the object actually rolled. Children may experiment with measurement to compare the distance the objects rolled. Finally, the children record their experiment on a graph so other children can compare results with them. These young scientists will be developing spatial relationship, prediction, observation, graphing, and cooperative learning skills (Kamii & DeVries, 1993; Sprung, 1996).

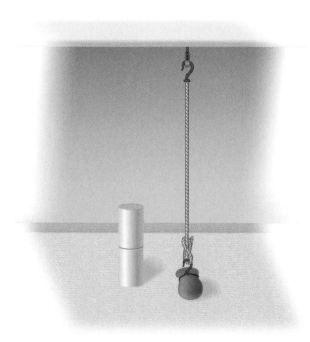

Figure 16–6 A pendulum is suspended from the ceiling.

Activities with Pendulums and Pulleys

Ceiling Pendulum Hang a **pendulum** on a long string from the ceiling or from the arch of an open doorway in an out-of-the–way location. The **bob** can be a rolled up sock. Children can predict where to place a cylinder block or other object and where to start the pendulum to knock down the target (Fig. 16–6).

Comparing Pendulums The goal in comparing pendulums is to experiment with pendulums that differ in length of the cord, weight, and size. Children may want to explore how changing the length of the line, the weight, or the size of the bob affects the distance of the swing and the speed of the swinging bob. Make a standing frame with a wood dowel attached (taped or clamped) to two chairs. On two cords of different lengths, hang pendulum bobs made of heavy and light materials, such as a rock, ball, sock, pompom, wooden bead. S-shaped hooks at the end of the cords make it easy to switch the bobs from large to small or from heavy to light. Children arrange two pendulums of different materials on the standing frame. They will experiment with the path of each pendulum and vary the materials and the length of the pendulum (Fig. 16–7).

This activity can be done outdoors by suspending a horizontal bar about 5 feet from the ground. It will be easier to compare distance and speed of the path the pendulum takes in the larger space outdoors.

Pendulum and Pulley In this activity the goal is to hit a predicted target by altering the height and length of the pendulum using the **pulley.** Experiment with

A pendulum is an object suspended from a fixed point so as to swing freely.

A bob is the swinging object that is fastened to the lower end of the cord on the pendulum.

A pulley is a simple machine made with a cord wrapped around a grooved wheel.

Figure 16–7 Children can compare two pendulums.

various changes in position, target, and length of pendulum. A pulley is mounted on a long board that is placed over chairs and taped down. A tennis ball is attached to a clothesline cord. Next to the pendulum and pulley, a flannel board is placed. On it place a circle target made out of felt. Before each attempt to hit the target, rub chalk on the tennis ball to mark where the ball hits the flannel board.

The child places the target on the flannel board and alters the height, length, and placement of the pendulum bob (tennis ball) to attempt to hit the target.

Figure 16–8 A pendulum with a pulley, suspended from the ceiling, adds more challenge.

When using a location with more space, attach a pulley to the ceiling. Ask another child to place the target and suggest how the other can hit the mark (Prairie & Selman, 1995) (Fig. 16–8).

Swinging Sand Pendulum Using a pendulum, children will explore making the path of sand as it pours from the funnel (placed as the bob) on a pendulum and observe the resulting pattern that will be made of the sand. Suspend a dowel rod between two chairs; attach a funnel with three or four holes punched near the top rim to an 18-inch cord suspended from the rod. Place a large plastic sheet under the apparatus. Using a large serving tray, cut white construction paper to fit the tray. Pour fine sand into the funnel and allow the funnel to swing across the paper, making a pattern. Children can experiment with the path the sand makes with the pendulum swing (Fig. 16–9). Another way to construct the swinging sand pendulum is to place the frame over the sandbox indoors or outdoors. When doing this, limit the path of the pendulum to stay inside the sandbox (Prairie & Selman, 1995).

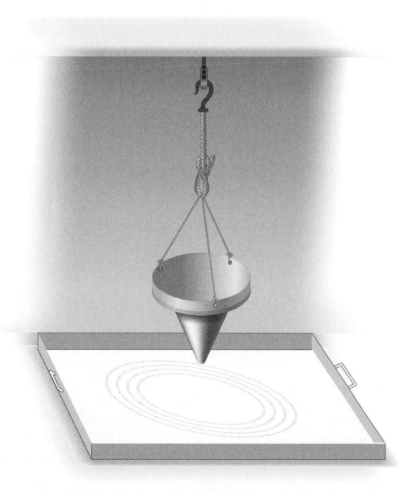

Figure 16–9 Sand pours from a swinging pendulum.

Physical Science in Blocks

In addition to the math learning with blocks, block building involves physical science. The very young child stacks blocks and takes pleasure in knocking them down. This transformation is seen in the sense of power she exhibits in making the clatter and disassembled pile. Then she begins again to transform the pile into a structure. Each block that she adds when building a tower is a mark of precise balance. Balance is a challenge when trying different combinations with shapes of the unit block set—cylinder, triangle, and arch. For the older child, building towers becomes more intricate, and so does the challenge of the balance. Balance is seen in complex forms in the architectural form of the arch, bridge, column, **lintel,** and **cantilever.**

A lintel is a long piece that spans two columns and usually carries the load above an opening.

As children lift unit, cardboard, and the heavier hollow blocks, children sense the force needed to move them with their hands, arms, and sometimes their whole bodies. When children explore different ways to move the blocks, planning at clean-up time could be instrumental in transporting blocks in ways children envision. In addition to the math concepts of symmetry and relationships of shape, children encounter physical science concepts in lifting, knocking them down, building, balancing, moving, and transporting all kinds of blocks.

Tinkering and Helping with Repairs

A cantilever is a projecting beam supported at only one end.

Because children have little opportunity to tinker, they will be delighted to take things apart to see how they work. To help children be aware of the make up of

Building a tower requires precise balance.

an increasingly technological world, **tinkering** becomes a part of the early childhood curriculum (Sprung, 1996).

As teachers find small repairs to make on the playground or in the classroom, sometimes children can work at the repair, hold the tools, or steady the ladder with an adult. Maintenance personnel who enjoy sharing their work with children can be greeted by curious helpers so daily tasks of keeping the school functioning do not seem such a mystery to the children.

Tinkering is to experiment mechanically by taking things apart.

Woodworking

Working with wood is both satisfying and rewarding for young children because of the aesthetic value of the wood itself and the use of real tools. Teachers carefully plan for setting up a safe experience, providing tools and materials where children accomplish real work, and teaching safe use. Children can have hours of satisfactory experiences in woodworking when proper use of tools is modeled, firm rules are adhered to, and children work singly or in groups of two with constant supervision.

Water as a Force

Water can be explored in many ways: as a sensory medium, as a force, and in understanding the source of water and transportation of it to home, schools, and parks for our use. The Inquiry Topic: Waterworks in this chapter explores the flow of water, and in Chapter 17, the Inquiry Topic: Water Source is the study of how water is transported from the water source to buildings.

INQUIRY TOPICS ON EXPLORING PHYSICAL SCIENCE

INQUIRY TOPIC

TINKERING

Purpose

Children will explore simple and complex machines, hypothesize how they work, and investigate the parts. Dismantling appliances is an investigation of the science behind technology (Ross, 2000).

Teachers Prepare

Study Examine parts of simple machines and appliances. Use simple tools yourself so you can support children learning tool use. Become familiar with unsafe parts and chemicals (such as in batteries) in appliance parts. Determine community locations where children are welcome and they can safely observe. These may be appliance/TV repair, shoe repair, machine shop, or car mechanic. Find technicians, male or female, such as a parent, repair person, or maintenance personnel of the school who would visit the classroom or welcome children at their location to view a repair process.

Questions   Are children curious about how things work? Do they converse about complex appliances such as the VCR, television, or computer? Are they capable of handling tools for disassembly? Can they manage lots of small items by categorizing and storing them in containers? Are they mature enough to keep small parts out of their mouths? Is there a way for the children to observe an adult completing a repair process?

Materials   For disassembly and assembly of simple machines, you will need two or more items to take apart, trays, a basket for each set of pieces of the simple machine, and recipe cards (see below). For tinkering you will need throw-away appliances, such as clocks, VCRs, or cassette players. Tools needed are four sizes of Phillips-head and flathead screwdrivers, and several needle-nose pliers. Acquire several containers to hold small parts.

Safety concerns   All electrical plugs are removed before children handle appliances. Be sure that children know that no parts or wires are to be inserted into electrical outlets (unused outlets in the classroom will be covered). Explain the electrical current and its potential harm. Teach safe tool use and the basics of what they are doing. No tools or objects should be used like a hammer or a pick. Be sure that they know they should not take apart anything at home unless an adult says they can. For your own guidelines, ask a knowledgeable person about hazardous parts of an appliance that children will disassemble. Because real tools are used on real appliances, closely supervise the children's work at taking apart appliances.

Recipes
1. Disassembly and assembly of simple machines. Select simple machines such as a garlic press, a spray mister, a food grinder, or a plastic balance scale. On recipe cards show a diagram (or photos) of the simple machine disassembled and then assembled. On a separate recipe card, describe with words and pictures the tasks to accomplish with the tool, such as assembling the garlic press, using it at the play dough table, taking it apart, and washing it before returning it to its container (Sprung, 1996).
2. For tinkering, after showing children the materials and appliances, work with them to develop "work rules" so children are safe and materials are stored neatly. Post the rules and readdress them as children and teachers find need for additional rules.

Use technology   Photocopy instruction pamphlets that come with the appliance. Look for assembly instructions available on a short teaching video or CD (request from manufacturer). Take photos of assembled and disassembled appliance. Videotape children's discussions of parts and ideas of how the machine works. Use these to review what children thought as they gain more understanding. Look up the names of appliance parts on www.encarta.msn.com. Look up appliances on the Internet for descriptions of what they do and download pictures of appliances in use.

In Experiences About This Inquiry Topic, Children Will

Explore   Children will explore the simple machines and how they can assemble them and use them. They will explore the tools for the tinkering and try out using them. They will use various tools to investigate different appliance parts. In handling these parts children will see how they look and feel and see some moving parts. They will discover electrical circuits, pulleys, springs, levers, magnets, and other components, some of which they may recognize in daily life.

Identify   Children will learn the parts of the simple machine, the appliance, and the tools they use, the actions of the simple machines, and the actions of their work. Some terminology learned could be: circuit board, gear, lever, transistor, capacitor, and resistor. (Teachers may also be learning these names as well.) A resource person knowledgeable in electronics may be helpful in identifying basic parts. Then go to the Encarta on-line encyclopedia (www.encarta.msn.com) to obtain descriptions of identified parts.

Classify   Sort the kinds of screws and other parts that are removed from the appliance into separate containers. Each container is labeled by taping an example of its content on the lid. As the collection of loose parts grows, bring them together and ask children what they would like to do with them. This could involve resorting and using some items for other purposes.

Compare and contrast   Compare parts that come from different appliances. Discuss whether a particular part that looks the same does the same task in both appliances. Through the photos taken at different times, children can compare the differences in the look of the appliance as it becomes disassembled.

Hypothesize   Children will question how a tool they use works. Children will question what a particular part does when they discover it in the appliance. They will wonder what was wrong with the appliance and how it can be fixed. For the disassembly/assembly process of simple machines, they will form ideas of how the simple matching is put together and how it works. As they look at the more complicated systems of the appliances, they may have questions or ideas to share with a technician in a repair shop. This will be the time to plan a field visit to view technicians at work. You may plan to take a repairable appliance to the technician. First hypothesize with the group why it may not work and what part could be fixed. Videotape the technician at work and photograph close-up views of the repair. Use these photos and video to review what children saw the technician do and review their questions and new understanding. They may want to compare what they do in their tinkering with what the technician has done.

Generalize   Children can state how they see the tools and simple machines work. While many of the understandings of the working of an appliance are too complicated for them to understand, they can generalize about some of the processes, such as the mechanical workings when a video is inserted into the VCR. Children can discuss theories of what appliances need to work and how to fix them.

Extended Experiences   The group may want to revisit the technician to ask more questions or observe the repair process closely. Again take photos and videos and revisit. If children are focusing on a particular repair process, talk with them about replicating it in their tinkering work. They can draw steps of this process and post it in the tinkering center. Children may want to explore things they can make work using an electrical board. Children may be interested in developing dramatic play areas that depict the technician and repair shop. They can incorporate the loose parts from the tinkering area into dramatic play. For this play, substitute plastic tools for the real ones. Some children may want to make a book about the use of an appliance or tool. Groups could make "care books" that describe the safe use and care of appliances at home and add them to the family home library.

INQUIRY TOPIC

WOODWORKING

Purpose

Children will explore working with wood to understand its properties and to learn tool use. For advanced work children will cut and shape wood and combine two or more pieces to create an object from their ideas or from a model.

Teachers Prepare

Study   Study how to work with wood and learn tool use. Look for sources of wood. Look for a location where carpenter work is being done where children can visit, such as a house under construction. Look for a cabinet maker or carpenter who can show children their skills

Questions Are children interested in wood, in tool use? Can the children in the group use tools safely? Can there be enough adults to supervise this activity closely at least some parts of the day or some days each week?

Gather materials Tools: These are real tools, but of lighter weight, so the child can feel the satisfaction of real tools doing real work. These tools consist of 10-oz claw hammers, hand drills, assorted drill bits, 12- to 15-inch saws with a blunt end, C-clamps, miter boxes, lathe, and safety goggles. A solid workbench with at least one vise is necessary (see Web sites for catalog resources). Add 50-size sandpaper, a try square, pencils and rulers, short nails with large heads (roofing nails), and large wood screws to make up the basic supplies (Sosna, 2000). For small parts, place in a clear plastic container and tape an example of its contents on the lid. Hang woodworking tools on a pegboard mounted above or beside the work bench. On the pegboard, outline the shape of the tool as it hangs in place.

Wood Pine wood pieces (2 by 4s) can often be obtained from scrap at a lumber yard. Purchase a small amount of other soft woods such as balsa and poplar.

Additional materials to use with wood: wood shapes such as spools, wheels, strips, large washers, bottle caps, fabric scraps.

Children's Books *Force and Motion* by Lafferty

How a House Is Built by Jackson

The Magic Toolbox by Araki

Tools by Morris

Recipes For simplified experiences using hammers and first experiences hammering wood, Styrofoam one-inch thick and golf tees can be used and reused with a small wood hammer (Fig. 16–10). Or tape together several thicknesses of cardboard for use with the golf tees.

For beginning experiences with wood, a tree trunk or log can be used. Either the cut end of a stump or a side of a log with bark can be used as a surface for pounding in large headed nails.

Safety considerations Use tools with groups of children who can abide by basic safety rules. Use only with constant supervision by a knowledgeable volunteer or staff. Teach safe and correct tool use. Allow only two children to work with tools at one time. If children are sanding or gluing, this can be done at a nearby space large enough for several children. Whether indoors or outdoors, plan the woodworking area away from traffic and arrange so saws in use are directed toward a wall and away from other children. Anyone doing woodworking wears safety goggles.

Use technology Take photos of children's progress. Use close-up shots to show details of work. Videotape carpenters at work or the woodworking skill of a visitor. Access simple woodworking projects on the Internet.

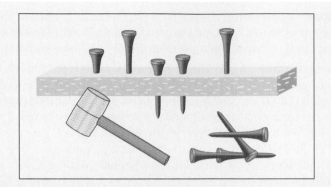

Figure 16–10 Materials for easy hammering experiences for a young child include thick Styrofoam and golf tees with a wooden hammer.

In Experiences About This Inquiry Topic, Children Will

Explore   Children will experiment with what they can do with a tool. They will saw, sand, hammer, drill, and insert screws. The accomplishment of joining two pieces of wood or sawing a 1" × 2" into two pieces will be prized work.

Identify   Name tools, processes of hammering, sawing, drilling, joining, and measuring. Children can name what skilled workers do with wood. Plan field trips to view carpentry work and/or invite a carpenter or cabinet maker to show her work during a classroom visit. Children can use drawing to record the woodworking being accomplished. Also videotape to show the process, and on return visits continue to videotape to show the change in work from day to day.

Classify   Match the tool with its outline when putting it away. Nails and screws can be sorted into containers.

Compare and contrast   Compare the skills children accomplish. Contrast what one task accomplishes as compared to another. Compare sizes of nails, pieces of wood, and kinds of wood. Compare the length of the nail or the screw with the wood piece or pieces that it will be nailed or screwed into. Informal and formal measurement can be used in these comparisons.

Hypothesize   Children will ask how two pieces can be joined. They will question how long to make a piece of wood. They will want to find out if they put a nail into two pieces will the nail hold the pieces together. They will question making wood smooth, smaller, or rounded.

Generalize   If I measure the nail and the thickness of the wood, I can find out if I can join two pieces. I can change the shape and size and combine wood pieces through different woodworking tasks.

Extended Experiences   Children can add to their products through gluing additional pieces, or painting, or adding a clear finish. Wood not appropriate for woodworking can become materials for gluing projects.

Combine woodworking with the Inquiry Topic   Trees (see Chapter 18). Collect branches and cut small logs for a group woodworking project. If group ideas for woodworking projects become advanced beyond the skills of the children, incorporate a carpenter or wood sculptor to work with their plans, or access woodworking plans on the Internet. Most work of young children will not advance to wood projects, yet some of the older and more experienced children may want to explore building a particular project. If so, teachers can work with them on using models, if that would be a project that builds satisfaction.

INQUIRY TOPIC

WATERWORKS

Purpose

Children will experiment with the flow of water. They can explore water flow in a variety of ways by finding out ways it flows and experimenting with transporting water through pipes and tubes. The goal is for children to explore materials and ways to vary the water flow by altering these materials.

Teachers Prepare

Questions   Are children interested in the feel of water when involved in water play or washing hands? In water play are they curious about the flow of water from one container to another? Is this a good time of the year for using water outdoors?

Study   Work with the various tools and materials for studying the flow of water. Experiment with different combinations of materials where water flow can be altered.

Gather materials   Materials for waterworks experiences include the water table and/or clear storage bins, a pegboard base to mount waterworks materials, pegboard hook, pitchers, plastic bottles, a valve, nail and hammer, clear plastic cups, twist ties, clear tubing and connectors, PVC pipes, and connectors for the pipes (or purchase from an early childhood catalog [see Web sites]). Outdoors, add empty dish soap bottles or other squeezable bottles. To the water table add funnels, basters, clear tubing, water play cups (with holes in the bottom), clear water pumps, and water wheel/sandmill.

Recipes   To make a water fountain, waterworks experiment station, water flow experiment and pipe connections, follow the directions in Appendix C in Tables C–6, C–7, C–8 & C–9.

Use technology   Take close-up photos or short videos of what children explore with waterworks. Review these with individual children to help them review what they have discovered. Photos may be collected for documentation on water flow. Research the Internet to download photos of waterfalls and river rapids.

In Experiences About This Inquiry Topic, Children Will

Explore   Children will first explore water as a sensory material and then experiment with what water will do using the materials added to the water table. As children work in water play, support them in setting up simple experiments in water flow following the recipes to make fountains, water works, and water flow experiments. Use I wonder statements following children's ideas. The experimenting will continue with the waterworks experiences indoors and/or outside. Children will make simple fountains and explore pouring water into cups on the waterworks experiment station, beginning with water flow in one cup, then two, and expanding more. They will experiment with water flow through a tube, directing the water and finding ways to start and stop it (DeVries et al, 2002).

Outdoors children can squirt water with the dishwashing liquid bottles and connect clear tubing and PVC pipe to experiment with water flow through pipes.

Identify   Name actions of the water: It flows, goes down, goes fast, goes slow, makes a fountain, and makes a spray. Water comes out of the holes flowing downward. Water flows out or the tubes or pipe or stops flowing.

Classify   Children make fountains the same; make additional plastic cups with one hole, two holes, or more; and make plastic cups with side holes or bottom holes.

Compare and contrast   As water flows out of the holes in the plastic cups, compare the water flow with another cup. Ask if children can change the water flow or make it match the flow out of another cup. Water flows the same, different, faster, slower, more, or less.

Hypothesize   How can I get the water to go faster? Slower? Stop? How can I make the water flow in another direction? How does water flow from one location to another? What is needed in pipes to allow water to start at one place and move to another? What can I construct to make water flow? How can I make water flow from one location to another (outside)?

Generalize   If you pour the water here, it will come out there (Nichols & Nichols, 1990). If I pour water in a cup with two holes, water comes out both holes. I can catch the water coming out of one hole. If I pour the

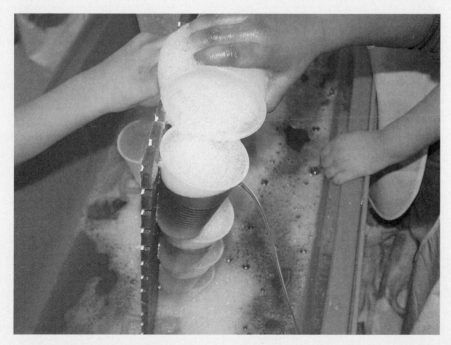

Children explore water flow in water works.

water in this end, it comes out here. I can put pipes or tubes together to make the water flow to a different place.

Extended Experiences   With these water flow materials children will explore for a long time. Follow their interest for expansion and reexamining their questions. The children could develop a pipe extension to allow water to flow from the spigot to the sandbox outdoors. Children could use plastic troughs for water and sand play (Fig. 17–1). Children could observe water flow in a river or stream and view the photos of waterfalls and rapids. If there is interest, combine this study with the Inquiry Topic: Water Source in Chapter 17.

SUMMARY

The four physical knowledge criteria provide a framework for all the sciences for young children. The physical science experiences here are motivating and meaningful for preschool and kindergarten children. The open-ended time for discovery of cause and effect in physical science will bring satisfaction and a sense of self-confidence through ongoing discovery. As you follow children through experiences in the other sciences, these same important components of physical knowledge will be seen. These will become apparent in the earth science you will encounter in the next chapter.

TO FURTHER YOUR THINKING

1. Discuss your remembrances of chemistry experiments from your schooling. What do you remember learning? What was your attitude about the experiments? Compare this with a possible response of children if they saw Example D, the volcano experiment at the beginning of the chapter.

2. From the Additional Resources look for more physical sciences experiences in these books: Forman, 1984; Green, 1996; MacDonald, 2001; and Wellhousen and Kieff, 2001. Select two experiences that promote the four criteria of physical knowledge. Assemble the materials and experiment with these yourself, and, if possible, try them with a young child. What makes your choices appropriate learning—or not—for young children?

3. Use a set of unit blocks incorporating the different shapes into building a structure. As you build, pay attention to the way you balance blocks and construct arches, bridges, lintels, and cantilevers. Compare your process of working with blocks as physical science with your earlier experience of finding math concepts in block building (Chapter 15).

4. Brainstorm with a colleague on uses of ramps, pulleys, pendulums, and balance for a family at home and/or in businesses in your community. If you were to implement a study on any of these topics, which examples of use could children view in the community? For example, a ramp is used for delivery trucks to lower the truck bed for unloading shipments of food at grocers and tiny pulleys are incorporated in the cords on pleated window shades.

5. Using one of the glossary terms from this chapter or a concept in physical science that you are curious about, go to Ask Jeeves for Kids www.ajkid.com and type in your question to expand your knowledge.

6. Look up information on the Froebel philosophy and the creation of unit blocks by Caroline Pratt on Froebel Web www.froebelweb.org. Compare the Froebel philosophy with the constructivist approach to physical science presented in this chapter. How does the creation of unit blocks by Caroline Pratt support physical science in block building and understanding of shape and space in mathematics?

7. Select an inquiry topic of tinkering, woodworking, or waterworks from this chapter. Discuss a way to introduce this topic to a selected group of children. What materials would you need to introduce this topic? What do you think children would know, and what would they want to find out? What information would you need to study before beginning this inquiry topic?

8. For each of the three inquiry topics in this chapter, imagine that you are the facilitator in these experiences. Consider your comfort level in these topics. What could you explore in order to increase your comfort level?

REFERENCES

Chaillé, C., and Britain, L. (2003). *The young child as scientist: A constructivist approach to early childhood science education* (3rd ed.). Boston: Allyn & Bacon.

DeVries, R., Zan, B., Hildebrandt, C., Edmiaston, R., and Sales, C. (2002). *Developing constructivist early childhood curriculum: Practical principles and activities.* New York: Teachers College Press.

Kamii, C., and DeVries, R. (1993). *Physical knowledge in preschool education; Implications of Piaget's theory* (2nd ed.). New York: Teachers College Press.

National Academy of Science. (1996). *National science education standards* [Book version, on line]. Washington, DC: National Academies Press. www.nap.edu

Nichols, W., and Nichols, K. (1990). *Wonderscience: A developmentally appropriate guide to hands-on science for young children.* Santa Fe, NM: Learning Expo.

Prairie, A. P., and Selman, G. (1995). Pendulums. Unpublished.

Ross, M. E. (2000, March). Science their way. *Young Children, 55*(2), 6–13.

Sosna, D. (2000, March). More about woodworking with young children. *Young Children, 55*(2), 38–39.

Sprung, B. (1996, July). Physics is fun, physics is important, and physics belongs in the early childhood curriculum. *Young Children, 51*(1), 29–32.

ADDITIONAL RESOURCES

Scholastic Early Childhood Today. (2002, June/July/August). The beauty of boxes & blocks. *Scholastic Early Childhood Today. 16*(8), 34–43. Creative problem-solving activities for children using simple boxes.

Forman, G. E., and Hill, F. (1984). *Constructive play: Applying Piaget in the preschool.* Menlo Park, CA: Addison-Wesley. Innovative materials in physical science to try with young children. The authors developed a variety of constructions for children to explore aspects of physical science.

Green, M. D. (1996). *474 science activities for young children.* Clifton Park, NY: Thomson Delmar Learning. Extend children's interest in physical science activities through a variety of activities in Woodworks, Marvelous Motion, and Thingamajigs. www.Delmar.com

Hirsch, E. S. (Ed.). (1996). *The block book* (3rd ed.). Washington, DC: National Association for the Education of Young Children. This classic book relates block play as learning in all developmental areas. www.naeyc.com

MacDonald, S. (2001). *Block play: The complete guide to learning and playing with blocks.* Beltsville, MD: Gryphon House. A simple idea book that goes far beyond block building. Check out simple machines and ramps. www.gryphonhouse.com

Wellhousen, K., and Kieff, J. (2001). *A constructivist approach to block play in early childhood.* Clifton Park, NY: Thomson Delmar Learning. A very complete text on blocks for learning and play. It does not limit itself to wooden blocks alone but emphasizes all kinds of constructive materials. www.Delmar.com

Videos

South Carolina Educational Television. (Producer). *Block play: Constructing realities.* [Video]. Washington, DC: National Association for the Education of Young Children. Shows children's learning from blocks and stages of block play. www.naeyc.org

Science anytime anyplace Motion & machines. [Video]. Crystal Lake, IL: Magna Systems, Inc. Depicts children experimenting with inclined planes, electricity, and magnets. www.magnasystems.org

Children's Books

Araki, M. (2003). *The magic toolbox.* San Francisco, CA: Chronicle Books.

Ardley, N. (1992). *The science book of motion.* San Diego, CA: Harcourt Brace Jovanovich.

Burton, V. (1999). *Mike Mulligan and his steam shovel.* New York: Houghton Mifflin.

Hoban, T. (1975). *Dig, drill, dump, fill.* New York: Greenwillow.

Jackson, C. T. (1994). *How a house is built.* New York: Scholastic. Contains illustrations of common tools.

Lafferty, P. (1992). *Force and motion.* Boston, MA: Dorling Kindersley Books.

Morris, A. (1998). *Tools.* New York: HarperTrophy.

Rau, D. M, and Billin-Frye, P. (1997). *A box can be many things.* Minneapolis, MN: Children's Press.

Web Sites

www.ajkid.com Ask Jeeves for Kids enables teachers and students to enter questions and get related responses. Teachers can get some quick answers to questions children ask.

www.childcraft.com and www.lakeshorelearning.com are catalog sources that have woodworking tools and woodworking bench. Lakeshore Learning has "Build and Play Tubes" that can be used in waterworks.

www.encarta.msn.com An on-line encyclopedia for research. Without subscribing, one can have access to explicit print information on a wide variety of science topics.

www.froebelweb.org Froebel Web: An Online Resource. This Web site focuses on Froebel philosophy as well as Caroline Pratt, who developed the well-known unit blocks used widely in schools for young children.

Chapter 17

Exploring Earth Science

OBJECTIVES Through the process of discovery in this chapter, you will be able to:

1. Describe earth science explorations that children can understand.

2. Depict the interrelationships of the four kinds of science.

3. Discuss the learning experiences in exploring mud, sand, and water.

4. Discuss exploration in the phenomena of rocks, sand, and soil.

5. Describe weather experiences for young children that they can understand.

6. Apply the focus of field trips on inquiry.

7. Describe young children's understanding of light and shadow and the light spectrum.

8. Discuss development of inquiry topics in rain, light and shadow, water source, and ecology.

9. Describe young children's concepts about ecology.

IDEAS TO PONDER

- What can young children understand in earth science?

- What can young children grasp in understanding weather?

- How can I continually use field trips to augment classroom learning?

- How can children study shadows?

- What can children learn about saving the earth?

Another kind of freedom for children, and adults, comes from being out of the owned space of schools and houses. The sky, the clouds, the rain, the wind are for everyone equally. . . . They lift our spirit. (Rivkin, 1995, p. 12)

You can participate in children's ponderings by offering your thoughts as a peer. Simply affirming that you share their curiosity is better than trying to give them answers. Join in the wonder and go where it takes you! (Ross, 2000, p. 12)

EARTH SCIENCE DEFINED

Earth science is the study of nonliving elements or inanimate matter on the planet and elements that affect the planet. These include meteorology or effects of weather, including temperature, moisture, sun, and wind, that are felt by a young observer outdoors. As the study of the materials of the earth, geology is at the heart of earth science. Basics of water, sand, and mud provide the sensory materials highlighted in Chapter 5. Earth science includes light and shadow, the source of water, and ecology. Young children will not understand everything about these elements, yet it is with the sense of wonderment that teachers connect with children as they encounter earth science.

STANDARDS

Properties of earth and sky.

Objects in the sky.

Changes in earth and sky.

Content Standard D. Reprinted with permission from *National science education standards.* (1996). The National Academy of Sciences, courtesy of the National Academies Press, Washington, DC (p. 107).

As with physical science, in earth science young children become most involved with what they can act on and change. The curriculum in this chapter centers on those experiences in which children have direct action on elements of the earth:

- The child selects a rock. By marking it with a penny or a pencil, he can directly see the result.
- The child pokes a stick in the ground. She digs around to find weeds with roots and several ants that stream away from her.
- The child walks in the rain. He lifts his face to the softly falling drops and opens his mouth wide.

FOUR KINDS OF SCIENCE INTERTWINED

As you work with the four types of science areas, it soon becomes evident that the study of these sciences (as presented in Chapters 16 to 19) are often interrelated. For example, in the study of the earth, soil is formed by decaying plant and animal life. This process helps make the soil a composite rich earth for plants to be sustained and grow and to support animal life. As this chapter shows, all is intertwined.

Ecosystems are biological and/or earth systems that form a living unit.

Young children can experience small areas of earth as **ecosystems.** Children can dig up a section of earth and discover elements of both plant and animal life. Children can see an ecosystem in miniature by creating a terrarium (see Chapter 18). Playgrounds can be seen as ecosystems with places for different types of play and spaces for plants, animals, and children (see Chapter 13). By keeping the playground space environmentally healthy, this spot of earth is preserved.

ECOLOGY

The first step toward concern for saving the environment for future generations is for young children to experience and enjoy it. Kupetz and Twiest (2000) confirm this by saying, "Teachers have responsibility to expose children to the delights and mysteries of the great outdoors. Before children learn how humans impact the environment in harmful ways, they need opportunities to learn to care about it" (p. 62).

Ecology is the study of conserving earth and living systems.

As evident from **ecology,** effects of humans on the environment show countless negative influences. Many of these influences are outside what young children experience. Yet in small observable ways, children can picture the changes humans can make to keep our spaces on earth for the people, animals, and plants and to preserve resources for the future.

OBSERVABLE COMPONENTS OF WEATHER

Weather is experienced almost daily, yet young children understand only some components. Children are involved in what they see around them; what is far away has little meaning to them. So focus with them on what they experience in their environment. They can

- Examine the water puddle after a rain and step over it or jump in it.
- Feel the force of the wind blowing their paper streamer or feel their scarf being whipped away from their face.
- Observe that water changes to ice and back again and compare the melted ice to other ice.

This is what children can experience directly. Clouds are too distant to provide direct involvement. Yet their shapes, movement, and beauty can be observed often and notations about the clouds can be made when weather changes.

In the early elementary years children can begin to understand concepts about the water cycle because of their concrete operational thinking. For the early childhood years, focus on what children can see, not what is unseen. Because steam itself cannot be observed the resulting condensation when it hits a colder surface is not understood. Because young children cannot see the water vapor that leaves the earth and eventually makes up the cloud, young children cannot grasp all the steps in the water cycle.

WATER, SAND, AND MUD EXPLORED

Rich and satisfying play comes from the mediums of water, sand, and mud. Teachers prepare the environment both indoors and outdoors for water, sand, and mud and gather a variety of materials to use with these mediums. Children can be prepared to use these safely and in ways that shoes and clothing are not harmed.

The play value of water is tremendous because of its multisensory character of sounds, textures, changes of state, and soothing feelings of wetness. Water is a primal element and holds endless fascination for young children. It excites and relaxes. Children seldom miss opportunities for water play, whether they are in the bathtub, in puddles, or in swimming pools. Water is also a valuable addition to other play elements, particularly sand or dirt.

These substances are from the earth. Using the mediums in the classroom and outdoors has great value to young children as these areas of earth science are close to the children. Table 17–1 describes the settings and materials for these experiences in detail.

TABLE 17–1   Materials for Water, Sand, and Mud Experiences

WATER, SAND, AND MUD EXPERIENCES

Sand Areas

Sand is an excellent medium for creative play and exploration. It is easy to move and mold. It can be dug, sifted, sculpted, poured, and drawn upon.

A large sand area outdoors provides for dry sand or water and sand play (see Chapter 13). Indoors, sand can be experienced in a sand/water table, especially during long periods of time spent indoors in temperate climates. Clean, fine sand that does not give off dust is appropriate. Some graininess in the sand also provides a different texture.

Children like to play in sand with small toys—especially pocket-sized trucks, animals, and vehicles—or they find other props, including on-site vegetation outdoors. Many types of plants are feasible for play, from grass and wild plants to parts of mature trees (Moore, Goltsman, & Iacofano, 1992, pp. 150, 160, 163).

In addition, a set of kitchen and tableware add to sand play. Plastic shovels, molds, and containers for holding and transporting sand add to the various kinds of sand play. Teachers can be aware of the kinds of play of the children and add the materials that support that play.

Troughs

The flow of water and sand is a force that children can experience outdoors freely (see Chapter 16 for Inquiry Topic: Waterworks). Children can work with adults to arrange troughs (the kind used for rain gutters). These can be suspended over the sand area so that one flows into another, end to end. Experiment with the angle of the trough so that water and/or sand will flow from one trough to another and then to the sand area underneath (Fig. 17–1).

Water

For indoor and outdoor experiences with water, children can use small pumps, water wheels, funnels, and containers of all shapes and sizes from short and wide to tall and narrow. Different kinds of experiences in water depend on the materials used at the water table and other areas of the classroom or outdoors. Materials can be organized for varied water play experiences: pouring and filling, sieves and containers with holes (small/large holes, high or low in container, one hole to many holes), pumps and wheels, sponges, and materials for washing (like different kinds of fabric). As teachers observe the play of children in water throughout the day they can learn what the children are interested in with this medium and follow accordingly.

When weather is freezing, the children can decide to create changes with water, snow, and ice. They can gather snow for the indoor water table, place water in containers outdoors overnight for their "homemade ice," and observe changes of these when brought inside or observed outside on a warmer day. If melted snow or ice is saved, it can be compared with where it came from, can be examined for its properties, and can be put outside or in the freezer to change its form again.

Soap and Water

Soap can be added to water. Longer-lasting bubbles can be made with $\frac{3}{4}$ cup mild dish detergent such as Dawn®, $\frac{1}{4}$ cup glycerin (from the drug store) or sugar, and 2 quarts warm water (Hill, 1977). Add an egg beater to make bubbles. Give each child a straw (for his use only), and the children can collectively create a bubble mountain together, or each child can make bubbles in his own small container. A short straw placed in the side of a Styrofoam cup makes a simple bubble machine. Children can experiment with berry baskets, shapes made with chenille stems, and plastic rings that secure a six-pack of water bottles.

Mud

Mud is also used indoors or outdoors. Indoors, teachers can supply the soil from outside or purchase planting soil. In wash tubs or water table, children can explore this medium with water. For an outdoor digging area, boots or Ziploc bags over shoes, and smocks over clothes help keep children clean. Add short plastic shovels, buckets, tablespoons, and cups to the digging area. Children gain an absorbed sense of satisfaction from working with soil (Hill, 1977).

ROCKS, SOIL, AND SAND IN INQUIRY

Rocks are of interest to children, especially when they can collect them firsthand. They can be sorted, seriated, and measured. Children can experiment with volume by seeing how many rocks of different sizes can overflow a large jar of water (Fig. 17–2). Children can build forms with rocks or make paths outdoors.

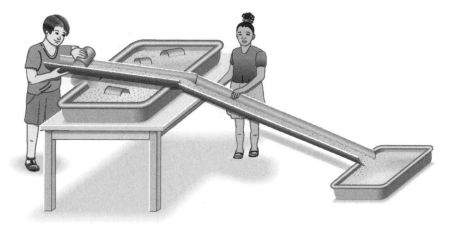

Figure 17–1 Children explore flow of sand with troughs constructed from plastic gutters.

Some stones can be drawn with; others can be sanded down to obtain sand. Change of characteristics of rocks can be observed in water. Some rocks can be cracked open (use safety goggles). A beam of light shown on some rocks shows different consistencies. Combine stones and sand to explore different ways of creating.

Sand and gravel can be sorted with a sieve, compared wet and dry, molded and shaped, and poured and piled. Gravel can be rubbed on hard surfaces and soft, such as a plastic frame and flannel. A magnifying glass can show the size of the granules.

The soil can be dug up outdoors, compared to sand, and used wet, damp, or dry. It can be mixed with sand, small rocks and crumbling leaves, grass, bark, and flowers. With these other natural ingredients, soil is a rich ingredient for dramatic play.

Figure 17–2 Children explore volume and displacement of the water when rocks are added.

For comparing portions of the earth in different areas of the playground, mark out a one-foot square. Using small trowels, spoons, and table knives, collect about a cup of earth from each area. Label each cup with the source of the earth, such as sandbox, garden, under the tree. Bring these samples indoors and provide a tray for each sample. Provide tea strainers, colanders, pencils, spoons, bug catchers, magnifying glasses, and/or microscope to examine each cup of earth. Children may draw the results they find. These examinations will no doubt show that the earth is made up of many things.

REFRACTED LIGHT

Refraction is deflection (or bending) of light as it passes from one medium to another so the colors in the light spectrum are made visible.

When children are working with bubble making outdoors in the sun, they may come upon light **refraction** in the bubbles. This may bring on new discoveries. Teachers can add acrylic **prisms** to capture and spread the light **spectrum.** One can also find the colors of light in oil suspended in water. In the sunshine, make a rainbow by adding a sprinkler either at a low volume in the water table or on the cement.

The formation of the light spectrum is one of the earth science phenomena that preschoolers cannot yet understand. Yet because they can make the colors of the rainbow occur, they will be interested. Telling children that sunlight is made up of all colors does not make sense to them because they do not see this without the refraction. Better to wonder with the child at the beautiful array of colors they find.

A prism is a transparent object that is shaped to refract a beam of light.

LIGHT SOURCES AND SHADOWS

In addition to the daily experience of the changes in light and dark as a pattern each day, children can enjoy working with a light source. With a small flashlight a child can control this source safely. Along with the child, compare the impact the flashlight has in the classroom and outdoors. Use the flashlight on a sunny and a cloudy day, in the classroom, and in a room without windows, such as a closet. Look at the distance the light can project. The child can compare the light shown in a box, under a shelf, in a sock, and through a tube.

A spectrum is a continuum of colors (rainbow) formed when a beam of white light is dispersed.

Children can explore materials using the light source of a transparency projector or light table. Children can arrange transparent, translucent, and opaque materials directly on the light source and compare the results. They can try all kinds of materials, such as aquarium glass, buttons, plastic sunglasses, paper clips, rocks, plastic containers, crayons, and a collection of bottle tops, feathers, and pompoms.

Children can experiment with many materials on the light table. They can create with manipulatives made from transparent plastic, color paddles and colored cellophane, and found materials made of transparent or translucent plastic. Provide them with thin paper and markers or watercolor paints. Use graph paper or lined paper. Try examining items from nature, such as flowers, grass, stems, bark, and seeds.

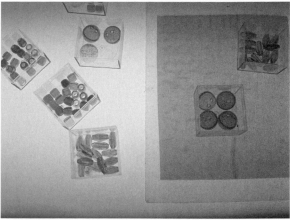

On the light table children see the vibrant red in flower petals and tints of color in buttons and beads.

From the study of light children may discover their own shadow. From this point their shadow and shadows of objects can be followed. Preschool children will have only an elementary understanding of shadows (see Additional Resources). The Inquiry Topic: Light and Shadows examines fascinating experiences with shadows.

WEATHER

Children can observe weather more closely if they are out in it rather than remembering it from the trip to school in the morning. Here is one system to observe weather with young children.

Designate a "weather reporter" for the week. She, with the help of her parents, can record the temperature and weather conditions or other **climatic data** before coming to school in the morning. The teacher can explore with the child and parents the most effective way to do this from home (radio, television, or computer). Or the weather and climatic data can be checked on the classroom computer each morning.

During outdoor play the weather person can interview several people about their experience of the weather at the moment. These descriptions can be more explicit than sunny, windy, warm or cool, or rainy. The child can record responses through drawings or tallies. Or she can use a copy of a chart with a variety of weather conditions displayed. During outdoor play she can mark the conditions she observes. If that day has inclement weather, the weather reporter can be asked to step outside a moment to get a report of the weather herself. The information is reported during group time and drawings or charts are posted for the day.

Any straight-sided container can serve as a weather gauge. Try to keep it clean and use it for observation only. When there is precipitation, measurements can be taken in centimeters and inches so children will be familiar with both measurements.

Climatic data is a collection of weather information both past and present.

In a temperate climate during spring or fall, the morning temperature that is recorded each day is compared over time. As the climatic data over a couple of weeks is followed, the differences in the weather and signs of the changing season are noted.

CLOUDS

By taking a sheet or blanket outdoors on warm days, the group can lie down and watch the clouds. Take photos of the cloud formations. The photos taken with the children can be added to the weather chart. With their own observances, the cloud formations will be meaningful to them. If children are interested, find the names of cloud formations on the Internet and keep a record of clouds seen tracked over that day and others. Do any of these clouds bring rain? To be sure children are not looking into the sun, do this early or late in the day and position them to look away from the sun (Seefeldt & Galper, 2000).

Cloud formations are photographed and labeled.

> **TABLE 17–2 Field Trip Focus on Inquiry**
>
> For inquiry the attention is
> - On noticing things in more or less detail depending on the child's age;
> - On comparing or contrasting new things to known or familiar objects or experiences;
> - On wondering how things get to be where and what they are; and
> - On enjoying and learning from our environment (Redleaf, 1996, pp. 4–5).

Watch the shapes and movement. After sharing *It Looked Like Spilt Milk*, by Shaw, play a game of I Spy as cloud formations remind you of objects (Huffman, 1996). If children show interest, bring out clipboards and charcoal pencils for them to draw the shapes they see. They then can dictate their imaginative ideas.

FIELD TRIPS

Short excursions or site visits that show components of what children are studying are effective in seeing how things work beyond the classroom. Field trips can introduce or solidify what children know on a topic of study. If the field trip is nearby, recurring visits can provide the avenue for children to find out and revisit what they know. Rhoda Redleaf (1996) explains, "a field trip is more a frame of mind, an approach to an experience either indoors or out, which focuses attention on inquiry" (p. 4) (Table 17–2).

Of course, field trips will be about any kind of science or math and also may include social studies. Field trips can enliven any topic that can be studied through observing and interacting. Teachers will need to research what is available in the community and what aspects of a study can be viewed closely. The excursion or site visit is only one aspect of a study on a topic. Following is the development of the inquiry topic on rain incorporating field trips.

INQUIRY TOPICS ON EXPLORING EARTH SCIENCE

INQUIRY TOPIC

RAIN

Purpose

Children will feel and see the effects of rain right after the rain has stopped by taking an excursion to experience the weather.

Teachers Prepare

Study   Find an area in the neighborhood that has a variety of materials and vegetation that will show effects of the rain. Study what different animals and insects do when it rains. Look up average rainfall in the current month, and the amount of rainfall in your climate that will provide enough moisture for plants to grow.

Questions   Do children notice the effects of rain or lack of it? Are they interested in rain itself? Is the weather warm and calm enough to be comfortable outside?

Materials   Rain gauge placed outdoors, centimeter and inch measurers, boots and jackets (if it is cool), camera, clipboards with pencils and paper, colored pencils, Ziploc bags, scissors, spoons.

Children's Books

Drip Drop Splash by Tresselt

Where Does the Butterfly Go When It Rains? by Garelick

Come On, Rain! by Hess

The Rain by Laser

Cloud Dance by Locker

Technology   Look up climatic data on the Internet to find weather predictions, number of days it rained recently, and amount of rainfall recorded. Show the weather symbols used on weather predictions and weather maps (with your location highlighted).

Take photos of cloud formations and display them. Use the Internet to label types of clouds observed and photographed. Take photos early in the day from the classroom window and during changes in the weather before going on the rainy day walk. Take a close-up photo of the rain gauge with no measurable rainfall and later when the group goes to measure the accumulated rainfall. As you go on the rainy day walk, take close-up photos of evidence of the rain and return later to the same photo locations to record evidence of what happens later.

In Experiences About This Inquiry Topic, Children Will

Explore   Look up to observe the presence, the movement, and the look of the clouds. If there is sunshine, look for the rainbow, which can be observed with the combination of water vapor and sunlight. Ask children to smell the air. How does the air feel? What did the air outside feel like when it was raining? How is the air different now? Look at and touch cars, grass, branches, dirt, sidewalks to see what evidence is left of the rain. Look for colors after the rain. Dig in the dirt to find out how wet it is on top and farther down (Redleaf, 1996). Listen and watch for birds, squirrels, worms, and insects.

Children select the things that change because of the rain.

Identify   Ask children to dictate a list of the things that changed be-cause of the rain. Discuss descriptions of moisture, dampness, wetness, and standing water. Take close-up photos of these items as children talk about them.

Classify   Look for colors after the rain. If children are interested, ask them to find the color of pencils that matches the color of the item ob-served and record it on the clipboard. For items that can be gathered into bags, collect two identical items, one kind per bag, to take back to the classroom.

Compare and contrast   Record the amount of rainfall reported on the Internet and the amount measured on the rain gauge.

Measure the moisture level depth of the soil in both centimeters and inches and compare with the amount of rainfall reported on the Internet and the amount in the rain gauge. Notice water standing on sidewalks or in puddles and compare with the dryness before the rain. Measure the size (diameter) and depth of puddles. Before coming inside, measure these again. Compare with earlier measurements. Take photos both times.

Compare the kinds of clouds seen early in the day and after the rain. Compare with other photos of clouds. Discuss possibilities of clouds when none are observed, on a cloudy day.

Pay attention to the smell of the air before and after the rain. Compare brightness after rain with that before or during rain.

Once back in the classroom, take out the pairs of items collected and explore putting them in water and compare colors. To take this further, ask if children want to leave a wet object in the bag and the one like it out on the windowsill to compare after it dries.

Hypothesize After first going out after the rain, ask children what they think will happen next. After gathering together indoors after the trip, use photos and the dictated list to ask children what happened to each item because of the rain. Wonder with them what happened to the clouds as it stopped raining. What happened to the water in the puddle? What do you think will happen to the puddle later that day? (If children cannot go back and see for themselves, take another photo later in the day.)

Generalize From the list generated on the walk, ask children to dictate stories about what happens to these items in the rain. Read the stories to the group and, using the photos to remember the events of the rainy day, help children decide on a "Rainy Day" play that depicts the coming of the rain and what happened to the items in the rain and afterward. Copy their lines to the play and read the lines as they act it out. Take photos of the play. Use these photos along with their dictated stories and their play in a class book.

Extended Experiences For ongoing study, track the amount of rainfall over several weeks. Count the rainy days and nonrainy days. Dig a hole and fill with water. Measure the amount of water left after 10 minutes, 30 minutes, and one hour. Compare with the record of what happened to the puddles after the rain. Go back to visit the same items that you saw on the rainy day walk after it has been dry for a while and note any changes. Look for the same insects and animals on nonrainy days.

INQUIRY TOPIC

LIGHT AND SHADOWS

Purpose

Children will explore light and the absence of light, create shadows, and explore shadows of themselves and objects.

Teachers Prepare

Study Read the stages of children's reasoning about shadows (see DeVries et al, 2002, Appendix). Experiment with various light sources: sun, flashlight, overhead classroom lights, transparency projector, slide projector, and light table. Determine the best light source for different effects. Observe the shadows at different times on sunny days. Determine the available and added light needed and best time of day to see shadows in the playground and in the classroom.

Questions   Are children aware of their shadow? Are they interested in following their shadow with different light sources? Is there usually sunny weather at this time?

Gather materials   Obtain flashlights, transparency projector, slide projector, light table, camera, large box from appliance store with materials to paint the inside black, screen or white sheet, colander, a fancy doily, a square of lace, and other fabrics of translucent material. Add tag board, tongue depressors, and masking tape to make shadow puppets.

Recipes   The dark box is used with a flashlight to explore shadows, and the shadow puppet theater provides the stage and materials for shadow puppets. The directions for making these two items are found in Appendix C, Table C–10, and Table C–11.

Use technology   Digital camera, slide projector, and transparency projector.

In Experiences About This Inquiry Topic, Children Will

Explore   Explore the concept that shadows are the result of light being blocked. Children can explore this phenomenon both indoors and out. Start with a slide projector indoors with the light on a blank wall or sheet. Children can vary the distance of their bodies from the light source and the screen and explore making their shadows tall and short, large and small.

Children can examine the shadows they make with stick puppets. Try making a puppet with holes for eyes and other forms with cut-out shapes.

Identify   Identify shadows in the outdoors on sunny days. Ask children to find a shadow and then identify what object blocked the light to make the shadow.

Take photos of children with and without their shadows. With a small group examining the photos, see if they can name the child by looking only at the part of the photo showing the child's shadow.

Classify   Experiment with a light source from different places in the room. Compare the light in the room with the ceiling light on and off. Add a clamp-on light that can be placed in different areas, the ceiling, the window, or a dark corner of the room (for safety, keep out of reach of the children). Try out what can block the light and what can allow the light to shine through. Try umbrellas, scarves, large sheets of clear and translucent plastic, and large sheets of poster board or card board. Doilies, snowflake patterns, lace, and transparent and opaque fabrics can also be explored. From these experiences children can gain a basic understanding of things that make shadows and things that do not. Develop a list of materials that light will shine through and those that will not. Try these same materials in the sunshine and compare the results.

Take the shadow exploration outdoors by engaging children in shadow play of following and leading with their shadows. What makes it change its shape? Compare shadows of teachers and children, of different children, of siblings. Look at shadows in the early morning, at noon, and in the late afternoon. Look for shadows on sunny, cloudy, and misty days. Keep a class log of findings. Ask families to look for the child's shadow in the evening inside and outside. Ask parents and children to complete a simple chart of their findings and add to the compiled list of shadows.

Compare   Use the dark box indoors. Children can compare the light they see from a flashlight both inside and outside the box. Then try the colander and different materials to see if they can make different patterns of light and shadow (Fig. 17–3).

Contrast   Using a strong light source, such as the slide projector, tape a large piece of paper on a blank wall and with pairs of children, ask them to position one child so that his shadow shows on the paper. Experiment with this over several days so children have experiences of making the shadow large or small. At one point one child or an adult can draw the shadow of the other on the large paper.

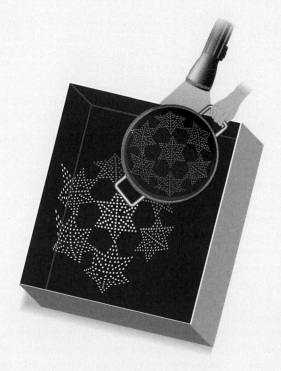

Figure 17–3 Children can explore the patterns made with a flashlight in a dark box.

With the transparency projector children can experiment with small items such as miniature animal figures to find outlines of these on the screen. Children may want to investigate other items or cut out their own.

Hypothesize   Ask questions outdoors, such as, If it is a cloudy day, where is your shadow? If it is a sunny day, where is your shadow? Where does your shadow go when you go inside?

Generalize   Indoors with the light source you can ask, experiment, and then conclude: If I want to make my shadow big, I can be here. If I want this object to be little, it can be here.

Ask children to explain to a parent or other visitor what makes shadows and how they can be altered. Make a shadow puppet theater and ask children to make the shadows large or small on the stage. The story of the Three Billy Goats Gruff could be used with only one puppet representing the three goats. Children can decide how big they want the troll to appear. (Be conscious of fears children may have.)

Extended Experiences   If families want to work with the shadows and shapes that appear in the night, parents can work with their child by looking at objects in the half dark, then turning on the light to see what caused the shadow or shape.

Outdoors on a smooth-surface area in the afternoon sun, ask one child to draw, using colored chalk, the shadow of another child while he is standing. Ask what happens when the child who is drawing walks over the shadow. Experiment with the child lying down on the traced shadow. Does her body fill the space of the shadow? Ask what happens when the standing child moves or sits (DeVries, Zan, Hildebrandt, Edmiaston, & Sales, 2002; Green, 1996).

INQUIRY TOPIC

WATER SOURCE

Purpose

To look for the source of water in the city or town and see how clean water is prepared and sent through a system of pipes to buildings and houses.

Teachers Prepare

Study   Study source of water in the area and school building. Find the system of pipes for incoming water into the school building, and trace it to faucets and toilets. Compare a city water system with a well or other source. Look for other water pipes, such as in sprinkler systems, sewer pipes, and heating systems. Find the water meter for the building. Explore the neighborhood for other water uses, such as a fountain, fire hydrant, or drinking fountain. Find a diagram of a fire hydrant. Find information on the testing of water and its treatment in city or community filtration plant.

Children's Books   *Drip, Drop, Splash* by Tresselt

Questions   Are children interested in where water comes from? Are there water filtration plants that children could visit? Do they notice pipes along the floor or ceiling?

   Are the water pipes in the school building observable and are they in a safe location for children to observe? Is there a house under construction where children can observe the pipes before the walls are enclosed? Are children mature enough to understand systems of pipes connected from the water plant to a water main to the school building?

Gather materials   Plastic PVC pipe and connectors or commercially made pipes and connectors sets, clear tubing to fit the pipes with connectors, and funnels and pails. Use individual clipboards with paper and primer pencils. Locate copies of architectural drawings of the classroom and building or plans of a house under construction (if available), old faucets that can be taken apart, and materials for a clean water machine.

Recipes   To change dirty water to clean, build a clean water machine (Appendix C, Table C–12).

Technology   With a digital camera, take photos in the community of drinking fountains, display fountains, hydrants, hydrant connections on buildings, and pipes that are evident in the school, kitchen, bathroom, janitor's closet. Look up the city or community water treatment facility and source of water on the Internet.

In Experiences About This Inquiry Topic, Children Will

Explore   Observe the pipes and trace their paths in classroom and to other areas of the building. Explore the PVC pipe materials by joining them together in different formations. When using the PVC pipes outdoors, add water to observe the water flow. Explore the parts of the faucet and adapt a connector to join this with a PVC pipe. Experiment with water flow through pipes in different ways, including turning the faucet on and off. Experiment with the clean water machine to determine what the filtering process will clean and not clean, such as muddy water, flour mixed with water, Styrofoam pebbles, oil and collections of many small items in nature.

Identify   Find and photograph water fountains, display fountains, and hydrants in the community and pipes and fixtures in the school. If pipes are visible, trace the path a pipe takes from the place it enters the

Children see the obvious difference in the water when poured through the clean water machine.

building to the classroom. List all the places water is found throughout the school, such as sink, dishwasher, toilet, and janitor closet.

Classify Classify the diameter of pipes found in the school building for different purposes. Decide the uses of different pipes for different purposes in the school building.

Compare and contrast Compare the water fountain with display fountain. Compare pipes with small and large diameters. Compare clean with dirty water. If there is a house under construction where pipes can be seen, compare this with water pipes in the school building.

Hypothesize As children study the pipes in classroom and building, ask how the water gets to the school and to the classroom. On a visit to a construction site, children may be able to see the way water comes through pipes. If there are architectural drawings of the school or drawings of a house under construction, children can examine these to locate the water pipes on the plan. Children can draw their ideas of how water enters the building and is distributed to their classroom. Using diagrams, children can apply their emerging ideas of how a drinking fountain or

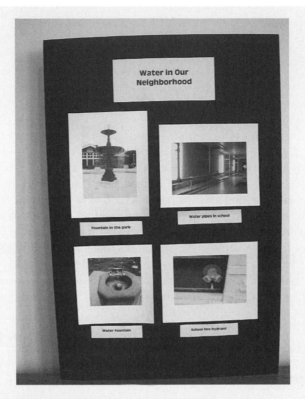

Photos taken of water in our neighborhood.
Photos courtesy Hattie Cooper

display fountain works. With diagrams and photos they can explain their ideas of the inside of a fire hydrant and its use in a fire. They can predict how to make water flow in PVC pipes to a certain location.

Generalize   Water is transported through pipes to reach the school building and the classroom. So when the faucet in the sink is turned on, the water flows out. Water can be cleaned for human use. Using the children's diagrams of pipes in the school, water fountains, and display fountains, ask the children to dictate what they know about how water flows. Retrace the locations visited in their field trips; use the architectural plans, photos, and diagrams; and apply their understandings to what they revisit. New hypotheses may arise as they apply their first generalizations. They can try out other ideas, as they gain further knowledge on how things work from the groups' ongoing hypotheses.

Extended Experiences   Visit the filtration plant in the community to inquire about how water is tested and treated to be clean and how it is carried to homes and other buildings. Other locations to visit include a car wash, the kitchen of the center as dishes are being washed, and the maintenance personnel using the janitor closet.

INQUIRY TOPIC

ECOLOGY STUDY

Purpose

Children will observe attractive and unattractive places in their neighborhood and change an unattractive area to a place of beauty. Children will find out that they can make a difference in ecology.

Teachers Prepare

Study Observe attractive and unattractive spots in the neighborhood and decide to make one place in the neighborhood inviting. You may decide ahead of time and inform children about the area they will change, or allow children choices of what to accomplish. Whether this area is in their own playground or a nearby park, you will need to obtain permission to change this area and discuss plans with appropriate personnel. Some areas will require the support of others, such as bringing in dirt and mulch or continuing the care of new plants.

   The decision will need to be made as to what is possible and what resources are available. If the plan includes planting flowers, attempt to make these perennials so they will continue to grow year after year. Consider requesting the help of parents, high school students, community members, and businesses in this project. Gardening supply stores may want to support the project by supplying materials.

Prepare materials Tools for cleanup such as rakes, shovels, garbage bags, and gloves for children. Clipboards and primary pencils for recording and drawing spaces they are interested in. Photos of selected places in the neighborhood and the chosen area before, during, and after the steps of the project. Seeds, plants, mulch, and source of water.

Children's Books

Wanda's Roses by Brisson

Niki's Walk by Tanner

In Experiences About This Inquiry Topic, Children Will

Explore As you take neighborhood walks, notice with children beautiful places and places that are sore spots because of garbage or lack of care. Take photos of areas of interest. As you share photos with children, ask how they think these places got to be this way.

   After looking at things they find in their environment that are pollutants, collect some examples (these will need to be washed), such as plastic soda bottles, paper, aluminum foil, and water soluble and nonsoluble packing pellets. Try these in water and see what happens to the different items. Discuss what happens when we throw these things on the ground. Will a particular item go away when it rains?

Look at photos of attractive and unattractive places nearby the center. Visit these and talk about what the class might do.

Identify List names of the places they visit that are beautiful or sore spots. List items found in each type of area. Discuss the job of an ecologist.

Classify, Compare, and Contrast Classify what happens to trash when exposed to water.

Develop lists of what makes a space beautiful or a sore spot. When the project is decided, make a web of what they know and what they need to know. List the steps and materials and resources they need.

Hypothesize If there is continued interest, select a place to improve in the environment. Ask children how they think they could make this place beautiful. List the children's ideas. Possibly ask children to go back to the space and draw what could be a beautiful space. Provide input on possibilities and limits and available resources. The project may start with clean-up of trash (before starting, look for hazardous materials). With children wearing gloves, clean up the garbage. You may want to look at what is collected and classify the types of garbage found.

Discuss how the garbage got there and what people could do to prevent this. Include the children in this discussion through questions about what they can do on their playground and at their homes.

Enroll the help of others in this project by taking children's dictations of requests for help. Send these as letters or e-mail. As answers are received, share these with the children.

For the beautifying project, make up work group plans for small groups, inviting volunteers to work with small groups of children.

Generalize Take photos of the sore spot before the work begins. As the group progresses, take photos of the planning and of the work groups. Discuss the changes children are making in this one location. Talk about what they now know about making change. Discuss how they were able to get help from others and how, by working together, people can make effective changes. Discuss the problems they encountered and how they were solved. Send letters, with children's contribution of dictation and drawings to others who helped with the project.

Extended Experiences Keep a record with photos to share in the classroom and on the school Web site or in the school newsletter. Consider contributing an article to the local newspaper (Green, 1996).

SUMMARY

The subject of earth science combines with the other sciences for integrated experiences in exploring the world. With attention to topics that interest children, many aspects of earth science will be transformed into extended study. The following chapter, on Biological Science: Plants, will extend children's understanding of the bountiful earth.

TO FURTHER YOUR THINKING

1. Reflect on your early childhood experiences spent in natural surroundings. Were these experiences only occasional, or often? What did you encounter in these nature areas? How involved were you in exploring while there? How have these experiences affected the time or the desire for time that you spend in nature now?

2. Consider how the general elements of the four kinds of science are related. With a colleague or small group, develop a diagram depicting the four areas of science: physical science, earth science, biological science (plants), and biological science (animals). Under these categories, list four to five examples of each. Then draw lines to show the interconnections between and among these items. From this draw conclusions on the interrelatedness of these science areas for children.

3. When you experience the weather, do you embrace it despite whether you respond to it positively or negatively? Use this as a background to develop some pondering or open-ended questions (see Chapter 6) about today's weather for a young child or adult. Engage a child or adult in conversation about the weather today, attempting to obtain a detailed response to the weather including descriptions and personal thoughts. Exchange these responses with a colleague and determine ways children or adults can discuss weather beyond the customary responses to "How's the weather?"

4. In the neighborhood of your home or school, explore an area with a child or a colleague. Look for what both you and your companion, adult or child, take in through your senses: what you see below and above you, noticing items large and small; what you hear in small and overwhelming sounds; what you

smell in the air and in items close by; and what you feel as you touch items around you, whether natural or manmade. From this experience discuss with a colleague what is possible about children's learning from experiencing simple outdoor excursions.

5. From your day-to-day life, experience natural phenomena to compare and contrast observations like these: before and after a rain, wet and dry dirt; natural light and darkness in the day and night; the presence and absence of shadows; a beautiful natural space and one spoiled by lack of care. Discuss your impressions with a colleague and list vocabulary that can be used to compare and contrast what you experienced.

6. Plan to interview young children and elementary-age children about their shadows. Either indoors or outdoors, provide some time for them to look at their shadows. Ask questions about where shadows come from, how they change, and where they go. Record the children's answers and their ages and compare these with colleagues. Then compare your findings with stages of children's reasoning about shadows (see DeVries et al, 2002, Appendix).

7. From daily experiences at home or at school, consider the constant availability of access to clean water. With a colleague, list pondering questions for children about water sources. Discuss what young children would be curious about in discovering water sources. In a study of a water source in your community, what would young children be able to understand and not understand?

8. Select two children's books from the list at the end of the chapter and/or books suggested in the article by Kupetz and Twiest (2000). Discuss with a colleague or the class the way your choices support and extend children's experiences in nature through observing closely, handling natural resources, and/or appreciating natural and beautiful environments. Refer to the Kupetz and Twiest article for further application of these connections for children.

9. List possible ways an adult could be involved in ecological issues in your community, state, or nation. From this list, consider a possible goal for young children to pursue in ecology. What role, if any, could a group of young children take to accomplish this?

REFERENCES

Brisson, P. (1994). *Wanda's Roses,* Honesdale, PA: Boyds Mills press.
DeVries, R., Zan, B., Hildebrandt, C., Edmiaston, R., and Sales, C. (2002). *Developing constructivist early childhood curriculum: Practical principles and activities.* New York: Teachers College Press.

Garelick, M. (2001). *Where does the butterfly go when it rains?* Madison, WI: Turtleback Books.

Green, M. D. (1996). *474 science activities for young children.* Clifton Park, NY: Thomson Delmar Learning.

Hess, K. (1999). *Come on, rain!* New York: Scholastic.

Hill, D. M. (1977). *Mud, sand and water.* Washington, DC: National Association for the Education of Young Children.

Huffman, A. B. (1996, July). Beyond the weather chart: Weathering new experiences. *Young Children 51*(5), 34–37.

Kupetz, B. N., and Twiest, M. M. (2000, January). Nature, literature, and young children: A natural combination. *Young Children. 55*(1), 59–63.

Laser, M. (1997). *The rain.* New York: Simon and Schuster.

Locker, T. (2000). *Cloud dance.* San Diego: Harcourt.

Moore, R.C., Goltsman. S. M., and Iacofano, D. S. (Eds.). (1992). *Play for all: Guidelines* (2nd ed.). Berkeley, CA: MIG Communications.

National Academy of Science. (1996). *National science education standards* [Book version, on line]. Washington, DC: National Academies Press. **www.nap.edu**

Redleaf, R. (1996). *Open the door let's explore more! Field trips of discovery for young children.* St. Paul, MN: Redleaf.

Rivkin, M. S. (1995). *The great outdoors: Restoring children's right to play outside.* Washington, DC: National Association for the Education of Young Children.

Ross, M. E. (2000, March). Science their way. *Young Children, 55*(2), 6–13.

Seefeldt, C., and Galper, A. (2000). *Active experiences for active children: Social Studies.* Upper Saddle River, NJ: Pearson Education.

Shaw, C. G. (1993). *It looked like spilt milk.* New York: HarperCollins

Tanner, J. (1987). *Niki's walk.* South Melbourne, Australia: Macmillan.

Tresselt, A. L. (1987). *Drip, drop, splash.* New York: Lothrop Lee & Shephard.

ADDITIONAL RESOURCES

DeVries, R., Zan, B., Hildebrandt, C., Edmiaston, R., and Sales, C. (2002). *Developing constructivist early childhood curriculum: Practical principles and activities.* New York: Teachers College Press. The appendix contains an excellent description of the stages of children's reasoning about shadows.

Green, M. D. (1996). *474 science activities for young children.* Clifton Park, NY: Thomson Delmar Learning. This book has a full-color section on an ecology project that can be adapted for younger children. **www.delmar.com**

Seefeldt, C., and Galper, A. (2000). *Active experiences for active children: Social studies.* Upper Saddle River, NJ: Prentice Hall. Two chapters, Chapter 6, Earth: The Place We Live, and Chapter 7, Way Up in the Sky, explain ways to bring an understanding of the earth and sky to key experiences for young children.

West, S., and Cox, A. (2001). *Sand and water play: Simple creative actives for young children.* Beltsville, MD: Gryphon House. From the basics of sand and water, teachers can develop many learning activities. www.gryphonhouse.com

Video

Science anytime anyplace: Weather, light and shadows [Video]. Crystal Lake, IL: Magna Systems, Inc. www.magnasystems.org

Children's Books

Brisson, P. (1994). *Wanda's Roses.* Honesdale, PA: Boyds Mills Press. Wanda wishes to make her community beautiful.

Garelick, M. (2001). *Where does the butterfly go when it rains?* Madison WI: Turtleback Books. Questions what different animals do when it rains.

Hess, K.(1999). *Come on, rain!* New York: Scholastic. A plea for and celebration of rain.

Laser, M. (1997). *The rain.* New York: Simon and Schuster. Rain is beautiful and appreciated.

Locker, T. (2000). *Cloud dance.* San Diego: Harcourt. Beautiful drawings of clouds.

Locker, T. (1993). *Where the river begins.* New York: Bt Bound. The book follows the flow of water.

Shaw, C. G. (1993). *It looked like spilt milk.* New York: HarperCollins. Depicts many imaginative forms of clouds.

Tanner, J. (1987). *Niki's walk.* South Melbourne, Australia: Macmillan. A wordless book showing environment.

Tresselt, A. L. (1987). *Drip, drop, splash.* New York: Lothrop Lee & Shephard. Beautiful prose that describes water, from the raindrop to the ocean.

Web Sites

www.eichild.com Environments catalog has small-sized Pipefitters.
www.eNasco.com Nasco catalog has pipe connectors called Build It!™
www.intellicast.com One of many weather forecast sites.
www.nws.noaa.gov Local forecast by city and state has clear graphics showing day and night.
http://iwin.nws.noaa.gov Interactive Weather Information Network has hourly reports of listed cities in states.

Chapter 18

Exploring Life Science: Plants

OBJECTIVES Through the process of discovery in this chapter, you will be able to:

1. Describe what children can learn from the study of plants.

2. Discuss children's understanding of germination and the life cycle of plants.

3. Identify concepts of children seeing themselves as caretakers of the environment and comparing life processes of plants with their own growth.

4. Discuss the planning for growing plants with children from container gardening to large garden plots.

5. Describe development of inquiry topics of growing plants, making a terrarium, and trees.

6. Discover use of information and fiction books on plant life for ongoing curriculum.

IDEAS TO PONDER

- How can children become interested in plants?

- What can children understand about germination?

- How can I approach growing plants when I am inexperienced in gardening?

- How can children begin to appreciate care of the environment?

- How can children's literature support learning about plants?

Ask any adult who cares intensely about acting responsibly toward the environment and she will be able to tell stories of how she bonded with nature at a young age. When we garden with children, we allow them to become responsible for a small part of their world and give them the opportunity to connect with the earth and its creatures. Through gardening, children begin to make the connection between what is sold in the supermarkets and the earth from which it comes. They begin to see their place in the ecological web that is our world. (Starbuck, Olthof, & Midden, 2002, p. 4)

GOALS IN EXPLORING PLANTS

Children can gain a connection with the earth whether they build a terrarium or dig in a garden. This simple act of gardening will open a world of discovery and understanding of how earth systems work. In the process of gardening, sensory experiences will get children in touch with the materials of dirt, seeds, and plants.

Children will learn to respect plants as part of the environment. They will find that vegetables, fruits, and flowers are products at the end of the growing season that can be enjoyed. Through gardening children can experience the ecological view that if they plant it they can pick it.

As a teacher you can engender appreciation for all plant life. This includes plants usually categorized as weeds (named as a weed when a plant is not wanted in certain places). Others, such as wildflowers and prairie grasses, are left to grow so that they can complete the life cycle and begin again.

Taylor carefully plants the seeds.

STANDARDS

All students should develop understanding of

- ▪ The characteristics of organisms
- ▪ Life cycles of organisms
- ▪ Organisms and environments

National Science Education Standards: Content Standard K–4. C. Reprinted with permission from *National science education standards* (1996). The National Academy of Sciences, courtesy of the National Academies Press, Washington, DC (p.106).

GERMINATION

Germination is a good place to begin. For young children, germination is nothing short of a miracle. For seed germination, the child is able to experience the result, but not immediately. Because this occurs over time it is harder for the child to understand. In applying the criteria for physical knowledge (Chapter 16), germination does not occur together in time with planting. Germination will need to be

Germination is to begin growth or cause to sprout from seed.

After waiting seven days, young sprouts are visible.

observed over and over. In order for children to grasp germination, follow these two guidelines for planting: Plant seeds that germinate quickly at first, and plant seeds many times. Through experiencing this miracle many times, children can come to expect the seed to sprout.

PLANTING INDOORS AND OUTDOORS

Planting seeds can be done easily inside and outside at planting times. The wide variety of ways to start seeds provides various experiences in germination.

There are some steps teachers use to help ensure germination. Always try planting the same seeds at home before trying to plant them with children. If seeds do not sprout, turn this into an advantage by looking at what happened. Discuss the result and try again, changing the way the planting is done. For seeds planted by children, the most common mistake is overwatering. By using a spray bottle, this can be minimized, and you can teach the children to avoid leaving standing water on the soil.

What grows from seed is the plant, whether it is grass, vegetable, or flower. What blooms on the plant is the flower. So as sprouts emerge, identify them as plants. Although gardeners focus on the vegetable produced, it is interesting to note that most plants do reach flower and seed stages if allowed to mature. For vegetables, different parts of the plant are eaten: lettuce—leaf, radish—root, beans—pod and seed, zucchini—fruit.

GARDENING

To transplant is to move a sprout or plant from one growth medium to another.

Children will get the full experience as gardeners when they prepare the soil, plan the garden (or planters), plant seeds, and **transplant** seedlings. They can see themselves as caretakers for living things smaller than themselves. And in a small part they may connect this with caring for the environment. As small things sprout and grow, children may compare this to their own growth as they are seeing themselves as growing and changing.

Some forethought is needed in planning to harvest plants in temperate climates. In these areas of the country, plan to plant vegetables directly in the garden that mature quickly from seed. (See those listed in Outdoor Plots.) For other vegetables and flowers, start some of these indoors earlier and transplant after danger of frost is past. Or buy plants already started. Some choices for beginning seeds indoors or purchasing young plants are parsley, chives, spinach, cabbage, zucchini, tomatoes, marigolds, pansies, salvia, and zinnias.

Planter Boxes

The small pots used to start seeds or hold small plants are usually not suitable for most plants to produce flowers or vegetables. Plants need more "foot" room to grow roots. Small plants can be transplanted to planter boxes (about 24" × 8" and

8" to 10" deep). Or the seeds can be planted directly in the planter box. If the planter box gets enough sun during a regular growing season, often these plants will produce. Planter boxes are more successful outdoors.

Outdoor Plots

Small garden plots in an area that receives direct sun can be quite an adventure for a group of children. A three-foot-square garden can grow small vegetable plants and a small tomato plant for very fresh salads (Clemens, 1996). With the young children, sow the seeds for radishes, lettuce, and peas just after the danger of frost is past. Buy one small tomato plant. Place a row of miniature marigolds around the edge to keep the aphids off the tomato plant. Or import ladybugs to eat the aphids (and for enjoyment of these small creatures). Depending on the area of the country, before school vacation you may be harvesting.

When there is room for the class to have a 20-by-20-foot garden, the class can work for a bigger and more varied harvest (Clemens, 1996). More tomatoes, rows of sweet corn, and sunflowers can be planted. Plants from early harvests can be dug up and the area replanted with cucumbers and even pumpkins and a peanut plant (select a fast-growing variety for temperate climates).

If you are new to setting up garden plots, work with an experienced gardener to select the plants best for your area and to prepare the soil. The extension service in your state will be glad to get you started; in addition, garden centers often offer expert advice.

Kendal harvests tomatoes in a midsize garden.

Butterfly Gardens

For a garden that can attract butterflies to your area, a sunny outdoor space can be planned with annuals and perennials. Use the information in Chapter 13 and Additional Resources in that chapter for basic information to get you started, and then request information locally on the best choices of plants.

FROM SEED TO HARVEST

From the seed and sprout to the harvest, children can experience the full life cycle of plants. Or, conversely, the sequence of experience may be first finding seeds from the harvested crop and then planting them for the continuity of the plant's life.

Dandelion: The Children's Flower

While the life cycle can be seen over time in gardening experiences, the dandelion can show this most easily. Within a mature plant, one can find bud, flower, developing seed pods, and seeds ready to parachute into the wind. Because of its common status as a weed, children can learn that this particular plant can be picked, examined, and taken apart. Children can search for the plants from large to small and wonder at the presence of so many plants close together. When the seed kites are ready, they can be blown away. Children can harvest the seed, plant it in a planter box, and time the start of dandelion seedlings (Fig. 18–1).

From Flower to Seed

There are many ways children can explore the life cycle of plants over time. A common plant, marigolds, is easy to grow from seed. After the flower blooms and dies, the seed forms. These seeds can be discovered inside the flower. The cut

Figure 18–1 The dandelion from bud and flower to seed.

Figure 18–2 The marigold from bud and flower to seed.

flower and the seed head can be examined; and seeds are saved to be planted the following spring. In temperate climates, the seeds can be sown in small pots indoors and transplanted outdoors in six weeks (Fig. 18–2).

Examples of the Harvest

Varieties of squash and pumpkin can be harvested or purchased. Inside these vegetables children will find the seeds to scrape out. Some of these seeds can be washed, baked, and eaten. Others can be saved to plant the following spring.

In the fall the skin of the pumpkin can be decorated with magic markers. This decoration is easy for young artists to create. When it is time to change fall decorations, the pumpkin can be cut open to expose the seeds and pulp.

The pulp of the pumpkin or squash can be baked, then separated from the skin, processed in a food processor, and used in recipes, including the favorite pumpkin pie. For a healthy snack, prepare pumpkin pie batter and bake it crustless in a casserole. It will be sweet, healthy, and probably a taste preferred by young children.

If the pumpkin is carved in the traditional manner in the fall, the leftover pumpkin shell can be cut up and added to the compost pile or buried directly into the soil to be refound in the spring. Through this process children can experience the process of decaying material returned to refurbish the soil.

Sunflowers are grand flowers to grow and harvest in a midsize garden. While watching the sunflower grow taller than themselves, children can measure its growth. During the bloom time children can track the position of the flower in the sun. One mature flower can be brought inside while others are left in the garden for the animals. If the flowers are near a fence, children may be able to view spry squirrels hop along the fence, jump onto the large blooms, and sequester the seeds away for the winter.

The sunflower is a fascinating flower to view and harvest.

Children can enjoy picking out the sunflower seeds and take on the challenge of counting them. This monstrous task can be made manageable by asking each child to find 10 seeds, and each group of 10 can be placed in its own section in a large container. Then older children can count how many groups of 10 they have made. After counting, some of the seeds can be roasted and eaten, a few can be set aside for planting the following year, and the bulk of seeds can be food for the birds and squirrels in the winter.

FROM BULB TO FLOWER

A bulb is a fleshy structure of the root that contains sprout and food for the coming growth season.

Bulbs are a refreshing surprise when these plants emerge from the ground in spring. Bulbs can be buried deep in the ground in the fall for their beautiful spring blooming. Another way to enjoy bulbs is to force their growth indoors. From late fall to spring, paperwhite narcissus are a bright addition to the classroom.

The paperwhite narcissus bulb is placed in a tall glass over black marbles. Or several bulbs can be placed in a shallow bowl with rocks around them to hold each bulb in place. In the first weeks, water consistently to keep the water level to a point halfway covering the bulb. Within one week the white roots and stems will grow. In two to three more weeks, there will be a delicate group of paperwhite flowers. If the stems lop over during the growth period, tie some twine loosely around them to bind them together (Fig. 18–3).

Children can see the whole plant when planted singly in a clear glass. They may enjoy sketching the stages of growth on a graph or drawing the flowers using either black markers on white paper or white chalk on black paper.

Figure 18–3 The narcissus bulb grows into a fragrant flower indoors.

INDOOR PLANTS

The care, feeding, and watering of indoor plants can be an ongoing source of study. Bring the plants to the attention of the children by focusing on them. When humidity is low, plants can be misted with a simple spray bottle. Place the plants on a low table or in a large sink where children can spray the water on them.

In the classroom teachers take opportunities to examine plants with children as they take care of them. Plants will need to be repotted, to give the roots more room and by dividing up plants that have developed new growth through the root system. Also, the familiar spider plant shows its growth of new plants among the leaves, and these will need to be potted for their ongoing growth For some plants like the philodendron, **cuttings** of leaves can be placed in water to start new roots.

A cutting describes the process of severing a plant section to start a new plant.

Indoor plants will need to be repotted.

EXAMINING SEEDS

Natural collections of seeds children find can be examined. The many seed pods of weeds, pine cones from the current season, and wilting flowers from a bouquet can be taken apart to examine and view through a magnifying glass.

During food experiences children can examine the parts of the fruit or vegetable where seeds are found. Whether the classroom harvests food and flowers or purchases fresh foods, as the food is prepared children can realize the connection between foods they eat and the life cycle of the plant when they see the seeds inside the pod.

Because seeds and berries are easily put in the mouth, keep a chart of poisonous parts of plants for easy identification. Additional Resources in Chapter 13 lists Web sites and books for this important reference. Contact your local poison control for information on harmful plants in your area.

VISIT AREAS OF LUSH VEGETATION

The best way to enjoy and know plants is for children to see them in their natural habitat. They can walk through a field, a nearby forest, or a field of prairie grasses. Guide children to look in all directions, especially up and down, look closely, and look through a camera lens. Record what they see in drawings and photos. Later these can remind them of the visions experienced.

A collection of seeds can be examined.

Because children cannot always experience plants in natural habitats, take field trips to places where the vegetation is planned. Visit a conservatory, a park, a neighborhood garden, or a nursery. In this experience you may want to focus on a certain kind of plant, again take photos, and perhaps make a plan to grow your own. Revisit these places and assist children in recording what they see through writing and drawing.

INQUIRY TOPICS ON EXPLORING LIFE SCIENCE: PLANTS

INQUIRY TOPIC

FROM SEED TO PLANT

Purpose

Children will experience germination and growth of seed to plant and see the result that planting one kind of seed emerges into one kind of plant. Over a growing season they can observe the life cycle of plants.

Teachers Prepare

Study   Study the process of germination and information on seed packets. Find out the times for planting various plants in your area, and time this with germination and the growth period before transplanting or planting directly outdoors. Experiment with germination of seeds you will try with the children. Plan places to plant and transplant indoors and outdoors. Decide how plants will be cared for on a regular basis during weekends and vacations especially during germination and sprouting.

Questions   Is this the right time to plant? What do children know about plant life? What are they interested in learning? How can planting be accomplished in the classroom and outdoors? What preparation is needed to develop this study? What cooperation from school personnel, parents, volunteers, and expert gardeners is needed?

Gather materials   Seed packets and seeds saved from previous seasons and pictures and directions (in addition to the seed packets). Materials for various means of starting seeds (see the following recipes). Garden tools, real tools sized for young and adult hands. Planter boxes, prepared area for garden, fertilizer, mulch for outdoor planting. Masking tape or stickers, markers, bamboo stakes, or dowel rods. Materials for charting growth of plants, camera.

Children's Books

A Carrot Seed by Kraus

The Tiny Seed by Carle

Planting a Rainbow by Ehlert

A Seed Grows: My First Book of Plants by Hickman

The Reason for a Flower by Heller

Recipes

Grass seed: Shallow container with dirt, or small sponge in plastic container, or eggshell halves with dirt, grass seed (found in hardware stores).

   For the quickest germination use grass seed. Sprinkle grass seed over the shallow layer of dirt in a container or eggshell half, and cover with a sprinkling of dirt. Or spread grass seed on the top of the sponge. Keep the seeds moist but not sitting in water. When the grass is tall enough, it can be trimmed with scissors.

Bean seeds: Lima beans from seed packets (or any form of dry lima bean), Ziploc bags, cotton ball, masking tape, marker, and spray bottle of water.

   Place each bean seed in the medium of a cotton ball that has been dipped in water and then squeezed out. Place the seed inside the cotton ball in a Ziploc bag and close it. Use masking tape to mark the child's name and the date planted. The bag is then taped to a window where it can get light (not direct sunlight). Mist the cotton as needed. As always, try this at home and then correlate the germination time with school days. After the seed sprouts the child can carefully open the cotton ball to investigate. These seeds can also be transplanted directly into a planter box or the garden.

Bean Sprouts:

Mung beans (dry mung beans can be purchased from oriental or health food stores)

Baby food jars

Cheesecloth or nylon hosiery

Among the fresh vegetables in the market there are all kinds of sprouts that have started from seed. The most familiar is the bean sprout from the small round mung seeds. First soak the beans for three hours, then rinse and place about one teaspoon of seeds in a small jar such as a baby food jar or a clear plastic glass. Cover with cheesecloth or nylon. Place in a dark cupboard. Rinse and drain three times a day. In three or four days the bean sprouts will be ready to eat. Rinse thoroughly to remove the small husks and enjoy in a salad or in a stir-fried dish over rice. If needed, the rinsed bean sprouts can be refrigerated.

Plant stakes: Use bamboo stakes or dowel rods, one per growing plant, to make plant stakes that identify the plant with picture, name, and the mature height of the plant. From seed packets or catalogs find the height of mature plants you will grow and record these in centimeters or inches. Cut bamboo stakes or dowel rods to the height of mature plant plus 10 centimeters (or 4"). Label with the name and picture of the plant near the top of each stake. On the lower end, mark off the 10 centimeters (or 4") with black tape or magic markers to indicate the portion of the plant stake that will be placed in the soil (see Fig. 18–7 later in this chapter).

Technology   Look up Web site information on the weather zone for your area (for planting times) and for plants that thrive best in your area. Download pictures of plants you will grow and planting directions. Use the Internet as a resource for problem solving when plants do not survive. Take close-up photos of germination and plant growth from planting to producing vegetable or seed. Share stories of plants growing with parents through e-mail.

In Experiences About This Inquiry Topic, Children Will

Explore   Begin with children exploring the potting soil and seeds and using plastic garden tools. The soil can be manipulated in the sensory table with their hands and tools. For lima bean seeds, the dried seeds

The mung bean is a small round bean that produces bean sprouts.

can be used in the sensory table. The tiny seeds can be placed in shallow plastic containers to be touched and looked at through a magnifier. Each type of seed can be stored later in a Ziploc bag along with the seed packet for planting later.

At the same time that children are involved in the planting seeds, set up the sensory table as a planting area with potting soil dampened and plant been seeds. As children explore they can observe firsthand the swelling of the seed, then its sprouting of roots and shoots (Starbuck, Olthof, & Midden, 2002).

Identify   Identify the names of plants from the seed packet (or pictures if using saved seed). Identify parts of the plant: seed, sprout, stem, root, flower bud, flower, seed. Identify the process of growth. Discuss and label what seeds need to grow: soil, water, light. As children do the gardening, discuss digging, planting, watering, weeding, hoeing, and harvesting. Take close-up photos of children participating in gardening and review these when discussing the actions of gardening work.

Classify   Mix several kinds of dried beans (navy, kidney, pinto, lima) for children to sort. From seed catalogs or the Internet, find pictures of the plants that will be grown from seed. Make these into two sets of laminated cards with the plant name on each card. Children can match these pictures of plants. Later they can work at grouping the plants according to type: flower, vegetable, grass.

Compare   Start the process of planting by first planting grass seed so children have only a short time to wait for germination. Next start the lima bean seeds in Ziploc bags and the bean sprouts where children can see the beginning sprout from seed (see the preceding recipes) (Figs. 18–4–18–6).

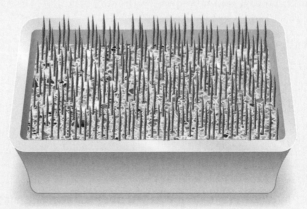

Figure 18–4 Grass seed grows on a wet sponge.

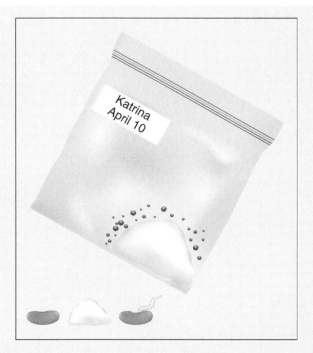

Figure 18–5 The lima bean seed will sprout in a Ziploc bag.

The sprouts of grass, lima beans, and bean sprouts can be compared using magnifiers and by examining close-up photos. From there, children can compare the germination of plants that will grow in the garden.

Children can use the prepared plant stakes to compare heights of the future garden plants by classifying and seriating them on a rug or table, by standing them up in the sand box, or by taping them to a wall display (mark the soil line on the background of the display and arrange stakes so the black lower section is placed below the soil line). If some of these plants will be planted in the garden, a small group of children can plan with you where to put the plants by organizing the plant stakes in the garden plot. These same stakes can be used to mark the plant location in the garden after transplanting. The growing plants can be compared to the height of the plant stake. As plants grow, children can mark on the stakes the current height of a plant with color-coded tape and date (Fig. 18–7).

Contrast   Contrast the look of the different kinds of seeds, and, as photos are taken of the seeds sprouting, contrast how the sprouts are the same as and different from each other. After a plant has started, place its stake next to it and compare the stake height with the growing plant. You can ask children how much the plant has to grow to be mature. When seeds are planted, set aside some seeds to compare with seeds the plant produces at the end of the season.

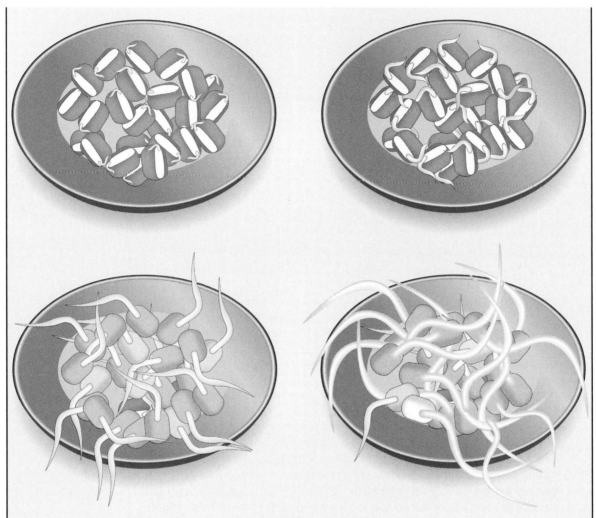

Figure 18–6 Bean sprouts grow from mung beans.

Hypothesize   After one planting, and as you plan the next planting experience, ask children what these seeds will need to grow. As time for planting outdoors draws near, children can start plants indoors, and, later, plant in the planter boxes or garden. If plants do not sprout, ask children what they think happened and what they might try next time they plant.

Generalize   With many experiences of growing plants from seed, children can write stories of "from seed to plant" that can be shared with families by e-mail. They can share what they know with parents, another class, or visitors. Individual children can volunteer to give tours of their indoor or outdoor garden.

Figure 18–7 Plant stakes can be used to measure the young plant's growth.

Extended Experiences Follow the growth of plants after transplanting in planter boxes or garden plots. Nearby field trips during the plantings add to children's understanding of growing plants. Identify where the same or similar plants are growing nearby in the community. Visit a garden store or nursery to purchase plants to transplant. Ask to visit when plants are being cared for to see the work of a **botanist.**

After vegetables have sprouted, visit a farmers' market or produce department to buy bean sprouts and the same vegetables that are growing in the garden. Back at school, examine the sprouts to find evidence of the seed. For the vegetables that contain seeds (beans, peppers, corn, peas, zucchini), open them to discover the seeds contained inside. Of course, prepare the vegetable for eating as a harbinger of the bounty to come.

A botanist is one who studies and cares for plants.

INQUIRY TOPIC

THE TERRARIUM

Purpose

The building of a terrarium can be a way for children to experience an enclosed ecosystem for plants and/or animal life.

Teachers Prepare

Study Explore the purpose and the creation of a terrarium. This system can be an enclosed one for plant life (with little extra water) or the plants and environment can support insects (such as crickets), snails, lizards, anoles, and frogs or toads (Cohen, 1994). If animals will be inhabitants of the terrarium, study the habitat and care and handling of this animal. If you add an animal from the lizard family, check the classroom temperature during the night and weekends and determine needed care for weekends and vacations.

Questions Are children interested in plant life, and/or animal life? Is the long-term care for the terrarium arranged? Where will the terrarium be placed in the classroom? Are children capable of handling small plants to transplant into the terrarium? Is there a botanical garden or plant nursery where children can visit to study the needs of plants and/or obtain supplies?

Gather materials Terrariums can be made with large pop bottles, a clear gallon plastic or glass bottle, or an aquarium. Materials for a terrarium include charcoal or sand, potting soil, mister, and small plants such as philodendron, ivy, and African violets.

Recipes Directions for preparing each type of terrarium is found in Appendix C, Table C–13.

Technology Look up terrariums on the Internet. Find species of plants that can grow in a small space. Order catalogs through the Internet. Photograph the steps as children put together the terrarium and as plants grow, and photograph close-up views of the animal. Tape record or videotape discussions of the planning stage with children. Communicate through e-mail with a botanist regarding children's questions on starting a terrarium.

In Experiences About This Inquiry Topic, Children Will

Explore This topic can emerge from the ongoing experiences of planting or as a way to continue the study of plants after gardening. Children can first visit an indoor environment of a botanical garden or nursery. Here they can feel the warmth and moisture, smell the plants, see how plants thrive, and find out how botanists care for plants.

As they continue study, they may also visit a pet store to select an animal to live in the terrarium.

Identify Identify the ingredients of an ecosystem, names of plants, parts of plants, and steps in starting the terrarium.

Classify Classify sizes of plants, where plants grow best, and what plants need in the terrarium.

Compare and contrast Compare what plants need in a terrarium with what plants need indoors and outdoors (Fig. 18–8).

Hypothesize What do these plants need to grow in the terrarium? What do plants like best? What happened to this (sick or dead) plant? What does the animal need in order to live in the terrarium (Fig. 18–9)?

Figure 18–8 This terrarium made from an aquarium is for plants only.

Figure 18–9 This terrarium is planned for plants and an anole.

Generalize All plants (outdoor, indoor, in a terrarium) need these things to grow. Plants and animals can live together in an ecosystem. After completing the terrarium, ask children what they put into the terrarium and how these items help the plants and/or animals. For a collage, provide materials that look or feel similar to the items children put in the terrarium, such as decorative grass for plants, sandpaper for sand, and black tissue paper for dirt. Set up these materials along with markers and colored pencils around the terrarium so children can represent the terrarium. Take dictation on lined paper or on the computer. Share children's stories about the terrarium and their list of items in it. Review these stories at group times (Chalufour & Worth, 2003).

Extended Experiences After many extended experiences in planting, older children may want to study what plants need through eliminating one of the ingredients that are a part of individual terrariums (light, dirt, moisture). Try many different kinds of plants in terrariums. Study the work of a botanist through visiting, e-mail communication, and photos.

INQUIRY TOPIC

TREES

Purpose

Children will observe characteristics of different kinds of trees and shrubs and their parts. By adopting a tree in spring, children can follow its growth through the season.

Teachers Prepare

Study   Study the species of trees found in your area, the annual cycle of the different kinds of trees, and characteristics of tree systems. Find out the kinds of trees in the neighborhood around the school. If the group will plant a tree or shrub, contact the people about the planting in the area where this will take place, including permission, obtaining the tree, and ongoing care.

Questions   What interest do children show in trees around them? Is this a season when children can study and plant a tree or shrub? Consider where a tree or shrub could be an addition to the landscape on the school grounds or in a nearby park.

Gather materials   Nursery catalogs with trees and shrubs, tree book, clipboards, paper and primary pencils, tape measure, Ziploc bags and paper bags, camera. Large box with dividers (such as container for crayons or markers purchased in bulk). Different kinds of wood, including a supply appropriate for woodworking, branches, and a crosscut slice of a stump.

Children's Books

Sky Tree: Seeing Science through Art! by Locker

The Giving Tree by Silverstein

The Apple Pie Tree by Hall

Recipe

Leaf rubbings: For the deciduous leaves that children collect, place them in large Ziploc bags until time to use them to make leaf rubbings. Use crayons without their paper wrappers. Place tracing paper or newsprint over a leaf and rub the side of the crayon on the top of the paper until the pattern of the leaf shows through. As children work they may want to experiment with making rubbings of several leaves on one paper. Taped to a sunny window or on a light table, the light shows off the intricate pattern and color.

Technology   On the Internet research information for species of trees that grow in your area, sources of trees (consider Arbor Day in the spring), growing conditions for new trees, and planting directions. As you study trees in the neighborhood, send an e-mail to parents asking them to do tasks with their children on this inquiry topic. Photograph the trees you visit and keep seasonal photos of selected trees and shrubs. For photos take both close-up and distance shots. From the items collected on site visits to the trees, scan a selection of these and print the images to have them for display.

In Experiences About This Inquiry Topic, Children Will

Explore   Take children on a visit to a nearby tree that they can adopt as "their tree" and return to it often. From the ground level help them discover the parts of the tree and explore it in different ways. The children can lie on the ground and look up, explore the ground to find evidence of roots, put their arms around the tree, examine its shadow, feel the bark, feel the roots (if exposed), and feel branches, leaves or needles, and any bloom or seed. Ask children to close their eyes and listen for sounds in the tree (Redleaf, 1996). Ask children to look for any living beings who are in or on the tree. Take photos of what children explore, including the shadow, and take a distant photo of the whole tree and record the visit through a group photo. Children can make a record of what they see by drawing a representative of the tree's characteristics. Help them collect parts of the tree found on the ground in their paper bags and collect a few leaves to place in the Ziploc bags. Collect many old and new leaves on the ground, both from this tree and others. Put this large collection of leaves in the sensory table for children to feel and crumble.

Identify   Name the species and main parts of the tree. Children may want to name their tree. If there are unknown parts of the tree that were discovered, explore the information books to find the name of these parts. Read with children about the parts of the tree that were seen on this trip. As children classify the items found, help a few of them make labels of each item on the computer.

Use new vocabulary: wood, bark, root, trunk, stump, branch, twig, flower, leaf, needle, conifer, deciduous, and season.

Classify   Children can display all they collected and decide how to organize them. Provide a sectioned box for classified items and label them. Keep some leaves in Ziploc bags and put others out to dry.

Compare   Compare sizes of items collected. Children may seriate the items by size, dryness, or color. Compare the size of the tree with another nearby, such as circumference of trunk, height, width. Compare the size of the tree with children's height, adult height, and nearby buildings. Decide how to measure the circumference of the trunk and width of the whole tree by measuring the diameter of the shade of the tree.

Return to the tree they adopted to examine and photograph the tree in the different seasons: spring, summer, fall, and winter.

After reading *The Giving Tree* by Silverstein, compare the length of life of a tree and a person. Look closely at a crosscut slice of a stump to examine the rings and explain that each ring represents a growing season (one year). Explore ways to count the rings and compare with ages of people in the classroom and school.

Contrast   Using pictures of **conifers** and **deciduous** trees, discuss ways they are similar and different. Include a trip to see and experience these different kinds of trees. Children can also collect what they find around the trees during this trip.

A conifer is a type of evergreen tree and shrub.

A deciduous tree is a type of tree or shrub that sheds its leaves seasonally.

The changes of a tree through different seasons are recorded.

Hypothesize   Question children on who uses the tree and how the tree can help us. Bring in the different kinds of wood, collect branches on the ground from the same kind of tree as the class tree as well as others, and bring in a crosscut slice of a stump.

Ask how the classroom tree started to grow and what it needs to grow (especially relevant to the children after germinating seeds). If seeds were found, ask what these seeds would need to grow. Look for new sprouts that are the same as the classroom tree. Try planting the tree seeds.

Generalize   Children can dictate what the tree needs to grow. As a culminating project, plant a tree or shrub on the school grounds or other place nearby. Decide the care needed to help the tree to grow over time. One consideration can be planting a tree of the same species as the classroom tree. If possible visit a tree nursery to obtain the tree.

Extended study   Extend this study by incorporating the Inquiry Topic: Woodworking from Chapter 16. Use the branches and stump in woodworking and ask what they find out about the different kinds of wood. Discuss the different uses of wood in the classroom and the school and ask parents to help follow this at home.

With children, create a replica of the classroom tree for the classroom or hallway by drawing the tree, as nearly life size as possible, on roll paper with markers, paint, and sponge painting. Plan with children to include all parts of the tree. Work with the children on how to plan, draw, decorate, and display (no small task) their creation.

With children write a "thank you to our tree."

Return to the classroom tree many times, especially timing visits with the different seasons (Redleaf, 1996). Continue to photograph and collect items to display. Using children's knowledge of the classroom tree, identify other trees of the same kind.

In examining shrubs, both coniferous and deciduous, watch for signs of growth in spring. Keep a record of shrubs that bloom and form berries (guard children against picking flowers and berries as most of these are nonedible).

At the end of the project children may decide to make the record of the classroom tree and the displays of different trees into class books.

SUMMARY

The in-depth experiences of plants and planting bring extensive study into the classroom and beyond. With outdoor and indoor experiences the children will be involved in study of plants over a long period of time. Your involvement in extensive planting will help children understand the growth of plant life and therefore relate to plants as part of ecosystems. As you study animal life in the coming chapter, you will find ways to combine these two aspects of biology.

TO FURTHER YOUR THINKING

1. Plant a seed and chart its growth. You can examine it in its stages of germination if you follow the directions for placing it in the cotton ball and Ziploc bag. Start mung seeds, and after they sprout, wash and stir fry them for eating. (See recipes on page 324–325)

2. Take apart flowers such as dandelions or marigolds to see the start of seeds inside the flower. Draw a diagram of this flower.

3. Visit a gardening center or conservatory. Ask for identification of local plants and study plants that are easy to grow in your area. Make notes on what you need for starting these plants.

4. Walk in the neighborhood during a growing season. Find evidence of different stages of growth.

5. Find several of the children's books in Additional Resources plus others on plant life. Review these, noting the age range best for the book and making brief notes on how you might use the book along with an inquiry topic.

REFERENCES

Carle, E. (1990). *The tiny seed.* New York: Simon & Shuster.

Chalufour, I., and Worth, K. (2003). *Discovering nature with young children.* St. Paul, MN: Redleaf Press.

Clemens, J. B. (1996, May). Gardening with children. *Young Children, 51*(4), 22–27.

Cohen, R. (1994, April). Creatures in the classroom. *Scholastic Early Childhood Today, 9*(5), 51–57.

Ehlert, L. (1988). *Planting a rainbow.* New York: Harcourt.

Hall, Z. (1996). *The apple pie tree.* New York: Scholastic.

Heller, R. (1983). *The reason for a flower.* New York: Penguin Putman Books.

Hickman, P., and Collins, H. (1997). *A seed grows: My first book of plants.* New York: Tonawanda.

Kraus, R. (1989). *A carrot seed.* New York: Harper.

Locker, T. (1995). *Sky tree: Seeing science through art!* New York: HarperCollins.

National Academy of Science. (1996). *National science education standards* [Book version, on line]. Washington, DC: National Academies Press. www.nap.edu

Redleaf, R. (1996). *Open the door let's explore more! Field trips of discovery for young children.* St. Paul, MN: Redleaf.

Silverstein, S. (1964). *The Giving Tree.* New York: Harper & Row.

Starbuck, S., Olthof, M., and Midden, K. (2002). *Hollyhocks and honeybees: Garden projects for young children.* St. Paul, MN: Redleaf.

ADDITIONAL RESOURCES

Burns, D. L., and Garrow, L. (1998). *Trees, leaves and bark (Take along guide).* Minnetonka, MN: Northword Press. An easy guide for teachers to use with children.

Green, M. D. (1996). *474 science activities for young children.* Clifton Park, NY: Thomson Delmar Learning. While there are a wealth of ideas in this book, use it as a resource for following children's ideas. There are duplicable examples of charts made for children's recording. See the contents for Diggable Dirt, Seed-Sational, Growing Potatoes (within Tater Time), and Woodworks. www.delmar.com

Lawrence Hall of Science. (1997). *Terrarium habitats.* Berkeley CA: Author. This teacher's guide provides the background on setting up terrariums in the classroom.

MacCaskey, M. (1999). *Gardening for Dummies* (2nd ed.). Hoboken, NJ: John Wiley & Sons. One place to start if one is a beginner in growing things.

Pranis, E. and Gifford, A. (2003). *Schoolyard mosaics.* South Burlington, VT: National Gardening Association. www.kidsgardening.com

Children's Books

Anthony, J. (1997). *The dandelion seed.* Nevada City, CA: Dawn Publishers.

Baldwin, A. (1970). *Sunflowers for Tina.* New York: Scholastic.

Carle, E. (1990). *The tiny seed.* New York: Simon & Shuster.

Carlstrom N. (1989). *Wild wild sunflower child Anna.* New York: Macmillan.

Ehlert, L. (1988). *Planting a rainbow.* New York: Harcourt.

Hall, Z. (1996). *The apple pie tree.* New York: Scholastic.

Heller, R. (1983). *The reason for a flower.* New York: Penguin Putman Books.

Hickman, P., and Collins, H. (1997). *A seed grows: My first book of plants.* New York: Tonawanda.

Kite, L. P. (1999). *Dandelion adventures.* New York: Bt Bound.

Kraus, R. (1989). *A carrot seed.* New York: Harper.

Locker, T. (1995). *Sky tree: Seeing science through art!* New York: HarperCollins.

Paolilli, P., and Brewer, D. (2001). *Silver seeds: A book of nature poems.* New York: Viking.

Posada, M. (2000). *Dandelions: Stars in the grass.* Minneapolis, MN: CarolRhoda Picture Books.

Silverstein, S. (1964) *The giving tree.* New York: HarperCollins. Later editions of *Arbol alma* (Spanish) and *L'arbre genereux* (French) are also available.

Web Sites

www.reeusda.gov Access this Web site to find your local state extension office staff who can assist with planning gardens and plants that are right for your area.

www.kidsgardening.com This Web site is sponsored by the National Gardening Association, helpful for information on children's gardens and grants to support children's gardens. Gardening books, tools and supplies are also available.

www.lhs.berkeley.edu Lawrence Hall of Science is a rich source for science curricula. Check out Gems on this site.

www.kidsdomain.com A recipe for a simple terrarium from a pop bottle can be found at Kids Domain Family Resource.

www.msue.msu.edu The Michigan State University Extension Web site has information on terrariums, including choices of plants.

Chapter 19

Exploring Life Science: Animals

Photo courtesy Patrick Clark

OBJECTIVES. Through the process of discovery in this chapter, you will be able to:

1. Describe what children gain from study of animals:
   a. Appreciate diversity of living beings in the world.
   b. Compare life processes of animals with the processes of their own body.
   c. Learn aspects of animal care according to the needs of the animal.

2. Decide concepts of animal life that are understood by young children.

3. Discuss what children can understand about their own bodies and the full span of life: birth, growth and change, reproduction, and death.

4. Describe development of inquiry topics on insects and arachnids, birds, and earthworms, and compare life processes of the child and the baby chick.

5. Use information and fiction books about animals and children's bodies.

IDEAS TO PONDER

- How can I help children appreciate animal life when I know so little about animals and their care?

- How can I teach respect for animal life and support children observing that life close at hand?

- What can I do when a pet dies?

- What can I teach about the body systems?

- How does literature support learning about animal life?

One warm fall day at the beach Alana followed a yellow moth as it flitted in the sun. At one point if flew toward her and landed on her index finger. She held her hand still as we all watched it hang on. Alana was fascinated that this beautiful creature would stay with her so long. Even when her father tried to release it without touching it, the little legs held firm.
(Author)

CHILDREN LEARN FROM ANIMAL LIFE

Children are fascinated by the beauty, movement, and bodily functions of very small creatures—from moths to squirrels. Since each one has its unique characteristics, each provides a focus for study over time. As in Alana's attention to the moth's, legs on her finger, children's attention is often drawn to one or two tiny features of a living being (Worth & Grollman, 2003).

STANDARDS

All students should develop understanding of

- The characteristics of organisms
- Life cycles of organisms
- Organisms and environments.

Content Standard K–4. C. Reprinted with permission from *National science education standards* (1996). The National Academy of Sciences, courtesy of the National Academies Press, Washington, DC (p. 106).

RESPECT FOR ANIMAL LIFE

One important value to pass along to young children is to respect animal life, as Alana certainly did. One day a group of four boys encountered an **ant colony** on the playground. They proceeded to stomp out the life of all the ants they could find. It seemed the message received from the adults in their lives was that **insects** were to be purged from existence around them. Still today, people work hard to rid insects from homes, and, yes, some of these are harmful and some compete for food systems. In reality, humans have coexisted with these small beings since early time.

Concerning the animal kingdom, many people enjoy animals in the wild, but when the woodchuck or rabbit destroy their productive gardens or skunks penetrate the environment with their pungent odor, their attitude changes. At these times people would like that animal destroyed, or at least out of the places that they inhabit. An attitude of respect can be shown by allowing the sharing of food, or moving the animal to another location, or providing a barrier around the tree

An ant colony is the organization of ants for living and working.

An insect is a small invertebrate belonging to a class of arthropods and has three body sections and six legs.

A woodchuck eats from a garden.
Photo courtesy Patrick Clark

or plant. While these aren't always workable solutions, adults can strive to follow that value.

Children can learn respect for each animal by getting to know its characteristics and by keeping it healthy and alive. At the same time that children are observing the animal, they will also learn about the animal's care. This often means observing the animal at a safe distance and leaving it be in its natural environment. For example, some small beings are harmed by the oil on our hands if we touch them (like the moth). Humans leave the animals alone because they can harm the animal, or animals may harm the humans. Many kinds of wildlife need to be free in order to survive as healthy beings. As adults demonstrate this respect, children learn these positive attitudes.

People in our modern world have changed the habitat of many animals, with the result that many species are either endangered or extinct. This is a loss of one of earth's benefits. How much better our future world would be if people learned to coexist with the animals and plan environments so each species can continue to live well. By getting to know animal life and its need for certain habitats and freedom, children can begin to appreciate each species and the need to preserve its environments.

CARE OF ANIMALS

Some insects may be captured without harm, but these need to be let go in their natural habitat (where they were discovered) in an hour or two. With careful planning some can be kept in captivity for a period of time to view a portion of their life cycle, such as the painted lady butterfly. These are brought into the classroom with the right timing to let them go free at the best time of the year.

While a few small animals make good pets for the classroom, some teachers question the value of a pet in a classroom over a period of time. Too often, pets live under poor conditions, are handled poorly, or have inadequate care on weekends. This promotes a negative message on the dignity of life (Seefeldt & Galper, 2002). If the decision is to have a pet over time, care needs to be taken to find an acceptable pet and carefully plan its care. Select a pet that can be proven to be disease free (and continue periodic testing for this). Find a pet that will not bite or harm a child. Bring a pet in the classroom that can withstand rough handling by a child, and supervise children for careful handling. Carefully plan to care for a pet on weekends and vacations. Also consider the room temperature throughout the year as being suitable for this pet. Before bringing a pet into a classroom, check with the state licensing representative for your school. States and municipalities may limit some pets because of prevalence of disease in select kinds of animals.

With these guidelines teachers have successfully added pets to the classroom life. Some of the pets that have lived long and healthy lives in classrooms are rabbits, gerbils, guinea pigs, hamsters, mice, anoles, frogs, toads, snakes, canaries, and fish. Visit the pet shop, talk with a small animal veterinarian, and look up informational Web sites, such as zoos, for habitat, care, and handling of pets.

The pet can be an ongoing source of satisfaction for young children. Children relate the body processes of the pet to their own. They compare characteristics and daily patterns of a certain pet to other kinds of animals and to their own bodies. Observing the birth of offspring can be an additional learning experience. The death of a pet can also be an unexpected outcome that the whole class would feel.

COMPARING LIFE PROCESSES

As the child examines the moth hanging onto her finger with spindly legs, she is asking questions such as, "What is she doing? How does she do that? How is she different than me?" The child is at work comparing the life processes of the moth with processes of her own.

While watching the guinea pig in its cage, children can be absorbed in watching it "poop." In doing so, they are comparing the guinea pig's body function in order to better understand their own. As the children first see tiny baby gerbils nestled together, they are reminded of their own growth, that they were small babies not so long ago.

STANDARDS

Organisms have basic needs. Organisms can survive only in environments in which their needs can be met. The world has many different environments, and distinct environments support the life of different types of organisms.

Content Standard: K-4. A. Reprinted with permission from *National science education standards* (1996). The National Academy of Sciences, courtesy of the National Academies Press, Washington, DC (p. 106).

STANDARDS

Plants and animals have life cycles that include being born, developing into adults, reproducing, and eventually dying. The details of this life cycle are different for different organisms.

Content Standard: K-4. C. Reprinted with permission from *National science education standards* (1996). The National Academy of Sciences, courtesy of the National Academies Press, Washington, DC (p. 106).

As children get to know the animal, they compare growth and change, eating and sleeping, eliminating and activity. Over time, children may experience birth, babies, reproduction, and death. These basic processes in animal life can be experienced in the school.

TALKING WITH CHILDREN ABOUT REPRODUCTION AND DEATH

As children pose questions and theories about birth and growth, teachers may be uncomfortable about handling these questions. There is some basis to this. Adults may be uncomfortable themselves about a topic. Teachers may feel that parents would not approve of these topics being discussed with their children. Teachers and parents may simply feel they don't know what to say to young children. With colleagues adults can discuss their reluctance to address these topics. The staff of a center may want to air this subject with parents to gain their view (which also may help parents broach this subject with their children).

Principles that can guide teachers in responding to questions on talking to children about birth, reproduction, and death are as follows:

- Children do not understand what they cannot see. They are working on theories of how important things happen in their lives. And they probably cannot grasp the whole picture.

- As children ask, listen to the exact question, and try to find the intent. One way to explore intent is to ask them what they are thinking about.
- When you decide to answer, answer only what they have asked.

If an adult does not know the answer or feels uncomfortable answering, the immediate response can be, "You have asked a question important to you. I need to find information [or ask other people, or think about this] to know how best to answer you. I will remember and talk to you about it tomorrow." This way the adult has the time to talk with others (including the child's parents, if needed) and reflect on what to say. This kind of answer shows respect for the child's thinking. If the child's questions are brushed aside by the adult, the child may believe that it is wrong to question a topic. The adult can confer with others, find the information and/or a book, and get back to the child within the allotted time.

Teachers can prepare for answering these questions by thinking through possible answers. This can be done effectively through the class you are taking or discussions with colleagues. Be careful about using allegorical answers that may lead the child to faulty thinking, such as a seed being planted in the tummy for the baby gerbils to grow. The child may take this information literally so she may believe that if she eats a seed she will have a baby. Most often the questions of young children do not entertain how growth began because they cannot think of what they have not seen (Chrisman & Couchenour, 2002).

The question from young children could be, "Where do the baby gerbils grow?" The teacher could answer, "They are very tiny beings in a special place inside the mother." Most times children of preschool and kindergarten age are not thinking of reproductive questions. Prospective teachers can discuss answers to possible reproductive questions to increase their comfort level.

Another aspect of life, death, may also be observed in caring for animals. Teachers can be matter of fact if death of an animal occurs in the classroom. For example, upon arrival in the morning the teacher sees that two of the baby gerbils are dead. She resists her first impulse of wanting to hide this fact of life from the children. Instead she leaves the nest as it is and waits for the children to discover what is amiss this morning. After children talk about the babies not moving, the teacher questions what they think is happening.

The teacher's frank discussion will pave the way for children to understand death. A common misconception children have about death is that the animal is only sleeping. Research possible causes of death of the gerbils, if possible. With the children, plan what to do with the babies who have expired.

CHILDREN UNDERSTANDING THEIR BODIES

Young children have developed some concepts about the life cycle, yet since their growth extends over such a long period, it is likely that the human life cycle will be incomprehensible except for the short time that they can remember. But given opportunity to see the life cycle in several organisms, both plant and animal, children are given a stepping stone to understanding their own (Worth & Grollman, 2003).

It seems that children would be able to study what is closest to them, their own bodies, yet they develop concepts based mainly on what they can see. Most body systems remain a mystery because children cannot see under their skin.

What can be learned skin deep? Comparison of themselves to others: skin tone, hair, height, teeth, and the size of hands and feet. Comparison of what they can do: run, jump, climb, draw, write, build, and balance. Children can make sense of what their body tells them, such as feeling of fullness or emptiness in eating, being tired or awake, feeling sick or well.

Since hair, fingernails, and toenails grow rather fast and are the objects of grooming by adults, these hold the fascination of children. Hair and nails can be magnified and compared with those of peers. If tangled hair is seen magnified, it is easier to understand why a pick or comb is needed to straighten or smooth it out (Holt, 1989).

Teachers are aware of common fears of young children. Because children think that all parts of the body are extensions of themselves, they believe that cutting hair and nails will hurt. They may also think that when blood oozes from a scratch, all the blood will come out. Perhaps to the child, a bandage fixes the scratch because it keeps the blood inside their body.

INQUIRY ABOUT ANIMALS

The inquiry topics that follow focus on insects and arachnids, earthworms, and birds. In the previous chapter the inquiry topic of The Terrarium includes preparing the terrarium for a small animal. The last inquiry topic in this chapter compares the children's own growth process with a chicken or other baby animal. With ongoing observation of a small animal, children can know more of its life cycle in order to compare with their own growth.

Insects and Arachnids

Arthropods are a family of invertebrate animals including insects and arachnids.

Arachnid is the class of land invertebrates, including spiders.

These small beings can be examined in the play yard and in the classroom. Alert teachers have prepared in advance to take children on classroom walks when aware of the preponderance of **arthropods.** The habitat, actions, and characteristics of insects and **arachnids** can be observed. These can be examined closely and then left alone or taken for a brief time for observation (and returned to the same spot).

Children can observe the arthropod, compare the live animal with photos or drawings, and draw it. If outdoors, they will enjoy having harmless insects on their hands, arms, and clothing. While most insects are harmless, it is wise to confer with books and local understanding. Most varieties of spiders are harmless, but a few can bite, so it is best only to observe all except the daddy longlegs. These are easily identifiable and harmless. Yet these gentle creatures need to be handled with care as their delicate legs can be harmed. Teach children to hold them in an open palm or allow them to crawl on a jacket sleeve (Starbuck, Olthof, & Midden, 2002).

The ladybug is examined closely.

INQUIRY TOPICS ON EXPLORING LIFE SCIENCE: ANIMALS

INQUIRY TOPIC

INSECTS AND ARACHNIDS

Purpose

Explore the arthropods found outside, study their movements, life cycle, and habitats. Children will compare arthropods with others of the same and different species, and even with themselves (Chalufour & Worth, 2003).

Teachers Prepare

Study   Observe for insects and arachnids outdoors. Look up Internet and library resources to become familiar with some of the arthropods in your area. Learn to identify creatures in the area that may bite, such as some spiders and some ants. Prepare materials for observing outdoors and capturing specimens for short periods of time.

Question   Are children finding arthropods and noticing them? Are children able to respect these creatures without harming them? Is this the time of year that many of these creatures are seen?

Prepare materials   Homemade or purchased bug jars and viewers (purchased bug viewers have magnifiers built in), magnifiers, clip boards and primer pencils with paper for drawing specimens, digital camera,

Ziploc bags, flashlight, *Caterpillars, Bugs and Butterflies (Take Along Guide)* by Boring and Garrow, or downloaded photos of arthropods.

Recipes   Make bug viewers by cutting off the tops of detergent bottles and cutting out large holes on the two sides of the bottom portion. Place the bottom portion inside a section of nylon stocking. Leave the top portion of the stocking untied. The child can hold onto the top portion and open it to put his newfound bug inside.

For a large specimen jar, use empty plastic jars such as a peanut butter jar. Using a nail, make one small hole in the lid. When catching a specimen, place the jar upside down over the insect or spider. Slide an index card under the specimen, turn the jar over, and then remove the card and screw on the lid.

Children's and Information Books

Bright Beetle by Chrustowski

Bugs by Parker and Wright

Caterpillars, Bugs and Butterflies (Take Along Guide) by Boring and Garrow

Inch by Inch by Lionni

The Very Busy Spider by Carle

Technology   Download photos and drawings of insects and arachnids in your area. Use a computer add-on microscope (see Appendix B) to view these small creatures you find. Take close-up photos of arthropods before letting them free. Using Kidspiration, ask children to develop a web on arthropods.

In Experiences About This Inquiry Topic, Children Will

Explore   Children will explore through discovery when finding arthropods in the playground or park. Insect hunts can take place in the play yard and on nearby walks in parks and fields. Children can look under rocks, boards, and rotting logs. Teachers and children can place a board in a damp area of the playground a couple of days ahead of time to provide a place some arthropods like. You can supply bug viewers (commercial or homemade) or magnifying lenses to look at children's findings close-up. These can also be examined under the computer add-on microscope. As children become comfortable with these small creatures, they can allow them to crawl on their hand or sleeve.

Identify   Place insect books for children's viewing, and read books such as *Inch by Inch*, *Bright Beetle*, and *The Very Busy Spider*; then discuss what children know about insects and where to find them. List what they know and graph the children's predictions on finding them. Using the magnifier to look at a specimen, identify the three parts of the insect body: head,

thorax, and abdomen and six legs and two antenna. Also, identify the two parts of the spider: **cephalothorax** (the head and thorax combined), with the strong **chelae** (jaws), and abdomen, with eight legs (Johnson, 1996). Look up the common names of the arthropod and label these with the children. Discuss what the arthropods do as children observe them. For different arthropods children may observe and name the spider web. Identify the location where different specimens were sighted.

Classify   Match the picture of the insect to the actual insect captured for study or a drawing of the insect by a child. Chart sightings of particular insects day by day. Children can draw what they find outside and then dictate what they have seen. They can add small sketches or drawings to the chart of sightings. If specimens are brought in for observations, gather a little dirt and the leaf or stem that the arthropod was on or near when found.

Compare and contrast   Take a paper plate and some tiny food scraps outdoors and place near an anthill. Set a timer for children to come over to check every 10 minutes. Children can observe the ants find and take the food away. Record what they take (Kleinsinger, 1991). On another day set out the paper plate with scraps for other identified insects. Compare what each insect takes. Compare photos of bugs with species children have drawn or captured.

Create a concept web using Kidspiration and compare what children know with what they now want to find out.

Hypothesize   Questions children have could be: What is it? How does it move? What does it eat? Where does it live?

In the classroom, use the recordings, chart, and close-up photos done by you and the children to research more on their findings. Compare findings to the list of what they know and to descriptions and pictures in information books and the Internet.

Observe the arthropod move and eat. Or try an experiment of placing leaves from several sources found around an insect and checking back later to see if any of the leaves have changed (Holt, 1989, 1990).

Generalize   Define what arthropods eat, how they move, and where they live. The children's findings can be added to lists and/or a web display of their experiences and knowledge.

Extended Experiences   If the children have discovered insect or spider eggs, a **caterpillar,** or a **chrysalis,** these can be placed in a specimen jar with food and observed over time. As spider eggs hatch or the chrysalis opens, let the arthropods go back to their natural habitat. Or painted lady caterpillars with butterfly kits can be ordered at the right season to let the butterflies go free. Use books such as *The Hungry Caterpillar* by Carle or *Waiting for Wings* by Ehlert, downloaded photos showing the stages of **metamorphosis,** and photos you take to review

The thorax is the central body part of an insect on which are the legs and wings.

The cephalothorax is the head and thorax (joined) of an arachnid.

Chelae are the pincer-like jaws of an arachnid.

A caterpillar is the larvae of a butterfly or moth.

A chrysalis is the pupa of a butterfly or moth in the stage of metamorphosis.

Metamorphosis is the change in the form or structure of an animal (i.e., butterfly, moth, or beetle).

and discuss the changes. Children may not recognize the reality of the change from caterpillar to mature adult butterfly.

If butterflies are seen in your area, planning a butterfly garden (Chapter 13) will attract more butterflies to your playground or garden. Even a butterfly feeder (From Insect Lore catalog) can attract them to visit.

INQUIRY TOPIC

EARTHWORMS

Purpose

Children will discover the characteristics of the earthworm, its habitat, and its benefit to plant life. They will prepare a habitat that the earthworms can thrive in.

Teachers Prepare

Study Look up information on characteristics of earthworms and how to care for them. Study the care of earthworms (see Additional Resources). Decide on how you will build an earthworm compost and/or viewing station. Determine location of earthworms in your area and time of year to find them.

Question What are the children's interests in and knowledge of this topic? Is this the season when earthworms can be found, or if purchased, can they live outdoors when let go? Is there a location where digging for worms can take place?

Gather materials Earthworms, digging tools, materials for compost and viewing station (Appendix C), trays, materials to make "dark" box, materials for graphs.

Children's Books

Wonderful Worms by Glaser

Earthworms (Animals) by Holmes

Recipes Directions for a compost home for earthworms and an earthworm viewing station are found in Appendix C, Table C–14, and Appendix C, Table C–15.

Technology Use the Internet for pictures and information on earthworms and how they help the soil. Also find photos of other creatures in the soil and in the garden. Download photos to compare them. Place a photo or drawing of earthworms in a plastic sleeve and place on the tray when children are handling the worms. Take close-up photos of the worms, where they were found, and development of the compost for worms. Take dictation by handwriting or on computer to record children's experiences and understanding of earthworms.

In Experiences About This Inquiry Topic, Children Will

Explore   Children will look for earthworms outdoors in the garden or on sidewalks after a spring rain. An alternate choice is to purchase red worms used for fishing at a sports store. Dig up some of the soil where earthworms are found for children to examine. Support children looking at the shape, color, and movement of the earthworm and handling the worm when ready (plastic gloves may help). Provide a large magnifying glass for examining at closer range. Exploration can continue indoors as you set the stage for developing an indoor habitat for earthworms. Children may be able to observe the **castings** the worm leaves on a paper towel. These castings are beneficial to the soil.

Identify   Provide the name of the species, earthworm, and the class of this worm, **annelid,** and parts of the worm: head, tail and the banded area, called the **clitellum** (klih-TEL-um) (Fig. 19–1).

Support children describing how they see the worm move and how it feels in their hands. Ask children what is needed for the earthworms to live in the classroom (Worth & Grollman, 2003). Use additional vocabulary: soil, compost, nutrient-rich castings.

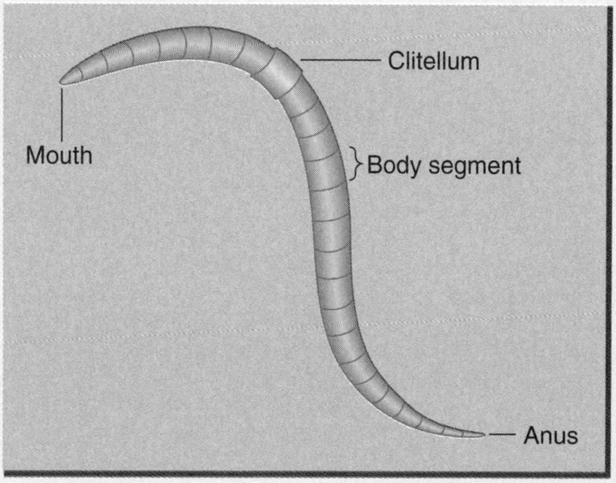

Castings are excrement of the earthworm that is beneficial to the soil.

Annelid is the name of the class of common earthworms.

Clitellum is the middle banded area of the earthworm.

Figure 19–1 Anatomy of the earthworm.

Classify   Prepare a graph for children to record the individual worm's response to touch on its head, middle, and tail (the pointed end of the worm). Several children can try this on different worms (Starbuck, Olthof, & Midden, 2002).

Compare   Set up experimental trials if children are interested in comparing whether earthworms like wet or dry, or light or dark. This can be done by placing dampened paper towels on a tray. Worms need the dampness of the towels so they won't dry out. To set the stage for the wet/dry trial, replace the paper towels on one side with dry ones. To set the stage for the light or dark trial, prepare a shoe box, cut a 1-inch opening along the rim at one end, and cover the inside with black paper. Place the box upside down on one side of the tray. For each trial put down one worm at a time on the middle line and observe which way the worm chooses to go. Discuss where the worm goes and graph the preference observed in each trial (Starbuck, Olthof, & Midden, 2002).

Contrast   Use drawings and photos of other creatures to compare differences in the appearance of other creatures found in the soil, such as sow bugs, ants, millipedes, and creatures found in other places, such as caterpillars, snakes, snails. Contrast these differences as you provide the names, and, possibly, the classes of these different types. If you

Children show fascination with earthworms.

Figure 19–2 Viewing station for earthworms.

collect some of these types from the soil and other parts of the garden or playground, compare the size, shape, and movement of these with the earthworms.

Hypothesize   After discussing the results of the trials of what earthworms did, then wonder with the children what worms prefer. Ask them what they think the worms would like to eat and how they could find out what they like. Plan to make an earthworm viewing station (Appendix C, Table C–15). Place selected food in certain spots in the viewing station and mark its location with masking tape on the outside. When observing the worms children can describe what the worms are doing (Fig. 19–2).

Ask children what they think they would need to make an indoor home for the worms, or how they can find out how the worms move in the soil.

Generalize   After children decide what earthworms prefer and have experimented with what the worms like to eat, decide plans for a compost home for worms. Build the compost home and add the worms and the food that the children choose for them. Observe worms in their new habitat and ask children what they know about worms. Ask children to dictate their understanding of these possible topics: Our Earthworms Prefer the Dark, What Earthworms Choose to Eat, or The Earthworms' Home. You can add close-up photos to these class dictations.

Using their understanding of what worms prefer and what they need to live indoors, communicate their accomplishments through e-mail, a class newsletter, or documentation. The children may want to invite a group to see the earthworm compost home, earthworm viewing station, and the earthworms.

Extended Experiences   Over time the earthworms may grow and/or reproduce in their rich compost home. To check this, periodically find all

Earthworms live well in their large compost home.

the worms in the compost, measure some of them, and count them to determine how well they are doing in their home. Before moving on to a new topic, find an outdoor location for the earthworms. The compost home could become part of a compost for gardening, or dig a spot for the earthworms in the soft earth of the play yard.

INQUIRY TOPIC

BIRD WATCHING

Purpose

Children will observe the characteristics, movements, and habits of birds in their neighborhood, and compare these findings for one kind of bird with others. Children will investigate the habitat of a particular species they observe.

Teachers Prepare

Study   Find out types of birds in your area, including birds of different types, such as robins, sea gulls, ducks, and chickens.

Question   Are children watching birds? What are children noticing about them? What birds are nearby to observe? Are nests observable at different times of the year?

Gather materials   For observing, several clipboards with paper, primer pencils and a selection of colored pencils, Ziploc bags, plastic tweezers, magnifying glass. Add an information sheet on birds in your area (see Technology) placed inside plastic sleeves to be used inside and outside the classroom. Laminate two sets of the bird picture cards to use for matching. Obtain ingredients for children to create pine cone birdfeeders and/or set out a purchased birdfeeder. If it is the time for nest building, place small scraps of yarn, tissue paper, grasses, and small twigs near a feeder. Request that parents or others bring pet birds in a cage for a brief visit.

Children's and Informational Books

Birds in Your Backyard by Herkert

Birds, Nests, and Eggs by Boring and Garrow

Smithsonian Kids' Field Guide: Birds of North America (East) by Kittinger

Recipe

Pine cone bird feeder: Peanut butter, bird seed, sunflower seed, string, pine cones from a previous season. With plastic knives spread peanut butter on the pine cones; then roll them in bird seed or sunflower seeds. Hang them in the playground in a quiet location or outside the classroom window (Kleinsinger, 1991) (Fig. 19–3).

Technology   After determining the birds in your local area, download pictures of these birds, their nests and diet, and description of characteristics. Use this to make an information sheet on local birds. In addition, make two sets of the pictures from the Web for bird picture cards that are about 2" square. Photograph birds at the bird feeder or anywhere birds are observed. Tape record bird songs.

In Experiences About This Inquiry Topic, Children Will

Explore   Since most of the information gathered will occur through looking, support this through watching with a child. Set up birdfeeders where its visitors can be seen from the classroom window. If birds can be seen from the classroom window, observing birds can be done throughout the day.

Model with children how to be very quiet when observing—or waiting—for birds outdoors. Ask children to look for what birds find or carry in their mouth. When anyone hears the birds' songs you can alert others to listen. And this can be audio recorded to hear later.

When feathers or bird nests are found on the ground, have children use tongs to handle these finds. Put items in Ziploc bags. When indoors children can view these specimens inside the bags with a magnifying glass.

Identify   Names of the species of birds sited, parts of the bird: feather, wings, tail, head, beak, feet, wingspan, diet, nest. Children can draw and describe movement on the ground, flying position, color, size, or shape.

Figure 19–3 A pine cone bird feeder.

Classify As children get to know the characteristics of different birds, ask them how they would classify them, using the bird picture cards. Encourage children to classify in different ways according to the characteristics they know. Use the bird picture cards for matching or lotto games. If photos are taken of birds observed, add these to the bird picture cards for classifying species or other characteristics.

Compare and contrast Ask children to record what they see and later compare the information they have with the information sheet you made. Or use the information sheet to compare at the time the bird is observed.

From children's interests select a part of the bird's body and contrast how this differs from one bird to another. Some differences could be

A cardinal visits the bird feeder.
Photo courtesy Patrick Clark

color differences between birds and between male and female of the same species, type of beak, the size and shape of the feet, and the wing span.

Hypothesize   From a list of differences, ask children what these differences could mean in what the bird can do. If this relates to something observable, such as type of diet, watch for evidence of this and record with drawings or photographs.

Frame suggestions relating to habitat of birds such as

Birds that live high in a tree would need:

Birds that live near water would need:

Birds that live mainly on the ground would need:

Or use hypothesizing for a particular species children have observed. For a particular species, discuss places to live, diet, nest, and raise young.

Generalize   Using the information from hypothesizing plus ongoing observation to verify children's predictions, plan a diorama on the birds observed, gathering the specific materials children decide birds need to live in an area. Use photos, children's drawings, and the actual materials to be shown in a large open box. Take dictation on children's understanding of the bird habitat. Create the diorama of all the things a selected species of birds would want in their environment.

Extended Experiences   Continue observing birds, and if interest continues visit a bird sanctuary, a zoo, or a farm with chickens, ducks, and turkeys to extend children's knowledge of different species. Children can ask questions of a farmer or zookeeper about care of birds.

INQUIRY TOPIC

COMPARE LIFE PROCESSES OF CHILD AND BABY CHICK

Purpose

Children will gain an understanding of themselves and their growth process from baby to adult through comparison of growth with a baby animal such as a chicken.

Teachers Prepare

Study   Look up the life stages of the chicken (or other animal observed), noting weight and height at different ages. Study ways to depict weight of animal and child at different ages, by collecting materials that combined will equal the weight of each: the baby chick and the infant.

Question   Is there an animal that children can observe from birth onward? Some animals that work well besides baby chicks are young gerbils (although children will probably not be able to see the newborns), mice, and hamsters. Are children asking questions about their own growth? Is there a good place for the chicken or other animal to safely grow and thrive when (if) they are too mature for the classroom?

Gather materials   Photos of children as infants, their birth weights, heights. Obtain accurate scales to weigh animal, measurement tools for recording children's height, and bathroom or medical scales for weight. Add butcher paper on rolls and lengths of yarn to record height. Collect photos of the teachers from infancy to the present. Find materials to make graphs. Select information books on infant development of humans and the selected animal and pictures of stages of growth of the animal.

Recipe   For comparing weights make bags of the same weight of an infant child and the newborn animal, see Appendix C, Table C–16.

Technology   Find information on the life stages of the animal on the Web. Take photos of the children and teachers at the same distance from the camera and in front of a background that has a posted measurement so children can use photos for comparison of height (Buckleitner, personal communication 2003).

Children's Books

Poem, "The End," in *Now We are Six* by Milne

When I Was Little: A Four-Year-Old's Memoir of Her Youth by Curtis

Everywhere Babies by Meyers

How Kids Grow by Marzollo

In Experiences About This Inquiry Topic, Children Will

Explore   Support children observing the animal. If children can be close to the animal, use a magnifying glass to observe body covering and body parts. Observe body processes of eating, drinking, eliminating, sleeping. Look at photos of baby animal, young animal and adult, infant, young child or kindergarten child and adult (especially photos that show height). Use senses of touch, sight, hearing, and smell to observe the animal closely. Request a parent to bring a young baby for the children to observe, and ask children to use their senses to observe characteristics of the baby. Ask them to find out, through observing, what the baby can do. Ask the parent the child's birth weight and height, and present weight and height.

Observe the baby animal over time and discuss what children see as the animal grows. Ask children to record what they see in pictures or describe it to put in the class journal (dictation).

Identify   Age of animal and human at different stages, name used for that age stage, name used for males and females. Identify weight and height in pounds, grams, inches, and/or centimeters. Describe what each baby, animal and human, can and cannot do.

Classify   After observing what the baby animal and an infant can do, discuss what the children can do and what the animal can do as it grows up. Ask children to draw the things each can do and place them under "human" or "chicken" columns on a chart. They could also place the items in order according to what, for example, the human baby can do first, next, what the young child can do, and follow the children's ideas all the way up to what adults can do.

Compare   As children observe differences between infant and baby animal, between themselves and the animal, these differences can be graphed. Develop the two baby weight bags (for baby chick and human baby) with the children and compare them, and compare the infant weight bag with their own weight and the weight of an adult. This can be done through use of scales and trying to lift each other—and the adult.

Matching   Use the contributed baby pictures and classroom shots of each child and teachers. Put each photo in a plastic sleeve or clear picture frame (write child's name on the back of each picture). Children can work at matching baby and "now" pictures. With the teachers' photos children can order them according to age of the teachers (Woods, 2000).

Compare with the children the height (or length) of the baby animal with the length of one of them at birth such as the baby who visited the class. For older children you may mark height in inches using a tape measure, using two colors of tape, one for the baby animal and the other for the human baby, and then count the inches for each. Create a graph large enough to show the full height of a human adult. Depict height of each of the following on the graph, using a color code or photos to identify each: baby animal, animal in youth (if possible), adult animal, infant, young child, young adult, adult. Children will be able to see the seriation from short to tall on the graph. (Note that by placing this graph with the lower line exactly at floor level, the children can continue to compare their height with heights depicted on the graph.)

Contrast   Using the graph about what the baby animal and infant can do, compare the differing abilities. With the children, create a "home" for dramatic play of the animal, such as chicken coop with an area for eating, sleeping, drinking water, and an outdoor area for the baby chick to find more food and exercise. Then in the housekeeping area create a "baby's room" for children to play out being the baby and taking care of the doll babies. During their play, and afterward at group time, ask children what they played and what they pretended in the actions or care of the chick or infant. Compare with the graph made earlier.

Use a journal to keep track of the growth of the baby chick and compare to information on the Internet. Discuss the number of birthdays the children have had and compare each birthday to one year. Make a timeline depicting the number of birthdays (years) for the oldest child; then, using the facts from the journal, make a timeline for the baby chick to contrast with the growth of the human. Compare the long time to grow for the children and the short time to grow for the chicken.

Hypothesize   Suggest the following concepts to discuss:

If parents were going to take care of an infant, they would need:

If parents were going to take care of a young child, they would need:

If a hen were going to take care of her baby chicks, she would need:

If farmers were going to take care of young chickens, they would need:

The class may plan a field trip to observe what is needed to take care of baby chicks on a farm or at the farm in the zoo. Or e-mail a farmer or zookeeper to find out.

Generalize   From their combined experiences take dictation about what children know about their growth and the baby chick's growth. Ask them to select photos taken throughout the experience that show what they know.

Ask children to dictate a letter to their parents describing what they know their parents did to take care of them as a baby. Send the dictations with an attached class photo or scanned baby picture, or compose a letter on the computer, scan the baby picture or current photo from the class photos, and print out for each child to give to her parents.

Extended experiences   Plan a field trip to take the young animal to its new home. Every three months, take more photos of the children against the background of the posted measurement. At the end of the year send copies of the child's photos home to each family.

SUMMARY

The study of animal life that is close to the child provides fascinating exploration. Whether this occurs in thorough examination of life outdoors or ongoing study of animal life in the classroom, children can gain a respect for various animals. While this chapter culminates the study of science, it opens the possibilities of sharing ongoing inquiry with children. You will be considering your approach to sharing science and math in the final chapter.

TO FURTHER YOUR THINKING

1. What have you learned about respect for all forms of animal life? Develop a statement that reflects your beliefs on the human relationship to all forms of life.

2. Discuss concerns you have regarding talking about any of the following subjects with young children you teach: birth, caring for young, elimination, reproduction, and death. What are cultural concerns in your community about the appropriateness of these topics for young children? If children address one of these topics, how will you respond? What can you do to be prepared to respond to questions on these topics?

3. With a colleague, list what you think preschool and kindergarten children do and do not understand about body processes. What limits children's ability to understand these processes?

4. List the animals that are found in the four inquiry topics in this chapter according to your comfort level for handling them. Considering that young children learn about animal species from firsthand experiences with them, what value do you place on bringing these animals into the classroom? What process can enable you to provide these experiences in the classroom even though you might not enjoy handling all the animals?

5. What are some ways children can have ongoing experiences in studying an animal that is not appropriate as a visitor or a resident in a classroom? From the list of animals that follows, decide if there are ways to provide opportunities for ongoing study considering the community of the school. If a study is not possible, cross off the name; if it is possible, list some ways to accomplish a study through ongoing experiences.

   duck
   lightning bug
   chameleon
   land snail
   deer

   For every item you crossed off, suggest another topic on animals that could be possible in your community.

6. From the list of children's books in this chapter, select two books that would enhance one of the inquiry topics in this chapter or other topics on animals. How would the two books extend the knowledge and experience about the animal(s) under study?

7. For the inquiry topic Compare Life Processes of the Child and the Baby Chick, select another small animal that could reside in the classroom. Develop a web on the changed topic. How does the change affect the way that this inquiry topic would develop with young children?

REFERENCES

Boring, M., and Garrow, L. (1998). *Birds, nests, and eggs.* Minnetonka, MN: Northword Press.

Boring, M., and Garrow, L. (1999). *Caterpillars, bugs and butterflies (Take along guide).* Minnetonka, MN: Northword Press.

Carle, E. (1985). *The very busy spider.* New York: Philomel Books.

Chalufour, I., and Worth, K. (2003). *Discovering nature with young children.* St. Paul, MN: Redleaf Press.

Chrisman, K., and Couchenour, D. (2002). *Healthy sexuality development: A guide for early childhood educators and families.* Washington, DC: National Association for the Education of Young Children.

Chrustowski, R. (2000). *Bright beetle.* New York: Henry Holt and Co.

Curtis, J. L. (1993). *When I was little: A four-year-old's memoir of her youth.* New York: Scholastic.

Ehlert, L. (2001). *Waiting for wings.* New York: Harcourt.

Herkert, B. (2003). *Birds in your backyard.* Nevada City, CA: Dawn Publishers.

Holt, Bess-Gene. (1989). *Science with young children.* Washington, DC: National Association for the Education of Young Children.

Holt, Bess-Gene. (1990, February). Setting the stage for science discoveries. *Scholastic Pre-K Today, 2*(5), 41–47.

Johnson, J. (1996). *Simon & Schuster: Children's guide to insects and spiders.* New York: Simon & Schuster.

Kleinsinger, S. B. (1991). *Learning through play: Science, a practical guide for teaching young children.* New York: Scholastic.

Lionni, L. (1999). *Inch by inch.* New York: Bt Bound.

Marzollo, J. (1998). *How kids grow.* New York: Scholastic.

Meyers, S. (2001). *Everywhere babies.* New York: Harcourt.

Milne, A. A. (1927). *Now we are six.* London: Dutton & Co.

National Academy of Science. (1996). *National science education standards* [Book version, on line]. Washington, DC: National Academies Press. www.nap.edu

Parker, N. W. and Wright, J. R. (1987). *Bugs.* New York: Scholastic.

Seefeldt, C., and Galper, A. (2002). *Active experiences for active children: Science.* Upper Saddle River, NJ: Pearson.

Starbuck, S., Olthof, M., and Midden, K. (2002). *Hollyhocks and honeybees: Garden projects for young children.* St. Paul, MN: Redleaf.

Woods, C. S. (2000, September). A picture is worth a thousand words—Using photographs in the classroom. *Young Children, 55*(5), 82–84.

Worth, K., and Grollman, S. (2003). *Worms, shadows, and whirlpools: Science in the early childhood classroom.* Portsmouth, NH: Heinemann and Washington, DC: National Association for the Education of Young Children.

ADDITIONAL RESOURCES

Boring, M., and Garrow, L. (1998). *Birds, nests, and eggs.* Minnetonka, MN: Northword Press. Another handy resource guide at a simple level.

Boring, M., and Garrow, L. (1999). *Caterpillars, bugs and butterflies (Take along guide).* Minnetonka, MN: Northword Press. A book written for the primary age is useful as a resource guide.

Creative Classroom. (1999, May/June). Beautiful butterflies. Author. A pullout guide of butterflies commonly found in the United States. www.creativeclassroom.com

DK Pockets (2003). *Animals of the world: Pockets full of knowledge.* New York: DK Publishers. Here is a convenient book for concise information on animals. www.dk.com

Green, M. D. (1996). *474 science activities for young children.* Clifton Park, NY: Thomson Delmar Learning. While there are a wealth of ideas in this book, use it as a resource for following children's ideas. You will find information for a study of feathers and duplicable examples of graphs made for children's recording. www.delmar.com

Howley-Pfeifer, P. (2002, November). Raising butterflies from your own garden. *Young Children, 57*(6), 60–65. This informative article sets up the process for attracting butterflies. www.naeyc.org

Kittinger, J. S. (2001). *Smithsonian kids' field guide: Birds of North America (East).* DK Publishers & Smithsonian. 140 species of birds and useful glossary. www.dk.com

Nancarrow, L., and Taylor, J. H. (1998). *The worm book: The complete guide to worms in your garden.* Berkeley, CA: Ten Speed Press. This book provides the background for understanding the earthworm.

Seefeldt, C., and Galper, A. (2000). *Active experiences for active children: Social studies.* Upper Saddle River, NJ: Prentice Hall. A section of Chapter 5, The Past is Present, offers curriculum about children's own growth from infancy to the present.

Tomich, K. (1996, May). Hundreds of ladybugs . . . *Young Children, 51*(3), 28–30. A preschool teacher's journal of emergent curriculum on ladybugs.

Zakowski, C. (1997). *The insect book: A basic guide to the collections and care of common insects for young children.* Highland City, FL: Rainbow Books.

Children's Books

Carle, E. (1985). *The very busy spider.* New York: Philomel Books.

Carle, E. (2003). *Panda bear, panda bear, what do you see?* New York: Henry Holt. In a lilting repeatable style, Eric Carle features endangered species.

Carle, E. (2003). *The very hungry caterpillar.* New York: Philomel.

Chrustowski, R. (2000). *Bright beetle.* New York: Henry Holt & Co.

Curtis, J. L. (1993). *When I was little: A four-year-old's memoir of her youth.* New York: Scholastic.

Ehlert, L. (2001). *Waiting for wings.* New York: Harcourt.

Fleming, D. (1991). *In the tall, tall grass.* New York: Henry Holt & Co.

Fleming, D. (1998). *In the small, small pond.* New York: Henry Holt & Co.

Glaser, L. (1994). *Wonderful worms.* Brookfield, CT: Millbrook Press.

Herkert, B. (2003). *Birds in your backyard.* Nevada City, CA: Dawn Publishers.

Holmes, K. (1998). *Earthworms (Animals).* New York: Bridgestone Books.

Lionni, L. (1999). *Inch by inch.* New York: Bt Bound.

Marzollo, J. (1998). *How kids grow.* New York: Scholastic.

Mayer, M., and Mayer, M. (1975). *One frog too many.* New York: Dial. An adventure about a boy in a wordless book.

Meyers, S. (2001). *Everywhere babies.* New York: Harcourt.

Milne, A. A. (1927). *Now we are six.* London: Dutton & Co.

Parker, N. W., and Wright, J. R. (1987). *Bugs.* New York: Scholastic.

Pattou, E. (2001). *Mrs. Spitzer's garden.* New York: Harcourt.

Pfister, M. (1992). *The rainbow fish.* New York: North-South Books.

Pfister, M. (1998). *Hopper hunts for spring.* New York: North-South Books.

Ryder, J. (1988). *The snail's spell.* New York: Puffin.

Scarborough, K. (1997). *Spider's nest (Watch it grow).* New York: Time Life.

Web Sites

www.geocities.com/wyllz This site has beautiful detailed photos of life cycle of the Monarch butterfly as well as hummingbirds, flowers, and insects.

www.insectlore.com Insect Lore specializes in butterfly kits and other species to observe in your classroom. This on-line and catalog store carries bug catchers and viewers and a wide variety of informational books on animal and plant life.

www.monarchwatch.org Learn about Monarch butterflies and participate in scientific research in tagging the butterflies through this Web site sponsored by the University of Kansas Entomology Program.

www.tolweb.org The Tree of Life Project is building a picture collection and information on all organisms and has a large array of insect photos. At this time Latin names are needed to select information. Also has a Treehouse for Kids.

Chapter 20

Inquiry as an Approach to Life

OBJECTIVES Through the process of discovery in this chapter, you will be able to:

1. Explain how advances in mathematics, science, and technology will change education.

2. Incorporate the disposition of inquiry into teaching and as an approach to life.

3. Ascribe to providing quality education in math, science, and technology for all groups in this country, including women and minorities.

4. Describe the inquiry process as the primary basis of learning rather than content, and dismiss the ideas that teachers will be the purveyors of information and know all the answers.

5. Determine the processes of following children's interests to develop topics and using ongoing assessment to make decisions in teaching.

6. Determine that the respect of children's thinking is the basis for all teaching.

7. Portray the value of the relationship between teacher and child.

IDEAS TO PONDER
- What is the most important component needed to prepare children for the future?
- How do I change my teaching practice?
- How does constructivist education apply to educating our children for tomorrow's world?
- How can I be the best teacher for children today?

The terms and circumstances of human existence can be expected to change radically during the next life span. Science, mathematics, and technology will be at the center of that change—causing it, shaping it, responding to it. Therefore, they will be essential to the education of today's children for tomorrow's world. (American Association for the Advancement of Science, 1989)

CHANGES IN SCIENCE AND MATH EDUCATION

As science, mathematics, and technology experience rapid change, an altered approach to education is necessary. No longer can teachers expect to pass on content knowledge as education. The meaning of knowing has shifted from being able to remember and repeat information to being able to access information and use it to solve problems (National Academies Press, 2000; Simon, 1996).

Research on learning has uncovered important principles for structuring learning to enable children to use what they have learned in new settings (National Academies Press, 2000). This also means structuring learning so young children can actively try out their developing ideas and use creative approaches to build new structures in their thinking. All of this is contained in the essence of constructivist education that has been followed throughout this book.

In their daily reflection, teachers continually ask themselves how they are challenging children at their level. Mallaguzzi (1998) of the Reggio Emilia programs states the complexity of reflection. "Teachers must possess a habit of questioning their certainties, a growth of sensitivity, awareness, and availability, the assuming of a critical style of research and continually updated knowledge of children, [and] an enriched evaluation of parental roles" (p. 69).

To prepare students to take their place in an ever-expanding world, teachers can continually prepare curriculum and the classroom environment in ways that enable children to apply actively what they are in the process of knowing. Dr. Rita Colwell, Former Director of the National Science Foundation, states, "In a knowledge-based economy, it is crucial that we educate all students and workers on how to use new knowledge" (Colwell, 2000).

Future careers will demand people who are more knowledgeable in science, math, and technology. "All students today need to know more fundamental science and mathematics than ever before. Science and engineering students must be adept in making connections across disciplines, not just in their own fields. Others need higher levels of math and science literacy in the workplace, and all citizens need a fundamental grasp of science and mathematics to make informal judgments and decisions in our complex society" (Colwell, 2004).

As we pursue universal education "we unequivocally need to include far more of our U.S. women and underrepresented minorities in the S & E [Science and Engineering] workforce. . . . Our demographics are changing, too. By 2050, it is estimated that our nation will be a majority of minorities" (Colwell, 2004). Inclusion of all diverse groups in this new focus on math, science, and technology from preschool on will mean that the potential of each person can be realized in these fields of study.

DISPOSITION FOR INQUIRY

In order to effectively prepare the next generation, you will need to exemplify the way children will need to be. To do this, take on the disposition of inquiry as a way of life. "A commitment to inquiry—as something that all humans must do to improve their lives and those of others—is an important theme for professional development" (National Research Council, 2000, p. 109). This will take many forms. In the classroom you will readily assess the thinking of children and implement this thinking into the evolving curriculum. You will also be involved with the children in applying inquiry to the subject at hand. As discoveries are made you will continue observing and applying and assisting children in their inquiry process.

Your process of inquiry should also continue beyond the classroom. Be open to inquiry as you marvel at events in nature and/or technology, such as noting the path of the Monarch butterfly as it begins its slow, fluttering journey south for the winter months, or the quick retrieval of information through the Internet, or the magnificent pattern of light on clouds that takes form in the digital photo appearing on the computer screen. As you experience the aesthetics found in nature and appreciate technology, these become an aspect of the inquiring person that the child can sense from knowing you.

In addition you, as an adult, will have an interest, a curiosity, a questioning attitude in life. With this investment in inquiry, this will be apparent as you become involved with the everyday acts of children. When you question why a toddler throws his hat into the wind or why he "messes" with his pudding instead of eating it, you are using inquiry as an approach to life.

When you explore a new photo program on the computer to discover ways to enhance a digital photo, you are using inquiry as a process in technology. When you look at the young plant shoots emerging from the ground in spring and examine how some are thriving and some are not, you are using inquiry in the process of gardening. When you will note advances in science, such as the genome project or development of a new disease in a developing country, you are using inquiry in your ongoing understanding of life. These qualities of inquiry become a part of you that will be shared in innumerable ways with the children you teach.

By living in ways that admire, enjoy, and investigate life, as teacher you will be able to admire, enjoy, and investigate life along with the children. In this way you are instrumental in supporting children's abilities to embrace the advancing world through inquiry.

YOUR ROLE IN INQUIRY

As you have arrived at this last chapter, you have had many opportunities to think through ways of incorporating math, science, and technology into your teaching of young children. You have experimented yourself with materials and numbers and computer information. Hopefully, you will soon try out experiences in teaching, see how children respond to your approaches, and reflect on ways that work for you. As a teacher of young children who will enter into the fast-advancing science-tech world, are you prepared to teach them to be creative thinkers and problem solvers, ready to research and apply what they find out?

Dismiss Having to Know

In this process there are two related beliefs of teaching that you can discard. The first is that you will always be the purveyor of information. Instead, because

> # STANDARDS
>
> Encourage and model the skills of scientific inquiry, as well as the curiosity, openness to new ideas and data, and skepticism that characterize science.
>
> Teaching Standard B. Reprinted with permission from *National science education standards* (1996). The National Academy of Sciences, courtesy of the National Academies Press, Washington, DC (p. 32).

children will be learning to find and use information themselves, you will be supporting that process as you research alongside them.

Second, like children preparing for a knowledge explosion, teachers can no longer expect to know all answers. So when you are willing to explore with children the avenues of the Internet or the content of a book, you show a more important disposition of the discovered process rather than having a knowledge base on the subject. Of course, seize these opportune times to add to your current knowledge as you take the road to investigate a topic, for as you learn you will be more prepared to take that knowledge further with the children.

Follow Children in Constructivist Curriculum

Teachers relate their own process of allowing children to develop the interest that will lead to a particular topic (Helm & Beneke, 2003; Jones, Evans, & Rencken, 2001). In taking her class on ongoing visits to houses in the community, Kay Rencken initiated the idea for these walks but allowed the idea to take hold with the kindergarten children. "If the children in Kay's class had not risen to the bait or shown enthusiasm about houses, there would have been no house project" (Jones, Evans, & Rencken, 2001, pp. 27–28). For teachers beginning to follow children's ideas, it can be a monumental task to let go of the tendency to lead and, instead, to engage children in finding the threads to carry the momentum of their interests into deeper study.

Use Assessment to Drive Curriculum

As you assess daily, this changes what you do with curriculum. The children themselves are the best predictors of what and how they will learn. Using all the skills of observing, collecting children's work, questioning, and listening, you and your colleagues will be able to make your best guesses of what and how to teach. Let that continually be your guide for making curriculum decisions.

Respect

Along with assessment and following the child for curriculum decisions, you will respect the thinking of the child. This respect will be seen in fully listening to his

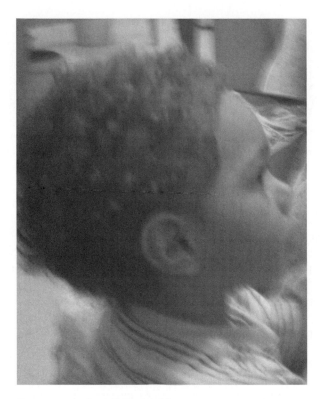

Respect each child's thinking.

ideas both through what he does and what he says, questioning to explore his thoughts further, and waiting and watching to see ideas take form. Your interest and support will open up more possibilities for the child in his learning, and your respect will be the scaffolding that supports the child in his encounters.

Respect will be revealed in preparing ways for the child to explore his ideas more thoroughly whether these seem (in the teacher's eyes) to be on the right track or not. DeVries and Zan (1995) explain that the outstanding characteristic of a constructivist approach is one that respects children's errors. This respect results in children being free to express their ideas and to take action on seeking results. Through this process the child will find she can rely on her own thinking. (DeVries & Zan, 1995, DeVries et al, 2002).

Relationships

Finally, teach with relationships in mind. In the Executive Summary of *Eager to Learn,* the conclusion states, "If there is a single critical component to quality [it] rests in the relationship between the child and the teacher/caregiver, and in the ability of the adult to be responsive to the child. But responsiveness extends in many directions: to the child's cognitive, social, emotional, and physical characteristics and development" (Bowman, Donovan & Burns, 2000, p. 16).

Responsive teaching occurs within relationships.

STANDARDS

Candidates know, understand, and use positive relationships and supportive interactions as the foundation for the work with young children.

Standard 4a. Reprinted with permission from National Association for the Education of Young Children. *NAEYC standards for early childhood professional preparation: Initial licensure programs,* 2003 (p. 29).

PROFESSIONALISM

Professionalism will be incorporated into your teaching. The NAEYC Initial Licensing Standards hold these values:

STANDARDS

Candidates identify and conduct themselves as members of the early childhood profession. They know and use **ethical guidelines** and other professional standards related to early childhood practice. They are continuous, **collaborative** learners who demonstrate knowledgeable, reflective, and critical perspectives on their work, making informed decisions that integrate knowledge from a variety of sources. They are informed **advocates** for sound education practices and policies.

Standard 5. Reprinted with permission from National Association for the Education of Young Children. *NAEYC standards for early childhood professional preparation: Initial licensure programs.* 2003 (p. 29). Bold added.

Ethical guidelines are organizational statements of accepted professional standards of conduct.

Collaborative *means the process of working jointly on a goal.*

An advocate is one who is a proponent for a cause.

SUMMARY

In order for early childhood education to meet the changing needs of today's world, current and future teachers must shift in thinking and embrace new ways of teaching. For children in all cultures, in all urban and rural areas, and from all families, rich to poor, teachers must provide the most advanced processes of thinking and learning to prepare children to face the scientific and technological age. Early childhood teachers are the first teachers children experience, so they must be the best teachers for the future of our children and for our world.

TO FURTHER YOUR THINKING

1. Take some time to reflect on the changes in math, science, and technology since you were in preschool, kindergarten, or first grade, depending on the earliest age you can remember those subjects. What does the young child do now in these subjects that you did not do at that age?

2. What does the young child need to accomplish now in the subjects of math, science, and technology in order to be prepared to enhance her daily life and to excel in her chosen career in adulthood? How does education need to change to prepare her for this?

3. What are educational differences that children experience, including those of different ethnic groups, different locations geographically (including urban and rural), and different socioeconomic groups? How can educators begin in preschool and kindergarten years to bridge the gap between these differences so all children have equitable education?

4. What changes in attitude and values have you experienced as you have moved through this book? How do you value inquiry in yourself? What is your attitude now for math? science? technology?

5. What values of inquiry, respect, and relationships with children will provide you with the best guidelines for preparing children for the future world?

REFERENCES

American Association for the Advancement of Science. (1989). *Science for all Americans.* Washington, DC: Author.

Bowman, B., Donovan, M. S., and Burns, M. S. (Eds.). (2000). *Eager to learn: Educating our preschoolers. Executive Summary.* Washington, DC: National Acadamies Press.

Colwell, R. R. (2000). The National Science Foundation: Turning 50 at the turn of the century. Speech given at 92nd Street Y, January 24, 2000 [On line]. Arlington, VA: National Science Foundation/Office of Legislative and Public Affairs. **www.nsf.gov**

Colwell, R. R. (2004). Limitless opportunities: Dynamic partnerships—Universities and schools making a difference in K-12 Education. Speech given at American Association for the Advancement of Science Annual Meeting, February 15, 2000 [On line]. Arlington, VA: National Science Foundation/Office of Legislative and Public Affairs. **www.nsf.gov**

DeVries, R., and Zan, B. (1995). Creating a constructivist classroom atmosphere. *Young Children, 50*(5), 4–13.

DeVries, R., Zan, B., Hildebrandt, C., Edmiaston, R., and Sales, C. (2002). *Developing constructivist early childhood curriculum: Practical principles and activities.* New York: Teachers College Press.

Helm J., and Beneke, S. (Eds.). (2003). *The power of projects: Meeting contemporary challenges in early childhood classrooms—Strategies & solutions.* New York: Teachers College Press.

Jones E., Evans, K., and Rencken, K. (2001). *The lively kindergarten: Emergent curriculum in action.* Washington, DC: National Association for the Education of Young Children.

Malaguzzi, L. (1998). History, ideas, and basic philosophy: An interview with Lella Gandini. In C. Edwards, L. Gandini, and G. Forman, *The hundred languages of children* (2nd ed.) (pp. 49–97). Westport, CT: Ablex.

National Academy of Science. (1996). *National science education standards* [Book version, on line]. Washington, DC: National Academies Press. **www.nap.edu**

National Academies Press. (2000). *How people learn: Brain, mind, experience, and school. Expanded Edition.* Washington, DC: Author.

National Association for the Education of Young Children. (2003). NAEYC standards for early childhood professional preparation: Initial licensure programs. In M. Hyson (Ed.), *Preparing early childhood professionals: NAEYC's standards for programs* (pp. 17–63). Washington, DC: Author.

National Research Council. (2000). *Inquiry and the National Science Education Standards: A guide for teaching and learning.* Washington, DC: National Acadamies Press.

Simon, H. A. (1996). Observation on the sciences of science learning. Paper presented for the Committee on Developments in the Science of Learnings for the Sciences of Science Learning. Department of Psychology, Carnegie Mellon University.

ADDITIONAL RESOURCES

Ayers, W. (1993). *To teach: The journey of a teacher.* New York: Teachers College Press. This classic offers an insight to teaching in elementary schools. This and others listed below may challenge you in enhancing your teaching values.

Copley, J., and Padrón, Y. (1999). Preparing teachers of young learners: Professional development of early childhood teachers in mathematics and science. In American Association for the Advancement of Science. *Dialogue on early childhood science, mathematics, and technology education* (pp. 117–129). Washington DC: Author. Integrating the teaching standards listed in this text through professional development in the Collaborative Coaching project.

Hawkins, D. (2002). Messing about in science. In *The informed visions: Essays on learning and human nature* (pp. 63–65) (Reissue). New York: Agathon. This brief but poignant essay provokes thought on science and education.

Katz, L. (1995). *Talks with teachers of young children: A collection.* Norwood, NJ: Ablex. In the developmental stages of teachers you may find your stage of teaching.

Kozol, J. (1995). *Amazing grace: The lives of children and the conscience of a nation.* New York: Crown. A trip to schools of New York City where the tough questions on the value of a child's life are asked.

Video

The amusement park for birds [Video]. Amherst. MA: Performatics. A project by a group of children in Reggio Emilia, Italy. This long-term project involved community and school collaboration to build an amusement park for birds in the park surrounding the school.

Web Site

http://www.childtrendsdatabank.org Child Trends presents data on educational outcomes in science and math as well as other topics concerning children.

Appendix A
National Standards

NATIONAL SCIENCE EDUCATION STANDARDS

Teaching Standards

The science teaching standards describe what teachers of science at all grade levels should know and be able to do. They are divided into six areas:

- The planning of inquiry-based science programs
- The actions taken to guide and facilitate student learning
- The assessments made of teaching and student learning
- The development of environments that enable students to learn science
- The creation of communities of science learners
- The planning and development of the school science program

Teaching Standards B and D

Teaching Standard B Teachers of science guide and facilitate learning. In doing this, teachers

- Focus and support inquiries while interacting with students.
- Orchestrate discourse among students about scientific ideas.
- Challenge students to accept and share responsibility for their own learning.
- Recognize and respond to student diversity and encourage all students to participate fully in science learning.
- Encourage and model the skills of scientific inquiry, as well as the curiosity, openness to new ideas and data, and skepticism that characterize science.

Teaching Standard D Teachers of science design and manage learning environments that provide students with the time, space, and resources needed for learning science. In doing this, teachers

- Structure the time available so that students are able to engage in extended investigations.

- Create a setting for student work that is flexible and supportive of science inquiry.
- Ensure a safe working environment.
- Make the available science tools, materials, media, and technological resources accessible to students.
- Identify and use resources outside the school.
- Engage students in designing the learning environment.

Professional Development Standards

The professional development standards present a vision for the development of professional knowledge and skill among teachers. They focus on four areas:

- The learning of science content through inquiry
- The integration of knowledge about science with knowledge about learning, pedagogy, and students
- The development of the understanding and ability for lifelong learning
- The coherence and integration of professional development programs

Curriculum and Content Area Standards: Grades K–4 Standards

Content Standard A: Science as Inquiry

A1. Abilities necessary to do scientific inquiry:

- Ask a question about objects, organisms, and events in the environment.
- Plan and conduct a simple investigation.
- Employ simple equipment and tools to gather data and extend the senses.
- Use data to construct a reasonable explanation.
- Communicate investigations and explanations.

A2. Understanding about scientific inquiry:

- Scientific investigations involve asking and answering a question and comparing the answer with what scientists already know about the world.
- Scientists use different kinds of investigations depending on the questions they are trying to answer.
- Simple instruments provide more information than scientists obtain using only their senses.
- Scientists develop explanations using observations (evidence) and what they already know about the world (scientific knowledge).
- Scientists make the results of their investigations public; they describe the investigations in ways that enable others to repeat the investigations.
- Scientists review and ask questions about the results of other scientists' work.

Content Standard B: Physical Science

B1. Properties of objects and materials

B2. Position and motion of objects

B3. Light, heat, electricity, and magnetism

Content Standard C: Life Science

C1. The characteristics of organisms

C2. Life cycles of organisms

C3. Organisms and environments

Content Standard D: Earth and Space Science

D1. Properties of earth materials

D2. Objects in the sky

D3. Changes in earth and sky

Content Standard E: Science and Technology

E1. Abilities of technological design

E2. Understanding about science and technology

E3. Abilities to distinguish between natural objects and objects made by humans

Content Standard F: Science in Personal and Social Perspectives

F1. Personal health

F2. Characteristics and changes in populations

F3. Types of resources

F4. Changes in environments

F5. Science and technology in local challenges

Content Standard G: Science as Inquiry

G1. Science as a human endeavor.

G2. Science and technology have been practiced by people for a long time.

G3. Men and women have made a variety of contributions throughout the history of science and technology.

G4. Science will never be finished.

G5. Many people choose science as a career.

Reprinted with permission from *National science education standards* (1996). The National Academy of Sciences, courtesy of the National Academies Press, Washington, DC (selections from pp. 27–74, 103–208).

NAEYC STANDARDS FOR EARLY CHILDHOOD PROFESSIONAL PREPARATION: INITIAL LICENSURE PROGRAMS

STANDARDS SUMMARY

Standard 1. Promoting Child Development and Learning

Candidates use their understanding of young children's characteristics and needs, and of multiple interacting influences on children's development and learning, to create environments that are healthy, respectful, supportive, and challenging for all children.

Standard 2. Building Family and Community Relationships

Candidates know about, understand, and value the importance and complex characteristics of children's families and communities. They use this understanding to create respectful, reciprocal relationships that support and empower families and to involve all families in their children's development and learning.

Standard 3. Observing, Documenting, and Assessing to Support Young Children and Families

Candidates know about and understand the goals, benefits, and uses of assessment. They know about and use systematic observations, documentations, and other effective assessment strategies in a responsible way, in partnership with families and other professionals, to positively influence children's development and learning.

Standard 4. Teaching and Learning

Candidates integrate their understanding of and relationships with children and families; their understanding of developmentally effective approaches to teaching and learning; and their knowledge of academic disciplines to design, implement, and evaluate experiences that promote positive development and learning for all children.

Sub-Standard 4a. Connecting with Children and Families Candidates know, understand, and use positive relationships and supportive interactions as the foundation for their work with young children.

Sub-Standard 4b. Using Developmentally Effective Approaches Candidates know, understand, and use a wide array of effective approaches, strategies, and tools to positively influence children's development and learning.

Sub-Standard 4c. Understanding Content Knowledge in Early Education

Candidates understand the importance of each content area in young children's learning. They know the essential concepts, inquiry tools, and structure of content areas including academic subjects and can identify resources to deepen their understanding.

Sub-Standard 4d. Building Meaningful Curriculum Candidates use their own knowledge and other resources to design, implement, and evaluate meaningful, challenging curriculum that promotes comprehensive developmental and learning outcomes for all young children.

Standard 5. Becoming a Professional

Candidates identify and conduct themselves as members of the early childhood profession. They know and use ethical guidelines and other professional standards related to early childhood practice. They are continuous, collaborative learners who demonstrate knowledgeable, reflective, and critical perspectives on their work, making informed decisions that integrate knowledge from a variety of sources. They are informed advocates for sound education practices and policies.

Reprinted with permission from National Association for the Education of Young Children (2003). NAEYC standards for early childhood professional preparation: Initial licensure programs. In M. Hyson (Ed.), *Preparing early childhood professionals: NAEYC's standards for programs* (p. 29). Washington, DC: Author.

PRINCIPLES AND STANDARDS FOR SCHOOL MATHEMATICS

Chapter 4: Standards for Pre-K–2

Algebra Standard for Grades Pre-K–2

Expectations

Instructional programs from prekindergarten through grade 12 should enable all students to:	In prekindergarten through grade 2 all students should:
Understand patterns, relations, and functions	• sort, classify, and order objects by size, number, and other properties; • recognize, describe, and extend patterns such as sequences of sounds and shapes or simple numeric patterns and translate from one representation to another; • analyze how both repeating and growing patterns are generated.

Represent and analyze mathematical situations and structures using algebraic symbols	• illustrate general principles and properties of operations, such as commutativity, using specific numbers; • use concrete, pictorial, and verbal representations to develop an understanding of invented and conventional symbolic notations.
Use mathematical models to represent and understand quantitative relationships	• model situations that involve the addition and subtraction of whole numbers, using objects, pictures, and symbols.
Analyze change in various contexts	• describe qualitative change, such as a student's growing taller; • describe quantitative change, such as a student's growing two inches in one year.

Geometry Standard for Grades Pre-K–2

Expectations

Instructional programs from prekindergarten through grade 12 should enable all students to:	In prekindergarten through grade 2 all students should:
Analyze characteristics and properties of two- and three-dimensional geometric shapes and develop mathematical arguments about geometric relationships	• recognize, name, build, draw, compare, and sort two- and three-dimensional shapes; • describe attributes and parts of two- and three-dimensional shapes; • investigate and predict the results of putting together and taking apart two- and three-dimensional shapes.
Specify locations and describe spatial relationships using coordinate geometry and other representational systems	• describe, name, and interpret relative positions in space and apply ideas about relative position; • describe, name, and interpret direction and distance in navigating space and apply ideas about direction and distance; • find and name locations with simple relationships such as "near to" and in coordinate systems such as maps.
Apply transformations and use symmetry to analyze mathematical situations	• recognize and apply slides, flips, and turns; • recognize and create shapes that have symmetry.
Use visualization, spatial reasoning, and geometric modeling to solve problems	• create mental images of geometric shapes using spatial memory and spatial visualization; • recognize and represent shapes from different perspectives; • relate ideas in geometry to ideas in number and measurement; • recognize geometric shapes and structures in the environment and specify their location.

Measurement Standard for Grades Pre-K–2

Expectations

Instructional programs from prekindergarten through grade 12 should enable all students to:	In prekindergarten through grade 2 all students should:
Understand measurable attributes of objects and the units, systems, and processes of measurement	• recognize the attributes of length, volume, weight, area, and time; • compare and order objects according to these attributes; • understand how to measure using nonstandard and standard units; • select an appropriate unit and tool for the attribute being measured.
Apply appropriate techniques, tools, and formulas to determine measurements	• measure with multiple copies of units of the same size, such as paper clips laid end to end; • use repetition of a single unit to measure something larger than the unit, for instance, measuring the length of a room with a single meterstick; • use tools to measure; • develop common referents for measures to make comparisons and estimates.

Data Analysis and Probability Standard for Grades Pre-K–2

Expectations

Instructional programs from prekindergarten through grade 12 should enable all students to:	In prekindergarten through grade 2 all students should:
Formulate questions that can be addressed with data and collect, organize, and display relevant data to answer them	• pose questions and gather data about themselves and their surroundings; • sort and classify objects according to their attributes and organize data about the objects; • represent data using concrete objects, pictures, and graphs.
Select and use appropriate statistical methods to analyze data	• describe parts of the data and the set of data as a whole to determine what the data show.
Develop and evaluate inferences and predictions that are based on data	• discuss events related to students' experiences as likely or unlikely.
Understand and apply basic concepts of probability	

Problem-Solving Standard for Grades Pre-K–12

Instructional programs from prekindergarten through grade 12 should enable all students to:

build new mathematical knowledge through problem solving;

solve problems that arise in mathematics and in other contexts;

apply and adapt a variety of appropriate strategies to solve problems;

monitor and reflect on the process of mathematical problem solving.

Reasoning and Proof Standard for Grades Pre-K–2

Instructional programs from prekindergarten through grade 12 should enable all students to:

recognize reasoning and proof as fundamental aspects of mathematics;

make and investigate mathematical conjectures;

develop and evaluate mathematical arguments and proofs;

select and use various types of reasoning and methods of proof.

Communication Standard for Grades Pre-K–2

Instructional programs from prekindergarten through grade 12 should enable all students to:

organize and consolidate their mathematical thinking through communication;

communicate their mathematical thinking coherently and clearly to peers, teachers, and others;

analyze and evaluate the mathematical thinking and strategies of others;

use the language of mathematics to express mathematical ideas precisely.

Connections Standard for Grades Pre-K–2

Instructional programs from prekindergarten through grade 12 should enable all students to:

recognize and use connections among mathematical ideas;

understand how mathematical ideas interconnect and build on one another to produce a coherent whole;

recognize and apply mathematics in contexts outside of mathematics.

Representation Standard for Grades Pre-K–2

Instructional programs from prekindergarten through grade 12 should enable all students to:

create and use representations to organize, record, and communicate mathematical ideas;

select, apply, and translate among mathematical representations to solve problems;

use representations to model and interpret physical, social, and mathematical phenomena.

SOURCES FOR STATE STANDARDS IN EARLY CHILDHOOD EDUCATION

http://edStandards.org/Standards.html

This site lists Boards of Education by states. Look for standards in early childhood/preschool/child development. There are standards for science, math, and technology in some states. If the Standards in the area and state for which you are searching are not on line, contacts within the Board of Education by state are listed.

Appendix B
Technology*

*Prepared by Warren Buckleitner and Arleen Pratt Prairie

SOFTWARE EVALUATION

I. Ease of Use (Can a child use it with minimal help?)

  – Skills needed to operate the program are in range of the child
  – Children can use the program independently after the first use
  – Graphics make sense to the intended user
  – It is easy to get in or out of any activity at any point
  – Getting to the first menu is quick and easy
  – Icons are large and easy to select with a moving cursor
  – Controls are responsive to the touch
  – Offers quick, clear, obvious response to a child's action
  – The child has control over the rate of display
  – The child has control over exiting at any time
  – The child has control over the order of the display

II. Educational (What can a child learn from this program?)

  – Offers a good presentation of one or more content areas
  – Graphics do not detract from the program's educational intentions
  – Feedback employs meaningful graphic and sound capabilities
  – Speech is used
  – The presentation is novel with each use
  – Good challenge range (this program will grow with the child)
  – Feedback reinforces content (embedded reinforcements are used)
  – Program elements match direct experiences
  – Content is free from gender or ethnic bias
  – A child's ideas can be incorporated into the program
  – The program comes with strategies to extend the learning

III. Entertaining (Is this program fun to use?)

  – Graphics are meaningful and enjoyed by children
  – Random generation techniques are employed in the design
  – Speech and sounds are meaningful to children
  – Challenge is fluid, or a child can select own level

    – The program is responsive to a child's actions

    – The theme of the program is meaningful to children

IV. Design Features

    – A child's work can be easily saved or printed

    – The challenge level automatically adapts to a child's level

    – The program knows if a child is struggling and adjusts the content accordingly

    – There are opportunities to put ideas or concepts into the program.

V. Value. How much does it cost, vs. what does it do?

(Adapted from Buckleitner, Orr, & Wolock, 2002, p. 9).

TECHNOLOGY SHOPPING LIST

For a computer station in preschool or kindergarten, the following list is helpful in planning or expanding technology resources. Because technology changes rapidly, check for current products.

Basic Set-Up

Two Windows-compatible or Macintosh computers with LCD screens

Two chairs per computer

Optical mouse for each computer

Surge protector power strip

Photo-quality inkjet printer

High-speed Internet access and firewall protection (for entire school)

Starter set of software (refer to list below)

Digital Camera, 3.1 mega pixels (or better) with rechargeable batteries or a charging cradle

CD storage racks (out of reach of children)

Optional Equipment

With the basic set-up installed, the following can be easily added to expand the technology in your program.

Camcorder with digital output

Audiocassette recorder

Scanner

Transparency projector

Light table

Computer microscope

SOFTWARE

These listings are intended to provide an introduction to software for children and teacher resources. All have been reviewed by Children's Software Revue, www.childrenssoftware.com. Each title has the publisher, copyright date, what the program teaches, suggested price, platform, and URL. Software changes often, so check for availability and price.

Classic Software

These products for preschool and kindergarten may or may not run on Windows XP or Mac OSX.

Arthur's Preschool 2002 Edition, The Learning Company, 2001, early math, early reading, shapes, letters, counting and music, $19.99, Win, Mac, www.learningco.com

Fisher-Price Outdoor Adventures Ranger Trail, The Learning Company, 1999, science, animals, nature facts, music, logic, $19.95, Win 95, 98; Mac OS (CD-ROM), www.learningco.com

Just Grandma and Me, The Learning Company, 1997, early reading, creativity, English, French, German, Spanish, $29.95, Win 95, 98; Mac OS (CD-ROM), www.learningco.com

Kid Pix Studio Deluxe Version 1.0, Brøderbund (The Learning Company), 1998, creativity, art, $39.99, Win 95, Win 3.1, Mac OS (CD-ROM), www.learningco.com

LEGO My Style: Preschool or Kindergarten, LEGO Media International, 2000, counting, classification, numbers, letters, art, music, logic, $19.99, Win, Mac OS (CD-ROM), www.legomedia.com or www.kidsdomain.com

Mighty Math Carnival Countdown! Edmark (Riverdeep), 1996, math: counting, comparing, sorting, patterns, place value, $29.00, Win 95, Win 3.1, Mac OS (CD-ROM), www.edmark.com

Millie & Bailey Preschool, Edmark (Riverdeep), 1997, reading, math, logic, matching, classifying objects, $29.95, Win 95, Win 3.1, Mac OS (CD-ROM), www.edmark.com

Millie's Math House, Edmark (Riverdeep), 1995, math, counting, sets, sequencing by size, shapes, $19.95, Mac, DOS, Windows (disk or CD-ROM), www.riverdeep.net

Orly's Draw-A-Story, Brøderbund (The Learning Company), 1996, writing and creativity, $29.00, Win 95, Win 3.1, Mac OS (CD-ROM) Not Windows XP, www.learningco.com or www.geodonka.com

Sammy's Science House, Edmark (Riverdeep), 1994, weather, logic, sequencing, classifying, animals, $19.95, Windows, Mac (CD-ROM), www.riverdeep.net

Newer Titles

These newer titles should run on newer computers (XP and Mac OS and later).

Clifford Thinking Adventures, Scholastic Consumer Software, 2000, early reading, logic, sorting, classification, counting, sequencing, $19.95, Win, Mac OS (CD-ROM), www.scholastic.com

Bob the Builder™, THQ, 2002, logic, classification, music, $19.99, Win, www.thq.com

Curious George® Downtown Adventure, Knowledge Adventure, 2002, logic, problem solving, creativity, $19.99, Win, Mac, www.knowledgeadventure.com or gzkidzone.com

Dogz® 5, Ubi Soft Entertainment, 2002, creativity, caring for animals, language, logic, $29.99, Win, www.ubisoft.com

Flying Colors v. 2.11, Magic Mouse Productions, 2001, creativity, art, drawing and painting, $29.00 (including delivery), Win, Mac, Win XP, www.magicmouse.com

Krazy Art Room, GuruForce, Inc., 2002, creativity, art, $39.95, Win 95/98/ME/NT4/2000/XP, www.guruforce.com

Nick Jr. Little Bill Thinks Big, Scholastic, Inc., 2003, math, logic, $19.95, Windows, Mac, www.scholastic.com

Ollo and the Sunny Valley Fair, 4.9, Hulabee Entertainment, 2002, creativity, memory, logic, counting, patterns, sorting, sequencing, music deductive reasoning, $19.99, Win, Mac (OS X only), www.hulabee.com or www.gzkidzone.com

Smart Toys

No computer required.

LeapPad® Leapster Learning System, LeapFrog, 2003, reading, math, logic, music, memory, $80, Leapster, www.leapfrog.com

Teacher Resources

Digital Blue QX3+ Computer Microscope, Compuvisor.com, science, computer add-on, magnifier from 10xs to 200xs, $49.45, Win, www.compuvisor.com

Encarta Reference Library Premium 2005, Microsoft, information reference, videos, chart maker, online resource, plus articles and multimedia for young readers, $69.99, Win (5 CD-ROMs), or 1 DVD. Also Children and Computers Recommendation, www.microsoft.com

The Graph Club 2.0, Tom Snyder Productions, 2003, graph making, charts, tables, $79.00, Win, Mac (CD-ROM), www.tomsnyderproductions.com

Kidspiration and Inspiration Software, Inc., 2000, planning, classification, logical thinking, $69.00, Win, Mac OS, www.inspiration.com

Mic-D Computer Microscope, Olympus America, Inc., 2002, science, computer add-on microscope, $1000, Windows XP, www.mic-d.com

World Book Encyclopedia 2004 Deluxe Edition, World Book, Inc., information reference, dictionary, videos, online resource, $39.95, Win, www.topics-ent.com

REFERENCE

Buckleitner, W., Orr, A. and Wolock, E. (2002). *Complete sourcebook on children's interactive media.* Farmington, NJ: Active Learning Associates, Inc.

Appendix C
Materials and Recipes for Preparing Math and Science Experiences

TABLE C–1   Materials and Organization for Basic Math Concepts

Classification

Counters of different colors of bears

Plastic bottle caps

Collection of small figures: animals, people, etc.

An assortment of beans

Bird seed

Assortment of buttons from Grandma's button box

Rocks of various colors

Materials found on a walk

Assortment of unshelled nuts

Plastic bowls of same colors as the items to be sorted

Grid of squares, laminated

Individual flannel boards (see below)

Thick yarn

Microwave containers

Plain place mats (Scoot-Guard Tableware)

Sections of a clear shower curtain liner with grid of squares, 1" grid for table work, or 3" grid for floor work Option: Window shade

Comparing/Matching
Plastic jars of different sizes with matching lids
Assorted small boxes with lids

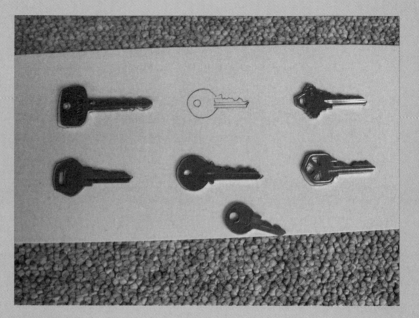

Matching keys and outlines of keys.

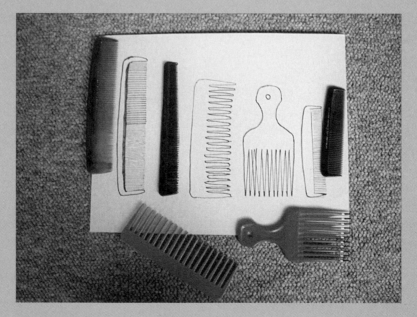

Matching combs and outlines of combs.

Ice cube trays, paper egg cartons, muffin tins

Assortment of keys and outline of each drawn on tag board

Assortment of combs and outline of each drawn on tag board

Plastic cups and saucers of different colors

A selection of materials or objects gathered on a walk, and outlines of these drawn on tag board

Contrasting

Paper dolls with a variety of clothes, some the same, some different.

A set of toy cars and trucks of different sizes from Matchbox® to Fisher-Price®, boxes with one end open, such as tea boxes of various sizes. Each box is a size to make a "garage" for each vehicle (Fig. C–1).

Various size soft balls, and card board tubes of varying diameters

Ordering or Seriation

Paint chips of one color such as chartreuse that go from very dark to almost white

Melody bells, or individual bars of xylophone that can be ordered in a series

Manipulatives that have different sizes: select an assortment so there is one of each size

Straws, yarn of various lengths

Tin cans with lids intact (make small holes to empty them of juice) of different sizes

Empty grocery boxes from toothpick boxes to cereal boxes

Graduated measuring cups

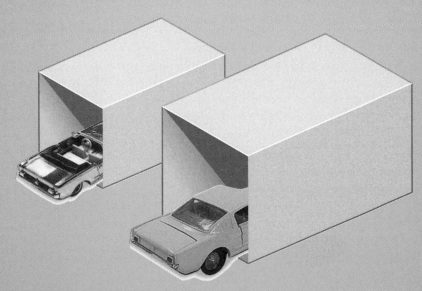

Figure C–1 Cars and garages.

Making Sets

Counters of different sizes and colors

Dry beans

Aquarium glass

Individual flannel boards of the same size. Glue squares of flannel to the cardboard backing of a writing tablet, turning the sides under. Glue the underside to tag board of identical size.

Thick yarn

Paper plates

Squares of heavy felt

Number Sense

Counters of same size and color

Cards with number symbol and dots representing numbers (see Fig. 14–1). The number symbol and dots representing the numbers can be on the same side or on opposite sides. Basic collection is 1 to 10. Make a full collection of 1 to 25.

Deck of playing cards (without face cards). Select the highest number that some children will know.

Dominos, basic set 0 to 6; extended set, 0 to 9.

Individual flannel boards

Thick yarn

TABLE C–2 Circular Path Board Games (Homemade)

General Directions for Making a Circular Path Game

A circular path game board is made by placing 20 white stickers in a circular or oval shape on a dark tag board. A colored sticker is placed over five of the white stickers at irregular intervals from three to five spaces apart. A single die (1–6) is used for each game. The movers can be pieces showing a person's head mounted on spools or commercially made movers (Moomaw & Hieronymus, 1995). The goal of the game is to complete the task together. This game board is planned for two players.

Game 1 Treasure Chest

Goal is to fill the treasure chest.

Materials

Circular path game board, 1 die, 2 movers

Treasure chest: Small treasure chest (decorated box or trinket box) is empty at the beginning of the game.

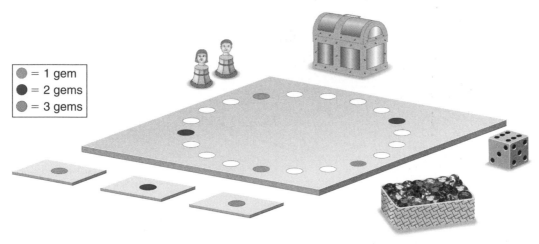

Figure C–2 Treasure chest game.

A basket of crystal gems provides the jewels to fill the treasure chest.

Cards of a particular color (match the colored stickers on circular path game board) direct child to add 1, 2, or 3 jewels to the treasure chest. These directions are printed using both signs and symbols (1, 2, or 3 gems).

Directions

Child throws the die and, using the number on the die, moves around the board the same number of spaces. When landing on a color the child follows the direction on the card of the same color. Older children can use tallying to add the number of jewels they add to the treasure chest (adapted from Treasure Chest Short Path Game, Moomaw & Hieronymus, 1995, pp. 138–39) (Fig. C–2).

Game 2 Blueberries for Sal

Goal is to fill the pail with blueberries which follows the theme of the story *Blueberries for Sal* by McCloskey.

Materials

Circular path game board, 1 die, 2 movers

Purple wooden beads or felt circles for blueberries

A small pail to hold beads or circles for the berries

Set of cards that match the stickers with the following drawings and symbols to indicate the player's action:

Pail turned over = lose 5 berries

Child eating berry = lose 1 berry

Bear holds pail = all blueberries are lost

A plant of berries = add 5 berries

Figure C–3 Blueberries for Sal.

Directions

Child roles die and, using the number on the die, adds berries to the pail *and* moves the same amount of spaces. When landing on a color, the direction of that color card is followed (Fig. C–3).

Game 3 Dress the baby

Goal is to dress the baby for play.

Materials

Circular path game board, 1 die, 2 movers

Small baby doll with baby clothes: shirt, pants, hat, pair of shoes, pair of socks

Color cards have drawings of each of the baby's clothes

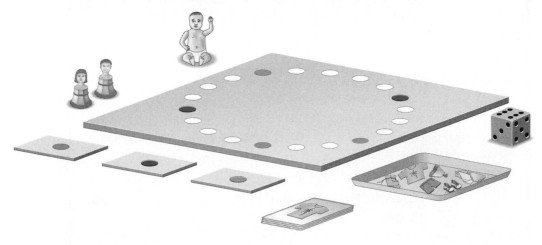

Figure C–4 Dress the baby.

Directions

Child throws the die and, using the number on the die, moves around the board the same number of spaces. When landing on a color the child follows the direction on the card of the same color. Child puts the item of clothing next to the baby doll. If the doll already has the item of clothing indicated, the child has another turn (Fig. C–4).

TABLE C–3   Directions for Graphs

Realistic Graphs

Vote with Their Feet

The teacher can ask children to choose which of two books they want to hear by "voting with their feet." This means walking to one of two story groups that has their favorite of the two books *The Very Hungry Caterpillar* or *The Secret Birthday Message,* both by Eric Carle. After the story the children can be directed to make a human graph by lining up, according to their choice. The two lines are then compared by each child reaching out to grasp the hand of a partner from the other group. The number of children without a partner is noted.

Graph of Leaves

After a fall walk collecting leaves, the teacher organizes a graph with a column for each category of leaf that the children decide. The teacher or individual children draw the kind of leaf (shape, size, or color) decided by the children at the bottom of each column. Then children place the actual leaf according to the category. When each leaf is glued on and sprayed with a fixative, it is placed in the discovery area. The next day children bring in more leaves from the playground and these are added to the graph.

Representative Graphs

Vote on Favorites

Voting can be accomplished by deciding on a question, such as, "Do you like red or blue?" "What is your favorite shape?" These graphs use a symbol of the object such as red and blue Unifix cubes or a cut-out shape of circle, rectangle, or triangle.

Vote for Favorite Book

A graph is made showing a selection of four of Eric Carle's books that have been read to the class. Each child shows his favorite story by drawing a picture of himself or printing his name on sticky notes and placing it under the picture depicting the story of his choice.

Bar Graphs

Choose Color of New Rug

Bar graphs may be used by older preschoolers or kindergarteners. To help children understand the bar graph at an early level, the teacher can ask children their favorite color, then ask them to place their choice by using a Unifix cube of the same color in front of a vertical bar graph. Then the representation of the blocks is transferred to the bar graph by cutting the same color and number of squares represented with the cubes and placing these onto the bar graph (Charlesworth & Lind, 2003) (see Fig. 7–3).

Estimation Graph

Children can use graphs to depict estimations. For example, the question may be, How many days for the narcissus to bloom? One to three children can interview classmates and adults on the chosen question. On this bar graph the estimated number of days is across the bottom and the number of persons who estimated the amount of days is on the left side. Using a poster that has a grid of rows and columns, the columns for each guess are filled in to match the number who made that estimate. For example, if the estimates ranged from 2 to 10 days, each day, from 1 to 10 has a column. As the narcissus plant is examined each day, comparison of the estimates are made.

TABLE C–4   Bead Bracelets and Display

Recipe for Bead Bracelets and Display

Materials

3' by 3' pegboard with 10 hooks for display, 30 5" by 7" index cards, small beads

Ten 10-inch sections of thin wire (such as telephone wire) (for four-year-olds, use ten 10-inch pieces of heavy string, and medium sized beads)

Tape and colored markers

Directions

Ask a small group to develop repeated patterns of beads on their wire. Then ask each child to draw the pattern he made on an index card, repeating his pattern twice. Each can color the pattern he drew with markers. Later the same (or another) child can put the index card on the display board and find its match to place on the corresponding hook. Decide on a price and label for the display and add this to the display board.

TABLE C–5   Weekly Calendars

Examples of Weekly Calendars

A Wall Calendar

Each day a child is selected to add a sticker symbol representing an event of that day. Some simple ideas are a main activity in the classroom, a book that was enjoyed, a birthday celebration, or a holiday. If the class is anticipating an event such as a trip to the library, the symbol for the event is placed on the upcoming day. Children can count days left to the event (Fig. C–5).

Velcro Board Calendar

Symbols of school days and nonschool days are made that represent the particular classroom and the lives of children during nonschool days. A school bus

Wall Calendar

Extra Stickers

Figure C–5 Wall calendar.

Our Week in Head Start						
Monday	Tuesday	Wednesday	Thursday	Friday	Saturday	Sunday

Figure C–6 Velcro calendar.

might represent school days. For nonschool days, children might select a symbol showing a house or a family watching television. Each day a child adds one of these symbols under the day of the week. On Friday the children talk about the nonschool days of Saturday and Sunday, placing the chosen symbols on the calendar. On Monday, the past week is discussed before the weekly symbols are removed and the weekly calendar is begun again (Fig. C–6).

TABLE C–6   The Water Fountain

Recipe for Water Fountain

To promote the children experimenting, start with one bottle with one hole on the side. As children explore their ideas, more bottles and more holes can be added. When the bottles are stacked, ask whether the water flows from one bottle to another, and how to enable that to happen.

Using a variety of three or four empty plastic bottles, such as peanut butter jars, or juice or water bottles, punch a variety of holes in the side with a thin nail and hammer. Also punch a large hole in the bottom of each bottle, except one used for the bottom. Filling a bottle with water and capping it provides needed stability for punching holes. To begin the fountain fill each bottle with water and stack them in the water table. The completed fountain will continue to flow when the top bottle is filled with water (Nichols & Nichols, 1990).

TABLE C–7 The Waterworks Experiment Station

Recipe for Waterworks Experiment Station

Mount a pegboard that is 24" by 48" (or the length of the water table) behind the water table. Punch holes in clear plastic cups and mount them on the pegboard using twist ties. Start with two cups each with one hole placed far apart on the pegboard. Add small bottles or pitchers to fill the cups. As children experiment with these, they can incorporate using other cups placed nearby. At first children may catch the water with a cup and then want to hold the cup in place. Then the idea of mounting a second, then third cup can be carried out. As children continue exploring the water flow, ask them if they would like to reposition the cups on the pegboard and change the placement of the holes to add more, or add holes in the bottom. Children may develop a system so the water cascades from one cup to another (DeVries et al. 2002).

TABLE C–8 Water Flow Experiments

Recipe for Water Flow Experiments

This set-up can be attached to the pegboard used in Table C–16. Remove the bottom of a 1-liter pop bottle and attach a valve (from a hardware store) to the cap end of the bottle. To the valve attach 1/2" clear plastic tubing (from a hardware store) that is 12" to 18" long. Using twist ties or hooks to mount objects on pegboards, mount the inverted pop bottle high on the pegboard and fill with water. Place additional hooks on the pegboard to hold the tubing where children choose to place it. Children experiment with turning the valve on and off, and placing the tubing in different positions to make water run. As children explore more cups can be placed on the pegboard as well (DeVries et al., 2002).

TABLE C–9 Pipe Connectors

Recipe for Pipe Connectors

For pipe connectors, obtain (from a hardware store) various lengths of $\frac{3}{4}$" PVC pipe and $\frac{3}{4}$" clear tubing of various lengths from 1 to 3 feet and connectors for these of various types (elbow, t-shaped, and straight). Using a water source, fill a small bucket or bottle and a funnel. Children will experiment putting together pipes so the water will flow and find out the pipes will carry water from one place to another (such as the sandbox) in the outdoor playground.

TABLE C–10   The Dark Box

Recipe for The Dark Box

Obtain a large appliance box from an appliance store and cut out a three-sided door on one side (this should be able to be opened and closed). Ask children to paint the inside with black paint and allow to dry. Then children can explore using a flashlight inside and outside the box (in dark and light). Let them try shining the light onto the colander placed both inside and outside the box and compare (Green, 1996) (see Fig. 17–3).

TABLE C–11   Shadow Theater and Puppets

Recipe for Shadow Theater and Puppets

Small table

Slide projector or strong flashlight

Shadow puppets made from tagboard

Tongue depressors

Masking tape

The stage will be formed from a small table turned on its side. Using masking tape, you can tape the stick of each shadow puppet on the edge of the table with the puppet above it. Position a beam of light from the slide projector (or flashlight) to shine horizontally from behind the stage onto the wall or a sheet, so the shadow puppets appear on the wall in a clear outline. You can make figures of animals or design puppets to tell a story (Green, 1996).

TABLE C–12   Clean Water Machine

Recipe for Clean Water Machine

Gather the following: Gallon glass jar, large clear funnel (or clear vinyl folded in cone shape with the point cut off), sand, gravel, soil, 2-cup clear measuring cup. Fill funnel $\frac{1}{4}$ full with gravel, then $\frac{1}{4}$ full with clean sand, and add additional $\frac{1}{4}$ full with gravel again. Fill measuring cup with water and muddy the water or add other materials such as coffee grounds, oil, crumbled leaves and so on. Slowly pour muddied water into the funnel. As the water is filtered through the sand and gravel layers, it comes out clean (Nichols & Nichols, 1990).

TABLE C–13 Terrariums

Recipes for Terrariums

The terrarium can be made from 2-liter pop bottles, any large clear gallon bottle of glass (with a wide mouth) or plastic, or a 5- to 10-gallon aquarium.

For the large pop bottles, remove the label and wash the bottle. Cut around the bottle 4 to 5 inches from the bottom, prepare the terrarium in the base, and place the top portion over the base. You may have to force the top portion inside the base (Fig. C–7).

For the gallon bottles, cut away the top portion of the plastic bottle, and keep the lids from the glass ones. If animals are going to be added, make a cover or screen from a porous material like net or nylon from hosiery and fasten securely with masking tape or heavy rubber bands. Or punch holes in the metal or plastic lid of the glass bottle.

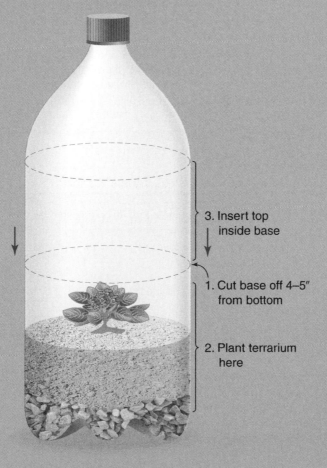

3. Insert top inside base

1. Cut base off 4–5″ from bottom

2. Plant terrarium here

Figure C–7 Two-liter pop bottle terrarium.

The larger terrarium works well for a selection of larger animals such as lizards or frogs. With animals, the cover will need to be a tight-fitting screen.

Choose plants that will do well in a moist environment and ones that will stay small in size. Philodendron and ivy grow easily and will provide vines of leaves for an attractive environment. African violets thrive in humidity and provide long-lasting attractive blooms.

The terrarium needs light, which can be from a growth lamp. Do not place the terrarium in direct sunlight as the inside temperature can become too hot. With animals in this habitat, in a cold climate the temperature of the room on nights and weekends needs to be monitored. The feeding of the animals will also need to be planned for weekends and school vacations.

To put the terrarium together, first lay down 1 inch of gravel or charcoal for drainage. Then add 2 inches of potting soil. If this is a plant terrarium, gently place the plants in the soil, tap them down, and water for moisture. The completely closed terrarium for plants will not need much water. This can be checked every week. Misting the air may be the only moisture needed. If droplets form on the glass or plastic surface, the environment has enough moisture (Holt, 1990) (see Fig. 18–8).

If this terrarium is planned for animals, plant the chosen plants in small pots. This way the plants can be removed easily so the whole environment can be cleaned periodically. Because it is not an enclosed environment, moisture will be lost from it. Animals may need misting daily. (see Fig. 18–9).

TABLE C–14 Compost Home for Earthworms

Recipe for Compost Home for Earthworms

Materials

Large container 12 or more inches deep

Newspaper

Soil

Water

Earthworms from garden or play ground (or purchased redworms).

Food scraps, lettuce, eggshells, coffee grounds

Directions

With the children, fill the container with finely shredded newspaper, and then dampen the paper (with no water at the bottom) and add soil to a depth of about 6 inches and mix the paper and soil. Add the worms and cover lightly with a sheet of dark plastic with holes in it. Add small pieces of leftover food scraps, eggshells, and coffee grounds. Moisten the soil every few days, but don't let the soil be wet. If you need to leave the worms for a few days, put them in a cool location (refrigerator works fine).

TABLE C–15   Earthworm Viewing Station

Recipe for Earthworm Viewing Station

Materials

> Select a large wide-mouthed clear glass jar and a peanut butter jar or other small jar that will fit inside the larger jar.
>
> Soil
>
> Sand
>
> Spoons
>
> Coffee grounds
>
> Lettuce and other food scraps

Directions

Place the smaller jar in the center of the large jar and layer the sand and soil alternately until the large jar is $\frac{3}{4}$ full. Place some coffee grounds in the soil in one spot. Put the worms on the soil, and add small bits of lettuce and, later, other food bits. Label each area where you bury the food so you can tell what the worms have eaten (Starbuck, Olthof, & Midden, 2002). When not viewing the worms, cover the jar with a paper bag or dark terry cloth towel (Kleinsinger, 1991) (see Fig. 19–2).

TABLE C–16   Comparison of Weights of Newborns

Recipe for Comparison of Weights of Newborns

For comparing weights, make bags of the same weight of an infant child and the newborn animal. Select nonperishable food items that have the weight stated on the box (such as 5 pounds of flour, 1 pound of rice, 11.5 oz of vegetable juice in a can, $1\frac{1}{4}$ oz of paprika) to equal the weight of one of the children at birth. Then weigh the baby animal as soon as it can be handled after birth and make up that weight with comparable kinds of items (such as two paprika cans). Put each group of items in a cloth bag and allow children to hold and compare them.

For an alternative plan to add up weights of newborn baby and animal, use a precision balance scale (weights with these come in grams, so you will need to convert ounces to grams) or a platform scale (measures weight up to 10 pounds) to find items in the classroom that add up to the total weight of the baby animal and newborn child.

A third alternative is to place a bag of sand on scales and adjust the amount to equal the weight of the human newborn and then make a second bag of sand to equal the weight of the newborn animal.

REFERENCES

Carle, E. (2003). *The very hungry caterpillar.* New York: Philomel.

Carle, E. (1986). *The secret birthday message.* New York: Harper Trophy.

Charlesworth, R., and Lind, K. (2003). *Math and science for young children* (4th ed.). Clifton Park, NY: Thomson Delmar Learning.

DeVries, R., Zan, B., Hildebrandt, C., Edmiaston, R., and Sales, C. (2002). *Developing constructivist early childhood curriculum: Practical principles and activities.* New York: Teachers College Press.

Green, M. D. (1996). *474 science activities for young children.* Clifton Park, NY: Thomson Delmar Learning.

Holt, B.-G. (1990, February). Setting the stage for science discoveries. *Scholastic Pre-K Today, 2*(5), 41–47.

Kleinsinger S. B. (1991). *Learning through play: Science—A practical guide for teaching young children.* New York: Scholastic.

McCloskey, R. (1948). *Blueberries for Sal.* New York: Viking.

Moomaw, S., and Hieronymus, B. (1995). *More than counting: Whole math activities for preschool and kindergarten.* St. Paul, MN: Redleaf.

Nichols, W., and Nichols, K. (1990). *Wonderscience: A developmentally appropriate guide to hands-on science for young children.* Santa Fe, NM: Learning Expo.

Starbuck, S., Olthof, M., and Midden, K. (2002). *Hollyhocks and honeybees: Garden projects for young children.* St. Paul, MN: Redleaf.

Glossary

Abstraction rule   The rule that dissimilar objects can be counted in a set.

Advocate   One who is a proponent for a cause.

Aesthetic   Relating to the beauty in the environment, either natural or planned.

Analyze   Find patterns in information, find evidence, and draw conclusions.

Animism   The belief that what moves is alive and objects take on human characteristics.

Annelid   The name of the class of common earthworms.

Ant colony   The organization of ants for living and working.

Arachnid   A class of land invertebrates, including spiders.

Arthropods   A family of invertebrate animals including insects and arachnids.

Artificialism   The belief that objects and events are caused by humans or are made for human benefit.

Authentic assessment   Capturing the individual and group process, concerns, and current thinking in order to implement applicable curriculum.

Basic math   The skills of classifying, comparing, contrasting, seriating, and making sets.

Bob   The object that is fastened to the lower end of the cord on a pendulum.

Botanist   One who studies and cares for plants.

Bulb   A fleshy structure of the root that contains sprout and food for the coming growth season.

Butterfly garden   An area planned with the kinds of plants and environment that attracts butterflies.

Cantilever   A projecting beam supported at only one end.

Cardinal principle   The final number counted equals the total number in the set.

Castings   Excrement of the earthworm that is beneficial to the soil.

Caterpillar   Larvae of a butterfly or moth.

Cause and effect   The belief that if two events happen together, one has caused the other.

Centration   The focus on one aspect of a situation and not considering any others.

Chelae   The pincer-like jaws of an arachnid.

Cephalothorax   The head and thorax (joined) of an arachnid.

Cerebral cortex   The area of the brain where conscious behavior and thinking occur.

Chemical change   A change in the composition of materials.

Chrysalis   The pupa of a butterfly or moth in the stage of metamorphosis.

Circular path game   A noncompetitive board game organized with a circular path for players to follow.

Circular process   Stages of inquiry that move from one step to another and return to an earlier step.

Classifying   The act of putting like objects in groups.

Climatic data   A collection of weather information both past and present.

Clitellum   The middle banded area of the earthworm.

Co-construction   The process of two or more people who construct concepts together beyond what the individual can accomplish.

Collaboration   The collective work of actively listening and developing ideas.

Collaborative   The process of working jointly on a goal.

Comparing The act of examining two objects to determine if they are the same or different.

Concept of number Knowing the total amount in a set.

Concrete operations Occurs as the third stage of cognitive development when the child has the ability to apply logical processes to concrete problems.

Conifer The type of evergreen tree and shrub.

Conservation The understanding that amounts remain the same if nothing is added or taken away.

Constructive play A kind of play where physical manipulation of objects is used to build or construct an object that represents the child's ideas.

Constructivist curriculum A framework for children to construct their knowledge about how the world works through active engagement in meaningful inquiry.

Constructivist learning Putting together (hence constructing) one's own ideas through action and thought processes.

Content What children learn in identification of objects and processes such as names of flowers or stages of growth.

Contrasting The act of finding the dissimilarities in two items.

Corpus callosum The connection between the right and left hemispheres of the brain. It is made up of a large band of neuron fibers.

Cutting The process of severing a plant section to start a new plant.

Daily schedule The general organization of a classroom day into time periods.

Data analysis Collecting data, organizing and representing it.

Decentering The act of taking in more than one aspect of a situation.

Deciduous The type of tree or shrub that sheds its leaves seasonally.

Decompose To take apart a number and arrange it in one or more subsets.

Density The mass of a substance per unit volume.

Descriptor A word or phrase that describes sensory input.

Developmentally appropriate practice A set of principles and guidelines that follow the way children develop and learn in programs for children from birth through eight.

Dictation The process of recording a child's thoughts or story so it can be saved for others to read.

Digital camera The type of camera that uses digital imaging which can be transferred and viewed on the computer.

Discovery area A table or other area that provides space and materials for exploration.

Disposition A prevailing inclination or a habit of mind.

Divergent thinking A thinking process that uses information to develop different ways of tackling a problem.

Documentation Using a variety of approaches to record and display the learning of a child or group of children.

Drill-and-practice software Children's software presents an academic task for the child, provides feedback, and takes the child to the next higher level.

Ecology The study of conserving earth and living systems.

Ecosystems Biological and/or earth systems that form a living unit.

Egocentrism Seeing events and experiences only from one's viewpoint.

Electrical board A system of electrical devices, wires, and battery that can be arranged to turn on and off the devices.

Ellipse A two-dimensional compressed sphere.

E-mail A process of sending messages usually in typed form to be received by a user on another computer through the Internet.

Emergent curriculum In-depth study for learning that develops out of children's and teachers' interests and questions.

Emerging literacy The beginnings of communication and understanding language, especially through reading and writing in the early childhood years.

Equitable Dealing fairly and equally with everyone.

Estimation Providing a rough guess.

Ethical guidelines An organizational statement of accepted professional standards of conduct.

Fast mapping A process of quickly increasing vocabulary by relating a new word to a similar word already known.

Finalizing a study The culmination of a long-term project.

Food experience A planned experience where children prepare a food for tasting and eating.

Functional play A kind of play where movement of the body or objects is done for the sake of movement or to experience the sensory aspect of the motion.

Games with rules Using board games or outdoor games that have a set of rules, including turn taking and a prescribed way to complete the actions of the game.

Gender inequities Attitudes that show a difference in expectations of boys' and girls' experiences.

Generalize Apply previous experience to new events.

Germination The beginning of growth or cause to sprout from seed.

Graph A systematic representation of data usually shown two dimensionally.

Group project The representation of the object of study.

Habitat A natural or planned environment where a particular plant or animal will thrive.

Hypothesize Using data from experiences to make guesses about what might happen.

I wonder statements To phrase an extension of an idea or suggest possibilities to consider in response to children's ideas.

Inclined plane A slanted surface of varying degrees from the horizontal.

Inquiry A close investigation in a quest to find out.

Inquiry topic Curriculum based on the inquiry process.

Insect A small invertebrate belonging to a class of arthropods and has three body sections and six legs.

Integrated curriculum Curriculum that encompasses many areas of learning no matter what the topic.

Intent The focus or direction of thought and action.

Interest areas Well-planned spaces for particular kinds of activities to take place in an early childhood classroom.

Internet A collection of interconnected computers that provide easy access to a vast amount of data and material from any connected site in the world.

Intersubjectivity The process of two people adjusting to be within the same intent.

Intervening force A phenomenon not caused directly by the child acting on it and which is usually not observable by the child.

Intuitive thinking Using appearances over logic.

Irreversibility The lack of ability to see that reversing a process will bring it back to its former state.

Kinesthetic The sense of movement felt in the body.

Language expansion A response to what a child says by expanding the word, phrase, or sentence using a complete sentence or a more complex one.

Light table A table top that projects a diffused light through a translucent surface where children can explore materials.

Lintel A long piece that spans two columns and usually carries the load above an opening.

Logicomathematical knowledge The understanding of relationships between and among objects.

Magical causality Attributing actions to magic when they cannot be understood logically.

Magnetism The force exhibited in magnets and other phenomena.

Manipulatives Various kinds of materials that children use to create their constructions.

Manuscript The accepted form of print in letter size and formation for early childhood classrooms.

Meaning-centered curriculum A study that focuses on a worthwhile topic that advances learning in depth.

Metamorphosis The change in the form or structure of an animal (i.e., butterfly, moth, or beetle).

Mindless curriculum Activities of children that do not involve them in understanding more about their world through inquiry and investigation.

Mung bean A small round bean that produces bean sprouts.

Myelination The insulation (myelin) of the long parts of the neuron that makes the transfer of information in the brain efficient and faster.

Neuron A cell of the nervous system where messages are transferred from one to another or to a particular part of the body.

Number sense The understanding of how numbers work.

Object permanence Knowing that an object continues to exist when out of sight.

One-to-one correspondence Putting two objects into relationship; one item goes with one item.

One-to-one rule In counting only one counting word is used for each object.

Open-ended questions A type of question that stimulates thoughtful responses and does not have one specific answer.

Open-ended software A type of program where children learn through discovering rather than being told right or wrong.

Order irrelevant principle The rule that a group of objects can be counted in any order as long as each item is counted only once.

Ordering The act of arranging in order.

Ordinal number The label of the position of an object in a series.

Orff instrumentation Uses instruments such as xylophones with removable tone bars.

Parallel talk Commentary that follows what the child is doing.

Part–part–whole The ability to decompose a number or an object into subsets and recompose it into a whole.

Part–whole relationships Seeing objects as whole and subdivided into parts.

Patterns The result of repeating elements in a regular fashion.

Pendulum An object suspended from a fixed point so as to swing freely.

Perennials Plants that grow and bloom year after year in their natural habitat.

Physical knowledge The knowledge about characteristics of objects and materials through exploring and acting on them.

Planter boxes Containers for small plants for indoor or outdoor use.

Pondering questions Questions that pose ideas that children can choose to think about.

Portfolio A collection of a child's work which shows growth in areas of development.

Preoperational thought The cognitive stage during the years from two to six where thought processes are prelogical and intuitive.

Pretend play This play uses roles or objects to take on imaginary roles seen in everyday life or learned through the media.

Prism A transparent object that is shaped to refract a beam of light.

Probability The exploration of the concept of chance.

Process How children learn such as exploring or experimenting.

Project approach A curriculum approach that uses a project for the focus of an in-depth investigation of a topic.

Project narratives Children can tell what they discover or want to know through recorded narratives.

Pulley A simple machine made with a cord wrapped around a grooved wheel.

Realism The belief that what is imagined is real.

Rectangular prism A three-dimensional form containing right angles.

Reflective thinking The process of using past information and knowledge combined with new information to compose new understanding.

Refraction The deflection (or bending) of light as it passes from one medium to another so the colors in the light spectrum are made visible.

Reggio approach The pedagogy of schools for young children in Reggio Emilia, Italy, that is based on the co-construction of knowledge and collaboration of children, teachers, and parents.

Representation The ability to use a mental symbol to stand for an object or an action.

Research Take formal or informal steps to look closely at phenomena to search for answers.

Reversibility The ability to reverse operations and use information presented earlier.

Rhombus A two-dimensional diamond shape.

Rote counting The process of saying the numbers in order with no reference to counting objects.

Safe search filter A program that limits access on the Internet to include only Web sites that are deemed appropriate for young viewers.

Scaffolding The structure the teacher provides so the child can master the task with help.

Scanner A device that inputs an image into the computer to be saved or processed.

Search engine A tool used to find Web sites containing information on a given topic.

Sensorimotor The first stage of cognitive development in which the child learns through senses and action on the environment.

Sensory processing Making sense of the intake from all senses and registering the input in a particular part of the brain.

Seriation The act of ordering according to a known characteristic.

Set A group of objects with certain characteristics.

Signs The spoken word or the written numeral in the number system.

Smart toy A toy with a computer chip that is programmed to perform certain activities for the child.

Social constructionist learning Involvement with others in the construction of ideas.

Social context Includes sharing in the immediate experience, the individual social history as well as the cultural social history.

Social knowledge The knowledge gained from and shared by people.

Sociocultural theory The concept that learning occurs in a social context.

Sociodramatic play Pretend play with one or more peers where children take on social roles they know.

Software Software is a computer program made for a particular purpose that can become portable by storing on a CD.

Spectrum A continuum of colors (rainbow) formed when a beam of white light is dispersed.

Sphere A three-dimensional shape of a ball or orb.

Stable order rule Counting words, $(1, 2, 3 \ldots)$ must be used consistently and in the same order.

Static states The process of believing the appearance of what is seen at the moment, not using information of the process to understand the result.

Study A process of learning that children and teachers involve themselves through discussion, design, and representation of a topic.

Substance in context The knowledge of a material or object in relation to the actual use of these materials.

Symbols Marks used to represent a number (○○○, ✔✔✔, ■■■).

Symmetry Regularity of form.

Synapse The connection between two neurons where the transfer of information take place.

Synthesize Combine data found at present with other data to compare and put into whole to make predictions or create hypotheses.

Tally The act of using marks to represent the number of objects in a set.

Thematic planning Curriculum developed on a topic that is preplanned by teachers.

Thorax The central body part of an insect on which are the legs and wings.

Tinkering To experiment mechanically by taking things apart.

Transductive reasoning The thinking of relationships from object to object or event to event without a hierarchy of relationships.

Transparency projector A machine used to project a transparent image onto a wall or other vertical surface.

Transplant Moving a sprout or plant from one growth medium to another.

Web A diagram depicting ideas or information on a particular topic showing interconnections and relationships of concepts.

Web site A particular place accessed through the Internet with its own code (address) where particular information and images can be viewed.

Weekly calendar The representation of days into a period of a week.

Zone of proximal development The area of learning at the point where the learner can accomplish the task with the help of another.

Index